I

AN OPEN BOOK

JOHN HUSTON

AN OPEN

BOOK

Alfred A. Knopf New York, 1980

This is a Borzoi Book Published by Alfred A. Knopf, Inc.

Grateful acknowledgment is made to Viking Penguin Ltd. for permission
to reprint an excerpt from *Memo from David O. Selznick*, edited by
Rudy Behlmer. Copyright © 1972 by Selznick Properties Ltd.
Reprinted by permission of Viking Penguin Ltd.
Excerpts from unpublished letters by B. Traven printed by courtesy of
Mrs. Elena Lujan Traven.

Library of Congress Cataloging in Publication Data
Huston, John, [date]
An open book.
Includes index.
1. Huston, John, [date] 2. Moving-picture
producers and directors—United States—Biography.
I. Title.
PN1998.A3H75 1980   791.43′0233′0924 [B]   80-7619
ISBN 0-394-40465-3
Manufactured in the United States of America
First Edition

A U T H O R ' S   N O T E

Many people have helped me with this book. I would like to express
my thanks to all of them and especially to William Reed for his
invaluable advice and assistance.

AN OPEN BOOK

For the better part of the last five years I have been living in Puerto Vallarta, Jalisco, Mexico. When I first came here, almost thirty years ago, Vallarta was a fishing village of some two thousand souls. There was only one road to the outside world—and it was impassable during the rainy season. I arrived in a small plane, and we had to buzz the cattle off a field outside town before setting down. There was one taxi and one hotel, the Paraiso, which catered to sailors, muleteers and traveling salesmen. It was best to have a room on the top floor—the Paraiso had one toilet for each floor, and they all ran over.

Over the years I came back to Vallarta a number of times. One of those times was in 1963, to film *The Night of the Iguana*. It was because of this picture that the world first heard of the place. Visitors and tourists flocked in. Before *The Night of the Iguana* the population was some 2,500. Afterward, it grew prodigiously and it's now close to 80,000. Today hotels and condominiums rise, naked as mushrooms, out of the abundant green jungle.

I am now living in Las Caletas, where I've leased one and a half acres from the Chacala Indian Community; the Mexican government has granted these Indians a long stretch of coast and a large interior region. To get to where I live you drive about fifteen miles south of Puerto Vallarta to a small fishing village called Boca de Tomatlan, where the highway leaves the sea and turns inland over the mountains. From Boca you take a *panga* (an open fiberglass boat with an outboard motor) south some thirty minutes to Las Caletas.

I have my place on a ten-year lease, with an option for another ten. After that, the land and whatever I've built on it go back to the Indians. I'm not too concerned about what happens twenty years from now.

Las Caletas is my third home. The first was in the San Fernando Valley outside Los Angeles. The second was St. Clerans, in County Galway, Ireland. I dare say Las Caletas will be my last. There are no roads to it, and it's unlikely there will ever be—the nearest village is about half an hour away by jungle trail. Las Caletas faces the sea and its back is to the jungle, so for this reason one thinks of it as an island. It lies within the boundaries of a huge bay—Bahia de Banderas. Hurricanes strike to the north and south. They've played havoc with Mazatlan and Manzanillo, but the surrounding mountains deflect the heavy storms from Bahia de Banderas. It gets big waves but never the great winds themselves.

Las Caletas consists of six dwellings on different levels. They are shelters rather than houses, for there are no real rooms apart from storerooms. The occasional wall is for privacy's sake. We're protected by sailcloth from wind and weather.

Gladys Hill, my longtime secretary, lives here. So does a Mexican girl in her twenties, Maricela, whom I salvaged from my last marriage. Maricela runs everything, including me. There would be no Las Caletas without her.

Life here is lived in the open. At night wild creatures come down to inspect the changes I've made in their domain: coatimundis, opossums, deer, boars, ocelots, boas, jaguars. We find their spoor or trails in the mornings. Flocks of frenetic parrots come winging in at first light, full of talk. They climb, dive, wheel as one bird, alight in the treetops, all talking. They take off, do another quick turn or two and disappear—talking.

After sunrise the jungle quiets down, but there is always something going on at sea. Pelicans in tandem, skimming the waves—gulls and other seabirds, diving when the surface of the bay seethes and boils with sardines or schools of other small fish. There's a manta ray who performs regularly about fifty yards offshore. He always jumps twice. The first time is to get your attention. Then he throws all three thousand pounds of himself so high out of the water that you can see the freckles on his white underbelly. Gray, humpback and killer whales and porpoises ply the offshore waters. We're trying to keep a record on the grays because this is the farthest south they've ever been seen.

The winters are sparkling clear. There is almost no rain for nine months. By spring the jungle greens have faded to olive drab. In late June clouds begin to gather. They thicken and lower until they're halfway down the mountainsides. The atmosphere gets heavier and heavier. Then one day the heavens open and the torrential rains beat down. Instantly there are explosions of color throughout the jungle: orchids, birds of paradise, all manner of bromeliads. And every night there's an electrical display out at sea, lighting up the horizon like a great artillery duel between worlds.

Now that I'm of a certain age, I'm following a piece of old Irish advice in going to live by the sea: "It stops old wounds from hurting. It revives the spirit. It quickens the passions of mind and body, yet lends tranquillity to the soul."

I'm content having arrived at this moment in eternity, but for the life of me I don't know how I got here. I've lost track of the years. It's incredible being seventy-three, but, in the face of the evidence contained in this book, I have to accept the fact. It used to be that I was the youngest in every group. Now, suddenly, I'm the oldest.

I've lived a number of lives. I'm inclined to envy the man who leads one life, with one job, and one wife, in one country, under one God. It may not be a very exciting existence, but at least by the time he's seventy-three he knows how old he is.

I've lost a number of friends, but quite a few are still alive and kicking: Willy, Paul, Hank, Billy, Peter, Giacomo, Sam and another Sam. More women have survived, but they are all younger than the men: Suzanne, Marietta, Lillian, Olivia, Maka, Cherokee, Irene, Liz, Dorothy, Lesley, Annie, Betty and Gladys. I count those names like a pirate counting his spoils at the end of a long voyage.

My life is composed of random, tangential, disparate episodes. Five wives; many liaisons, some more memorable than the marriages. The hunting. The betting. The thoroughbreds. Painting, collecting, boxing. Writing, directing and acting in more than sixty pictures. I fail to see any continuity in my work from picture to picture—what's remarkable is how different the pictures are, one from another. Nor can I find a thread of consistency in my marriages. No one of my wives has been remotely like any of the others—and certainly none of them was like my mother. They were a mixed bag: a schoolgirl; a gentlewoman; a motion-picture actress; a ballerina; and a crocodile.

My only recurrent dream is one in which I'm ashamed of being broke and having to go to my father for money—something that happened only a time or two, and then he pressed the money on me. There was an instance when I was flat-assed broke and didn't go to him and, when he found out afterward, he was deeply hurt. Why, then, should I have that dream in which I feel weak, dissolute and shiftless? It doesn't match up with anything, symbolically or otherwise. It's a random dream. . . .

He left a few things: an ivory-handled .44 Colt revolver; a gold watch; and a pair of straight-edged razors. I was named after him: John Marcellus Gore. He was my Grandpa.

2   I remember Grandpa Gore as having white hair and a white, flowing mustache, and being tall and thin. Of course everyone seems tall when you are three or four, but I think he really was. He was also an alcoholic who went on periodic sprees, in the course of which he would simply disappear. Occasionally—my father told me this —Grandpa would declare his intentions in advance: he was going to a certain hotel in such-and-such a town, and Dad was to come for him on a given date. Dad would appear on schedule and say, "All right, John, it's time to sober up. You told me you would on this date."

"Did I say that?"

"Yes."

"All right. Now I'll stop." And he would. "Whatever his other faults," people said, "John Gore's word was gospel."

Sometimes Grandpa would go without drinking for a couple of years— then he would start a bat which might last for weeks, or even months. There would be no word from him for a long time, and then the family would receive a letter or a telegram reporting his whereabouts. He would be at the end of his rope, holed up in a hotel room in some Godforsaken town, sometimes hundreds of miles away. It was usually my mother who would go to him and, as a rule, put him into a hospital to go through the ordeal of sobering up.

Mother took me along on one of these excursions. It was to Quincy, Illinois. It was raining; Mother was carrying an umbrella and we were walking under big trees that must have been maples. We came to a white house sitting back on a lawn in the middle of which there was a large tree. By the time we arrived, it was raining very hard. Grandpa was sitting on the front porch of the house. He stood up as we approached, and Mother greeted him and kissed him on the cheek. She held me up to do likewise. I remember his cheek was unshaven. Then Mother sat down on the porch swing with me beside her.

"How's Deal?" asked Grandpa. Deal was what he called Gram.

Suddenly there was a blinding light and a tremendous crash. The air was full of ozone. My mother fell off the swing onto her knees.

"Is Deal in good health?" asked Grandpa.

I stared at the tree in the front yard, seared down the middle and smoldering, and thought: "This must be what it means to be drunk . . . Grandpa doesn't even know when lightning strikes!"

John Gore had been a drummer boy in the Confederate Army. He came up the Ohio River some years after the war and visited Marietta, Ohio, where he met Adelia Richardson. Adelia had two sisters, Ada and Metta. Ada was later to marry a wealthy contractor and make her home in Greensburg, Indiana, and Metta's husband-to-be was an Episcopalian minister with a parish in Hartwell, Ohio. Security played no part in Adelia's choice. She married the adventurer John Gore. Their daughter, Reah Gore, was my mother.

Adelia's father, William P. Richardson, had been breveted to general after Chancellorsville, where he fought as colonel of the 25th Regiment Ohio Volunteer Infantry. I have a sword presented to him by the privates and non-commissioned officers of the 25th Ohio just before the Battle of Chancellorsville, where he lost an arm and saw his regiment decimated. I have a copy of Richardson's acceptance speech.

> The value of this gift is immeasurably enhanced by the fact that it was given to me by men who have proven their valor in their country's cause on many a well-fought field. . . . Wealth, influence or favoritism might procure such a gift as this, but the esteem and confidence of brave men cannot be bought.

When my mother was still a little girl, Grandpa Gore took part in the Oklahoma Land Rush, where he rode a thoroughbred in the race for land. People not only raced for individual parcels, but got together and staked out towns. Then, of course, they tried to get their town made the county seat. Whichever town got the county seat got the railroad, ensuring success for the town and its inhabitants, while the towns that lost usually sank into oblivion, becoming hamlets or ghost towns. Everything was at stake; bad blood rose between competing communities and often ended in gunplay. Wherever new land was opened up for homesteading—in Oklahoma, Texas, Kansas—such battles would be fought.

John Gore was a part of all this. He started newspapers in a number of new little towns—after persuading the city fathers to invest in a printing press. But even when Grandpa's business efforts were successful, he would move on after a time, leaving Gram to keep an eye on things while he searched for fresh pastures.

Gram told me that on one occasion, during the conflicts called the County Seat Wars, the town in which she and John Gore lived was invited by a rival town to come over for a peaceful discussion of their problems. A half-dozen men went, among them my grandfather. Riding into the town, they noticed that all the windows were shuttered and the blinds drawn. Sensing danger, they wheeled their horses and rode back down the main street at a gallop. Three of them were killed by rifle fire. John Gore was one of those who escaped. After that it was open warfare.

A week later my grandmother was standing on the front porch of the general store with a number of other people. A man drove up in his buckboard, got out and started up the steps past her. Gram recognized him; she'd known his family back in Ohio. They greeted each other warmly and talked about mutual friends. Gram asked where he was living now and, of all places, he named the rival town. He would of course have been shot dead on the spot if Gram hadn't stepped between him and the others. She questioned him and discovered that the man had been away on a trip for some weeks and hadn't an inkling of the recent bloodshed. She ignored his confused queries and said, "It is no time for questions. Get in your wagon and be on your way. Don't even look back." Her friend did as she said, and no harm came to him.

"Once in Boulder, Colorado, Grandpa won a large sum of money gambling, got drunk and bought three saloons. Then he opened the doors and invited the whole town to belly up. Gram left their hotel to find him and discovered what he'd done. She stopped the first sober man she saw on the street and sold him all three saloons for a dollar.

My grandparents knew some of the well-known frontier figures of the time, including the frontier marshal Bat Masterson. One time when Grandpa had been off to God knows where for some time, Masterson came to see my grandmother. He asked, "Are you all right, Mrs. Gore?"

She said, "Yes," but Bat then took out his wallet and gave it to her. It was full of bills of large denomination.

"What's this, Bat?"

"Well . . . it's until John gets back."

"I couldn't possibly."

"Of course you can. I know John. He'll pay me back."

Gram thanked him and said, "I don't need it yet, Bat, but I'll know where to come if I do." One of my mother's earliest recollections was being given a "pony ride" on Bat Masterson's knee.

Sometime during this hectic period of moving from town to town with Grandpa, Gram placed my mother in a convent school in St. Louis. It was in St. Louis, at the World's Fair in 1904, that my mother met and married my father—an itinerant young actor named Walter Huston.

My father was born in 1884 in Toronto, Canada, of a Scottish mother, Elizabeth McGibbon, and an Irish father, Robert Huston. The family can be traced back to the thirteenth century and a soldier of fortune whose arms and exploits aided the King of Scotland. His name was Hugh de Padvinaw, and he was rewarded for his services with what now constitutes the Huston Estate near Johnstone, Scotland—then known as "Hugh's Town."

The branch of Hustons from which I am descended moved to Northern Ireland in the early seventeenth century, and in 1840 my great-grandfather Thomas left County Armagh for Canada. His son, my grandfather Robert, was a cabinetmaker whose pieces were sought after in a period of fine craftsmanship. There may be unsigned pieces by him in Canadian museums today; according to my father, his work was of that quality.

My father had one brother, Alec, and two sisters, Nan and Margaret. He was the youngest of the family. While the children were still in school, their father, Robert, went off hunting one day with a group of friends. As the party climbed a steep hill, Robert outdistanced the others and disappeared from view. When his friends arrived at the top, Robert lay there dead.

Alec took over and supported the family. He had some talent as a draftsman, and he became a signpainter as well as an inventor of sorts. Alec not only put the bread on the table for his mother, brother and sisters, but it was also owing to his efforts that the others were able to continue their schooling and, later, to pursue careers. Nan received good musical instruction and became a piano teacher. Margaret sang from the time she was a child. She sang in churches and, in her teens, also appeared in private recitals in the homes of the well-to-do. When she was eighteen, a group of Toronto women made her their protégée and arranged for her to give a formal recital. It was billed as the Margaret Huston Benefit Recital. The money collected on that evening, plus private donations, sent Margaret to Paris to study. Within a few years she became a dramatic soprano of considerable reputation.

Walter started acting at home at about age ten, using his mother's bedsheets as costumes. At fifteen he had a walk-on in a play starring Rose Coghlan called *White Heather*. From that moment acting became his life.

In his late teens he went on the road with a repertory company. Years later, what he mostly remembered was being hungry, a series of trains and sheriffs and boardinghouses and muddy streets and dilapidated show houses and doing his own washing. But, for all the hardships, he reveled in being an actor, in strutting up and down the streets of the small towns he played and bragging about his worldliness and travels.

Walter got a job during the summer of 1902 in Detroit as the Hero in a play called *In Convict Stripes*. The Villain was the warden of a prison where the Hero was incarcerated. At the climax, having been spurned by the Heroine, the vengeful Villain placed a child dear to her heart on a box of dynamite, lit the fuse and retired. Whereupon the Hero, in the nick of time, seized a rope fortuitously dangling from a rafter, swung across the stage and snatched the child to safety. Only then did the "dynamite" —an ingenious contrivance somewhat along the lines of a big mousetrap —explode, showering the stage with rubber rocks.

Rather than endanger a child, a dummy was used in this scene. Sometimes, as Walter swooped down and snatched it up, the doll would come apart, leaving our Hero holding a torso leaking sawdust. Apparently this didn't spoil the illusion for the audience, for the applause was always enthusiastic. Later Walter would reappear with a real child on his shoulder, and the applause was even more clamorous. The Villain would likewise reappear at the end of the play, stalking across the stage baring his teeth, to hisses and boos. Prior to Walter's joining the company, Mary Pickford had played the child; Lillian Gish replaced her in the part.

After leaving Detroit the company toured the Midwest and the West on the ten-twenty-thirty circuit, which derived its name from those standard prices of admission—ten, twenty or thirty cents. (There were at the time two other classes of touring companies, the one-dollar top and the two-dollar top. The ten-twenty-thirties were the bedraggled beggars of the theater troupes.)

After *In Convict Stripes* ran its course, Walter signed on with other repertory companies, all of which went bust on the road. He and four other young actors then pooled their money and went to New York, where on 38th Street they shared a room containing one bed. Each night they'd toss a coin to see who'd get the bed. In three weeks Walter managed to get one job—which paid three dollars—as a supernumerary in the Metropolitan Opera Company's presentation of *Le Cid*, featuring a new tenor from Italy named Caruso.

Dad's big break came a few weeks later when he was chosen from among some seventy starving hopefuls to play a bit part in the Richard

Mansfield production of *Julius Caesar*. The salary for the job was $25 a week, and Walter was jubilant. It wasn't just the money; he actually had lines to say in a play with Richard Mansfield! It was a golden opportunity. The lines were:

> Prepare you, generals!
> The enemy comes on in gallant show;
> Their bloody sign of battle is hung out,
> and something to be done immediately!

On opening night Walter got as far as "Prepare you, generals!" . . . and went completely blank. After a period of terrible silence he looked into the glowering face of Richard Mansfield and heard him hiss, "Get that idiot the hell out of here!" Dad described that as one of the lowest points of his life. Shamed and bitterly disappointed, he decided to give up the theater—forever.

Dad had been a good hockey player as a boy in Toronto, and for a while he played for a Brooklyn team before going back to the theater—in spite of his vow—by the back door. In 1903 he was engaged as assistant stage manager in a production titled *The Bishop's Move*, with W. H. Thompson in the leading role. Thompson, then about fifty, was a gentleman of the old school, a fine actor and a kindly, understanding man. He took a liking to my father and helped to restore his faith in himself. By the time *The Bishop's Move* closed, Walter was sufficiently recovered from his debacle in *Julius Caesar* to again seek work as an actor, and was immediately engaged by a company to go on tour with a play called *The Sign of the Cross*—salary, $30 a week. Walter was touring in this play when he met my mother at the St. Louis World's Fair.

I've read accounts that say my mother was dead-set against Walter being an actor. This is not true. After they were married in 1904, she accompanied Dad on the road in a company that went as far west as Arizona. Dad told me that in the Midwest, when they played to good houses, they made a practice of getting out of town fast—local posses would otherwise go after them for taking away too much of the town's money! And in the Far West the audiences took the performances so seriously that Dad and the other actors had to put on brass knuckles to protect the villain from the townspeople, who would lie in wait for him outside the stage door.

That road company must have encountered too many posses, for it eventually went broke, and Mother and Dad were stranded in the wilds of

Arizona. They telegraphed John Gore for money, which he sent along with an invitation to come and stay with him and Gram for a while. They were living in Nevada, Missouri, because John Gore had won the light-power-and-water company of that town in a poker game. When Mother and Dad arrived, Grandpa made Dad the chief engineer of the company.

Nevada, Missouri, was where I was born on August 5, 1906, but I wasn't there for long. A few months after Dad assumed his engineering duties a fire broke out in town. The fire chief called for more water pressure and Dad gave it to him. Apparently he shouldn't have, or perhaps he turned the wrong valve, because the water main broke. The entire town on one side of the tracks burned down. We left precipitously—in the middle of the night, by buckboard—and headed for the state line.

Although Dad's heart was really in the theater, he now had a wife and a child to support, so he continued in his efforts to become an engineer. His next job was with a hotel in Indianapolis, managing the power plant. Presently he was offered a job with the light-and-power plant in Weatherford, Texas. My first memories are of Weatherford: being in the saddle in front of my mother at night, mesmerized by the sound of the horse's hooves striking cobblestones. And it was there that I spoke my first recorded words. My parents came into a room and discovered me with one of Dad's neckties around my neck. I held up one end of the tie and said, "Poison fangs!" They'd taken me to a carnival snake-show the day before.

My childhood memories of Weatherford are pleasant, but it was there my parents' marriage began to fall apart. Dad was doing his best to be a good husband and father, but he was a born actor and couldn't get it out of his system.

His sister Margaret deplored what he was doing with his life. She felt he was wasting his talents. After a concert tour of Europe, Margaret was on her way back to New York and wanted Walter to meet her there. Dad wrote her, but he didn't say anything about New York. Mother asked if he was going.

"No," said Dad. "I'm not going."

"Why didn't you tell Margaret so?"

Dad didn't answer.

"You want to go?"

"Yes."

"Well then, go!"

He went, and that was the end of the marriage. He wrote frequently and sent us money, but he never returned home after that.

Sister Margaret's plans for him came to naught. He stayed with her for a while in a fine New York apartment. Margaret took the stickpins out of his ties and urged him not to buy such loud clothes. Dad tried to humor her, but secretly he had no use for her high-class friends. He thought they lived vapid, colorless lives, and couldn't understand why they wore clothes no one would notice.

It wasn't long before he was back on the road. It was this period of his life that he described as playing "rep, tent and tab," sometimes doubling as a glass-eater and wire-walker. He toured every city in the country over 20,000 in population, and he once told me of hotels in the hinterlands where there were signs: NO DOGS OR ACTORS ALLOWED! After a few years of working solo he did an act with a headliner named Bayonne Whipple that took off. Billed as "Whipple-Huston," she and Dad toured the Keith and Orpheum circuits. Walter wrote his own sketches and songs, made up his own dance routines, played the drums and thought up mechanical trick effects. One of his inventions was patented: a rubber-face contraption he used in a sketch called *Spooks*. Titles of a few of his songs were: "I Haven't Got the Do-re-mi." "I've Got a Good Job" and "Why Speak of It?" He sang these to me years later, along with others whose titles I've forgotten.

Dad and Bayonne performed the *Spooks* skit, among others, for some five years, standing up and delivering lines to each other that Dad described as bordering on the idiotic, while hanging breathlessly on the reaction of an audience sophisticated to roughly the degree of a third-grade education. In one of these skits Dad played a porter. He made his own cap, cut out letters in brightly colored material and sewed PORTER across the brim. Then he looked at himself in the mirror and noticed that the letters were backward. Confused, he took a pair of scissors, cut them off and tried to rearrange them. Telling about this years later, Dad said, "You know, that comes close to being feeble-minded!"

Thinking back on that period of Walter's life, I am amazed at the transformation that took place within the next twenty years. I marvel that this was the same man who later became a close friend of people like Bernard Baruch, George C. Marshall, Arturo Toscanini and Franklin D. Roosevelt. If ever there was a caterpillar who became a butterfly, it was my old man.

Gram read aloud to me throughout my childhood. One of my favorites while we were still in Weatherford was a long piece of doggerel called "Yankee Doodle Dandy." I loved it, and had her read it to me over and over. One day she couldn't find her glasses, so I "read" it to her. I couldn't read, of course, but I knew the verses by heart, and when to turn the pages. The next thing I knew, I was on a stage in Dallas, reciting those verses in an Uncle Sam suit. During my act I stepped out of a large bandbox in the middle of an announcer's spiel that I remember contained the phrase: "Forty-eight verses . . . and only three years and seven months old. . . ."

I made several appearances in the theaters around Texas, and my mother praised me extravagantly. She told me I was supporting the family, and she showed me a new hat and a purple dress that she said I had bought for her through my "work." Later, when I was sitting with my face to the wall as punishment for something I'd done, I asked my mother, "How can you do this to me . . . after all I've done for you?"

"What have you done for me?"

"I bought you a purple dress, that's what!" There I had her, hoisted on her own petard.

During this same period I had a playmate called the Hoppadeen. He was something like a dinosaur, I suppose, because he was as high as a telephone pole, and he had eyes as big as washtubs. And he was magical; he could shrink down and come into the house and sleep under my bed. In the theater he always waited patiently under my seat. When we'd get ready to leave, I'd call the Hoppadeen, but sometimes—like a dog—he wouldn't come, and I'd have ushers shining lights under the seats, looking for my pet.

The Hoppadeen played a major role in my life for a couple of years. Mother and Gram used him for all he was worth. When I'd go out to play, the Hoppadeen was given his instructions: "Don't let John run into the street." And I wouldn't. I couldn't let him down.

Grandpa was away—God knows where, in California or Alaska—so Gram spent her time between her two sisters and Mother and me. Now and then Grandpa would put in an appearance, then be gone again. He was almost always away.

Mother had a diamond ring John Gore had given her. Whenever she was low on funds, Mother would hock the ring. In Greensburg once Uncle Alec and Aunt Ada noticed it was not on her finger. They went through her purse, found the pawn ticket and redeemed the ring for her. Uncle Alec was one of the town's eccentrics. I remember there being great laughter about him the day he took Ada's coat—a particularly feminine number—off the hall rack, got into it and wore it downtown to his office. He never knew what he had on.

I went to first grade in Greensburg. After Greensburg—I suppose because she didn't want to burden her aunts—Mother put me in a boarding school. I was unhappy there so she sent me to another. I was even more unhappy in the second place so, finally, I didn't go to school at all and Mother and Gram taught me the three R's themselves.

It was around 1910 that Mother went to work as a reporter. She worked for various newspapers: the St. Louis *Star*, the Cincinnati *Enquirer*, the Niagara Falls *Gazette* and the Minneapolis *Tribune*. I remember being in one of these cities when Mother appeared in a state of high excitement and talked about the *Titanic*. The word, unrelated to the event, stayed in my memory.

I never tired of traveling from town to town with Mother. I've always loved trains. I remember so well the smell, look, taste of soot, the sounds of passing over trestles and bridges, walking through the cars, feet braced and struggling for balance. There was the thrill of sleeping in upper berths and the splendor of the dining cars. And I admired the porters and waiters who are now disparagingly called "Uncle Toms" by some blacks. They were a breed unto themselves: dignified, courteous, soft-spoken. I lament their passing. Of all Americans, they had the best manners.

Now and again, when Gram wasn't there, Mother had to hire a nurse-maid to look after me, and that led to my introduction to sex. I recall lying on a bed with the maid. Her skirt was up and her behind was bare. I patted it and stroked it and laid my cheek against it. I remember being keenly disappointed when not long afterward Mother fired the maid.

Aunt Margaret gave a concert in one of those towns in which Mother was working, and after the concert we went to visit her backstage. I remember later being alone with Margaret in her hotel room. She sang to me. It was a different kind of music than I'd ever heard—probably Debussy. Years later I was told that Margaret was the first woman to sing Debussy in the United States, and I understand she was also one of the foremost interpreters of the songs of Hugo Wolf.

Mother divorced Walter in 1912, and he and Bayonne Whipple were married in 1915. Grandpa Gore moved to San Francisco that same year, and Dad and Bayonne joined him there at his request. Grandpa wanted Walter's help in consummating a scheme of some sort which he said would make them all richer than Rockefeller.

Mother became angry when she heard that Dad and his new wife were staying with her father. She had always sent John Gore six very fine neckties for Christmas. Now, full of spite, she went to the bargain basement of a department store, purchased six cheap, vulgar neckties and sent them to him with the price tags attached.

Mother also married again. Her new husband was Howard Eveleth

Stevens, the chief engineer—and later vice-president—of the Northern Pacific Railroad. Stevens was a widower with two small children, Howard, Jr., and Dorothy, both younger then I. All his suits were the same color: dark gray. All his shoes were black, and all his shirts were white.

Mother, Gram and I went to live with Stevens in Miriam Park, a pleasant suburb of St. Paul, Minnesota. For the first time in my life we lived on a street and had neighbors—and Mother gave parties. I'm sure that Mother's flair and unconventionality appealed to Stevens. As for her, our new stability must have been attractive compared to the life we had been leading.

Stevens was a kind man. He used to take me to baseball games. There was a billiard room in the house, and he taught me to play pool, at which I became not quite a slicker but good enough, in later years, to win the Ira Gershwin Pocket Billiards Cup! Stevens had a private railroad car, and he took me on trips with him occasionally. I grew to like him very much.

Dad visited us while we were in St. Paul, and I remember this posed a problem for me. Mother had instructed me to call Stevens "Dad," and that's what I'd been doing. Obviously I couldn't call them both "Dad." For a fleeting moment I considered calling Walter "Papa." I finally solved the dilemma by not addressing either of them directly. This took some fancy footwook on my part, but somehow I managed it.

After we moved to St. Paul, Mother lost track of her father. He just disappeared. Then one day Gram received a telegram from Waco, Texas, saying that John Gore had died there. Mother went down alone and saw to his burial.

He had died one night in a little rundown hotel on the edge of town. An empty half-pint whiskey bottle was on the floor beside his bed. There were two telescope cases full of raincoats, which he had been selling door to door. In a corner of one of the cases Mother found six cheap neckties, with the price tags still on them.

When I was ten or eleven years old, a doctor came to our house to attend a sick maid. He didn't like the look of the dark circles under my eyes and asked my mother if he could examine me. She agreed, and the doctor listened to my chest with a stethoscope. He then announced that, in his opinion, I had an enlarged heart. Alarmed, my mother took me to a heart specialist, who confirmed the diagnosis. He also ordered that various tests be made. Albumen was present in the urine. This indicated that, in addition to an enlarged heart, I had chronic nephritis, or "Bright's Disease," which was then considered a terminal illness.

I was born with circles under my eyes. I have them to this day. My heart was not enlarged. It was a big heart, yes, but designed for what was to become a big body. The mild nephritis was inherited, and I have passed along this physical imbalance to my second son. But in 1916 doctors didn't know nephritis could be congenital, and were unable to judge its severity.

Mother then took me to the Mayo Clinic for a series of appointments with various specialists. Their findings were the same.

We returned to St. Paul. I was put to bed. No exercise. A bland diet. No red meat. No eggs. No condiments. No salt.

In the fall the St. Paul specialist recommended I be taken to a warmer climate to avoid the rigors of a Minnesota winter. Mother and Stevens didn't hesitate—all their thoughts were for my welfare. It was agreed that Mother and I would go to California. Although she was unaware of it, I suspect something in my mother welcomed this as an escape. She was bored with that narrow, formal society of the St. Paul suburbs.

We never went back. Stevens visited us from time to time, but he and my mother never lived together again. Some twelve years later they were divorced.

Our route to California was roundabout. We traveled first to New Orleans, where I saw more specialists and had more tests. The results were the same. From there we went across Texas, stopping off to put flowers on John Gore's grave.

When we arrived in California, we stayed at the Alexandria Hotel in downtown Los Angeles. There were no good hotels out in Hollywood then, and the Alexandria was where people from the motion-picture colony congregated.

Another specialist was consulted. No change in diagnosis. Complete bed rest. No exercise. No change in diet.

I still remember the names of the specialists who attended me: Dr. Lyman Green in St. Paul; Dr. Bell and Dr. Soniet in New Orleans; Dr. Palmer in Phoenix; Dr. Wernich in Los Angeles. I remember them because they cast the Shadow of Death over my childhood—a shadow I was to live under for more than two years.

One day the telephone rang. My mother talked for a few minutes, put down the phone and said excitedly, "John, I have a wonderful surprise for you!"

"What?"

"That was Charlie Chaplin! He heard there was a sick boy in the hotel, and he's coming up to see you!"

A few minutes later there was a knock at the door. Mother opened it, and Chaplin came in. My heart was pounding. I couldn't contain my excitement. No one today holds a position in a child's world even remotely comparable to the one Charlie Chaplin held then. He was more than a picture star; he was myth incarnate; nobody thought of him as a real being. Yet here he was, flesh and blood, standing before me. After shaking hands with me, Charlie turned to Mother and said, "My dear, you must have something to do, . . . some shopping perhaps? You go on out. Take as long as you like. I'll stay with John."

She was gone for more than an hour, and it was an enchanted hour for me. To see Charlie Chaplin on the screen was a joy, but to see him in person, to be an audience of one for my idol, was beyond words wonderful. He was a trainer in a sideshow performing with invisible fleas. He folded a handkerchief and did a little puppet show. Then we talked. I asked how they made everything go slow in movies, and he explained the principle of slow motion to me. I asked how somebody could jump off a diving board and, before hitting the water, reverse and come back up. He told me how that was done. His explanation was simple and clear, and I understood perfectly. It seemed as though only a few minutes had passed before I heard the sound of Mother's key in the lock.

I didn't see Chaplin again until I came to California years later to work in pictures. We were reintroduced in David Selznick's house, but some reticence kept me from reminding him of our previous meeting.

After that I saw Charlie from time to time. I used to play tennis with him and Tim Durant. Charlie and I were good doubles partners—with my height I'd play the net while he covered the back court.

One night there was a party at the French Consulate. Charlie, Oona and I were by ourselves for a moment in a corner of a room. It was probably the good champagne that prompted me to speak about our first meeting.

"Charlie, do you recall, some twenty years ago, coming to see a little sick boy in the Alexandria Hotel?"

He stiffened, gave me a strange look, then abruptly turned and hailed someone across the room. It was a mystifying reaction. It was as though he was ashamed of my mentioning a good deed. I saw Charlie often after that, but there was no reference to this subject again, ever.

Charlie had his share of troubles. Some woman once claimed that he was the father of her child. It was proved conclusively that he wasn't, but it was messy. He was harassed and knocked about, and the press had a field day. Later, during the McCarthy era, he was accused of being a Communist. Finally the IRS got on him, and he fled the country to avoid some exorbitant tax, which I am sure was levied as a punishment for his suspected Communist leanings.

In 1965 I happened to be at the Shepperton studios in London where Charlie was making *The Countess from Hong Kong*. The cast and crew were having a party to celebrate his seventy-sixth birthday, and I joined them on the set. Charlie rushed over and embraced me with tears in his eyes. It was the only time I ever saw him emotionally demonstrative.

From Los Angeles we went to Phoenix, Arizona. For the heat. Sweating would help the kidneys throw off the albumen. For six months I had sweat baths twice a day and the same debilitating diet: no meat, no eggs, no salt, no condiments. I kept getting worse. All my hair fell out. I was bald as an onion. Mother was convinced that I was dying, and her ministrations intensified. My doctor, considered to be the best in Phoenix, even went so far as to caution me against whistling in bed—the strain might be too much for my heart. I disliked him thoroughly.

Finally Mother called in another doctor. He was equally well known, but he was in high disrepute. He was thought to be on drugs, and he probably was. His behavior was quite eccentric: he was known to slap his patients around on occasion. His name was Willard Smith.

Dr. Smith came to the house and talked with my mother. Looking at the diamond rings on her fingers, he remarked that she could apparently

afford his services. He examined me, then said to Mother, "Well, whatever else is wrong with your son, he is dying of malnutrition. You're
killing him!"

Dr. Smith insisted that I be put on a growing boy's normal diet, including eggs and meat and all the things I'd been deprived of. Mother complied, but she was terrified. For her, this was a desperate gamble. But the
gamble paid off.

When I could go to Dr. Smith's office alone, I sat outside in his waiting
room with the other patients, and I was amazed at his behavior. Every
time he opened the door to his office, he abused everybody in the waiting
room—in choice language. He was said to have tuberculosis, and he
would yell at his dumbstruck patients: "You aren't as sick as I am! I'm
running a higher temperature than anyone here . . . and you have the
nerve, you bastards, to come to me for treatment!" Besides being violent
and vicious sometimes, he *looked* diabolic—a tall, gaunt man with a
widow's peak and dark brows. He always took me out of turn. He was
as gentle with me as he was mean to almost everybody else, and I liked
him very much.

It was when I was under the first doctor's care—and still confined to
bed—that I first "rode the waterfall." Now and then I had been taken out
for a drive in the car along a canal a block or so from our house. We
would follow the canal bank and then cross a bridge, near which I could
see people swimming. It looked like heaven to me. To get to this canal
and go swimming became an obsession.

I had overheard enough of Mother's conversations with the various
specialists to know that I was doomed. I said to myself, "Well, if that's so,
I'm going to swim in the canal before I die!" One night I got out of the
window after everyone in the house was asleep, walked to the canal and
went swimming. I was so weak I floated more than I swam, but, oh, I had
the most marvelous time. I returned to the house, got back in through the
window to my room, and nobody knew the first thing about it!

A couple of nights later I did it again. But this time I was swimming
near the bridge, which was fronted by large watergates which were
lowered and raised to regulate the flow of water in the canal. When these
locks were opened, it caused a suction which swept the water under the
gates to erupt on the other side, creating a great geyser of water similar to
rapids below a waterfall. I got caught this night in the current and suddenly found myself being sucked under the water. I thought I was
drowned for sure, but then I found myself being ejected on the other side
and I was perfectly all right! I got out and made my way back to the

house. The next time I sneaked out, I rode the waterfall intentionally, and then two or three more times. So when I was transferred to Dr. Smith's care and was eventually allowed to go swimming, I went down and put on a show, going over the waterfall. It was a sensation! *Nobody* had gone over the waterfall until then, but from that time on, it was the thing to do.

Dr. Smith encouraged me to walk daily as far as I could, and after a few months I was walking some miles each day and eating like a horse. Finally I was pronounced well enough to go to school.

My initiation to public school was not without its hazards. Mother dressed me in short pants, long stockings, a jacket and a necktie! My classmates wore Levis and cowboy boots. The teacher had been told that I'd been ill, but the kids knew nothing of this, and I took a bit of pushing around for a few days. The leader of the pack was a kid named Eddie Strand. He was a tough guy and I was a sissy, or so they all thought, because of my clothes.

One day Eddie shouldered into me and tried to push me down the stairs. We scuffled. Our teacher separated us, but Eddie said he'd be waiting for me after school. The teacher overheard this, so she kept me inside for more than an hour after class. When I came out, Eddie Strand had gone. I knew there was no avoiding the issue, whatever the cost. So the next day, when I had a chance, I approached Eddie and said, "Eddie Strand, if you want to fight, meet me at the cement works after school."

The cement works were near the school. When I arrived, there was a fair-sized group waiting to see Eddie Strand knock my block off. The boys made a circle around us, and Eddie and I squared off. Now, at this time I was convinced that any violent exercise would kill me; the idea had been so thoroughly drilled into me that I couldn't throw it off. As I put up my hands to start the fight, I remember thinking: "Well, I didn't die in the canal, but this'll probably do it."

After the first few blows were exchanged, I realized that Eddie didn't have a chance. He might be tough, but he sure didn't know how to fight. Before swinging, he'd pull back his fist, telegraphing the punch. I hit straight. I could throw two and still step aside in time not to be hit. I was astonished at how easy it was. Pretty soon Eddie's nose was bleeding profusely and one eye was swelling up. He decided he'd had enough and stopped fighting. I hid my elation under a mask of insouciance, threw him my handkerchief, turned and walked away. I knew the onlookers were duly impressed and the news would quickly spread.

It was one of life's sweeter moments.

From then on, everything opened up. Eddie and I became buddies. I was a great guy in school; I was invited to every party; and I was popular with all the "little mice."

By 1918 we were back in Los Angeles, where I fell under the diabolic influence of one Sherman, a boy two or three years older than I. Sherman was a young Edison gone rotten. He conducted exotic and highly dangerous experiments in the attic of his house. Most of all Sherman liked to make bombs. He taught me how to get nitroglycerin by boiling sticks of dynamite, which we stole from a building site. We skimmed the nitro off the top of the kettle with a spoon, and with an eyedropper trickled it into three-ounce bottles held slantwise. We filled them all the way up so the nitro couldn't shake around, and put a cork in the bottle. This was the nucleus of the bomb, around which we packed black powder and whatever else came to hand.

In order to accumulate the equipment necessary for Sherman's experiments, we became accomplished thieves, regularly shoplifting from the local hardware stores. When we weren't stealing something—in the name of scientific knowledge—or hand-crafting instruments of death, we engaged in pranks that should have been good for at least three to five up the river. Things like letting the brakes off railroad cars parked on a steep incline, riding them down a slope and jumping clear before they derailed at the bottom.

Our most spectacular job was the blowing up of Anaheim Landing. The landing had been condemned by the town, so Sherman and I saw no reason why we shouldn't save the wrecking crew the trouble of tearing it down. We planted a string of Sherman's bombs at the base of the thing, lit the fuses and retired to safety on the strand. But we had no idea the pier would disintegrate as it did. Sherman's parents were fishing from the shore nearby, and their friend Mr. Simmons was unfortunate enough to be rowing past the landing in a small boat when the bombs went off. Boards and debris came raining down all around him. He lost one oar, and I had a fleeting vision of him pulling frantically on the other oar and going around in a circle. It's a wonder he wasn't killed. Sherman and I tried to hide behind a dune, but it was no use. We were picked up by a posse that came galloping out from town on horseback. Sherman's father had to pay quite a sum to get us off.

Sherman's parents were up against it. Sherman wouldn't go with them on their fishing forays unless they took me along; and they sure as hell couldn't leave Sherman home alone. Before a planned trip to Lake Arrowhead, Sherman and I stood meekly by while our bags were searched. But then, just before they were loaded into the car, he managed to smuggle two bombs into one of them.

At Arrowhead we were lodged on the top floor of a three-story hotel, and our only exit was through Sherman's parents' room. The question was how to get the bombs out without being discovered. Sherman solved the problem. He would go downstairs alone and I would toss the bombs to him from our bedroom window. That sounded logical enough, and the next morning Sherman left the room and I watched for him below. Presently he appeared, took up a position before a toolshed a few yards back and signaled the "all clear." I lobbed the first bomb out the window, and Sherman caught it perfectly. The second one I didn't throw too well. Sherman managed to round the corner of the hotel before the bomb hit the ground, scattering the toolshed and all its contents over two acres of orchard and breaking every window on that side of the hotel. That finally did it. Not only were there to be no more trips, but Sherman and I were not even allowed to see each other. Of course, we did.

One weekend we broke into an old brick building that had been an adjunct of Occidental College but was now condemned. We planted flares at every window. Then we tore big pieces of sheet metal from the roof and took them to the top of an elevator shaft on the upper floor. After nightfall, when all was in order, we lit the flares and sat back to watch the show. While waiting for the fire department to arrive, I found a bucket of red paint and, in a bid at immortality, painted my name in giant red letters on a white wall.

The fire trucks, followed by police cars, arrived with squealing tires, clanging bells and screaming sirens. We waited until the confusion subsided and, from an upstairs window, watched police officers and firemen cautiously circle the building. Then, in a moment of tense silence, we began dropping the pieces of sheet metal down the elevator shaft. It sounded like the whole place was falling apart. Policemen entered the building with drawn guns, and of course we were arrested.

Sherman was old enough to be booked at the city jail. I was taken to the Juvenile Detention Hall and held overnight. His father and my mother showed up in the morning and got my release. They already had Sherman in tow. No one spoke to anyone. I risked a glance at his father's face. It could have made a fifth at Mount Rushmore.

Shortly afterward I was sent to military school. Sherman and I never really got together again. We saw each other a couple of times, but my days as a sorcerer's apprentice were over.

I wasn't unhappy to leave the public school that I had been attending. The curriculum bored me; I made poor marks. In fact, I was abstracted to such an extent that the principal once called my mother in for a talk and asked her if she thought I might be on drugs. For this reason, nothing much was expected of me when I arrived at the San Diego Army and Military Academy. It was a year ahead of the public school curriculum. I got there about a week before mid-term exams. It was decided that I should take them, if only to help determine my academic aptitudes. I hit the books for a week, took the exams and got straight A's. I was top man in several subjects.

In spite of my momentary pleasure at having proved a point, I found life in the Academy intolerably dull. The only relief was an absolutely hideous girl who lived near the school. She was the object of amorous pursuit even by the kids who called her Hatchet Face. I captured her favors by the unspeakable device of telling her she was beautiful. She was willing, and we went to the beach one night. But virtue, which is always lying in wait for the young, triumphed. We got sand on our private parts—and that was the end of that.

After a semester or so at the Academy I prevailed upon my mother to let me return to Los Angeles and live at home. I enrolled in high school and, in spite of the fact that I had already covered the subjects at the Academy, promptly dropped back to being a C student.

I made friends in the neighborhood with two older boys: Charlie Wright and Harold Hansen. They were upperclassmen and I was in my second year, but we hit it off from the start and spent a lot of time together. Harold was middle-sized, had heavy eyebrows, no chin, a long neck and arms like a gorilla. Charlie, on the other hand, had yellow hair and stood well over six feet. He was handsome, well liked and a straight A student. The three of us were highly critical of the whole public-school system, so we undertook to educate ourselves. Fortnightly, on Sunday afternoons, we read among ourselves one major and two minor papers. I remember one meeting when Harold read the major paper: "Hesiod, the Didactic Poet." Charlie's paper was on Mesmer, and mine on Edgar Allan Poe.

One night I went with Charlie and Harold to see a school play called *Prunella*. I became enamored of the heroine. She happened to be in the same class as Charlie and Harold, and they took me backstage after the play and introduced me. I had no idea at the time, but "Prunella" was to become my first wife.

Mother was enchanted by Charlie. She called him, justly, "a young

Greek god." She didn't approve of the simian Harold at all. Then, one morning, we opened the paper and discovered that the Greek god had robbed a bank—in cahoots with a bank messenger. The police suspected the messenger and cut into a telephone call he made to Charlie. Charlie confessed, told them where he had buried the loot, and the police went out to collect it. It wasn't there. They never did find it. Largely because of his youth, his school record and its being the first offense, Charlie was detained for only a few weeks and then released. He changed high schools and within a year became the student-body president.

Harold boxed, and that's the way I got into the sport seriously. The athletic instructor at a city playground, a Mr. Lott, had been a professional fighter, and offered boxing lessons at $1.50 each. Harold and I enrolled. Mr. Lott was good, and he gave us a sound education in the basics. First he had us punching through an imaginary circle, learning how to lock the wrist and turn the arm as the punch is thrown, to develop more power. Lott approved the style of James J. Corbett, and stressed footwork, timing and precise boxing technique, as opposed to the brawling tactics of most club fighters. When we did get to bag work, it was first with the light bag, and not for some months were we allowed to put our weight into a blow.

After we'd been with Lott about six months, he encouraged Harold to go down to the Los Angeles Athletic Club and spar a few rounds under the eye of George Blake, the man in charge of the LAAC boxing team. Blake was impressed. He took Harold under his wing and allowed him to use the facilities of the club with the idea of fighting as an amateur. I was only fifteen and not ready for this yet, but I used to go down with Harold and watch until Blake told Harold not to bring me along anymore. He didn't want me hanging around. I never forgot this. I never went back, and when I did start boxing, I made a point of refusing all fights at the LAAC.

During Harold's first real fight Lott coached from the corner and refused to let him use his right. He was instructed to use nothing but a left jab and a straight left during the whole fight, which he did. He won the bout, but gained an undeserved reputation of not being a puncher. Actually, he had a hell of a punch, as he subsequently proved.

Harold saw the fight game as a way of paying for his college education, and he did very well. He won the lightweight championship at LAAC, and eventually started boxing for money in other clubs—under another name, so as not to lose his amateur standing. After he finished high school, he went on to the university—paid for by his boxing—and took a doc-

torate in history. When last I heard of him, he was a professor at Clare-
mont College in Pomona.

After Harold graduated and Charlie changed schools, I transferred to
Lincoln Heights High School. Even though it meant riding an hour each
day on a streetcar, I was happy. This school was famous for its boxing
teams. There were two future world champions going to Lincoln Heights
at the time: Fidel La Barba and Jackie Fields.

Thanks to the excellent foundation in boxing basics received from Mr.
Lott, I—like Harold—had an edge over most of the other amateur fighters,
and I quickly took the Lincoln Heights championship in my division. I
had a natural feel for the sport. Standing close to six feet and weighing
around 140 pounds, I was a stringbean, but I used my long arms to good
advantage. I had excellent timing, a good left jab, and I could hit surprisingly hard.

Following in Harold's footsteps, I began to box in the little clubs for
money, starting out at five dollars a fight. I didn't really need it. I had a
good allowance—but I liked the idea of getting paid for fighting. I had
to hide what I was doing from my mother. She wouldn't have approved at
all. I fought the whole round of clubs: Azusa, Glendale, Monrovia, Glen-
dora and as far north as Bakersfield and Fresno. As I got better yet, I
began to get fights at Doyle's, the Lyceum, "Madison Square Garden" on
Central Avenue and the Old Legion.

Most boxers today carry their hands close to their face, whereas in
those days the predominant style was simply to keep one hand out—a
more open stance. I was unorthodox. I kept my right up and carried my
left low, a style which enabled me to take better advantage of my height
and reach. Muhammad Ali often uses that same technique to great effect.
My opponents were usually shorter than I, and I held back initially, not
throwing my left until they came within range. Most of my knockdowns
were solar-plexus blows, and in several bouts I broke my opponent's
lower ribs. I quickly caught on to the fact that most club fighters tend to
throw combinations exactly alike—an unvarying sequence of jabs, hooks
and crosses. When you learned the order of an opponent's combinations,
you could protect yourself from them automatically. Now and then I was
rudely surprised, but for the most part it went like that. I won twenty-
three of twenty-five bouts—getting a broken nose in the process—and
wound up one of the ranking lightweights in California before deciding
against making the fight game my profession.

It was at this point that I discovered the world of painting. Nothing has
played a more important role in my life. Yet I chanced upon it by accident.

One day I saw a page on modern art in the Sunday supplement of the Hearst newspaper. There were reproductions of Duchamp's *Nude Descending a Staircase*, a Picasso and a Matisse, and the article made fun of the artists, calling them "Futurists." I didn't know what the hell they were all about, but I was fascinated, and I sensed that the text of the article was idiotic. I'd had a certain gift for drawing from the time I could hold a pencil, but before I stumbled upon this article, art *per se* had never entered my consciousness. Now I caught fire.

I went to the public library and checked out a book called *Cubism and Post-Impressionists*, the only text in the library dealing with modern art. It was fully illustrated, and the reproductions were quite good. I was profoundly impressed.

I told my mother I wanted to go to art school. She accepted the idea, and I enrolled in the Smith School of Art in Los Angeles. I could see right away that this wasn't what I was looking for. They put a model on a stand, and although I got to look at a naked woman for the first time in my life, the excitement of that wore off quickly. The models were frozen into position, and the students drew them two-dimensionally, first outlining and then shading in the figure. It was an almost photographic process. The difference between one drawing and another was basically a difference in angle. Theoretically, all could have been done by the same hand.

I had attended classes at Smith for a couple of months when I heard about the Art Students League, a group of artists who paid the rent on a little place on Main Street where they met three times a week. The group consisted of about a dozen people, and I was allowed to join them and put my share into the kitty. I guess it was on the principle that a seventeen-year-old kid who was interested in this kind of art should be encouraged.

There was among us one of the finest painters I ever knew. His name was Val Costello, and he worked as a signpainter during the day. I can only compare his pastels with those of Degas. Other members were Al King, Nick Brigante, Jimmy Redmond, a man named Otto and a man named Boag. They didn't draw like the people at the Smith School. Each man here had his own style: each man's drawing was different, even though they were all working from the same model.

Shortly after I started attending, I overheard them discussing two painters: Stanton MacDonald-Wright and Morgan Russell. Wright and Russell had gone to France to study during that golden period between the two world wars. They met in Paris and, working together as closely as Picasso and Braque, started a school of painting they called Synchronism, in which color, instead of line or light or shade, was used to describe form.

Thus, as a tour de force, Russell rendered Michaelangelo's *Bound Slave* in terms of color—abstract planes. Wright and Russell were the first Americans to paint abstractions.

On the death of his father, Wright had returned to California and put down stakes. Members of the League invited him to come to our classes as a mentor. He accepted. Wright was a tall, slim man in his middle thirties. He had a stylish mustache, and his forehead was so high he looked almost bald. He was a fierce intellectual, with a sardonic turn of phrase that was both amusing and stimulating. What he said was pointed and purposeful. He spoke Spanish, Italian, German, and of course his French was flawless. We later discovered that he also spoke Chinese.

Wright taught us to draw according to a principle—*contrapposto*—of which Michelangelo was the supreme master. When there wasn't a model —and often there wasn't—we drew from a plaster-cast "slave." We drew twice a week at night, and on Sunday afternoons we painted—again to a principle: Cézanne and the relationship of colors.

Sometimes after class he would talk to us about the great art of oil painting. From him I first heard of Giotto, Ciambue, Duccio, Fra Angelico, Piero della Francesca, those fountainheads from which the quattrocento flowed. It was the best talk ever. I was enthralled by it and rightly so.

S. MacDonald-Wright furnished the foundation of whatever education I have. He steered me not only in art, but in literature. He led me to Rabelais, Flaubert and Balzac, and the poets Verlaine and Baudelaire. I read them in French, working with the aid of a dictionary and an English translation open beside me.

In 1924 I went to New York to live, and that severed my connection with the Art Students League. Over the years, whenever I was in Los Angeles I asked about Wright and the other members of the League. Most of them had scattered. Val Costello had died. I tried to find his paintings, pastels and drawings, but they had simply disappeared. I did locate one finally, and the work was just as beautiful as I remembered.

I saw Wright briefly just before World War II. The next interval was a long one. About fifteen years ago I was in New York and turned on the television set in my room. A man was being interviewed by a Princeton University professor. He was white-haired and -bearded but something about him was familiar, and suddenly I realized it was Wright. I called the station instantly; they told me the program had been taped, and that he was living in Japan.

Then about six years ago I was in Los Angeles and made my usual inquiry about Wright. He was back from Japan and living near Santa Monica Canyon. I had several long occasions with him and with Al King and Nick Brigante, two of the last survivors of the Art Students League.

I remember the last afternoon in Wright's house with King and Brigante. Wright, then in his eighties, was lamenting his years. He said that he felt like a nuisance and that he sometimes contemplated suicide. But for all his pessimism he thought it his duty to maintain certain standards of excellence. In discussing arrangements for another visit I said,

"How about Thursday?"

"Did you ever learn Italian, John?"

"No—not really."

"Oh, then Thursdays are out. I speak nothing but Italian on Thursdays."

Now, almost fifty years later, Russell and Wright are finally coming into their own. A recent exhibition at the Whitney Museum in New York featured their work. This is as it should be. Personally, I owe such a debt of gratitude to Wright that I can't begin to express it. I wish I had done better because of him.

In my teens I began to spend more and more time with Dad and his family in New York. After the war Aunt Margaret had married a man named William Carrington. Carrington had amassed a fortune as a grain merchant, and he lavished every luxury upon his wife. Besides a Park Avenue apartment they had an estate at Quaker Ridge, outside Greenwich, Connecticut, called Denby; another estate, called Villa Reposa, in Santa Barbara, California; and a villa on the Italian side of Lake Maggiore.

In the summer of 1923 I went to Denby for the first time. Dad was there, and so was Aunt Nan. Besides the main house there were three widely separated guesthouses, one of which—my favorite—was beside a little lake. The whole place was staffed with dignified, kind people, most of whom had been with Billy before he and Margaret were married.

Life at Denby was formal and different from anything I had ever known. We had tea on the lawn every weekday. On Sundays we would drive over to have tea with Mr. and Mrs. Clarence Wooly or the Eugene Meyers, or they would come to us. We went to a little Episcopal church in Quaker Ridge on Sunday mornings. I hadn't been to church for years. The pastor was a young man interested in teenagers. He claimed to have been an intercollegiate middleweight boxing champion and offered to put on the gloves with me. We never finished the first round. I did nothing but knock him down. He had a glass jaw, and I didn't know how to pull my punches.

We went to New York now and again. I heard concerts at Carnegie Hall, and Billy Carrington and I went to theater matinees, but the high spot of that summer was the Dempsey-Firpo fight. Dad took me. The only other thing I have ever seen to compare with this fight in sheer dramatic impact was the celebrated *mano a mano* between Lorenzo Garza and Manolete, the greatest matador of my generation, in Mexico City some twenty-five years later.

Dad and I were not at ringside but in the first tier of elevated seats, with a very good view. Firpo was a massive figure in a brown bathrobe. He stood head and shoulders above everyone in the ring—a towering, immobile shape. Dempsey came into the ring wearing a white sweater, and he was moving all the time. There was an awesome difference in the sizes of the two men. Dempsey looked like a kid compared to Firpo.

The fighters were introduced. The opening bell rang. At the very first exchange Firpo went down, and the crowd rose as one and went wild. The little man sitting next to me couldn't see and climbed up onto a narrow guard railing. Firpo was up, then he was down again. I glanced toward my neighbor. He wasn't there anymore. He had fallen to the passageway below. I paid no further attention, and neither did anyone else. He was probably dead or dying, but nobody had any time for him. That gives you an idea of the pandemonium of the moment.

Firpo could hit. He wasn't the façade that Jess Willard had been. He knew how to fight, and he was throwing long, straight punches. Dempsey fought with a kind of desperation, as though for his life, weaving in and out with that crouch of his, throwing left and right hooks that seemed to come from nowhere and everywhere.

The rule that a fighter has to go to a neutral corner when his opponent has been knocked down was in effect, but it was ignored in this fight. Each time Firpo went to the canvas, Dempsey stood over him—waiting. As Firpo's hands and knees cleared the canvas and he attempted to rise, Dempsey would hit him again. Had Firpo been able to stand up for a moment and clear his head, it might well have been a different story. As I said, he could hit. Toward the end of the first round he connected and knocked Dempsey clear out of the ring. Everyone in the arena was on his feet yelling, and then I saw hands pushing Dempsey back through the ropes. Immediately Firpo charged. He got Dempsey into a corner, but in a blind desire to finish his man, he lost his head. He began throwing lefts and rights wildly. Had any one of those blows connected, that would have been the end of the fight. But here Dempsey showed himself to be a true champion. He could hardly hold his hands up, but he stood in that corner slipping and blocking punches as best he could, and weathered the storm until the end of the round. In the second round he came out and put Firpo down for the count. Instantly fights broke out all over the Polo Grounds. There was a rush of mass emotion that defies description, and I still look back on the occasion with a sense of awe.

A year later, when Dad was playing *The Easy Mark*, he told me about hoodlums moving into the theatrical world. Now, in addition to dry cleaners, laundries and small businesses, they were asking payoffs from actors. A nightclub singer in Chicago had had his tongue slit. It was rumored that Al Jolson was paying protection money.

One night Dad came into his dressing room after the final curtain and stood with his back to the door, frowning.

"What's the matter, Dad?"

"It's trouble. There's a guy outside this door who thinks I need protection."

Full of myself, I jumped at the chance to let Dad see me in action. I said, "I'll take care of him." I pushed Dad aside, burst out the door and there stood Jack Dempsey, smiling at me. "Hello, John," Dempsey said, "your father's been telling me about you."

After years of working fly-by-night theaters in vaudeville, Dad got his first legitimate role in *Mr. Pitt*, a play by Zona Gale, produced by Brock Pemberton and largely financed by Aunt Margaret. I was back in school in Los Angeles. Dad sent me the reviews. One after another, they praised him to the skies, saying that his performance marked the emergence of a new, important actor in the American theater. He played a man who is so hopelessly gauche that even those who know how good and kind he is at heart can't help but treat him with cruelty. He realizes the effect he has on others and despises himself for it, but doesn't know how to change. In the end, he meekly accepts his isolation as ordained by the Almighty. I never got to see *Mr. Pitt*. Its run was over before my next trip to New York.

Dad's next role, in *The Easy Mark*, bore a superficial resemblance to *Mr. Pitt*. However, this play was written to formula and, in contrast to *Mr. Pitt*, was vulgar in conception and dialogue. Despite its being so patently aimed at the box office, the play had only a moderate run.

Later that year Dad received a manuscript from Kenneth MacGowan of the Provincetown Players, and when he'd finished reading it, he passed it along to me. When I'd read it, he asked me what I thought. I said, "I think it's one of the greatest things I've ever read." He nodded. "I think so, too." It was *Desire Under the Elms*, by Eugene O'Neill. Dad was engaged to do the part of Ephraim Cabot at $300 a week.

I attended all the rehearsals. Robert Edmond Jones, then the leading figure in stage design in the United States, if not the world, was the director. He sometimes directed as well as doing the sets, costumes and lighting. *Desire* was one of those occasions. Jones was all black, bushy eyebrows and dark mustache. He had a long, meaty neck and a sturdy body, but he fluttered his fingers when he talked and his speech was by turns breathless and gushing. I wondered if he was a homosexual, but in due time I learned that his manner was the result of his being reared by two maiden aunts. He was in fact a prude. The thought of sex outside the sanctuary of orthodox marriage scandalized him. This all became clear to me when, years later, he married my Aunt Margaret and I came to know him well.

O'Neill was delicate in appearance with fine, even features. He was of medium height, slender and stood very straight. At first he, Jones and the actors sat around a table with a rehearsal light overhead while the actors quietly read the play. Now and then one of them would ask a question. Sometimes Jones would answer and sometimes he would turn to O'Neill. O'Neill's voice was so low that, sitting down in the orchestra, I couldn't hear what he said. In the second week the actors put their lines away and moved about the stage. At this point O'Neill sat in the orchestra. He never addressed an actor from that distance. Sometimes he made notes and handed them to Jones. Presently I began to see the characters come to life. The dialogue fairly struck sparks. Scene by scene and act by act, the play came together and took on heroic proportions. By this time I knew it by heart—the rhythm and cadence and flow of the play had got into my bloodstream. What I learned there during those weeks of rehearsal would serve me for the rest of my life. Not that I was aware of it at the time. I only knew that I was fascinated.

Desire Under the Elms received but one review that reflected any understanding whatever. That was by Stark Young. Most reviewers found the play offensively salacious. It was denounced from the pulpit; a Hearst editorial called upon the city fathers to close it down, then fumigate the theater. Bluenoses went to the housetops and cried that if *Desire* were not closed it would bring about the collapse of an otherwise respectable community. The righteous protests reached such a point that the mayor appointed a civic committee to judge whether or not the play was likely to contribute to the delinquency of the New York theater-going public. With the committee members, he later attended a performance. They issued a solemn verdict: *Desire* was not a salacious play; rather, it was a work of art. That committee should have written the reviews!

But the cat was out of the bag. You couldn't fool the public. They flocked to the ticket office, dollars in hand, convinced that if they looked closely enough and listened carefully, they would uncover dirt somewhere. The play became so successful that the company moved uptown from the old Greenwich Village Theater to the Earl Carroll and Dad's salary was boosted to $500 a week and ten percent of the weekly receipts over $10,000. Gross receipts ran almost double that and the play settled down for half a year's run. Dad was in the chips for the first time in his life.

For the most part, O'Neill's plays were not well received. *Desire Under the Elms, The Great God Brown, Strange Interlude, Mourning Becomes Electra* were all attacked by the critics. Nothing, in their eyes, ever quite came up to *Anna Christie*, which is now conceded to be one of his weakest plays. *Ah, Wilderness!*, his single excursion into comedy, was approved of. *The Iceman Cometh* was excoriated, and the first production of *A Moon for the Misbegotten* never even got to New York. At a dinner party after the opening of *The Iceman Cometh*, everyone around me agreed that it was tiresome, pretentious and a dismal affair altogether. I differed strenuously, and my friend E. E. Cummings and I engaged in a shouting match. My feeling then and now is that if any play by any American will endure, it will be *The Iceman Cometh*. To this I might add *A Long Day's Journey into Night*.

After I became a director, it was always my hope that someday I could do something of O'Neill's. The opportunity finally presented itself in 1946, after my discharge from the Army. I was under contract to Warner Brothers at the time, and I had received permission from them to direct Jean-Paul Sartre's *No Exit* on the New York stage before returning to Hollywood. After *No Exit* closed, and before I had yet left for the Coast, I received a call from Theresa Helburn, one of the heads of the Theatre Guild in New York. The guild had staged all of O'Neill's late plays, and she asked me to lunch to discuss the possibility of my directing the newest play, which no one had read yet, called *A Moon for the Misbegotten*. What I felt for O'Neill amounted to reverence, and when Theresa asked if I would consider it, I said, "I don't have to consider it. I'll do it." She sent me the play. I read it immediately and called to confirm what I had said before. I had a problem, however: I was expected back at Warners on a certain date. I was sure that all I had to do was talk to Jack Warner and he would give me his permission and his blessing. It didn't work out that way. When I got out to California and saw Jack, he declared that Warners had already shown enough patience and forbearance by letting me do *No Exit*. He wanted me right there in Burbank, making films for Warners and fulfilling my contract.

I phoned Theresa to tell her that my directing *A Moon for the Misbegotten* was an impossibility. I expressed my disappointment and said, "You wouldn't know the debt of gratitude I feel to O'Neill. Please tell him this for me when next you see him."

"Wait a minute, John. He's here. Tell him yourself."

For once I was articulate, and I told O'Neill what those days during the rehearsals of *Desire Under the Elms* and *The Fountain*—another O'Neill play in which my father performed—had meant to me as a boy. I don't think I would have been able to speak so freely to him if it hadn't been over the telephone. O'Neill thanked me and said that it meant a great deal to him to hear this. God knows it was an honest expression on my part.

It was in 1924 that I had my first taste of acting. Kenneth Macgowan asked me to come down to the Playhouse and read with a group. The Provincetown Players had two theaters in the Village then, the Playhouse and the Greenwich Village Theatre. Both were off-Broadway or "little," theaters, as they were called in those days, with the Greenwich Village Theatre being much the larger of the two. The Players held readings occasionally, hoping to turn up new talent.

I don't suppose the Provincetown Playhouse held over two hundred people. It had a tiny stage, but Robert Edmond Jones and, after him, Cleon Throckmorton used it to splendid advantage. It was amazing what the Players were able to accomplish in such a limited space. O'Neill himself had come up by way of the Provincetown theaters with productions such as *The Long Voyage Home, Bound East for Cardiff, The Moon of the Caribbees, The Hairy Ape* and *The Emperor Jones.*

Not long after my reading at the Playhouse I was offered a part in Sherwood Anderson's *The Triumph of the Egg*, a long one-act play drawn from Anderson's story. With lots of makeup, a wig and a mustache to conceal my youth, I played the lead: an older man whose life has been one failure after another, most of them having to do with chickens —small chicken farms, that is, and the production and merchandising of eggs. His final defeat is assured when he frightens off a potentially important customer with a frantic monologue on his only subject, ending with a display of *gallus gallus* freaks preserved in formaldehyde. The reviews were lavish in their praise for both the play and me. *The Triumph of the Egg* was put on in conjunction with O'Neill's *Diff'rent*, and the two of them made choice little-theater fare. They had a better than average run.

My second acting experience was in a play by Hatcher Hughes called *Ruint*, also put on by Macgowan and the Provincetown Players. Sam Jaffe had a part in this, and that's where I first met him. *Ruint* was a play about Southern mountain folk, and when I heard Sam read his part, I wondered where they had dug up the real article. I thought he was a Southern hillbilly, and I modeled my accent on his. Then, during a break, I discovered he was born and raised on Cherry Street on the Lower East Side of New York.

Sam and I hit it off immediately. He admired the same writers I did; he knew about painters and painting; he was a fine pianist and composer; he'd studied philosophy at the New School for Social Research under Horace Kallen; he had done original work in mathematics; and he was a good boxer. A rare combination was Sam—and is to this day. I've known Sam Jaffe for over fifty years now, and it is hard to describe him without making a panegyric of it. He is a devout vegetarian who doesn't smoke or drink, but never tries to win you over to his views. He is marvelously quick of wit, with a rare talent for the comeback. He went on, of course, to become one of the finest actors on the American stage, and he has worked with me on two films: *The Asphalt Jungle* and *The Barbarian and the Geisha*.

Sam was in the process of getting married when I first met him. He was in his late twenties, a few years older than I, but he was still *virgo intactis*. I don't think Sam looked forward to the conjugal arrangements with any great eagerness. Marriage was a hell of a big step for Sam to take. When he did get married, he rented the room just below mine on Macdougal Street in the Village and then continued to live with his mother while he and his new wife, Lillian, proceeded to furnish the place piece by piece. The last thing was to be the bed. As soon as they bought the bed, they would move in and commence their lives as man and wife.

They finally went down to purchase that critical piece of furniture, and made arrangements for it to be delivered to their flat. At the first opportunity Sam called the store back and told them to hold the bed until further notice. He was getting his nerve up. After two or three days Lillian began to wonder what had happened, and she called the store herself. At last, the bed was delivered and Sam's last bridge was burned.

My ramshackle building in Greenwich Village was certainly a dubious place to bring a new bride. On the first floor was the 1920s version of a discothèque, where somebody played the piano while customers downed bootleg liquor. I had an arrangement with the proprietor, who kept part of his liquor supply in my storeroom in the hall. It was a good hiding place, and every so often I got a bottle of gin as a payoff.

In the process of moving in from my father's place I had left some of my belongings on the stairway, and somebody stole my typewriter. From then on I was systematically burglarized. My so-called apartment—really a living room with an alcove—was easy to break into. Any kid could break the lock, so I drove a big spike into the door to hold it shut. To get in and out, I would enter through Sam's place and climb up the fire escape to my outside window.

The Huston brothers and sisters were all assembled in New York that year. I quickly discovered that Margaret was the head of the family. There was about her a great sense of power—a forcefulness (amounting almost to ferocity), disciplined but all the more formidable for being so self-contained. I admired her, but didn't wish particularly to be around her. She was in her forties, good-looking, with hair the color of red gold, and the ample curves of an opera singer. When Margaret came into a room, all the other beauties faded. Everybody watched Margaret.

Once, in discussing my future, she suggested that I point myself toward Oxford. If I was good in my studies, she had influential friends in England who could help me. When I told her I preferred to go to Paris and study painting, she pretended not to hear me. I think even Dad was somewhat disappointed that I didn't fall in line with Margaret's ideas.

At the peak of her career Margaret had damaged her vocal cords by choking on a piece of shredded wheat. No longer able to sing professionally, she had developed a teaching system to enhance voice projection, based upon breath control and the exercise of little-used or latent muscles. Margaret's pupils in voice training included Lillian Gish, Alfred Lunt, John Barrymore and Orson Welles. It was entirely a labor of love for her. She made a deep and lasting impression on the theater and artists of her time. Stark Young, the respected critic of the *New Republic*—and an old friend of both Margaret and Dad—placed Margaret Huston Carrington among the "half dozen most distinguished and brilliant figures of the last two decades."

Margaret was a consummate actress in a drawing room. And so, for that matter, was her sister, Nan. I remember once at a party Margaret and Nan did a skit, and I'll swear they quite literally turned into a pair of Irish "shawlies." They blacked out teeth, put hats on backward, let their hair straggle, with tufts pulled out from under their hatbrims, and launched into a performance that was nothing short of inspired. The guests found them hilarious at first, but as they caught on to the brogue and better understood what was being said, the laughter stopped. The shawlies spoke in asides about their surroundings and all present. Their observations, punctuated with obscenities, were funny, all right, but they were also bitter and discomforting.

The Carrington apartment occupied an entire floor of a building on Park Avenue, and it was sumptuously furnished. In the drawing room were Aubusson tapestries, two Magnasco paintings and a Della Robbia. Margaret's bedroom had Chinese wallpaper. There was a fine library, of course, but the room that impressed me the most was the dining room.

It had silver-papered walls, silver candlesticks on the buffet and Georgian silver on the table, each item reflecting on the others from silver mirrors. One of the most embarrassing moments of my youth was at a Christmas-afternoon dinner in that dining room.

The table was laid with beautiful lace and fine silver. A string quartet was playing in the next room. Distinguished guests were present, including Robert Edmond Jones and the financier John P. Greer. Champagne was being served liberally, and I had three glasses. After dinner I smoked a cigarette. Everyone knew I was too young to be drinking or smoking, but champagne and cigarettes were offered, and I took them. After a while I smelled something burning and discovered that the coal of my cigarette had dropped onto my napkin. I put it out surreptitiously, smothering it in my napkin; then suddenly the tablecloth in front of me was on fire! Before I could move, somebody splashed water and extinguished the blaze. There was a long, dreadful silence. Then I heard my Uncle Alec attempt to come to my rescue with a diversionary disquisition on how good Glover's Mange Cure was as a shampoo!

Next to Dad, Alec was my favorite Huston. He had a full head of white hair, eyebrows like graying caterpillars and deep-set brown eyes. He had a square jaw and looked rather like George Washington gone raffish. He stood just under six feet, was solidly built and cared nothing about his clothes or the way he looked. He had three consuming passions: the seduction of women, fighting and the technique of oil painting—in that order.

Walter had a deep affection for Alec, but deplored his transgressions. Whereas Dad was a combination of tact, discretion and good manners, Alec was deficient in all those things. His basic animal nature would eventually get the better of him, no matter how hard he tried. Alec would get drunk at times when one wasn't supposed to, or he would make a pass at the wrong woman. The two brothers were superficially as different as night and day, but they really had a great deal in common: a way of looking below the surface of things; a deep regard for the truth; and, most of all, a delight in the absurdities of life.

Alec had come down to New York from Toronto to demonstrate an invention of his. This consisted of a big machine in which one could place a drawing or whatever and it would project the image in the size required up to a distance of fifty feet, distortion-free. This sounds simple, but in fact it is pretty complicated to work out an arrangement of lenses that will project clearly over that distance. Alec saw his invention as a boon for scene-painters. They wouldn't have to refer to scale drawings, sketches and the like. He was there to demonstrate the machine to various businessmen and artists whom Dad had lined up. I was as excited as Alec about the prospects for the contraption.

The furniture for Alec's apartment had been acquired by Dad from some play that had failed—bad reproductions of French antiques, all with lots of gilt. The windows looked right out on 14th Street, and I remember they were hung with red velvet curtains. I was often broke in those days, so I'd drop in on Alec. He was always good for dinner. He knew fights and fighters from way back, and we discussed the styles of Fitz-simmons, Jeffries and Corbett. We had long discussions on the theory of the left hook. Or we'd talk about art—about how the Old Masters obtained their pigments or prepared their canvases.

Alec almost always had a bottle. It was Prohibition times, but he'd made a connection with a bootlegger. Alec didn't approve too much of my drinking with him because he thought I should stay in shape and go on to become the Welterweight Champion of the world.

One day I got an earache that developed into a mastoid. This was before antibiotics, so I had to have an operation. During the two weeks I spent in the hospital Alec came at least once a day, sometimes twice. One evening he arrived in fancy dress. He explained that he was going to the annual charity ball at the Astor Hotel, a New York social event, and Margaret had insisted he wear this get-up, a Louis XVI costume. He had his wig in his pocket, and he took off his overcoat to reveal silk stockings and satin breeches. Alec also had a pint of rye whiskey in the pocket of his topcoat. He allowed me a short drink, took a slug himself and was off to the ball in high spirits.

I didn't see Alec the next day. This was quite an omission, but I thought he probably had had too much to drink and was simply sleeping it off. It wasn't until the following day that I heard from Dad part, if not all, of what had happened.

Alec had proceeded to get drunk immediately upon his arrival at the ball. Aunt Margaret had a suite reserved in the hotel with rooms for her guests to change in, and others in which supper was served. Alec got involved with a woman who was also drunk, got her to one of these rooms and made a pass at her. She was not compliant. There was a quarrel, during which the woman called his brother Walter a ham actor. Alec took a swat at her, she screamed and all hell broke loose. People came running, and it was a most embarrassing scene. Dad took the two of them out onto the ballroom floor and said, "Now you've got to dance together, to show that everything is all right." Alec took two steps and fell flat on his face. It was hopeless. They took him back to one of the rooms and put him to bed. Aunt Margaret declared she was finished with Alec forever! Aunt Nan echoed her sentiments.

Alec woke up in the hotel the next morning with a terrible hangover and guilt beyond description. My father was rehearsing for a play, and Alec didn't know where to reach him. He couldn't bring himself to call Margaret or Nan. He couldn't get his overcoat because he had lost his claim check. So he had to walk all the way from 43rd Street to 14th Street dressed as Louis XVI. Kids followed him, jeering. Alec told me later that it was one of the worst times he ever had.

Finally he made it to his studio. He staggered inside, sat down in one of his gilt chairs—and there was a knock at the door. It was the woman from the basement apartment below his, who was a dressmaker. Apparently Alec had left a tap running in his washbasin, which had overflowed and flooded her place, ruining a number of dresses the woman was working on. That was the end of a perfect day for Alec. He said, "Look, I don't have any money, and everything I own is in this apartment. Such as it is, it's yours. Look around and take what you want." The woman spied Alec's invention sitting in the corner and inquired about it.

I can close my eyes now and witness Alec demonstrating his machine for the last time: warming to his subject, oblivious of his knee breeches and silk stockings, eyes beginning to sparkle as he explains how it works, animated by the same enthusiasm and faith he has shown from the beginning. Infinitely sad and funny. He went back to Toronto a shorn, bald, nude sheep.

When Billy Carrington died in 1930, Margaret married Robert Edmond Jones. Margaret and Bobby were devoted to each other. Shortly after I went to work for Warners in 1937, I got a call from Margaret. She and Bobby were staying at the Villa Reposa in Santa Barbara, and she asked if I could come and see her; she had been ill, and there was something she wanted to talk about with me. By the time I got there, she was in a hospital. She had had a blackout. "John," she said, "I have a proposal. Don't tell me now what your decision is. I want you to think about it carefully. I'm ill. I don't know what's the matter with me, and I don't want to know. I don't want to have anything to do with it. Bobby is useless in such matters. Nan is a fool, and Wally is an optimist. For one reason or another, I don't want them to do what I'm asking you to do now. Take over. Take over entirely, have anything done that needs to be done, but keep me out of it."

"Of course, Margaret."

"No, no, I don't want your answer now. You go home and think about it."

"I don't have to think about it, Margaret. I'll tell you right now that I'll do it."

Her doctors told me that Margaret had cirrhosis of the liver. They said she might live another two years, but the likelihood was that she would not. Staying in bed offered her best chance of living longest. I brought a diagnostician from Los Angeles for a consultation, and he concurred with everything they'd said.

From this time on, Margaret called me beforehand to ask permission if there was any question concerning something she wanted to do. No one ever told her what was wrong with her, and she made no inquiries. I'd weigh her request and say, "Yes, Margaret, that will be all right," or "No, Margaret, I wouldn't do that if I were you."

In the latter case she would say, "Well, you aren't me, so just tell me—yes or no?"

"All right. No!"

One day Margaret phoned me. "John, I want to go East to Denby. I want to see the leaves turn. May I do that?"

I talked to the diagnostician, and he said, "If she goes East, it will take weeks if not months off her life. It depends upon how important it is to her."

I knew how important it was to her, so I called her back.

"Yes, Margaret. It will be all right."

Margaret and Bobby went to Denby. Bobby told me afterward that it was an enchanted period. Margaret said to him on one occasion, "I should have lived my whole life like this." She'd awaken in the night, and the two of them would go down and sit on the veranda. Bobby would get her a glass of champagne, and they would talk. "It was Margaret at her best," Bobby said. And it was also a wonderful and enlightening period for him. He loved Margaret deeply. Along with the first snowfall Margaret died.

When I got out of the hospital following surgery for the mastoid, it was midwinter. Dad thought it might be a good idea for me to get out of New York for a month or two; I said I'd like to go to Mexico. He gave me $500, put me on the *American Banker*, and I was in Vera Cruz after a few days at sea. The revolution had been over several years, but there was still evidence of the fighting. The town had a blasted, pitted look. Buzzards fed in the streets, which were the same unrelieved color as the tin-roofed adobe houses. Most of the houses flew red flags, which was a declaration that the peons were free from their landlords.

There was a restaurant in the main plaza with tables on an outside veranda. Each diner had a stack of small coins beside his plate. Beggars, going from table to table, were given a coin from each stack. There was an endless procession of beggars. The men would show you their stumps, and the women would reveal babies, all bones and swollen bellies, hidden beneath their rebozos. I'd been driven as a sightseer through New York's East Side and I'd been to Harlem a few times, but I'd never witnessed real poverty before—the bleak, dire kind that revolution leaves in its wake.

The train from Vera Cruz to Mexico City passed through tropical valleys full of flowers, vast corn and cane fields, then wound up through the pine forests surrounding Mount Orizaba and at last came out onto the plateau of Mexico. Our coal-burning engine had to slow on the steep grades, making the train an easy prey for *bandidos*. We carried fifty soldiers, divided between the first and last cars, which was standard procedure. I learned later that the train before us and the train after us were both hit.

I was fascinated by a Mexican *charro* who sat across from me in the coach. He was a fine-looking fellow with long, horizontally combed mustaches, a short leather jacket with silver buttons, skin-tight leather pants with silver buttons down the outside leg, a huge *charro* hat and, of course, the artillery on his hip. He offered me a cigarette, and I smoked it. The tobacco was heavy, sweet and biting. American cigarettes were tasteless forever afterward.

I don't know of any city that has changed as much as Mexico City in a single generation—from a leisurely Old World place to the screaming, fuming hell it is now. The Paseo de la Reforma—today a commercial thoroughfare lined with hotels and office buildings—was then all handsome colonial homes set back behind wide gardens. On Sundays the *charros* and their ladies and children paraded Arabian-type mounts, all highly collected, under silver-studded saddles, down the long green island that divided the traffic along the Paseo. The parade began in Chapultepec Park, continued to the end of the Paseo and then back again.

The buses alone were a prophecy of the future. They were meant to hold at most twenty passengers, but people would pack the roofs and runningboards by the score. From certain angles you could hardly see the bus—only moving clusters of people. They were always having accidents. Sometimes their casualty lists rivaled those of their remote cousin in disaster, the airplane, in later years. The Mexicans drove their cars with the same dash with which they rode their horses, like *charros*—going from standing still directly into the gallop, accelerator down to the floorboard, and reining in or braking to an abrupt stop.

The whole time I was in Mexico I lived at the Hotel Genova, a former hacienda. It was managed by a Mrs. Porter. She had a glass eye, a wooden leg, and wore a wig, but there her resemblance to an old maid of song and story ended. She had been through the Revolution, had lost everything, including the originals of the above-mentioned items, but this had not dimmed her spirit. She was a connoisseur of good living, and I soon discovered that she was very wise. There have been times in my later life when I've wished I had Mrs. Porter to consult. Not that she was loose with her advice: she always took into account the person to whom she was giving it. For instance, when she was asked about the bullfights by visiting Americans, she would usually tell them not to go—the spectacle was too revolting. But Mrs. Porter herself never missed a Sunday. When I found this out, she allowed me to join her. Mrs. Porter was a great *aficionada* and explained the *fiesta de los toros* to me so that before long I knew what to look for in a matador.

Sometimes her friend Hattie Weldon came with us. Hattie, a squarish German woman in her sixties, owned and ran the finest *manège* in Mexico. When she discovered my interest in horses, she invited me to come and ride. The first time I went, she watched me in the ring, saw I knew what I was doing, and from then on I had the pick of the mounts. It was in this way that I met Colonel José Olimbrada. His was already a familiar name in the show-horse world. He was a colonel in the Mexican Army and taught at Hattie's in his free time. His specialty was dressage. It was an area in which I'd had no training, so I decided to take private lessons from him. Olimbrada was a complete horseman in the class of Colonel Harry Chamberlain, Count Friedrich Ledebur, Liz Whitney Tippett, Count Piansola and Colonel Joe Dudgeon—a select group who will be remembered not only as great equestrians but as men and women possessing a knowledge of horses qualifying them as veterinarians, anatomists, horse psychologists, knowing the animal body and soul.

I enjoyed acquiring some skill in dressage, but I soon began running short of dough. I told Olimbrada I would have to be leaving him as a pupil. He said that if it was a question of money, he'd be glad to go on with me for nothing. I declined this, and he made another suggestion: How about my taking an honorary commission in the Mexican Army? There would be no pay, of course, but I could have meals at the barracks, a place to sleep if I wanted, and the best horses in Mexico to ride. I jumped at his offer and was given the temporary rank of lieutenant. Thereafter I trained with Olimbrada's crack squad—about all that was left of the once proud Mexican cavalry. Mechanization, as with every other army, was taking over.

As word spread of the gringo lieutenant, I became an object of curiosity; then, perhaps for the novelty of it, I was taken up by some of the high-ranking military. Many of the colonels and generals I met were Indians who had come up through the revolution; others were from wealthy families. One and all, they were a wild bunch. Many of them had Pierce Arrows with big brass headlamps and heavy bumpers. For diversion, a general would invite some fellow officers for a ride. His chauffeur would be put in the back seat of the car with a case of champagne. The general would then get behind the wheel, start the engine, put his foot to the floor and go hurtling through the streets, scattering pedestrians, while an open bottle of the bubbly was passed from hand to hand.

And there were the poker games. These were held in hotels, brothels and private homes, and if, in the course of a game, there was a big hand and a large sum of money was exchanged, someone usually drew and cocked a pistol, turned the lights out and threw the pistol up so that it hit the ceiling. It would go off upon striking either the ceiling or the floor, and then the lights were turned on to see who, if anyone, had been unlucky.

In the course of all this high living I met the powerful bureaucrat José Avelleneda. He was a dark-faced Indian with a gold ring in his left ear. The biggest private swimming pool I ever saw was at his home in the suburbs of Mexico City. There was a party going on, and the pool was full of girls without any clothes on.

Avelleneda had a mistress: Celestine de Compeamour. Using his influence, he got her face printed on certain bills of Mexican currency. One reason the Mexicans who were in power lived so high was that they knew the odds against surviving a change in government, or simply surviving. After President Obregón was assassinated, Avelleneda had a price placed on his head, and he was killed while trying to get away to Vera Cruz.

Curfew in the city was 11:00 p.m. If you were caught in the streets after that, you were taken straight to jail. My mother had come down from California for a visit, and one night we were guests at a party in an excellent little French restaurant. Our host was a South African named Alphonse de Vanderburg, a man in his forties. Vanderburg's chief claim to fame—so far as I know, true—was that he had made love to Mata Hari, the German spy, and lured her across the Spanish border into France, where she was caught and executed. The dinner party was for a red-haired Irish girl who was sailing for England the next day. The other guests were the girl's boyfriend—a Mexican bandleader—Hattie Weldon and Colonel Olimbrada. And there were two more: white bull terriers who belonged to the owners of the establishment. Each dog had his own chair and his own saucer of champagne. The Irish girl was distraught about leaving Mexico. Her feelings welled up suddenly while her lover was playing the guitar, and she began to swallow pills out of a little bottle. Someone knocked the bottle out of her hand, and the pills spilled all over the floor. Everyone was down on his hands and knees collecting pills, including the red-haired girl, who was still trying to put them into her mouth. Then, to add to the excitement, guns started going off outside. It was election day, and disgruntled factions were having at it. We waited for the shooting to die down, but it went on and got closer and closer. Then it was too late to go home, for it was after curfew. Olimbrada finally had to go out and get us a military escort. A memorable night.

Shortly after this I found myself challenged to an old-fashioned gun-fight. My antagonist was the redoubtable Vanderburg. He had been bothering the wife of a friend of mine for some time. She didn't want to tell her husband, and asked me what I thought she should do about it. I said, "Leave it to me." I told Vanderburg to lay off, and he threw a punch at me. We were separated by friends, but afterward I got a message from him to meet him at a certain corner of the Paseo de la Reforma, where we would settle our argument like gentlemen. This meant pistols. I went downtown and bought myself a pistol with the longest barrel I could find. There was a purpose behind this. I had no intention of having an armed confrontation with Vanderburg; I planned to shoot him in the legs as he came around the corner. The long barrel was so that I could sight the pistol better at long range. I waited at the appointed place and the appointed time, but Vanderburg didn't turn the corner. My mother did. She had heard about the "duel," so she came and disarmed me.

On this first visit to Mexico I was aware now and then of being in the presence of great art. The Sun Stone had been discovered, as well as the monumental figure of Coatlicue. I saw them, the red grasshopper and a number of the great feathered serpents at the museum on the Zocalo. Teotihuacán masks and monos from Colima, Nayarit and Jalisco appeared in shops from time to time and sold for practically nothing. I bought a few pieces, quite openly; there was no law against buying and selling them. I visited the pyramids at Teotihuacán, and was awestruck.

My mother wanted me to return to the United States and get to work at something—painting, theater, whatever. She didn't approve of the life I was leading, and in this she got the support of Mrs. Porter and even Colonel Olimbrada. The people I was going with were forever getting shot up in poker games or killed in car accidents, and she was sure I was headed for disaster. She used every argument, including, finally, the one that settled the issue: if I didn't agree to leave, she'd see to it my father sent me no more money. We came back together by train—I think to Laredo and then to Los Angeles.

In California I saw old friends again, and resumed my love affair with "Prunella," the heroine of the school play I had attended a few years earlier with Charlie and Harold. Her name was Dorothy Harvey, and she was beautiful, with a heart-shaped face and wide-set gray eyes with that heavy fringe around them the Irish sometimes have. She was a gifted student in college, majoring in philosophy, and meant to become a poet. She was the first girl to whom I had ever made love that I had any feeling for other than carnal.

With all the unreasonableness of youth—that lack of logic that borders on lunacy—I asked her to marry me. She had a little more common sense than I did. She agreed, but said we'd have to wait until she finished her last year and a half of school. That wasn't good enough for me. I wanted complete surrender or nothing. In a gesture to show her my own independence, I went back to Mexico. I heard about a boat going to Acapulco and promptly booked passage.

From Acapulco I accompanied a mule train to Mexico City. Right away I got fleas. I was simply alive with them and there was no way of getting rid of them, of course, before Mexico City. I went to the head of the train and stayed there for the entire seventeen days the trip took.

A few days out, there occurred an incident which I later used in *The*

Treasure of the Sierra Madre. Three Mexicans carrying guns came into camp and asked for tobacco. We gave them some cigarettes. They asked for food, and we gave them that. One of the men was carrying a muzzle-loader, and the others had .30-.30 carbines. They asked for a box of .30-.30 ammunition. The *jefe* of the mule train gave it to them. They wanted another box. The *jefe* said no and told them to get out of camp. I noticed that the weapons of my companions were shifting to bear on the trio, and I knew that if the men had gone for their guns, they would have been shot down right there. They knew it, too, so they left. That night, when we were around the campfire, the mules fed and tethered, packs removed, a single rifle bullet came out of the darkness and hit the fire. As coals flew, we rolled to safety. Then there was a yell from one of the invaders telling the captain that when we moved on in the morning we must leave them more cartridges, bolts of silk and various other items they knew we were carrying. The captain shouted back, telling them to go to hell. Shots were fired, interspersed with threats and curses on both sides. Then there was only silence. The captain assigned sentries to guard the mules, the goods and ourselves for the rest of the night.

The captain left nothing behind. We traveled all the next day, everyone on the alert, but we were unmolested. We began to think that what had taken place was a curious, isolated incident.

However, that night was a repetition of the night before: rifle bullet into campfire, roll into darkness, sporadic gunfire, except that the attackers were ominously silent, making no reply to the taunts of the captain and his men. We know what they wanted. Fortunately, none of us was hit on either occasion. The captain ordered a very early start the following morning, leaving four men to cover our backtrail.

The rear guard caught up with us in the afternoon, leading a prisoner on foot, hands tied behind his back and a rope around his neck. We recognized him as one of the men who had entered our camp.

Our men had lain in wait, and the three rascals had walked into the trap. One of them got away clean; another was wounded, but escaped; and we had the third one, whom we turned over to the *rurales* in the first town we came to, Chilpancingo. Poor devil, the penalty he faced was summary execution.

All this time I'd been thinking of little else than Dorothy. I was really in love. I'd committed myself to this trip, but after only a few days in Mexico City I caught a train back to California—and Dorothy. When I reappeared on the scene, all that I'd demanded of her was forthcoming. We went to a justice of the peace for a quick, private ceremony. We had no luggage, so we borrowed a suitcase from a friend of Dorothy's and spent the night in a hotel.

The first thing we did the next morning was to go to Dorothy's house. The dark looks that greeted us only got darker when I explained that everything was all right: we were married. Her parents were furious. We then went to my house, where Mother's and Gram's reactions were the same as the Harveys'. Although not unexpected, it was a thoroughly depressing reception. I then telephoned Dad. I could tell from his voice, although he tried to hide it, that my news upset him, too, but, knowing that I was broke, he told me our wedding gift would be a check.

We stayed in a two-room cottage in an orange grove owned by Dorothy's parents. The seriousness of what we'd done hit us both at once. For five minutes we hated each other. I said maybe we could get an annulment; if not that, a divorce. The fact that an escape was possible cleared the air. We decided to give ourselves a little more time.

We rented a beach shack up near the Malibu Colony, and there the marriage came together. I think we were both happier than we'd ever been—perhaps happier than we'd ever be again. As a result of that euphoric experience, I recommend young marriages to everyone. I was full of myself; there was nothing I couldn't do, and Dorothy shared that conviction. I wanted her constantly in my sight—wanted nothing so much as to shine in her eyes—and I was determined to be that paragon she thought me to be. I made scores of drawings of Dorothy while she read aloud to me from Kant, Leibniz and other philosophers she had been studying in the university. Sometimes I would become so totally absorbed in sketching or painting that I lost track of what she was saying, but I loved the sound of her voice.

During this time Mother went to Europe and, upon her return, smuggled in a copy of Joyce's *Ulysses*, which was banned in the United States. Dorothy read it aloud while I painted. It was probably the greatest experience that any book has ever given me. Doors fell open.

Meanwhile the creative paradise in which Dorothy and I had ensconced ourselves was being jeopardized by a hard reality. We had no money. The only paying work I had done until that time was boxing and the brief foray at acting in New York. We were broke except for the wedding present my father had sent, and that went fast. As the months went by, Dad didn't forget us. He'd send an occasional hundred dollars, but that was hardly enough to get by on.

One time we had no money at all, not even for groceries. I had been running on the beach and shadow-boxing every day, and thought I was in pretty good shape, so I decided I could pick up a few dollars fighting. It had been almost three years since I'd been in a ring, but I went to the Lyceum in Los Angeles and asked for a fight. They remembered me, and put me on the card. My opponent was a black boy from Spokane, and he gave me the worst beating I ever took. I had no timing. I could see the punch coming, but I couldn't avoid it. He hit me with everything but the ring post. My eyes were cut, my nose was broken again, and it was all I could do to keep from being knocked out. That was the kid's last fight.

It was time for a decision. I very much wanted to paint, but I knew I had to find a better way to earn a living. One of the major reasons I decided to give up painting as a profession was my knowledge of the wretched life that Morgan Russell had led. Only the patronage of Gertrude Vanderbilt Whitney kept him from starving. Here was a great painter, and he lived like an animal for years, doing anything to survive. I began to understand that to be a painter you have to have such dedication that even a wife scarcely matters. So I put the paints away and started writing. It was years before I painted again.

Eventually I turned out a story titled "Fool." I sent it to Dad, who in turn showed it to Ring Lardner. Lardner showed it to H. L. Mencken of the *American Mercury*. Some weeks later I received a letter from Mencken saying that he wanted to publish "Fool" in the *American Mercury*.

I will never forget that day. Mencken—the figure of Mencken—loomed so hugely when I was a young man. He was both arbiter and wit for that generation. He was editor *par excellence*, and the *Mercury* had no competitor. I remember how, every month, I waited for the *Mercury* to come out, and how I devoured every line. I suppose the biggest thing that ever happened to me was getting that letter from H. L. Mencken.

With this encouragement it seemed to me most logical to proceed immediately to New York and launch into a literary career. I thought all doors would be open to anyone who had had a story published in the *Mercury*. This turned out to be untrue. I had received all of $200 for "Fool"—which should have told me something, but I was happily insulated in my own dream world. One day I went to the *Mercury* offices and asked for a meeting with Mencken. He was busy with someone else. I waited and waited, and finally went away. I never tried again.

The best I could do, at last, was to land a job as a reporter for the New York *Daily Graphic*—not the *World* or the *Times*, but the *Graphic*—and that was mainly because my mother worked there. Mother—under the byline Rhea Jaure—was, along with Walter Winchell, one of the paper's star reporters.

Mother lived in a little two-room furnished apartment on Houston Street, within walking distance of the *Graphic*. She had almost no life beyond her work. I would drop in on her now and then, and she was always alone, either reading or writing. She would occasionally go out to dinner with someone—an associate at the paper or her best friend in New York, Thomas Wolfe, the author of *Look Homeward, Angel*. I never met Tom Wolfe, but Mother described him to me in affectionate terms. When I would invite Mother to go with Dorothy and me to the homes of our friends, she always had an excuse. I saw her from time to time, but we traveled in different worlds.

Sam and Lillian Jaffe introduced Dorothy and me to many interesting and talented people, and Dorothy was immediately beloved by everybody. I think Sam knew every one of the top musicians, writers and theater people in New York. It was through him that I met Lillian Hellman, Arthur Kober, Louis Untermeyer and others in that world—including George Gershwin.

There was something dazzling about George. He had sweeping eyebrows, a curling lip, beautiful, wide sloping shoulders and a long neck and jaw. I looked at him the way you size up a fighter. Eventually, Sunday afternoon with George and Ira in their separate penthouses on Riverside Drive became a regular event for Dorothy and me. I did a caricature of George that was his favorite. He had it printed as a Christmas card, and I remember seeing it reproduced in a book about him.

Dad and Bayonne Whipple had long since parted and he was at this time in New York with his third and last wife, Nan Sunderland. Nan was a fine actress and a lovely lady. One day she introduced me to a friend of hers, Paul de Kruif, a bacteriologist who had turned to writing. I recently reread two of his best-known works, *Microbe Hunters* and *Hunger Fighters*, and they're as good today as they were then. De Kruif and I hit it off famously, and Dorothy and I used to go out to Forest Hills and spend weekends with him and his wife, Rhea.

Those weekends were important occasions for me. De Kruif and I had long discussions about literature. He didn't like Shakespeare or James Joyce, and had little use for any poetry. For him, words had to serve a useful purpose. I remember, in defending *Ulysses*, I read to him the first page. He was unimpressed. Then he asked me for a translation of *"Introibo ad altare dei,"* which I had just read to him. I couldn't give it. His eyebrows went up, as if to ask, "What kind of an adversary is this? He literally doesn't know what he's talking about!" Since that bad moment I've made a point of being better prepared when I go to make a case.

When De Kruif went to Europe, he gave us his apartment in Forest Hills to use until his return. We corresponded often, and I used to receive great letters from him. He didn't just fill pages with information; he posed questions, teased your interest, made you think and made you want to measure up and learn more about yourself and the world around you. De Kruif was, after Macdonald-Wright, the most important formative influence in my life.

At the other extreme of my New York existence in those days was a poker club I helped form. We didn't have such glamorous names among our members as the famous Thanatopsis Club, but I'm sure we were better poker players. The group consisted of Bernard Bergman, George Seldes, Carleton Beals, Am Ram Scheinfeld, Sam Jaffe, myself and a few others who dropped in from time to time. One of the latter was George S. Collins, who was Mayor Walker's legman. Collins carried the payoffs, brought in the girls and represented everything that was crooked in American politics. We paid homage to George S. Collins. We made up a letterhead bordered by waving American flags, and called ourselves The George S. Collins Athletic and Social Club. At dinner, whether he was present or not, we always started with a toast to this paragon of virtue, who should have been in Sing Sing for his looks alone.

We played every Saturday night, and each member in turn gave a dinner the night of the game. Dinners became more and more elaborate as each member tried to outdo the others. Often one of the better New York chefs would be invited to prepare his specialty. All the members were good players, and while it wasn't a big game, it wasn't a small game either, and you could win or lose a thousand dollars.

Harlem was going strong in the late 1920s, and I spent a lot of time there. Billy Pierce had a dance school on Broadway, and I used to go there and watch him make up routines for the stars. They all came to him, including Tom Patricola and Jack Donohue. Billy was a black man, then in his seventies. He worked at night until two or three o'clock in the morning with a piano player and a dancer named Buddy. Billy sat in a chair and told Buddy what to do in the way of steps. We became friends, and I used to go to Harlem with him. Billy once made an observation that has stuck with me to this day: "The difference between white men and black men is that when things are going good for us blacks, we hang to-gether; it's only when things go bad that we start quarreling. For the

whites, it's just the opposite. When things are going bad, you stick together, but when things are going good, you fall out."

There were a number of tiny clubs in Harlem that served drinks. Most
of these places had no more than a half-dozen tables, but various artists
would drift through during the course of the evening, perform and then
move on to the next club. If you just sat in one place for a night, you got
to see some of the best talent Harlem had to offer.

Billy Pierce and that great fighter Jack Johnson were old friends, and
one night the three of us were sitting in a Harlem club when Jack became
reminiscent and talked about the only woman he'd ever loved—his first
wife, who was black, not the white woman he later married to such
public outrage.

Jack met this woman in Texas, and they got married. Later—I believe
it was in San Antonio or Galveston—he was to fight Joe Choynski. It was
agreed that he would be paid his purse at ringside and the fight wouldn't
start until he got his money, which was to be handed to his wife. Jack
waited in his corner the night of the fight until his wife gave him the nod,
and the fight started. Sometime during the fight Jack glanced over and
noticed that his wife's seat was empty. She wasn't in his dressing room
when the fight finished, and she wasn't there when he got back to their
hotel. She had flown the coop with the money. Jack went after her and
found her in Los Angeles. She had an explanation of some kind. Any
explanation would have served, for he was in love with the woman.

Things settled down for a while, then one day Jack came home and
discovered she had skipped again. This time she had taken all of her
things and all of *his* things, including his clothes. Through the grapevine
he heard that she had run away with a black jockey named Kid North.
Jack traced her to an apartment in Kansas City, but by the time he got
there she was gone again. He found his clothes in the apartment. They
had been cut down to the size of a jockey.

Years later he was in Chicago and read a small item in a newspaper
saying that a woman who claimed to be the ex-wife of Jack Johnson had
been arrested for shoplifting. He went down to the jail, and, sure enough,
it was she. He got her a lawyer, went her bail, took her to his hotel room
and put her to bed. She was really on her uppers and had no decent
clothes, so Jack went out to buy her some. I remember him saying, "And
I bought her this big box of lingerie, too." But when Jack came back to
the hotel with this armload of clothes and gifts, she was gone. He never
saw her again.

A long time afterward I was introduced to Kid North in a bar on

Central Avenue in Los Angeles. I asked him if it was true about Jack's suits. Had they really been cut down to his size? He said yes, they had.

In 1929 I met a girl who made marionettes and worked in a marionette theater for Tony Buffano: Ruth Squires. Ruth's marionette shows weren't very good, so I wrote one for her. *Frankie and Johnnie* turned out to be quite a success. Sam Jaffe improvised background music for the opening performance, and the damned thing went over like a house afire. Boni and Liveright offered me an advance of $500 to publish the play, and turned out a beautiful little book, illustrated by Miguel Covarrubias. George Gershwin had the idea of making *Frankie and Johnnie* into an opera, and we talked about it, but before we could get around to it, George died.

I was ecstatic when I received the $500 check. It was the most money I'd ever earned. I took a train to Saratoga with a friend who was running a horse there, and while waiting for the race to start I got into a crap game. I began rolling naturals. I let it all ride, and ran my $500 up to $11,000! Something told me to forget about my friend's horse, and, sure enough, he lost.

Meanwhile I was on and off the *Graphic*. God knows I was the world's worst newspaper reporter. My mother had left the paper and I was on my own. Bill Plumber was the city editor, and he liked me. The night editor, Scheinmark, hated my guts—for pretty good reason.

The most important assignment I had was in Elizabeth, New Jersey. There had been a famous "torch murder" there some time before, and now there was a rumor that a prime suspect was about to be arrested. It was only a rumor, otherwise the *Graphic* wouldn't have sent out someone as inexperienced and ill-equipped as I was. When I got to Elizabeth, I checked into a hotel. I had just entered my room when through a ventilator, I heard someone in the next room talking on the telephone. I went closer to the air vent and listened. He could have been in the same room, and it didn't take me long to figure out that the man was a *New York Times* investigator phoning in his account to the newspaper. The name of the suspect was H. Colin Campbell. He lived at such-and-such an address in Elizabeth and worked for an accounting firm in New York. He commuted to and from work, and was expected back home shortly, at which time the arrest would be made. Well, this was a stroke of luck unheard of! I ran downstairs to a public telephone and called the *Graphic*. It was too much for them to believe, but Plumber told me to stay with it. I took a taxi over to the suspect's apartment building and told the driver to wait for me. I found the name on the letterbox: *H. Colin Campbell, Apt. 1A,* and went up and knocked on the door. Campbell's wife answered the door and said that her husband hadn't arrived home yet from work. I was in time! I told the woman I was from the *Graphic* and asked if her husband had been a witness to a crime. She didn't know what I was talking about. I could see that from her face. She was very nice, but at a complete loss. Finally I asked her point-blank, "You mean he doesn't know anything about the Torch Murder?" She looked at me as if I were crazy.

I went out and got into the taxi. Immediately I was surrounded by police detectives. They had the place staked out and were waiting for H. Colin Campbell to come home. They yanked me out of the cab and questioned me about what I was doing there, and I told them I was from the *Graphic.* When I repeated what I had said to Campbell's wife, they were predictably furious and told me to get the hell out of there and never come back. While I was getting back into the taxi, one of the detectives slammed the door on my knee. I later discovered he had fractured the kneecap.

I went to a telephone and told Bill Plumber what had happened. He said, "My God, John! Get on it and stay on it. I don't care what you have to do, but get back there and cover the arrest." So I took a circuitous route over fences and through back alleys and finally got into the apartment building, where I found the janitor. I asked him if I could stay on the stairs, out of sight. He agreed, and I settled down to wait for the fireworks. Nothing happened. Finally it got so late that I knew something was wrong, so I went to the Campbells' door again. Nobody answered my knock. I called Plumber for the third time from the janitor's phone. Plumber said, "Where the hell have you been? The arrest was made over an hour ago. Get your ass over to City Hall."

Dejected, I went to the City Hall only to find that all the entrance doors were locked. There were no reporters outside, and the place looked deserted except for some lighted windows on the second floor. I threw a few stones at the windows, and somebody opened one and asked what I wanted. I explained who I was and why I wanted in, and they directed me to a door I had overlooked. I limped in and up the stairs, and there at the top of the landing was the detective who had slammed the door on my leg. He was standing near the balcony railing, and I never came closer to murder. One push and he would have been over the edge to the marble floor a couple of stories below. Stifling the impulse, I entered the room and found it full of reporters and detectives. Then the door to an adjacent room opened and there was H. Colin Campbell, a little green-faced man with glasses, surrounded by guards who cleared a way through our midst and disappeared down a hall leading to the city jail. I went back to write my story and then proceeded to a hospital to have my knee X-rayed.

I hobbled around on a few more assignments before pulling my next boner. This case involved a Broadway dance team, the female half of which owned a beautiful strand of pearls. The pearls were reported stolen, but I smelled a publicity stunt and went to the midtown hotel of the dance partners to question them. I said that I had knowledge of a strand of pearls, and would they be interested in recovering them? The woman played it close to the chest and told me to appear that night at the club where they were working. I went, and as I entered, the police closed in around me.

Johnny Broderick was a very tough, very famous New York cop. *The New Yorker* did a profile on him in which he was quoted as saying, "Gimme a gangster, give him a gun, and leave the rest to me." Broadway was Johnny's beat, and he was the detective who nabbed me, although at the time I didn't know who he was. Broderick began asking me questions about the pearls. I told him, "I'm a reporter for the *Graphic*. I'm trying to get to the bottom of this thing, just as you are."

"Let me see your card." I didn't have it. "Well," said Broderick, "maybe we'd better call your paper."

Scheinmark was on the desk, and Broderick spoke to him first. "There's a guy here who claims he's a reporter on your paper. Would you recognize his voice?"

"Certainly."

I got on the phone and said, "Hello, Scheinmark."

"Who's this?"

"Huston! John Huston!"

"No, it isn't."

"Scheinmark, what do you mean it isn't? You know damned well it's me."

"Oh, no, that's not Huston's voice. Let me talk to Broderick again." I gave the phone back to Broderick. Scheinmark said, "Yes, that sonofabitch is Huston. Kick his ass out of there!"

Scheinmark fired me for that, but Plumber rehired me, and I was sent out to cover a story in Astoria. A worker in a tobacco factory had stuck a knife into another worker, and the victim died. It was an unimportant homicide, as such things go. I was sent out to get the simple facts. I did precisely that, but then I got my notes mixed up. When the story appeared in print, I had the owner of the tobacco factory as the assailant. That ended my connection with the *Graphic*.

In 1929 I appeared as an actor in a short film called *Two Americans*. This was the result of my father trying to get me a day's work. Dad played both Lincoln and Grant in the same film. Grant he played in a kind of a crouch, blowing cigar smoke at the camera. As Lincoln he stood tall and straight and spoke in measured cadences. It was a *tour de force* unabashed in its theatricality. I had all of eight lines, spoken on a doorstep.

Herman Shulin and Sam Jaffe were working together at about this time on *Grand Hotel*, and Herman had the notion that I should direct it. I had never directed anything, but we talked about the script and I said, "Herman, why don't you direct it yourself?" Which he did, and of course it was a great success. On the strength of *Grand Hotel*, Herman was called to Hollywood to produce and direct for Sam Goldwyn.

Herman did not forget his friends. Once he reached Hollywood, he interceded on my behalf with Sam Goldwyn, and pretty soon I received an offer to work for the Goldwyn studio as a contract writer. This I accepted with alacrity and great expectations.

My father was on the coast making a picture called *The Criminal Code*. He met Dorothy and me at the little Santa Fe railway station in downtown Los Angeles, led us to a new Buick and handed me the keys: a "welcome to Hollywood."

6 Sam Goldwyn also welcomed me when I reported to the studio. It was the only time I was to see Goldwyn during my entire stay there. I'd come riding in on Herman's coattails, and it wasn't long before Herman's honeymoon with Goldwyn turned sour.

Goldwyn wouldn't agree to a project for Herman to get started on. Each morning Herman would drop by my office or I'd go to his and we'd discuss books that would make good pictures—*The Moonstone, Lavengro, The Riddle of the Sands, The Magic Mountain*. We'd get high on something, and Herman would go up to Goldwyn's office only to come back after half an hour with his tail between his legs.

It was as though Goldwyn, having invested Herman with authority, had become jealous of his prerogatives. Herman got the feeling that not only did Goldwyn not like our ideas, he didn't like Herman. It was rejection after rejection until finally Herman threw up his hands and decided to return to New York and the theater. He asked for his release and mine at the same time. Goldwyn had no objection.

Dad was offered a picture at Universal—*A House Divided*. He had me read the script. I suspect that this picture was inspired by *Desire Under the Elms*. They'd made O'Neill's old man a fisherman instead of a farmer. He brings in a mail-order wife—a young girl—who then falls in love with his son. This plot, in hands other than O'Neill's, had become bad melodrama. I saw how the script could be improved by bringing the dialogue down to an absolute minimum, making the characters inarticulate. A single word would take the place of a speech or a gesture be made to serve for a single word. This would give the picture both a certain starkness and a distinguishing style. Dad had me write a couple of scenes to show as examples to the director, William Wyler, and the associate producer, Paul Kohner. They both agreed with everything I suggested, and I was asked to see Junior Laemmle, who was then running Universal. Junior hired me to do a new screenplay.

Junior's father, Carl Laemmle, Sr.—the founder of the studio—had emigrated to the United States from Germany. Before his retirement, he had made it a practice, on his frequent trips to his homeland, to engage young men who were ambitious and promising. They got a ticket to the States and a job. The rest was up to them. Willy Wyler, a distant nephew of "Uncle Carl," was one of these recruits; Paul Kohner was another. Paul had worked as a personal assistant to "Uncle Carl," and when the old man handed the reins over to Junior, Paul became a producer. As for Willy, up to now he'd directed only two- and five-reel Westerns; this was to be one of his first feature films. Wyler, Kohner and I became friends and still are after some fifty years.

My script of *A House Divided* turned out well, and Junior Laemmle put me under contract to Universal. I was given another assignment— *Law and Order*, taken from W. R. Burnett's *Saint Johnson*. It, too, was for Dad. Next I worked on *Murders in the Rue Morgue*. I tried to bring Poe's prose style into the dialogue, but the director thought it sounded stilted, so he and his assistant rewrote scenes on the set. As a result, the picture was an odd mixture of nineteenth-century grammarian's prose and modern colloquialisms.

Willy and I often went to Ensenada on weekends. Dorothy usually came with me, and Willy sometimes brought along a girl. We stayed in a luxury hotel that had not only good food and rooms with private patios, but a casino. We always wound up broke, but we had a great time for a couple of days until the money ran out.

I used to work out in the studio gymnasium. There was an ex-pro in charge, and we'd box now and then. Willy often came by to watch. One day he asked me what you did if you got into a street fight. "Get in the first one, Willy. Just watch your man closely. He'll get a certain look in his eyes when he's about to swing. Beat him to it with a straight left to the nose, and nine times out of ten the fight will be over." I don't think Willy had ever hit anybody up till then, but not more than a week later he had an argument with a parking-lot attendant. Willy saw "that certain look" in the man's eyes and promptly decked him. This happened two or three more times, Willy watchful for "that certain look" and, when he saw it, getting in the first blow. Thereafter I always thought twice before giving Willy the benefit of my advice.

I had read Oliver La Farge's book about the Navajos called *Laughing Boy*. It impressed me, and I gave it to Willy. Willy liked it and got

Junior Laemmle to buy the property. Then Willy and I took a scouting trip to the Navajo Reservation. We drove to Flagstaff, Arizona, and took a dirt road up through the Reservation, heading for the northern section and the Wetherill Trading Post.

It was a trip into another country. I remember a meeting held in the front yard of Wetherill's place between a government agent who spoke no Navajo and various representatives of the Navajo people. The agent was there to inform the Indians that they would not get as much help from the government as they had been getting. Mr. Wetherill translated while Willy and I watched from the parlor window. There was a front lawn enclosed by a fence—the only lawn on the Reservation—and a flagpole, around which everyone gathered in a big circle and passed around an Indian pipe. As the agent spoke his piece, Wetherill translated to the Indians. When the meeting was over, the Indians stood up, shook hands and left. Coming back into the house, the government man was shaking his head and Mr. Wetherill had a grin on his face. It seems the last thing said by the Indians—now that they understood the meaning of the Great Depression—was that if the Americans were that poor, then let them come up to the Navajo country. The Navajos would take care of them.

One time we sat all day long in a hogan watching a sand painting being made. The artistry, precision and expertness of the shaman were remarkable. He had two helpers, and they prepared for him natural colors, ground from various earths found on the Reservation. The shaman took a handful of this earth and, closing his fist lightly, drew with the open bottom of his hand over the clay floor of the hogan. His lines were straight and true. The helpers filled in behind him. The shaman had a cigarette in his mouth as he worked. He smiled at us from time to time.

The sand painting was for a young girl. Before sunset she was brought in, and the shaman indicated she was to sit beside the painting. Her velvet top was removed. She was about eleven or twelve and her little breasts were just budding, while her ribs showed in stark outline. The shaman and his helpers began to sing. Then, using two fingers, the shaman daubed her torso with the various earth colors. You could see that she was dying of tuberculosis, against which the Indians had little or no resistance, but her great eyes were shining and she smiled happily as the "sing" went on. When the sun was down, the sand painting was destroyed.

Upon our return from this trip I wrote a screenplay, but it was never made into a picture. We couldn't find a Laughing Boy. I proposed doing the film with real Indians—Mexican or American Indians—but even Willy thought that was too wild a notion. The picture was delayed for one reason or another until finally the studio sold it to Metro, which proceeded to make a wretched, vulgar picture out of it in 1934, starring Ramon Novarro and Lupe Velez. It should be done again.

During the Depression there was an army of unemployed on the roads, and a large number of children: over five hundred thousand kids whose parents were victims of the Depression. Most of them were riding the rails. The railroads allowed this, but many towns and cities wouldn't let them off the trains. There were some very bad incidents; in Texas a number of such children died in a boxcar. Willy and I took a trip around California talking to kids, brakemen and hobos. Then we wrote a script.

The final scene in our screenplay involved two kids who'd tried to rob a pawnshop. One of them had been seriously wounded—dying—and the other held a menacing crowd at bay with a gun in his hand. Standing over his dying friend, he shouted to the crowd, "You killed him!" The camera then came around so the kid was pointing the gun into the audience, with the accusation "You killed him!"

The picture was never made, for the best of reasons: the day we finished writing the script Franklin Delano Roosevelt took office. Before the picture could go into production, the kids were off the roads, working in the CCC camps in the reforestation program. That tells something about the Roosevelt Administration. The change in public attitude was magical. Overnight it seemed there was a new spirit in the air, a feeling of high confidence which persisted throughout the first two Roosevelt Administrations—right on into World War II.

Everyone of consequence in the movie industry had a boat in those days, not only actors and directors but heads of departments, writers and producers. Dorothy and I were always being invited, and soon most of our weekends consisted of sailing back and forth between the mainland and Catalina Island. Sailing was the rage. Men who were mild-mannered and conservative behind their desks during the week put on yachting caps and brass-buttoned jackets and became Captain Blighs on their own quarterdecks each weekend. When you were on a small boat approaching a mooring, you'd be given commands that could be heard a quarter of a mile away. All the terms were nautical, of course. And you'd be asked to do things as a crew member that were incomprehensible to anyone who, like myself, hadn't read the book.

This could be dealt with. One could learn the terminology. But there were other difficulties, such as the captain's wife getting drunk and crawling into the sack with the handsome young actor who was a guest aboard. On a couple of occasions it seemed murder was in the making, so I gave up sailing.

Dorothy and I lived in an apartment house with a swimming pool. The rent was about double what we could afford. We had a black maid, and entertained and partied a great deal. Dorothy took tennis lessons, went to the most prominent Hollywood hairdresser and had luncheons with other motion-picture wives. We had a joint checking account, which was often overdrawn because we'd forget to make entries on the stubs. Whenever I came home, Dorothy would get the martinis going. How you prepared martinis was important. The hostess who served little pearl onions was one up on those who used olives. Both of us drank too much. I had too many one night, and on my way to the Clover Club, a gambling establishment on Sunset Strip, I bumped into a parked car. I was arrested and spent the night in jail. This was not an uncommon experience in the crowd that we moved with. The point of all this is that we were living a standard Hollywood existence. I'm surprised now that I could have endured it for more than a week or two.

By this time Dorothy had given up any idea of becoming a writer. She had become a wife, like all the other wives. Our marriage had become conventional—extending even to the point of conventional misbehavior on the part of the male animal. I began having affairs. There were so many pretty girls. It was completely inconsequential, never serious—until Dorothy entered a room at the wrong moment.

I think Dorothy tried not to believe her eyes. Afterward she appeared to be bewildered and confused. The possibility of infidelity had never entered her mind, and here, thrust before her, was something for which she was completely unprepared. It had been a perfect world for her. Now all of a sudden she was destitute. There was never an accusation or a confrontation; Dorothy simply went about trying to maintain her world by having more cocktails than before—until finally she became an alcoholic.

I got a house at the beach again and went to live there with Dorothy in complete isolation. Now there was to be no drinking for either of us. Dorothy refused to face her drinking as a serious problem, but she agreed to this arrangement. Then something strange and puzzling occurred. It had been Dorothy's practice to start drinking around five o'clock in the afternoon and go on from that hour until by midnight she would be unconscious. Now each day about five her eyes appeared misty and her gestures became vague. Even her speech was slurred. I thought I'd come upon some psychological phenomenon until I discovered she had hidden little bottles of drink around the house. Once I started looking I found them everywhere—on top of cupboards, even in her shoes. Dorothy, who had been the soul of truth, had become a liar.

There was no contending with it. Dorothy wouldn't discuss her drinking when she was sober. Perhaps she had just given up. In any case, there was a complete change of spirit in this woman whom I had only known to be warm, generous, loving and full of the joy of living. Now she was withdrawn, and in her eyes I saw occasional flashes of resentment, perhaps hatred. I had become her jailer. If I was away for any length of time, I'd return home to find her intoxicated. No matter how closely I watched, she'd find ways. I discovered a laundry man was bringing her bottles secretly.

I contended with it for some months; then the day came when, despite all my feelings of guilt and responsibility, I decided to cut and run.

The excitement of the hour consisted of Darryl F. Zanuck's leaving Warner Brothers, where he'd risen meteorically from dialogue writer for Rin-Tin-Tin to executive head of the studio. He'd devised a new genre of pictures, stories taken from the headlines—the "big city" stories, featuring actors like James Cagney and Edward G. Robinson. They called for a new technique—short, quick scenes. After making a few of them for MGM he started a new company, Twentieth Century Pictures, which later became 20th Century-Fox.

My contract with Universal had expired by this time and Zanuck had heard through contacts in the business that I was a free agent. I was called into his presence and given two volumes of a current biography of P. T. Barnum to read, with the idea of making them into a script.

Zanuck was a small man with prominent front teeth. He spoke in a voice several decibels too loud for the size of the room and the nearness of his listeners. He moved around as he talked, flexing a polo mallet with a shortened stick—an exercise to strengthen the wrist and forearm. I never saw Darryl play polo, but I was told he was low on skill and high on courage. I little dreamed at the time that in later years I'd get to know him very well and to like him very much.

I read all the available material on Barnum and saw, in the man's wild energy, boundless vulgarity and casual assumption that he was the shrewdest man alive, an exemplification of the nineteenth-century American dream of conquest and Manifest Destiny.

Meanwhile Dorothy had set sail for England with Greta Nissen, a Scandinavian actress friend who was going to make a movie there. Before leaving she filed suit for divorce, asking nothing of me, not alimony—nothing.

Zanuck's reaction to my script was a disappointment. He didn't like my approach and wanted to make changes that were out of keeping with my original idea. I said it would be better to write an entirely new script. He agreed, took me off the project and give it to two big-name writers to do. A year or so later I saw the picture. Wallace Beery as P. T. Barnum made appropriate grimaces but I didn't think the script, a flimsily constructed success story, held a candle to the one I'd written. I wonder if it was anything like as good as I thought at the time. I wish there were a copy around somewhere; apparently there isn't.

One evening, not long after Dorothy's departure, I was driving from my father's house to Hollywood when I picked up a hitchhiker at a stop signal. A few blocks later, when I was traveling in an outside lane in a stream of traffic, a figure suddenly appeared right in front of my car. In spite of the fact that I was going only about thirty miles an hour, there was no avoiding it. I struck it and saw it roll. I stopped, ran back and saw that it was a girl in blue jeans. She was unconscious. Other cars stopped, and people gathered around. I picked up the girl, carried her to my car and drove to the emergency room of a hospital a few blocks away.

I was interviewed by a detective, and my hitchhiker was questioned separately. Our stories matched, of course. Apparently the girl had stepped out in front of another car in the inside lane. It just missed her, and she then spun out in front of me. I only saw her a fraction of a second before I hit her. That knowledge didn't help much when I heard from the doctor on duty that she had died without regaining consciousness.

The fact that I'd had the previous accident and that my night in jail had gotten into the papers became background for this incident. I had had nothing to drink this time; the people in the car behind testified to the moderate speed I was going, and the hitchhiker was able to confirm that it had been an unavoidable accident. But because of the adverse publicity I had to appear before a grand jury. I again told what had happened, and once again all the witnesses concurred. No further action was taken, but the experience seemed to bring my whole miserable existence to a head. I felt like a fighter who has been tagged. You get one and you're a little stunned and you can't quite get your hands up. You get another, and yet another from a different direction, and each time you're going a little deeper into that darkness. It was the culmination of a series of misadventures and disappointments. Now I wanted nothing so much as to get away.

At this point, perfectly in accord with my state of mind, I received an offer to write scripts for Gaumont-British in London. Gaumont-British was owned by the Ostrer brothers, and Mark Ostrer was a friend of my father. Dorothy saw Mark Ostrer in London and told him that she was sure I would like to get away from Hollywood for a while. Though he didn't say it in so many words, my father was against my leaving. I think he was afraid that if I went to London, Dorothy and I would get back together and that would only lead to more pain for us both. We were now divorced, the final decree having been issued just before the accident. But my mind was made up.

Dorothy met me at the boat. She didn't look well, and her hands were shaking. She drove me to a hotel. I soon discovered that if there had been any change it was for the worse. I talked with her friend Greta, who had hoped the change of scene would benefit Dorothy. She told me she was giving up on her.

Dad was right. I shouldn't have gone to England. I should have left Hollywood, but not gone to England. Not for the reason that Dad feared, but because the atmosphere at Gaumont-British when I reported for work was anything but cordial. I had been imposed on them by the majority stockholder, who had no executive role in the operation of the studio, which was run by the Balcon brothers, with Michael Balcon as studio head. The Balcon brothers all but bared their teeth at me. Again I felt that the cards had been stacked. There was only one man who showed me any cordiality whatever: Angus MacPhail, a red-headed Scotsman who was the head of the story department. Much of the resentment against me stemmed from the fact that my salary was $300 a week, an enormous sum according to British standards. British writers were getting no more than $75 or $100, with perhaps $150 for a top writer. So here I was, and I realized that I had better perform.

I had several ideas for stories. One was about the founding of Oxford University, another was a dramatized biography of Richard Brinsley Sheridan, author of *The School for Scandal*. And yet another came out of an experience during my first few days in England when I had bought an MG car and taken it out to the country for a spin. Passing through St. Ives, I stopped at a curio shop and purchased a little wooden figure that interested me. It was Eastern in origin but not of any culture I knew—not Indian, not Chinese, nor Japanese. I decided it might be Burmese.

Coming back into town, I stopped at Dorothy's flat, where she was entertaining friends. Somebody present had a sheet of Irish Sweepstakes tickets, and it was proposed that we sign with a pseudonym. "Burmese" sounded like a good pseudonym to me, so I took some tickets jointly and some singly, and signed them "Burmese."

"Burmese" put an idea into my head for a story. Three strangers purchase a sweepstakes ticket and sign it using the name of a goddess. The ticket is drawn in the lottery but, meanwhile, it has become a clue connecting one of the trio with murder. Thereafter the goddess sees to it that nobody gets anything but his just desserts. I told Angus MacPhail this notion and he liked it very much. There was a director there who had a penchant for this kind of material, so Angus had me tell him the story of *Three Strangers*. The director—whose name was Alfred Hitchcock—liked it also, but apparently the Balcon brothers did not, and that was the last I heard of it.

The studio then put me on the story of the English music halls, which was fairly hopeless despite the amount of research and thinking time I devoted to it. Bryan Wallace, son of the mystery writer Edgar Wallace, was assigned to work with me, and in the end he wrote a treatment himself. He was well disposed toward me—in spite of the fact that I was earning four times as much as he was—and offered to put both our names on it. I wouldn't hear of that. I take no credit for magnanimity, because I thought the treatment was deplorable.

I dropped by Dorothy's place two or three days in a row, but she didn't answer the door. I assumed she had gone to the country, but thought it peculiar that she hadn't told me. After a couple of more days I went back again and got no answer at the door, but I heard her dog whining. I immediately called the manager, and we opened the door. Sure enough, her dog—an Irish terrier—was inside, frenzied and half starved; Dorothy herself lay in a drunken sleep on the bed. She had been smoking a cigarette, which had fallen onto her chest and burned the entire length, with the ashes still lying in the burn. She hadn't stirred. I got the name of a doctor from Bryan Wallace, and Dorothy was taken to a hospital. The doctor recommended a treatment for alcoholism employing strychnine. He said there was an element of danger in the treatment, but very slight. I had heard of this treatment before from other doctors who had seen Dorothy, so I said, "All right, go ahead."

I visited her in the hospital that night and she seemed all right, but when I came into her room early the next morning she said, "John, I'm dying." And I knew she was. She was shaking convulsively. Her complexion had gone green, and her lips and the area around her mouth were deathly white. What was to be feared in the treatment had occurred. Dorothy's doctor couldn't be found, and with that sometimes infuriating English insistence on protocol, the hospital staff didn't want to call another: her doctor had been notified, and if I'd have a seat, he'd be here shortly. I went over to the door of her room and began kicking it. I threatened to kick my way through every door in the hospital unless something was done for her at once. Another doctor appeared, treatment was started immediately, and finally her own doctor arrived. They saved her, but it was a close thing.

I had rented a little house in Chelsea, on Glebe Place, and when Dorothy got out of the hospital, I took her home with me. There was an upstairs room with a balcony overlooking the living room, and I put her there. We started the non-drinking schedule again, but the pattern soon showed itself again. I remember coming in one afternoon and Dorothy appeared on the balcony. She beckoned vaguely, and I went and stood beneath the balcony looking up at her. She threw a crystal inkwell at me.

One morning, shortly after this incident, there was a ring at the door. It was the postman, with a registered letter from the studio claiming that I had broken my contract. I suppose I had, but I wasn't concerned with the question of who or what was responsible. I only remember sitting on the sofa reading the letter and slowly but surely getting the picture of what a fix I was in. There was Dorothy upstairs, *non compos mentis*; I couldn't get another job in England because my work permit was good only for Gaumont-British; I didn't want to turn to my father because he had been against my going to England in the first place. I began to sweat.

Then there was a second ring at the doorbell. It was a telegram. I opened it and read: CONGRATULATIONS. YOU HAVE WON 100 POUNDS CONSOLATION PRIZE ON THE IRISH SWEEPSTAKES. One of my "Burmese" tickets had been drawn. The English pound was then worth considerably more than it is now; the money was enough to buy Dorothy a ticket to California and her parents. That's what I did. There was a boat leaving that same day that would go through the Panama Canal to California without interim stops. So I dressed Dorothy, drove her to the ship and put her aboard.

From then on it was steps going down for me. I gave up the house. Dorothy had fallen asleep on the sofa one day while I was away and set it on fire with a cigarette, and there was a big hole in the sofa. When the renting agent came to take inventory of the place before I left, I sat a friend upon the hole and directed the man's attention elsewhere. (Years later while I was in Ireland I received a letter from the woman who owned the house, inquiring if I was the John Huston who had burned a hole in her sofa. I answered her immediately: yes, I was the man and I was terribly sorry about it. I explained the circumstances and asked her to send me a bill; a check would be forthcoming. She wrote back that she didn't want money from me, she just wanted to know if I had changed since that time. She had faith in humanity and believed that people could change. There followed an extended exchange of letters in which I insisted on making restitution and she consistently refused. The matter was finally settled by my making a donation to the World Wildlife Fund.)

After I left the house, I called the place where I'd bought the car and told them to come and collect it. I couldn't keep up the payments. Then I went out and found a furnished room.

Eddie Cahn, who had directed *Law and Order* at Universal, had arrived in London in the meantime, and we fell in together. Eddie had come over under contract to make a film for a fly-by-night production company, but by the time he arrived, the company was defunct. His working papers were also limited to this one effort, so, like me, he was stranded and practically penniless. He took a room in the place where I was living, and things promptly got worse. The owner of the establishment, an epicene character who always dressed in a brown bathrobe, got wind of the fact that Dorothy had left me with a handful of large unpaid bills, and set up a little plot to blackmail me with them, holding my passport as a sort of ransom. In the end Eddie and I were left with no alternative but to walk out, leaving everything behind. The American Consulate subsequently issued me a new passport.

Eddie and I spent that night in the open, and the next and the next— either in Hyde Park or on the Embankment. Friends named Wellesley— Gordon was "Head of Scenario" in a small London studio, and his wife, Kay, had once worked at Universal—had us to dinner occasionally, but other than that it was pretty slim pickings. Then I received word through the grapevine that a doctor wanted to see me; he had a message from my father. I went to his office, and he told me that my father wanted him to check on my physical condition. Dad was worried about me. I said, "Sure, go ahead."

The doctor couldn't find anything wrong with me, and wrote to my father to say so. Dad later showed me the letter. I was in excellent physical condition, it said, but I had been "eccentrically" dressed. The inference was that I might not be all that healthy upstairs. In fact I was wearing just about all the clothes I had left: a pullover sweater, trousers and tennis shoes.

I could have called Dad and help would have been immediately forthcoming, but I refrained from doing this. I felt it would be no use. I knew
I couldn't get out of my bad streak that way. The sources of bad luck
reside in the unconscious. We inflict it on ourselves as a kind of self-
punishment. At the time I only thought of myself as unlucky—under a
dark cloud—but that fuming dark cloud undoubtedly emanated from my
own spirit. I examined myself to the best of my ability, but couldn't come
up with any answers. I didn't know where the illness lay, or how deeply
chronic it was. I had neither the equipment nor the inclination for analyzing myself in depth, nor did I have the wherewithal, time or money to
consult a proper analyst, so I did nothing. My hope was that if I left it
alone, my innate health, given time, would overcome whatever the hell
was wrong.

Meanwhile Eddie and I were on our uppers. We were actually walking
the streets singing cowboy songs for coppers and an occasional sixpence.
That's more or less how we survived. It was summertime or we wouldn't
have been up to it. Then one day Gordon Wellesley said to us that he had
been approached by representatives of a company which built racing cars
who were interested in making a picture about racing. Gordon told them
he knew of a very fine American director and an excellent writer who
just happened to be in London, and said he would do his best to interest
them in this project. Of course Eddie and I jumped at this, and in short
order we had a meeting with the principals of the company. Our clothes
had been pressed and our shirts laundered by the Wellesley maid, so we
were at our most presentable. They were frank in saying they knew
nothing about the motion-picture industry and looked to us for guidance.
I said I just happened to have a story in mind that I felt sure was exactly
what they wanted. I proceeded to write a treatment in about ten days,
and our friends had it typed and put into screenplay form.

Once the screenplay had been turned over to the automobile people,
Eddie went out with them for an evening. He was the front man. He had
half a crown in his pocket. They went to a bar before going to dinner,
and Eddie put the half-crown in a one-armed bandit and hit the jackpot.
With his winnings he was able to buy drinks with the rest of them.

They arranged to meet with Eddie the following day and come to a
final business arrangement. Eddie was gone for several hours, and when
he finally came back, I asked with bated breath, "How did it go?" He said,
"Not too bad." He took out his handkerchief, and a couple of £5 notes
fluttered to the floor. I picked one up and looked at it closely to make
sure it was real. Then Eddie took off his hat. It was full of £5 notes.

We had received an advance of £500 and the go-ahead to make the picture. Eddie was to be not only the director but also the producer, with the power to sign checks. He faithfully split everything with me, and we moved into the Dorchester.

Things went well enough with the film project until the first day of shooting. Eddie was sitting on top of a fence below the grandstand at the Seabrook race track, where we were to make some shots, watching his crew setting up the cameras. When he went to jump down, he caught his foot in the railing and broke his leg, right at the ankle. It was a very serious break. He had to go to a hospital and was unable to continue with the picture, so they brought in a new director, and the two of us were once more out of a job. But we had enough money to buy tickets home, and that's what we did. In New York I had a great reunion with my father. He was vastly relieved to see me alive and well. That night I saw him in *Dodsworth*.

I was twenty-eight years old now, and at loose ends. The past few years seemed to me a shambles. All in all, Hollywood had been a failure, and England had been a dismal experience. Nothing discernible had been accomplished, and I remember thinking that perhaps I should have stayed with my painting—and starved. It couldn't have been any worse than the knocking about I'd been taking. I thought I might try to write again— perhaps short stories. So I took a cottage outside Westport for the summer of 1935. My good intentions were torpedoed almost instantly by my next-door neighbor, who had a badminton court and a chess board and undertook to teach me both games. I was instantly very good at badminton. Before the summer was out, the New York State champion came to Westport and I played him and beat him. Badminton is a little like boxing: the timing is all-important. It's a matter of reflexes. I was better at it than at any other game I ever played.

Chess was another matter entirely. I was utterly fascinated. I worked hard at it and read books on it, but at the end of the summer I was unable even to follow the games of the masters. For someone as exposed to failure as I had been over the past few years, chess—unless one had a talent for it—was not the game to help restore self-confidence. I had no talent for it, so I took a solemn oath never to play the game again. It is one of the few pledges I've lived up to religiously.

Another neighbor in Westport was Franklin P. Adams—F.P.A. of the "Conning Tower" column in the *Tribune*. It was at his house that I met Monte Bourjaily, the editor of the *Mid-Week Pictorial* section of *The New York Times*. It was known that a new kind of picture magazine was soon to hit the market, a magazine to be called *Life*. *Mid-Week Pictorial* had always carried pictures, and the *Times* decided to sell *Mid-Week Pictorial* rather than try to compete with *Life*. Monte had no such fears. He bought *Mid-Week Pictorial* as an independent venture before the first issue of *Life* was published. He offered me a job on it, which I took at a very small salary. If the magazine was a success, we were all to share in it.

Mid-Week Pictorial was a good idea. If Monte had only had the capital—which he didn't—it would have worked as well as *Life*, which came out a few weeks after we went into publication. *Life* produced a number of dummy issues and spent lavishly on them before the first real issue hit the stands. *Life* became an instant success. By comparison, *Mid-Week Pictorial* looked pretty tacky, and it lasted only a few months. I left before it breathed its last gasp.

I ran into Robert Milton in New York. I'd first met Bob when I worked for the Provincetown Players and he directed a play for them. He was in London when I worked for Gaumont-British, and I'd visited his flat there occasionally. The first thing you noticed about Bob was his pink hair. He was mostly bald, but he had tufts of pink hair which he let grow long over his ears. You had to look at his eyelashes to confirm that it wasn't dyed.

It took me a while to discover that Bob was on his uppers. He'd had quite a position in the theater, but he hadn't had a successful play for a number of years and was now leading a hand-to-mouth existence. He approached me one day with a script by a young playwright named Howard Koch and asked me to read it and give him my comments. Bob then brought Koch and me together. Howard Koch was a tall, thin man, amiable, perceptive and extremely likable. He took in good part what criticisms I offered. Presently Bob called me again and said, "John, we have an offer to do this play in the WPA Theater in Chicago. Would you be interested?"

"In what capacity?" I asked. Koch had written the play, and it was a finished product, so there was no room for my assistance in that department.

"I mean," said Bob, "would you like to act in it?" At this time anything looked good to me. I agreed.

The play, called *The Lonely Man*, was a story about Lincoln reincarnated and set in a contemporary problem situation. It was a CIO labor theme: what would happen if Abe Lincoln returned and freed the industrial workers as he had freed the slaves? *The Lonely Man* was a success in Chicago, and for me it was an altogether enjoyable occasion.

One night Bob Milton asked me to join him and a friend for dinner after the show. His friend was a lovely Irish girl named Lesley Black. She was in her early twenties and on her first visit to the United States. Lesley was right out of the Arthurian legends—a Lily Maid. I spent every moment I could with her before she went on to San Francisco to stay with friends. I knew I was falling in love again. No, not again: when one falls in love, it is always for the first time.

Lesley stopped again in Chicago on her return trip, and this time I proposed. She accepted, and we decided that she was to return to Ireland, tell her mother and her sister her intentions, bring them back to New York in a month, and we would get married there. What I got out of the WPA was just enough to pay my bar bills, so it was quite feckless of me to think about taking a wife. Flat busted, I had no more business marrying Lesley than I had had marrying Dorothy.

The Lonely Man was to close in Chicago, so during the last two weeks I sat down and wrote a treatment of my "Burmese" story, *Three Strangers*. I then called Willy Wyler, asked him to put me up for a while, took a plane to California and sold the treatment to Warner Brothers for $5,000, with a contract to come back to California and write the screenplay. With that money I was able to meet Lesley, her mother and sister in New York, and Lesley and I were married.

After our marriage Lesley and I went out to Hollywood, where I went to work for Warner Brothers and finished the script of *Three Strangers*. Willy was also at Warners, preparing *Jezebel*. He was having some script problems which, fortunately, I was able to solve. Henry Blanke was producing the picture, and that's how I fell in with him. From that moment on, Blanke was my champion and mentor.

I didn't keep track of the hours when I worked for Warners. I'd write continually on a script until it was finished. If I wrote at night, I would

7 arrive at the studio the following morning around ten or eleven o'clock. This was not the Warners way. They liked to regiment their troops. Writers were supposed to be in at 9:30 in the morning and check out no earlier than 5:30 in the afternoon.

So one day I got a short note from Jack Warner, whom I hadn't yet met. It was typed on his blue Jack Warner stationery, and remarked upon the fact that I seemed to have a habit of coming in late. He concluded with the phrase: "What kind of a racket do you think this is?" I responded in kind: "I didn't know I was in a racket! This information comes as a considerable surprise to me. I don't associate with racketeers, but if such is the case, I prefer to terminate my contract here and now. . . ." The letter went something like that, assuming an absolutely insufferable air of righteousness.

Back came a letter from Jack Warner assuring me that Warners was anything but a racket. Its principles were of the very highest. That was the last I heard about coming in late.

Jack and I eventually became good friends. There was a funny, childlike candor to the man. He was never guarded in anything he said; words seemed to escape from him unthinkingly. He was accused—and there may be something to it—of playing the fool. He was anything but pretentious, and seemed to be constantly laughing at himself, but he was certainly a canny, astute individual when it came to his own interests.

The man who actually ran Warner Brothers was Hal Wallis. I doubt that there is anyone around today with his combination of imagination and executive ability. Under him Warners made a series of biographical pictures: *The Life of Emile Zola*, *The Story of Louis Pasteur*, *Juarez*, *Dr. Ehrlich's Magic Bullet*.

After finishing *Jezebel*, my first picture for Warners, I worked on *The Amazing Dr. Clitterhouse*, starring Edward G. Robinson and Humphrey Bogart. Shortly after that, Henry Blanke asked if I would be interested in writing a screenplay about Benito Juarez, the "father" of the Mexican

Republic. I couldn't have asked for a more attractive assignment. It seemed almost providential, tying in with my knowledge of Mexico and my love for that country.

Wolfgang Reinhardt was working at Warners with the hope of becoming a producer, and Blanke asked that he also be associated with *Juarez*. Considerable research had been done by a little Scot named Aeneas MacKenzie, and his work impressed me so much that I asked that he be allowed to collaborate with us.

The story was of the conflict between the deposed Mexican President, Benito Juarez, and the French puppet, Emperor Maximilian. It was a conflict of ideologies. Both were men of the highest principles. Each man was struggling for what he believed to be best for Mexico. Maximilian and Juarez, though antagonists, admired and respected each other deeply. The last scene in the picture was set in the cathedral where Maximilian's body was lying in state after his execution by Juarez. Juarez came into the cathedral alone, went to the bier, knelt down and asked forgiveness.

MacKenzie, Reinhardt and I worked in complete harmony. Wolfgang had a scholar's knowledge of Europe during the period of Napoleon III and the Hapsburgs; I was a Jeffersonian Democrat espousing ideals similar to those of Benito Juarez; and MacKenzie believed in the monarchical system—perhaps even to the point of defending the Divine Right of Kings. Thus the actual writing, when MacKenzie and I got to it, was by way of being dialectic. We worked on the screenplay for almost a year. Warner Brothers always kept a day-by-day account of script progress and how their writers were doing, but, thanks to Henry Blanke, we were spared the customary surveillance. Nothing was shown to the front office until the last line had been written. After we turned it in, I got a call from Hal Wallis, followed by a note saying it was the best script he had ever read.

That delighted us no end, but our pleasure was short-lived. Paul Muni, who was to play the part of Benito Juarez, insisted on changes to accommodate his own conceit. We had dramatized Juarez' Indian taciturnity. Whatever he said was in as few words as possible and always to the point. Muni complained because he didn't have as many lines as Maximilian. He was, in those years, a great star. His roles in several successful biographical films had taken him to the top. He was held in the highest regard, especially by Warners. In Mr. Muni's estimation, his contributions to the dramatic arts were for the enrichment of the world. It was heavy going around Muni.

Wallis and Blanke both tried to convince Muni that he was wrong in his requirements, but he was deaf to their arguments. The director, William Dieterle, a German of considerable talent who'd made two pictures with Muni—*Pasteur* and *Zola*—assured me that he had defended the script to the best of his powers, but Muni wouldn't listen to him either. Muni didn't have a very nimble intelligence; still, in argument he was hard to corner. And if one did succeed in cornering him, he simply issued a fiat: unless changes were made, he wouldn't do the picture. The studio had lent itself to the creation of his ponderous prestige; now it had to pay the consequences. So a new writer—Muni's brother-in-law—was put on the script. His changes did the picture irreparable damage. It was a beautifully mounted picture with outstanding performances by Bette Davis, Brian Aherne, John Garfield and, yes, Muni too. It would have been a great picture if his mentality had been equal to his talent.

Around this time Paul Kohner became my agent. When I was in England, "Uncle Carl" Laemmle had sold Universal, and my friend Paul, along with all the other "nephews" from the Old Country, had to find work elsewhere. He had a bad time of it. One job after another came to nothing. At last he decided to forget about being a producer and to start an agency. I was Paul's first client, and he is still my agent. Forty years, or near to it, must be some kind of record in a place where the relationship between agents and clients is as transient as that between husbands and wives.

I'd gone out to Warners to write the screenplay *Three Strangers* for $500 a week. When they took up my option, the salary went to $750. With the assurance that I had a future with Warners, I borrowed $25,000 and Lesley and I started building a house. It was located near Tarzana, then merely a crossroads in the San Fernando Valley. As I recall, the biggest industry there was the Adohr Milk Farm.

I designed the house, and got Rochelle Lewis, the man who had constructed a house for my father in the San Bernardino Mountains, to build it. The Tarzana land was some seven acres at the foot of a high hill, and it had two small knolls on it. The house was built on those two knolls with a bridge between them to serve as a gallery. A pool came out from beneath the bridge, and you could dive into it from the rear veranda. The Valley was quite hot, so I designed a small attic space with louvers running the length of the roof. The house was inspired more by stable architecture than any other style. It offset the heat and suited the terrain.

One day Lewis phoned and said that he was with Frank Lloyd Wright, who'd heard about the house and would like to see it. Might he bring him out? I said I'd be honored. Wright cut a somewhat theatrical figure with his silver-white mane, worn long for that period, a cape and a big Bohemian Quarter hat.

As he came into the house, he looked disapproving and said, "I see you have a threshold." Before I could ask him what, if anything, was wrong with that, he strolled into the living room and looked up, again disapproving. "I don't like high ceilings. I like the sense of shelter that a low ceiling gives. Why do you have high ceilings, Mr. Huston?"

I'm tall. I explained that low ceilings are uncongenial to someone of my height. You never feel you can stand upright. I like the sense of space and freedom that a high ceiling gives.

"Anyone over five-ten is a weed," Wright said.

After a while we went outside. Wright stood looking up at the high hill directly behind the property. With a long sigh he remarked, "How beautiful! I hate to turn around and look at the house." But he did so, and though I was now expecting a diatribe that would demolish me certainly and the house itself perhaps, he surprised me by expressing general approval of what I'd done. He had specific criticisms as well. It had been a mistake to use such heavy beams in the bridge section. It took away from the unity and flow of the whole. He was obviously right. He went on from there to give what amounted to a lecture, referring to the house to illustrate his points. It was an unforgettable lesson in architecture. In concluding his observations, he said it delighted him to see a natural expression from an amateur. Unlike the other arts, modern architecture tended to exclude amateurs—first, because in most cities having the plans drawn by a certified architect is mandatory and, second, because the building itself is so costly that the owner cannot afford to make mistakes and start over. These, he said, were among the reasons why, of all the arts, architecture was the least benefited by independent and original thought or feeling.

This was the only time I ever met Wright. After his death a few years later I received a call from someone at the University of Wisconsin telling me that among instructions left by Wright to be followed after his death was one that said if a film about his life was ever contemplated, he'd prefer that John Huston do it. I would like to.

Gram and Mother had come out to Los Angeles and taken an apartment. Mother was in great good spirits, and both she and Gram thought highly of Lesley. We saw a lot of them. Mother was very proud of her new driver's license. She had bought a car in New York—her very first car—and had driven it to Indiana, where she picked up Gram. From there the two of them had come cross-country. One Sunday afternoon, at her insistence, I took a ride with Mother—or, rather, she took me for a ride. She went at about fifteen miles per hour, hard over to the right side of the road; she steered a zigzag course first toward the right, then toward the left, alternately. We'd go off the asphalt onto the dirt borders from time to time, but this didn't seem to faze her. She was certainly the worst driver I have ever sat beside, and I marveled that she and Gram had made it. The trip to the Coast had taken them nearly two weeks, and now I knew why.

Not long after they arrived, Mother began to have headaches—so severe they'd bring tears to her eyes. They would last an hour or two. As the weeks passed, these attacks became more and more frequent, so I telephoned Loyal Davis.

Loyal, one of the foremost neurological surgeons in the world and a longtime friend of my father and mine, was then professor of surgery in Northwestern University. He recommended a diagnostician in Los Angeles. I took Mother to him. The doctor left the door to an inner office open. I heard him asking Mother questions, and I heard her replies. At first her answers were intelligent and to the point. Then, in responding to a query about her everyday activities, she began to talk in a random, illogical fashion, describing a life style that existed only in her imagination: friends, parties, joyous occasions.

Before long the doctor came out.

"Did you hear?"

"Yes, and I can't make anything out of it at all."

"Has this happened before?"

"No, it's the first time."

He said, "Either she's psychotic or there's a lesion in the brain."

When Loyal heard my account of what had happened, he was on the next plane. It was his opinion, after examining Mother, that she should be kept under observation for a time. A pneumo-encephalogram was not only extremely painful but somewhat dangerous, and we didn't want Mother to go through this if it was unnecessary. We put her in a nursing home, but she deteriorated rapidly. Speaking, she'd transpose syllables. She talked with apparent ease, in conventional tones, except that what she said was scrambled. After a few weeks she retreated into silence. A pneumo-encephalogram had to be made, and it showed that she had a brain tumor.

Shortly before Mother went up for her operation, I spoke to her. Now she had become entirely mute. She lay, her eyes closed, but conscious. I said, "Mother, they know what's wrong with you. They're going to fix it now." I had hoped only that some of this might get through to her. I knew she couldn't respond.

But she answered me perfectly clearly. "Can they fix it, John?"

"Yes, they can fix it, Mother."

It was as if a ghost had spoken to me. She smiled without opening her eyes, and nodded on her pillow. They gave her an injection and took her up to surgery. She never regained consciousness.

My writing assignment for Warners after *Juarez* was *Dr. Ehrlich's Magic Bullet*, another biographical picture. This film—the story of Paul Ehrlich, who discovered Salvarsan, a specific remedy for syphilis—was released in March 1940. The screenplay was nominated for an Academy Award.

My father had been working exclusively in motion pictures and living in Los Angeles. A New York producer, Montgomery Ford, sent him a play to read, *A Passenger to Bali*, by Ellis St. Joseph. Dad felt a return to the theater was in order. He liked the part and asked me if I would direct him in the play. I jumped at the chance. Warners gave me time off and, shortly, Dad and I were in New York and rehearsals began.

The play is a contest between a demagogue and a man of conscience. All the action takes place on a tramp steamer plying the China Seas. The captain is cursed with the presence of a lone passenger he can't get rid of. None of the ports of call will receive him. He's a known troublemaker, the instigator of race riots, religious conflicts. Now, at sea, for want of bigger game, he sets about undermining the captain's authority with the native crew. The captain finds himself a prisoner on his own ship. Only when the ship goes on the rocks does the crew comprehend the wanton destructiveness of the passenger. He's left to perish on the derelict. The question propounded by the play was: Should the captain have put the passenger adrift in an open boat some time beforehand and saved his ship, or was he right in having acted according to the law even at the cost of his ship?

It was an interesting theme, and the play was quite well written, but it was soft in the middle and lost impetus in the last act. What the passenger said became repetitive. It was an honorable failure, even though it closed after only a few performances.

I returned to Warners to work on *Sergeant York*. Howard Hawks directed. It's gone down as one of Howard's best pictures, and Gary Cooper had a triumph playing the young mountaineer.

My next assignment was to adapt W. R. Burnett's crime novel *High Sierra* into a screenplay. I have always admired Burnett, who seems to me one of the most neglected American writers: *Iron Man*, *Saint Johnson*, *Dark Hazard*, *Little Caesar*, *The Asphalt Jungle* and *The Giant Swing*—considerable novels all. There are moments of reality in all those books that are quite overpowering. More than once they've had me breaking into a sweat.

Mark Hellinger was the producer of *High Sierra*, and Raoul Walsh directed it. Paul Muni was offered the lead, and I was pleased when he turned it down and Humphrey Bogart got to do it. Before this picture Bogie was well down the list at Warners. *High Sierra* marked a turning point in his career.

Paul Kohner had written into my contract that if Warners took up my next option I would be allowed to direct a film. I selected Dashiell Hammett's *The Maltese Falcon*. It had been filmed twice before, but never successfully. Blanke and Wallis were surprised at my wanting to remake a two-time failure, but the fact was that *Falcon* had never really been put on the screen. The previous screenplays had been products of writers who sought to put their own stamp on the story by writing new, uncalled-for scenes.

This time it was George Raft who had to be offered the role first. Raft turned it down; he didn't want to work under an inexperienced director—so I fell heir to Bogie, for which I was duly thankful.

I came very well prepared to my first directorial assignment. *The Maltese Falcon* was a very carefully tailored screenplay, not only scene by scene but set-up by set-up. I made a sketch of each set-up. If it was to be a pan or a dolly shot, I'd indicate it. I didn't want ever to be at a loss before the actors or the camera crew. I went over the sketches with Willy Wyler. He had a few suggestions to make, but, on the whole, approved what he saw. I also showed the sketches to my producer, Henry Blanke. All Blanke said was, "John, just remember that each scene, as you shoot it, is the most important scene in the picture." That's the best advice any young director could have.

I had my set-ups, but I didn't want to be rigid in my approach. I would have the actors rehearse a scene, work it out for themselves without any instructions from me. As they spoke their lines and moved about, they would, for the most part, fall into the positions indicated in my sketch. Sometimes what they did was better than what I'd drawn, in which case we'd do it their way. Only about twenty-five percent of the time would it be necessary to bring them around to conform with my original idea.

The English actor Sydney Greenstreet had worked on Broadway, but this was, I believe, his first film. There's always talk about the difficulty of making the transition from the stage to the screen, but you wouldn't know it to watch Greenstreet; he was perfect from the word go, the Fat Man inside out. I had only to sit back and take delight in him and his performance.

I rehearsed with Mary Astor before the picture started, and together we worked out her characterization of the amoral Brigid O'Shaughnessy: her voice hesitant, tremulous and pleading, her eyes full of candor. She was the enchanting murderess to my idea of perfection.

Peter Lorre was one of the finest and most subtle actors I have ever worked with. Beneath that air of innocence he used to such effect, one sensed a Faustian worldliness. I'd know he was giving a good performance as we put it on film but I wouldn't know how good until I saw him in the rushes.

Elisha Cook, Jr., lived alone up in the High Sierra, tied flies and caught golden trout between films. When he was wanted in Hollywood, they sent word up to his mountain cabin by courier. He would come down, do a picture and then withdraw again to his retreat.

Bogie was a medium-sized man, not particularly impressive offscreen, but something happened when he was playing the right part. Those lights and shadows composed themselves into another, nobler personality: heroic, as in *High Sierra*. I swear the camera has a way of looking into a person and perceiving things that the naked eye doesn't register.

Bogie was then married to Mayo Methot, whom he called "Rosebud," probably after the sled in *Citizen Kane*. She was forever "on stage"—raucous and demanding. Bogie indulged her and did his best to placate her. But let her feel attention shifting away from her person and there would be hell to pay. She was known to throw plates in restaurants and wield knives. I can only marvel at Bogie's putting up with her as long as he did.

As a rule, at the end of the day everyone goes home, each to his separate domicile. But we were all having such a good time together on *Falcon* that, night after night after shooting, Bogie, Peter Lorre, Ward Bond, Mary Astor and I would go over to the Lakeside Country Club. We'd have a few drinks, then a buffet supper, and stay on till midnight. We all thought we were doing something good, but no one had any idea that *The Maltese Falcon* would be a great success and eventually take its place as a film classic.

During the entire filming not one line of dialogue was changed. One short scene was dropped when I realized I could substitute a telephone call for it without loss to the story.

There was a long scene in Sam Spade's apartment that, according to my sketches, would be made in a number of cuts, but in the rehearsal we decided to move the camera, dolly and pan instead. One camera move led to another until finally there were, I suppose, more moves in that scene than in any scene I ever made afterward.

We shot it in one take. The men on the dolly had to know the cues as well as the actors; the suspense during the take was electric, but Arthur Edeson, the cameraman, brought it off. I don't remember exactly how many dolly moves were made, but the number twenty-six comes to mind.

Blanke put me together with the composer Adolph Deutsch. Working with the composer was a privilege afforded only to top directors. This was another example of Blanke's confidence in me. Deutsch and I ran the picture many times, discussing where music should be used and where not. As with good cutting, the audience is not as a rule supposed to be conscious of the music. Ideally, it speaks directly to our emotions without our awareness of it, although, of course, there are moments when music should take over and dominate the action.

When the time came to preview the picture—in a neighborhood theater out in Pasadena—I was surprised that both Jack Warner and Hal Wallis attended. The heads of the publicity and editorial departments and various other top men were also there. It commanded considerably more interest than the average "B" film. The audience reaction was good, the preview cards were from good to excellent, and it was decided that no cuts were required. The publicity department wanted to call it *The Gent from Frisco*, but Hal Wallis persuaded Jack to let it remain *The Maltese Falcon*.

On the drive back to the studio with Hal I ventured to ask him how good he thought it was. "Good," he said. "How good?" "Good."

I spoke to Hal Wallis about Howard Koch, the author of *The Lonely Man*, and, on my recommendation, they brought him out to Warners. He later wrote *Casablanca*, the biggest success the studio ever had. What should have been a brilliant career was, however, irretrievably damaged when Howard was blacklisted during the Communist witch-hunt following the war. He wasn't one of the Hollywood Ten, nor was he a Communist, nor was he a fellow traveler, but he refused to grovel before his accusers, and that was enough to make him unemployable.

Koch's first assignment at Warner Brothers was *In This Our Life*, based on the novel by Ellen Glasgow. Wallis offered it to me. I didn't like the script, but Koch was there on my say-so and I couldn't very well shoot down his first effort. Also it was very flattering for me—a director with only one picture behind him—to be given a picture with Warners' top stars: Bette Davis, Olivia de Havilland, Charles Coburn, George Brent and Dennis Morgan. So I put aside my reservations and tried to make the best picture I could.

I never cared for *In This Our Life*, although there were some good things about it. It was the first time, I believe, that a black character was presented as anything other than a good and faithful servant or comic relief. Bette fascinated me. There is something elemental about Bette—a demon within her which threatens to break out and eat everybody, beginning with their ears. The studio was afraid of her; afraid of her demon. They confused it with overacting. Over their objections, I let the demon go; some critics thought Bette's performance was one of her finest. But I will remember this film mostly for what it shows about the old "dictatorial" studio system: how much sympathy and latitude could be granted even to someone as inexperienced as I.

Under the studio system, no one ever had any real idea how successful a picture was unless it was an absolute runaway. *Variety* gave weekly box-office figures for major houses, but those figures were only approximations, and no one could tell whether they had been padded for publicity purposes or reduced for other reasons. The books of the company were not open. You could tell, in general, whether the picture was making money, but you had no access to the details. Nor were you all that interested. You were paid a salary, and your main interest was in going ahead and making the best pictures you could.

Most major studios worked about the same way. First, the story was decided upon and the script written, and that script was more or less gospel. Under the present system, many pictures go into production with screenplays that are half-baked, and directors and writers continue to work on them as they're being shot. That seldom if ever happened in the old days. If there were changes to be made during the shooting, the changed pages had to be shown to the producer and sometimes even to the head of the studio and be approved. This would seem to give the director less authority than he might like, but, in my case at least, it never worked out that way.

Once a screenplay was accepted, it was given a budget. In doing this, the studio took into account which category the picture fell into. More time had to be allowed for an "A" picture with stars. Making a picture of that kind, you figured on filming about three script pages a day. A "B" picture was made faster—perhaps six pages a day. The production department timed each individual scene in advance and also determined the order in which the scenes would be shot.

I have always liked to stay in continuity as much as possible, for it allows greater freedom with the story. If you haven't locked yourself into a corner by shooting scenes toward the end of the picture early on, you are free to incorporate ideas that present themselves as you go along. For instance, the scene of Jack Nicholson in *Chinatown* getting his nose slit was not in the original screenplay. If they had shot later scenes prior to shooting this one, they would have had to re-do them, showing the sutures in his nose. But even more important is that sense of storytelling— the cadence and rhythm that's in the director's subconscious. Jumping back and forth in time is interruptive. However, this can be indulged only so far, and the privilege must be weighed against the cost. If maintaining continuity means leaving a distant location and going back to it—unlike leaving a sound stage and going back to it—it would, of course, be an unwarranted extravagance.

By this time the art director would have submitted sketches for your approval, and the set director, following the art director's ideas, would have verified styles and period with you. Even the china, glassware and silver to be used in a dining-room set would have been discussed.

The next step was a production meeting with heads of all the departments. The director sat at the head of a horseshoe table with his producer, and the head of production asked questions. If there were any unclear areas, the heads of the individual departments asked for clarification.

The department heads were necessarily experts in their particular domains, and this meeting was primarily to assure them that everything was in order. They didn't like last-minute surprises. If you said, "I'd like fifty extras for this scene," the production manager might well respond, "You shall have seventy-five." But if he tended to give you more than you asked for, you were expected to abide by the arrangement—it was like signing a contract. You would make the picture with these stated materials and resources. The head of the location department would report on the accessibility, weather and general physical conditions in the places where scenes were to be made away from the studio. By the time that production meeting was over, you would have signed on the dotted line, so to speak. After the production meeting the entire schedule was laid out on a production board.

A production board was a wooden board in fact, four or five feet long by one and one half to two feet high. Narrow strips of cardboard about one half inch wide were inserted vertically on this board. Each strip represented one day; the days were given their order, and the scenes located according to the best requirements of the shooting schedule. Different colors denoted "day" and "night," and there were colors for each sequence. For a feature picture you had a basic 49-to-60-day schedule, while a "B" picture would be shot on a schedule of 28 days or less.

After the picture commenced, your work was monitored. The rushes were viewed—usually by the heads of the studio along with your producer—before you had an opportunity to see them. If they thought you were shooting an inordinate number of takes, there would be an inquiry. If a picture fell behind schedule, they would want to know exactly why. If anything untoward happened on the set, it was reported to the Front Office. You never knew who reported it, but no infraction was overlooked; the spy system was thorough. If an actor was late for his call, or was redolent of martinis in mid-afternoon, this information found its way without delay to the Front Office. So did most other awkward facts. In every case, the director was the first to be questioned. Steps would be taken. Offenders would be talked to. The studios went to extraordinary lengths in keeping their houses in order.

When a script was written and passed on by the studio, it was immediately submitted to the Office of Censorship. The office was generally known by the name of the man in charge, who was appointed jointly by the various studios. It was the Hays Office at first; later it was called the Breen Office, then the Sherlock Office, and so on. After the censors had read the screenplay, you would receive a letter setting forth their objections. Words like "damn" and "hell" were strictly forbidden. There could be no hint of sexual perversion and no mention of drugs whatever. Adultery—indeed, fornication—had to be punished. I recall instances when those requirements set up chain reactions that resulted in the most unprincipled conclusions. For instance, there was a picture in which a young soldier returned to find that his wife had been unfaithful. As this situation developed, the scriptwriter's only way out of the tangle was to have the young soldier kill his wife. She had been punished. Then he, of course, had to be executed. Now he had been punished. This was the result of a twisted logic that had little to do with protecting morals, and much to do with following the letter of the law laid down by the censorship office. There was little or no permissiveness. Kisses were not to be "protracted." "Cleavage" had to be avoided scrupulously. Despite the fact that I have a poor opinion of censorship in any form, I must admit that no picture of mine was ever really damaged by the censors. There was usually a way around them.

The Asphalt Jungle, for example, had a scene in which the crooked lawyer, played by Louis Calhern, killed himself. According to the script, he was to write a short, moving note to his wife, then take a pistol out of his desk drawer and put it to his head. Suicide was high on the list of forbidden acts, so this scene was flatly rejected. But it was necessary that the man destroy himself; it was an integral part of the story. What made it objectionable to the censors was the fact that the man was in his right mind: no man in his right mind kills himself. I said, "Doesn't the act in itself prove that he is not in his right mind?" They didn't think so. So I came up with an idea to which they agreed. I had him write the note and—like a writer who is dissatisfied with what he's done—crumple it up. The man is a lawyer, literate and well read, but here he can't get what he wants to say down on paper. He tries again and crumples another sheet of paper; he's incapable of lucid thought. He just shoots himself. This was enough to indicate, for the censors' purposes, that he was not in his right mind. It turned out to be a better scene for the change, but I wouldn't recommend trying to outfox the motion-picture code as a way to achieve storytelling success. The censors were responsible for doing grievous damage to many films.

The presence of a star in a picture was at least a partial guarantee of its success; there would be a greater certainty of return on investment. This obtained as long as it was the right picture for the right star. A star in the wrong role stopped being a star. The major studios knew this very well, and they deliberately set about creating a distinctive public style for each star. They had Clark Gable play a certain kind of role so that when people went to see a Gable movie, they knew what to expect and that they would probably like it. It was the same with Gary Cooper or Tyrone Power. And you knew for sure that Cooper or Power was in no more danger of getting bumped off than the Lone Ranger. Getting killed was reserved for stars like Bogart and Cagney. You knew more or less what you were going to see, and if one of the stars appeared out of his familiar character, you resented it.

The idea that a star in a picture ensures its success at the box office still persists, unreasonably. Today, when casting a male star, a producer will send his screenplay off to one or more of the top ten on the box-office list. He will go after Robert Redford, Steve McQueen, Paul Newman, Burt Reynolds, Robert De Niro, Al Pacino or one of the others highest in the current ratings. It doesn't matter whether the actor is right for the part. It's his name that's wanted. His name and his reputation as a winner can be used as a means of financing the film.

If a producer has Steve McQueen as a star, he will receive advance bids from distributors all over the world, competing for the film in release. These pre-production sales can add up to such imposing sums as to guarantee the recoupment of the negative cost of a film and even show a profit. But the fact is a star's name on the marquee today means much less than it used to. A star can be in the top-ten list one week and out the next.

Most stars today are not as certain of their position as they were in the old days. The studios protected their stars because they had an investment in them. Now stars choose their own vehicles the way top jockeys choose their mounts. Robert Redford picks his pictures with a rare canniness, showing good judgment about the kind of picture that's going to be successful. He's made very few mistakes. Paul Newman, on the other hand, is more venturesome. He hits and misses. He likes playing dissimilar roles; this reflects his imagination and his willingness to take a flier. The majors would have frowned upon this sort of behavior. They always cut the cloth according to the star's public image, protecting it thereby.

Often an image would become so prepotent that a star would embrace it as fervently as his public did. Errol Flynn is a prime example— although, in his case, I'm not sure whether the horse or the cart came first. Fighting, drinking, brawling and whoring featured in both his screen image and his everyday behavior.

Following *In This Our Life*, Howard Koch and I wrote a play called *In Time to Come*, which dealt with Woodrow Wilson's fight for the League of Nations at the end of World War I. With Otto Preminger as the director, *In Time to Come* ran on Broadway from December 28, 1941, to January 31, 1942, closing after forty performances. The Japanese had bombed Pearl Harbor on December 7. We were at war and our subject matter probably seemed dated.

Meanwhile my marriage had ended. Lesley had wanted desperately to have a child, and she finally conceived. She was happy during her pregnancy. The prognosis was good for a normal delivery but, a month or so early, she went into labor and the child—a little girl—was born prematurely. She died. The recovery from such a bereavement can be long and difficult. Lesley's reaction was extreme.

I was not sufficient to the occasion—partly through unawareness of her deepest feelings but mostly through my involvement in day-to-day events. I, too, had felt the pain of our loss, but after a few weeks had got over it— or would have but for the atmosphere of unrelieved grief that enveloped the house. Lesley's mother came to stay with us. This enabled me to spend more time elsewhere. Sometimes I'd be away all night. My absences were hardly remarked. Then, when war was declared and I went into the army, Lesley filed for divorce. She thought that was what I wanted. I put the blame where it belonged—on my own shortcomings. I wished that I had tried harder, or had greater understanding. But it was too late. There was no going back for either of us.

I got into the Army through my friend Sy Bartlett, a writer whom I'd known since Universal days. Sy was in the Reserve. After Pearl Harbor he was called up and commissioned a captain in the Signal Corps. At the beginning of the war he acted as an intermediary between the Army and Hollywood. He visited me one day on the set of *Across the Pacific*, a picture that was a follow-up to *The Maltese Falcon*, with more or less the same cast, and asked if I would be interested in accepting a commission in the Signal Corps. Of course I said yes and signed a paper. A few weeks later I received in the mail a list of names of military personnel and various American Army posts. I puzzled over it briefly and dropped it into the wastebasket. Later I discovered that this was the Army's way of sending orders. One was supposed to go down the list alphabetically to one's own name and read the abbreviated instructions printed opposite.

Some time later I was on the set when I was called to the phone and someone said, "Lieutenant Huston, you are directed to report for duty in Washington on . . ." and proceeded to name such-and-such a date and hour, about four days away.

I said, "But I'm right in the middle of making a picture!"

"Lieutenant Huston, do you wish to resign your commission?"

"Certainly not."

"In that case, you will report to Washington as ordered."

"Yes, sir."

Actually, I was right at the end of the picture. The story involved a Japanese plan to pull a "Pearl Harbor" on the Panama Canal. Bogart had been captured by the Japanese—led by master spy Sydney Greenstreet—and was being held prisoner in a house near the Canal. I proceeded to make things as difficult as possible for my successor. I had Bogie tied to a chair, and installed about three times as many Japanese soldiers as were needed to keep him prisoner. There were guards at every window brandishing machine guns. I made it so that there was no way in God's green world that Bogart could logically escape. I shot the scene, then called Jack Warner and said, "Jack, I'm on my way. I'm in the Army. Bogie will know how to get out."

They put Vincent Sherman on the picture. Warners wasn't about to go the expense of re-doing anything I had already shot, so it was up to Vince to figure out a way to get Bogie out of that house. His impossible solution was to have one of the Japanese soldiers in the room go berserk. Bogie escaped in the confusion, with the comment, "I'm not easily trapped, you know!" I'm afraid that, from that moment on, the picture lacked credibility.

In April 1942 I reported to U.S. Army Signal Corps Headquarters in Washington for active duty. I spent weeks and weeks doing nothing. I remember we had on those woolen tunics and Sam Browne belts and it was the middle of summer. Christ, it was hot! By the end of the day my tunic would be dark, steaming and heavier by a pound or two with sweat. But time weighed even heavier with boredom. I begged to be sent to where the action was—China, India, England. I pulled strings to no avail. It looked as though I was going to see the war out from behind a desk in Washington. I remember walking down a street with Anatole Litvak and breaking into tears of frustration.

I finally got my orders. I was to proceed to the Aleutian Islands and document that theater of combat. I met my five-man crew on Umnak Island and we moved right on out the chain to Adak. Adak was less than 500 miles from Attu and only 250 from Kiska—both of which were Japanese-held; it was nearer to the enemy than any other American territory anyplace in the world.

Along with the rest of the personnel, we lived in tents. The only Quonset huts on the island were for Bomber Command, Fighter Command and the hospital. The SeaBees had laid down interlocking sheets of metal for an airstrip, on either side of which were built revetments for the aircraft. Anti-aircraft emplacements studded a number of little hills surrounding the area. Although operations were never of the magnitude of the African and European campaigns, the war in the Aleutians was nevertheless bitter and costly, with disproportionate casualties because it was waged by aircraft in literally the worst flying weather in the world.

So far the Japanese were unaware of our presence on Adak, but about two weeks after my crew and I got there, I was crossing the airstrip when I heard the drone of an engine overhead. It didn't sound like one of ours. I looked up, and there was a Japanese Zero at about 5,000 feet. He was gone before we could get pursuit planes in the air or even man anti-aircraft. The enemy now knew where we were, and the possibility of an

Adelia Gore, JH's
grandmother

Reah Gore, JH's mother,
before her marriage

JH at 6 months
(*Courtesy of
Mrs. Margaret
Huston Walters*)

Reah Gore Huston,
JH's mother

Walter Huston, JH's
father, aged 18, as the
hero of *In Convict
Stripes*

Alexander Huston
(Uncle Alec), at about
20 years of age
(*Courtesy of Mrs. Walters*)

With
Grandmother Gore
(*Courtesy of
Mrs. Walters*)

Margaret Huston
(Aunt Margaret),
photographed in Paris
in 1895 (*Courtesy of
Mrs. Walters*)

Early theatrics: above, "Master John Huston, Baby Orator.
Age 3 yr 7 mo." Below left, "And how I loved her—Sakes Alive!"
Below right, the prop cigarette was his mother's idea

Walter Huston in
two vaudeville roles

In Arizona, aged 10,
with his dog Rex

Left, after a high school fishing trip; JH
at left. Above, his graduation picture

"The fastest ostrich in the world.
I road him." Below, the ham operator

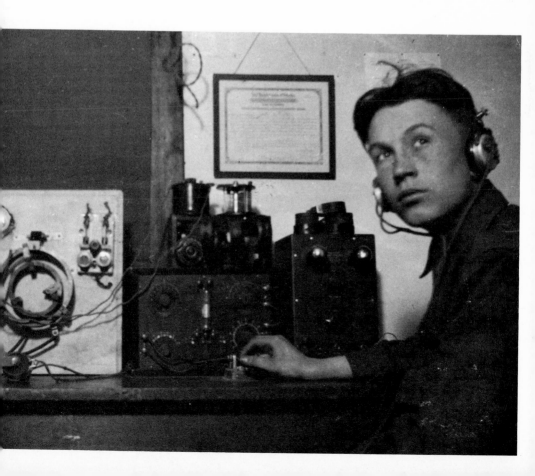

Left, the young painter, California,
1921 or 1922. Below left, JH and
mother at Teotihuacan, during his
first trip to Mexico in 1925. Right,
Jane Burley and John Huston
in 'Ruint' at the Provincetown"—
newspaper caricature, 1924

JH at the
start of his
acting career,
aged 18

Dorothy Harvey Huston,
JH's first wife, at about 18
(*Courtesy of Dorothy
Huston Hodell*)

With Lesley Black Huston,
his second wife, on a
hunting trip in Idaho,
late 1930s

Willy Wyler and JH at an
amusement park

The house JH designed and built near
Tarzana in the San Fernando Valley.
Below, with one of his horses

On the set of *The Maltese Falcon*.
Above, JH and his father. Below, with
Mary Astor and Humphrey Bogart,
JH directs Walter Huston

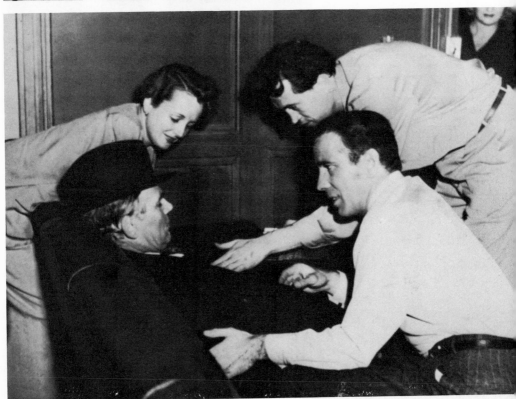

Coaching Bette Davis for a
scene in *In This Our Life*,
1941

With Olivia de Havilland
on a 1941 fishing trip

In costume for his stage
role in *The Lonely Man,*
Chicago, 1935

In the Aleutians, 194.
JH is at righ

Legion of Merit recipients, 194
From left, William Wyle
Sy Bartlett, JH and Anatole Litva

Lieutenant Huston of the
U.S. Army Signal Corps
with his father

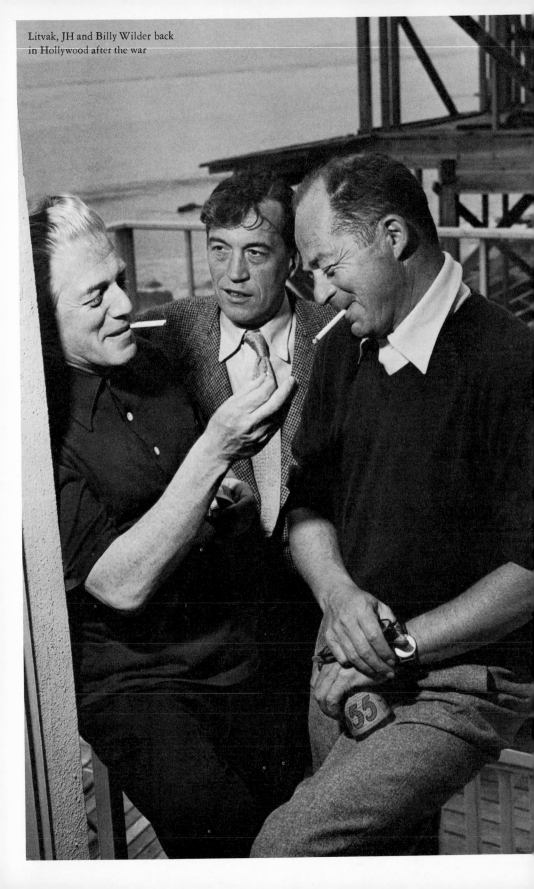

invasion could not be discounted. There were few facilities for defense, but we hastily dug slit trenches and arranged signals. They consisted of three cannon shots to indicate "Stand By to Repel Japanese Landing" and one cannon shot to indicate "All Clear." In the meantime we stepped up our bombing missions against Kiska and Attu, and I arranged for our photographic crew to go on these strikes and film the action.

Often the planes would take off in bright sunlight, but by the time the flight was formed, the airstrip would have been clouded over. The mission would have to proceed toward Kiska not knowing if there'd be a place to land when it returned. The next U.S. airstrip after Adak was 700 miles away. Many planes were lost to Japanese anti-aircraft and Zeros, but weather claimed just as many, if not more. They had only compasses and the seats of their pilots' pants to guide them. The losses in aircraft flying up from the States were also considerable, manned as they were by pilots and crews inexperienced in such flying conditions. On one occasion, out of twelve B-26 bombers routed up the Alaskan coast, only three reached Adak and all three cracked up on the airstrip as they tried to land.

Later came the B-17 or Flying Fortress, that masterpiece of design among the World War II bombers. It had speed, maneuverability, protective armor, six guns, three with moving turrets, and, most important of all, it had radar. After radar was introduced, the casualties dropped sensationally. There was no more bumping blindly into mountains.

Right away I got to be known as something of a hoodoo. Every time I got into an airplane, something happened to it. My first flight was on a B-24. The rest of the flight took off and headed for Kiska, but we were late getting off the ground because we couldn't find our tail gunner. We took off after he arrived, but ground control told us that if we didn't catch up with the rest of the flight within 100 miles, we were to abort the mission and return to base. That's what we had to do.

We returned to Adak to discover that there had been a great rainstorm while we were in the air, and the field was covered with water. We dropped in all right, but when the pilot put on the brakes, they froze. We went right through two other B-24s. Yes, right through them, shearing off wings. When we finally slid to a stop, the plane was a mess, and everyone looked around in a daze. Then somebody yelled, "Christ! We've got to get out of here before the bombs go off!" We tried one waist exit, but the plane had buckled and it was jammed. Everybody then piled out the exit on the other side of the aircraft in one hell of a hurry. I think I was the last able-bodied man out.

Nothing I had ever shot personally as a photographer turned out well—

and I'm afraid that holds true to this day—but I decided that this was my chance to get a good action shot. I went around to the nose of the airplane and began to film a rescue team of four or five men working frantically to extricate the unconscious pilot and co-pilot from the cockpit under the threat of the bombs going off. Everyone else had run to safety. I remember kneeling, trying to get a shot, and saying to myself, "Good man, Huston. Nerves of steel!" But just as I was congratulating myself, I began to shake uncontrollably. I put the camera down and ran. The bombs didn't go off.

On my second flight to Kiska, Zeros attacked us. I was trying to photograph over the shoulder of the waist gunner. Presently my camera wound down, and I lowered it to rewind. The waist gunner wasn't there. I looked down and saw him lying dead at my feet. The belly gunner motioned me to take over his gun while he took the waist gun, which was more important defensively. In order to facilitate his firing, he had to stand with one foot on the body of the waist gunner. The racket of the air battle continued for minutes. We were quite thoroughly shot up, but managed to limp back to Adak.

Among my crew there were two outstanding figures: Sergeant Herman Crabtree and Lieutenant Rey Scott. Sergeant Crabtree was a twin brother to Li'l Abner, some six feet four inches tall and weighing over 200 pounds. I remember his enormous, oxlike eyes. I used to conjecture how much one of his eyeballs would weigh. He was strong as an ox, too. We'd load him up with equipment—cameras, batteries, tripods—to take out to the planes. I could have jumped onto his back, too, and I swear he wouldn't have known the difference.

Sergeant Crabtree pleaded with me to take him on a mission. He alone of my five-man team remained behind, and he felt left out. I explained to him that there was nothing for him to do on a mission that would justify his presence. Every one else operated a camera. He said, "If I learn to use a camera, can I go?"

"Sure, Herman." I thought that would be the last I'd hear of it.

But Herman was serious. He took instructions from the other members of our crew, learned how to read a light meter, to load and unload the camera and so on—then he came to me one day and said, "I can operate an Eyemo, Lieutenant Huston. Now can I go?"

So I put Herman on a flight. It was a bad one. We lost two bombers out of our formation of twelve, and the remaining ten were considerably shot up, with a number of casualties. My plane sat down back at Adak before Herman's, and I waited to see if he got out. He did. I asked him if he'd got anything.

"Yes, sir. I think I got me a Zero."

This was early in the war, and no Japanese Zero had ever been filmed by an American camera.

"What, Herman? Are you sure?"

"Well, yessir. I think I got me a Zero. The Zero came at us and I could see it through the finder and the camera was running. I sure think I got him." We didn't know for certain until the report came back from Washington, where the film was developed, but Herman had got his Zero all right.

As we walked on across the field, I asked, "How did you like it, Herman?"

"Well, I don't know yet, sir."

"Would you like to go again?"

He debated that and finally said, "Yessir."

Just to test him, I asked, "When?"

"Well . . . about next Tuesday, when I get over being scared."

The other standout, Lieutenant Rey Scott, had a beard. You didn't see many beards in the military in those days, outside the submarine service, but you could get away with such things in the Aleutians—it was hard to get hot water, and overall conditions were such that many disciplines were relaxed.

Rey had done a picture in China on his own while still a civilian, an outstanding film about Shanghai during the Japanese bombings. He was a man who had no regard for appearances, and no particular regard for authority. In fact, he was a Bohemian in uniform; a bloody, no-good rogue and a lovely fellow.

Rey had been in the thick of it for some time and had acquired a fatalistic attitude regarding survival. At least that was his excuse for risking his neck at every opportunity. His talk was rather like the red Indian talk Ernest Hemingway used to affect, but Rey wasn't being funny, just succinct—a man of few words. He was also a drinking man, whatever was to be had and as much as. One night, after finishing off one of the bottles of rum I had brought from the States—black Jamaican rum that was the highest proof of any liquor this side of grain alcohol (it rolled rather than poured out of the bottle), he went down to the airstrip and commandeered a crew, saying that they had orders for a midnight raid on Kiska. This was most unusual, of course—we didn't have radar yet, and no night raid had been launched from Adak before. But it was a full moon, and, informal as things were on the island, they somehow believed him. They were piling into the aircraft when word got out what Rey was up to and the midnight raid on Kiska was canceled by the Bomber Command. I don't think Rey was really happy unless he was being shot at. During the raids, when he would run out of film, he would fire back at the enemy planes with his .45.

While on Adak, I made friends with Jack Chennault, the son of Claire Chennault of Flying Tiger fame. Jack's fighter planes had just been equipped with cameras which were synchronized with the airplanes' guns so that when the pilot pressed the firing button, the cameras recorded the flight of the bullets to their target. This was a new thing, and no action film had as yet been obtained. The cameras were adjusted to accept black-and-white film, but I convinced Jack he should let us modify them to take color film, and I supervised the operation myself so there would be no slip-ups.

An attack was made, and it was a marvelous success, with heavy dog-fighting in the air and a number of Zeros shot down. Everybody was ecstatic. The very first combat film, and in color! I sent it back to the States by special courier to be developed. Word came shortly that the film was absolutely blank. It seems I had fogotten to run out the leader—which was some six feet long—in any of the cameras! That was the biggest boner of my Army career.

One night we heard explosions in the distance and assumed they were guns from Japanese ships about to launch an invasion of the island. Sure enough, these explosions were followed shortly by our own signal cannon —three shots in succession indicating: "Stand By to Repel Japanese Land-ing." We were still living in tents, so we ran to our trenches, cocked our .45's and waited nervously for the enemy to appear out of the darkness. About an hour and a half later there was a single report—the "All Clear." We went back to our tents, rather shaken. Then more explosions in the background, followed by the *Boom! Boom! Boom!* of our signal gun. We ran back to our trenches. This sort of thing went on for four or five days, and we were all getting into a high state of nerves. Finally word got around that the distant explosions we had been hearing were not Japanese guns at all, but our own mines at the approaches to the harbor. They were going off spontaneously.

Then, one day, the U.S. Navy steamed into the harbor and dropped anchor. I went aboard one of the ships immediately to get a bath. God, what a luxury! It was my first shower in about ten weeks. It was aboard this vessel that I first heard the name "Blow-'em-up Brown." It seems he was the engineer who had planted the faulty mines.

The head of the Bomber Command on Adak was Colonel William O. Eareckson, a tall, angular man of rakish demeanor. He lived as his men lived, taking no privileges and leading all the more dangerous missions.

His men worshipped him. He rated the two stars of a major general, but no promotion ever came through, although he was decorated time and time again for bravery. It was he who first conceived the tactic of low-level bombing, bringing his planes in to Kiska no more than ten feet above the surface of the ocean—so low that the props left a wake in the water—before zooming up to drop delayed-action bombs on enemy ships and installations. The air war in the Aleutians was "Eareckson's War."

There was a journalist—I think from the *Chicago Daily News*—who went with the Colonel on a Mission. The plane was hit badly, and an enemy machine-gun bullet came through the instrument panel and dropped into Eareckson's lap, spent. On the way home from the target Eareckson showed it to the journalist, who got very excited.

"I'll give you fifty dollars for that bullet, Colonel."

"Sold," Eareckson said, and turned his plane around.

"What are you doing?" asked the journalist.

"Going back, of course. At fifty bucks a bullet, I can't afford not to!"

I remember a briefing he gave before an attack. He filled in all the details, then said, "Don't take evasive action on the bomb run. You're just as likely to turn into the stuff as away from it. Keep going in a straight line. And if someone plucks your sleeve and you look around and he's got a long white beard . . . why, you'll know you haven't another care in this sad world."

In one back pocket the Colonel carried a pint bottle of whiskey and in the other a little black book. One day somebody asked him what was in the book. "The names and next-of-kin of all the men who have died on my orders," he replied. He himself survived the war and died in his bed a few years ago.

There is a strange beauty about the Aleutians—undulating hills of spongy moss laced with salmon rivers, without a tree or anything like a tree for 1,500 miles. Most of the islands are mountainous, and a number of the mountains are volcanic, topped with white cones and streamers of smoke. The warm Japanese Current meets the Arctic flow up there, which accounts for the fogs and sudden precipitations. You are lost in a gray blanket one moment, and in the next the skies are clear and you are in bright sunshine. Over a period of two or three weeks a phenomenon occurred that I've never seen elsewhere. Each night the celestial dome was divided as if bisected—one half solid clouds and the other half dark blue and full of stars.

One day we photographed the funeral of a pilot who had been killed in action; his co-pilot had brought the plane home. The pallbearers were wearing black slickers, looking like the Aleutian ravens that this day, as always, hung in the air above our heads, seemingly motionless, as if on poles. It was pelting rain, and the fog folded around us, thick and heavy. The coffin with the pallbearers materialized out of the fog, and the ghostly ceremony began. The chaplain commenced the service with: "In my Father's house are many mansions . . ." and with those words the fog lifted. In the background I could see a smoking volcano, widely scattered thunderstorms and, finally, a half-dozen rainbows.

After four months I was satisfied that we had enough good film to cut into a picture. We were prevented from leaving by air because a hurricane was reported bearing down on Adak, so it was decided that we would go back by ship. One afternoon we loaded on board the troop transport U.S.S. *Ulysses S. Grant*, and were scarcely settled in when the hurricane struck. The *Grant* canted precariously from the force of the wind. Ashore, tents were floating around over the island. Airplanes, knocked upward out of their revetments, dropped into the sea.

The winds were unabated the following morning, and we were in danger of colliding with two other ships that were swinging uncontrollably nearby, on bow anchors only. The captain of the *Grant* took the initiative and by a magnificent feat of seamanship—playing the wind and the wave action with perfect timing—got us clear. As we passed between the other two ships, with only scant feet to spare, their crews were lining the rails, and they gave us a great cheer. We cleared the harbor entrance successfully and then rode out the storm at sea for three days.

When we came back in, *Grant*'s orders had been changed and we were transferred to a destroyer which was scheduled for a quick run to Kodiak. The seas were still heavy as we put out on this vessel. Almost everyone on board got sick, but for some reason I never get seasick. The man who was sharing my cabin finally crammed himself under his bunk, and only the whites of his eyes were showing. I couldn't take that, so I went into the wardroom and sat alone. Presently the slight figure of a man wearing glasses joined me, and we began to talk just to kill time. He asked what I did, and I told him. I discovered he knew all about emulsions and other things connected with films and photography, which was more than I did. That intrigued me, and I asked him what he did. He seemed reluctant to discuss it, but he finally said that he was a mine expert.

"What did you say your name was?" I asked.

"Brown."

"Not Blow-'em-up Brown, by any chance?"

"Yes. I'm afraid so."

It seems he was on his way to Washington to explain what had happened to his mines. Poor bastard.

After two more days at sea the destroyer was ordered back to Adak because it had been assigned another, more important mission. As we re-entered the harbor at Adak, I saw a large ship which was the sleekest thing I had ever laid eyes on. It was a modern oil tanker with great, long catwalks. It had come to Adak with a full load of high-octane petrol, but upon arrival it was discovered that the storage tanks in Adak were full. An administrative error. So we went aboard, along with Blow-'em-up Brown and other passengers, and started out for Kodiak for the third time.

Captain Carter Glass welcomed us as honored guests because we had been on missions over Kiska under fire. He and his crew had only been sailing around in submarine-infested waters with a cargo that one torpedo—one shell, even—would ignite and blow ship and man to Kingdom Come. I recall how one day a poker game was in progress when contact with a submarine was made. The Captain and his officers put their chips on their cards and hastened to the bridge. Depth charges were dropped. When the "All Clear" sounded, the game was resumed where we'd left off.

At Kodiak we were assigned quarters at the Naval Base. I was a first lieutenant, Rey was a second lieutenant, and we shared a room with an officer who must have been the oldest first lieutenant in the Army—a soft-spoken, white-haired gentleman from Arkansas. Late one night I heard him calling me, *sotto voce*, "Lieutenant Huston?" For a moment I thought I was dreaming. Then I woke up fully, and the voice continued:

"You got your .45?"

"Yes, what is it?"

"There's a b'ar in this room!"

Sure enough, there were grunting noises from the floor. I fumbled for my flashlight and took my .45 from the bedpost where we always hung them.

"Okay, I got my flashlight here. When I turn it on, let's both let him have it at once."

I turned on the flashlight. It was Rey. He was cockeyed and on all fours on the floor.

We stayed at Kodiak for three days, and Rey was on all fours a good part of the time. The fact that we had been out on Adak and had seen action gave us a special privilege. Colonels and rear admirals walked right around him and, when they had to, stepped over him; they never saw him.

From Kodiak we went by air to Anchorage, Alaska, and then to Whitehorse in the Yukon. There the weather closed in again. We had no communication with the outside world, not even radio contact. A pilot came into Whitehorse from the south with the information that the weather was clear over the inland route through Prince George in British Columbia. So we took off. It was the most harrowing flight I have ever been on, including any bombing mission. The weather closed in and it began to rain. The clouds got lower and lower. We were flying through mountain canyons, down valleys, and taking sharp doglegs. The moment came when I knew the pilot had to make a decision: go up above the stuff or stay down. He didn't want to go above it because there would be no radio communication over the landing area and we couldn't get down safely unless the weather happened to be clear there. So we stayed below it. There were veils of rain, so that you couldn't see anything for a minute or two, and then the veil would lift and we'd stand on our tail or wing to keep from hitting a mountain. This went on and on, until finally I wearied of being frightened, closed my eyes and said, "All right. Whatever comes!"

We made it to Prince George, set down for fuel and then went on to Vancouver and, finally, Seattle. Seattle was closed in. We had to turn out to sea and circle. The pilot remarked it would be a hell of a note not to make Seattle after what we'd just come through, but a hole finally opened up and we got down in one piece.

Back in Los Angeles, I did some preliminary work on *Report from the Aleutians* in the Army Photographic Center on Western Avenue and, in my spare time, visited friends and made the rounds of parties. Having just returned from working with authentic heroes, I was in no mood to put up with the screen variety. It was in this frame of mind that I encountered Errol Flynn standing in a hallway during a party at David O. Selznick's house.

I scarcely knew Errol. He had worked on the Warner lot as a contract player and I saw a little of him there, but he hadn't been in any of my films. I remember we had drinks in our hands. Errol must have been spoiling for trouble, or maybe he sensed my mood and picked up on it, for he very quickly got around to saying something wretched about someone—a woman in whom I'd once been very interested and still regarded with deep affection. I was furious at his remark, and I said, "That's a lie! Even if it weren't a lie, only a sonofabitch would repeat it." Errol asked if I'd like to make anything out of it, and I decided that I would. Errol led the way, and we went down to the bottom of the garden—just the two of us. No one knew we'd left the party.

We reached a place secluded enough to preclude interruptions, took off our coats and went at it. I was knocked down almost immediately, landing on the gravel drive on my elbows. I was up right away, and I was down again right away; and each time I landed on my elbows. Beginning some months later, and continuing for a period of years, little slivers of bone came out of my right elbow, but it didn't bother me during the fight.

I don't think my head was all that clear when we started, but it cleared up after a few punches, and then I began to get my licks in. It was a long fight. I was in very good condition, and Errol was a fine athlete and a good boxer; he knew how to handle himself and had some twenty-five pounds of weight advantage. By the time I finally began to get his range, he'd marked me up quite a bit. I was cut over the eye and my nose was broken again. But I paced myself, and I began to score on his body; I knew I was getting to him in the ribs. He started to clinch and wrestle then, and since he was stronger than I, I had some difficulty getting away from him in the clinches. I remember that the language on both our parts, although not heated, was about as vile as it could get. Errol started it, but I went right along with it. And those were the days when "motherfucker" was not a term of endearment.

The fight had now gone on for the better part of an hour. It was a clean fight. When I was first knocked down, I rolled, expecting Errol to come at me with his boots. He didn't. He stepped back and waited for me to get up, which I thought rather sporting of him. The fight was conducted strictly according to Queensberry, for which I take my hat off to Errol Flynn. Neither of us committed any fouls, and there was nothing we could complain about afterward.

The party started to break up, and some of the guests discovered us when we were illuminated by headlights as cars turned around in the driveway. Everybody came swarming down and we were separated. David assumed Errol had started the fight, since he had that reputation, and there were recriminations. David called Errol names and offered to fight him also. Errol went to a hospital that evening, and I stayed over at the Selznicks' and checked into a different hospital the next morning, where I received a call from Errol wanting to know how I was. He told

me he had two broken ribs, and I said that I had thoroughly enjoyed the
fight and hoped we'd do it again sometime. My father arrived in California a few days later, and he suggested that we fight again and sell
tickets for a charity. That didn't come off. I didn't see Errol again for
some twelve years, when we worked together in Africa on *The Roots of
Heaven.*

From Los Angeles I took *Report from the Aleutians* to the Signal
Corps Photographic Center at Astoria, Long Island, New York, for further work before taking it to Washington, D.C., to show it to the brass.
While working on the picture in Astoria, I stayed in New York. Rooms
were at a premium, but because I had been a client of long standing, the
St. Regis Hotel managed to provide me with a suite, which soon became a
gathering place for friends like Pete Hamilton. Our favorite pastime was
watching a lovely young lady who used to sunbathe each afternoon in her
roof garden, some four or five stories down. We would whistle, signal
and shout, but to no avail. She paid not the slightest heed.

Then I had an inspiration. I sent her a big box of flowers by bellboy,
enclosing a note asking if I could come to the door of her apartment—
only to the door—and make her a perfectly decent proposal. I didn't
expect her to invite me in. She sent back word for me to come over, so I
went to her place and told her what I had in mind. She was a good sport
and went along with the idea wholeheartedly. Later, when all the voyeurs
were in my suite, I left the room quietly. They didn't know I was gone
until I appeared below on the roof and lay down in bathing trunks beside the girl. I could hear their shouts over the sound of the traffic below.
I got to know the girl in this way, and I must say she was beautiful, if
distractingly innocent and simple.

I took her to dinner one evening to "21," and we sat in that little room
off the bar. Right next to us was H. L. Mencken. Now, as I've already
said, in my estimation Mencken was just about the greatest man of our
time, and I was hesitant about addressing him. Finally I decided to take
the chance.

"Mr. Mencken, my name is Huston."

"Not John Huston?"

"Yes."

"What are you doing these days?"

"I'm in the Army."

"Are you writing? You should be writing!"

"I've been doing some scriptwriting for motion pictures," I answered,
"and recently I've been directing films."

"Oh, well," he said, "you'll get over that. You'll come back to us after you get that out of your system. You were meant to be a serious writer."

Then came an accolade which took me completely aback. Mencken addressed himself to my companion and, oh, how I wished she were someone else. He said I should be writing a book; he compared me favorably to other writers—names that I don't wish to repeat, the comparison was so flattering.

When he turned back to his group, the girl asked, "Who was that?"

"H. L. Mencken."

"Who's he?"

Bob Flaherty, Oliver St. John Gogarty and Jed Harris were also in New York, and I saw a good deal of them. Most evenings were spent in the company of Flaherty and Gogarty. I'd met Bob in the mid-thirties in a projection room in London where we watched one of the first TV transmissions. A woman journalist appeared out of a snowstorm on the TV screen and declared that she was speaking from Crystal Palace some three miles away. Her image, she went on, was being conveyed to us at the speed of light—186,000 miles per second. Could we figure out how many thousandths of a second it took for us to see her blowing us a kiss?

I had seen *Nanook* and *Moana* and had great admiration for Bob's work. As the years passed and I got to know him, I felt a deep affection for the man. Bob was like a king or, rather, he was what kings should be like: his looks, bearing, courage, breadth of vision, and all those things, sans pomposity. An hour with Bob was refreshment for the soul. He believed in the virtue of man before the gangrene of civilization set in. It was up to us to discover the way back to our origins. What Bob thought and lived by and declared in all his pictures was opposite, in every sense, to the dogma of original sin.

Gogarty was the model for "stately, plump Buck Mulligan" in James Joyce's *Ulysses*. He held court in a bar in the eighties off Park Avenue that was the nearest thing in New York to an English pub. Its clientele was largely butlers, doormen, ladies' maids, chauffeurs. They had no idea who Gogarty was, but he always had an admiring circle around him. Oliver was a wonderful raconteur, but he never told the same story twice. Or, rather, it never came out twice the same way. For him, truth was a theme on which to practice variations. Whereas Bob's accounts of his own adventures were uncolored and could be taken word for word as gospel, Gogarty loved to fabricate or, I should say, improvise, for it was generally with the full knowledge and approval of his audience. They delighted in watching his imagination at work.

One night I took Flaherty and Gogarty to Jim Glennon's bar on Third Avenue: a hole-in-the-wall and one of my favorite places. Jim was a tall, thin man who was a classical scholar. Most of his customers had no idea they were being served by a man of such learning, but he kept the bar because he liked the atmosphere of drink. He never took the stuff as long as he stood behind the bar, but every few months would come the moment when he'd move round to the front and put his foot on the rail. That meant he was ready for a tear. Jim spoke Latin, Greek and Gaelic and knew Irish literature as well as anyone I've known; he could recite pages of *Finnegan's Wake* and knew Yeats by the yard.

The three Irishmen were delighted with one another. Jim was enthralled at having the living presence of "Buck Mulligan" in his bar. He sat with us in a booth. Things went famously for a time. Inevitably the talk turned to Joyce, for whom Jim felt something akin to worship. Gogarty, who felt nothing of the sort, withdrew from the conversation. Jim was quoting something out of *Anna Livia Plurabelle* when Oliver interrupted: "James Joyce was educated beyond his station in life." Dead silence. Glennon's face slowly drained of color, then he leaned toward Gogarty and spoke ever so quietly in Gaelic. Neither Bob nor I understood what he was saying. Gogarty got to his feet and left without a word, his back stiff with outrage. Glennon said only, "Sorry, John, Mister Flaherty," and returned to the bar. Bob and I left shortly after that, but we agreed that whatever Jim had said, Oliver had asked for it.

Jed Harris was the diametric opposite of Flaherty and Gogarty. He was cynical, sharp, bitter, hateful and vastly amusing. *Broadway* was his first great success and, after that, he directed hit after hit: *The Front Page, Coquette, Our Town, The Royal Family, Uncle Vanya. . . .* He dominated Broadway for a number of years. God knows how much money he made or where it went. He'd done a play with my father, *Apple of His Eye,* and Dad was one of the few people I ever heard him speak well of. His love of my father almost amounted to reverence and overflowed, in spite of himself, on to me.

As a director, Jed would have been a natural for pictures except that he was quite incapable of deceiving a fool into thinking that he considered him anything else. Since Hollywood never wanted for fools, the cards were stacked against Jed. I tried everything I could to convince the powers-that-were that they had missed a bet by failing to give him a picture to direct, but it was quite hopeless.

As I said, rooms were hard to get in New York during the war and, sometimes, I'd wake up in my suite in the middle of the night with the awareness that there was someone else in my room. Slowly, I'd make out a figure on the other bed. It was never who I hoped it might be: it was always Jed Harris, pale and hideous in sleep, his eyes closed but, beneath the lids, the eyeballs jumping.

Bob Flaherty's innocence was confounding—or should I say the complete absence of cynicism in his makeup. I witnessed a demonstration of it one night. We'd been with friends until all hours in an uptown hotel. I preceded Bob out of the lobby and hailed a cab. As the cab was making a U-turn, a little black man came running at me flourishing a knife. "This is my taxi," he said. "Get away or I'll cut your heart out." He was Puerto Rican. Bob hurried forward, "Here, young man, what's the matter?" My assailant pointed his knife at me and said, "He thinks he's better than me because he's white." Bob answered as though he were my counsel in a court of law. He said he knew me well and that I was without any color prejudice whatever. The Puerto Rican glanced at Bob and I hit him. The knife flew out of his hand, and he dropped to his knees. I picked up the knife, closed it and put it in my pocket. Bob was not at all pleased. "That was unnecessary, John." He helped the Puerto Rican get up, then asked where he wanted to go in the taxi. "To the Tombs," he said—the city jail. It seemed his brother was there, locked up.

"They'd only lock you up, too," Bob said. "You're under the influence of drugs, aren't you?"

"*Si.*"

"There's an all-night motion-picture theater on Fourteenth Street where you could spend the night. We'll take you."

We took him there. When he went to get out of the cab Bob turned to me. "Give him back his knife, John." It seemed to me that that was the last thing I should do until Bob added, "In his world you need a knife." We watched him buy his ticket and enter the theater.

The roster at the Astoria studio was colorful, to say the least: Gottfried Reinhardt, Irwin Shaw, Clifford Odets, Junior Laemmle, Sidney Kingsley, Burgess Meredith, William Saroyan and others of that caliber. Most of them were privates or non-commissioned officers. They were assigned to writing and producing training films. On the whole, their approach to their work was as serious as if they were doing feature films, and they did their best to serve their country. There were few recalcitrants. Bill Saroyan was one. He finally got someone in the State Department to agree with him that his talents were being misused. This resulted in his being sent to England to get a better feeling for the war and to write a

novel about it, which he did. The hero was a Nazi, and the villains were
U.S. and Allied officers and politicians. I don't think it was ever published.

Sound men, cameramen and other technicians of the motion-picture
trade all passed through Astoria and were then sent to the various theaters
of operation at the disposition of field commanders. Unit commanders,
such as myself, selected combat camera teams from these pools. I must
say that I found the volunteers who had been selected and trained by the
Army to be better qualified for such work than most of the Hollywood
professionals.

I was shuttling back and forth between New York, Washington and
Los Angeles with the Aleutian film. After the initial showing in Washington, I took the picture back to California, put in the opticals and added
the music. The picture was finished. I was still in California when I
received a telephone call to come back to Washington at once for a
special assignment.

Just before I returned from the Aleutians, the North African landings
took place, and a short while later President Roosevelt told General Har-
rison, then in charge of the Signal Corps Photographic Service, that he
would like to see film coverage of the action. There wasn't any. Anatole
Litvak and his crew had shot some pretty good stuff, but the ship carrying the exposed film had been sunk before it could even put to sea. So
there was absolutely nothing. The brass was acutely embarrassed. If it
could possibly be kept from him, the President was not to know that the
Photographic Services had assigned only one man and his crew to the
landings. That there should not have been several teams was an inadmis-
sible oversight. However, they had the solution: Frank Capra and I would
"manufacture" a North African film and be quick about it. Frank, as a
colonel, was placed in charge of the project. I was to be his assistant. We
went out to an Army training base in the Mojave Desert where the
terrain looked like Tunisia. We had troops moving up and down hills
under fake artillery concentrations—the worst kind of fabrication. Jack
Chennault had come back from the Aleutians, and we were able to get his
P-39 fighter planes to perform skip-bombing and strafing runs for us.

Then I went to Orlando, Florida, to simulate heavy bombing attacks on
North African fortifications. I set it up so that the fighters—which were
supposed to be German planes—would dive so close to the bombers from
which we were filming that you couldn't possibly identify them. There
were no casualties, thank God! It was worse than actual combat. The
bomber crews were sweating blood, and on several occasions were all for
knocking down the attack planes. My camera crew was utterly bewil-

dered by it all. I remember shouting to my first cameraman once, "They're coming in at two o'clock!" and seeing him look at his watch! When he was photographing in the waist of the aircraft, he didn't know where to stand, so the hot shells from the machine guns always hit him in the face.

We got this trash—now titled *Tunisian Victory*—together and took it back to Astoria, where Tony Veiller and I worked on the script while the film was being cut together. The material was so transparently false that I hated to have anything to do with it. Perhaps President Roosevelt was too busy with other theaters of war by then to care about "North African footage." I hoped so. In the meantime, promoted by now to the rank of captain, I was having myself a good time.

One afternoon at Pete Hamilton's I found myself conversing with an attractive, beautifully gowned woman whom I later discovered to be a full-blooded American Indian. She asked me where I was staying, and then offered me an apartment belonging to her and her husband, Norman Winston. They had just moved to the country; the apartment—at 270 Park Avenue—was empty and she saw no reason why I shouldn't have the use of it. The next morning, unbidden, a man arrived to pack and move me, and that night after work Frank Capra and I went to the apartment.

I caught my breath when we entered. It was one of the showplaces of New York. There were paintings by Picasso, Braque and Matisse on the walls, and there were sculptures by Modigliani. And there was a staff of four to take care of my every need. One day Norman Winston called to see how I was getting on, and urged me to try his brandy—a special stock. It was vintage, more than 100 years old! So, for a time, in a world of severe wartime shortages, I ate, drank and lived like a king.

Tony's Place, a restaurant on West 52nd Street, was one of the fixtures of New York then, and I was dining there one evening when Tony brought in his daughter. She was about thirteen and an absolutely beautiful child. She sat with me and we had quite a long conversation, during which I discovered that she had been studying ballet for years but had never seen a ballet performance. I said, "With your permission, Tony, I am going to take your daughter to the ballet." Tony was a mad Italian who stood on his head and sang operatic arias. He had no objection, so I planned it. There was a ballet opening about a week away, and I arranged that we would go from Tony's to the Met in a horse-drawn carriage, and that the young lady would have a corsage. I was going to do it in style. But the very next day I received orders to proceed immediately to Washington, and I had to cancel the date for the ballet.

Some six or seven years later I met a lovely young lady at David

Selznick's home. She sat next to me at the dinner table, and I was struck by her beauty and poise. She was under contract to David, and I remembered having seen her face on the cover of *Life*, as a modern Mona Lisa.

We chatted for a while and then she remarked, "You don't remember me, do you?"

"No, should I?"

"You failed to keep a date with me."

"I did? When was that?"

She laughed and said, "Quite a long time ago," and then told me her name. It was Tony's daughter, Enrica Soma. I never did get to the ballet with Ricki, but I did marry her.

The reason for my being ordered to Washington was that someone had had the idea that we should combine our fabricated film on the North African landings with that of the British, who had gotten some good authentic material of that campaign and were making a film also. After all, it was argued, they were our allies and a joint effort certainly was in order.

Frank Capra, Tony Veiller and I were issued emergency orders to proceed immediately to London. I'd brought no clothes or personal effects with me from New York and had no time to send for anything, but this turned out to be to my advantage when we arrived in England. In wartime England, ration stamps were required to buy just about everything, including clothing, and because of the special circumstances of my departure—which I explained to the issuing authorities—they were most generous in their issue of stamps. I was able to get two uniforms tailored by Kilgore and French, Sulka Army shirts to order, a cashmere robe from Harborough, and shoes by Maxwell. No one in the U.S. Army under the rank of general officer was as well turned out as Captain Huston.

It became immediately apparent that we, and not the English, stood to benefit by the collaboration. They had excellent combat footage as against our counterfeit material. Nevertheless the English film-makers agreed to abandon their project and proceed with us. I must admit that my heart simply wasn't in it and for the two months I was in England I left most of the task to Frank Capra and Tony Veiller.

It was the summer of 1943, and London was a remarkable place to be. The "little blitz" was going on, and there were blackouts at night. It was still a critical period and the English had tightened their belts yet another notch. Great excitement was engendered by the report that there was a shipload of oranges at the East India docks. I heard about it from a waiter at Claridge's who was hoping to get a couple—or even one—for his small children, who'd never seen an orange. All London knew about that ship and its cargo; it was a major topic of conversation. Then disaster struck. The ship got hit by a bomb at the dockside. There were oranges splattered all over the dock area. London mourned the loss of those oranges as though each one had been a human being.

But what the Americans and upper-class English thought of as next to famine, or at least very severe shortages, was actually an improvement over the pre-war fare of many working-class Englishmen. Because of government-controlled wartime distribution of food, they were living better than they ever had. The standard of living in England, per capita, actually improved during the war, which tells something about the reasons behind the apathy of so many of the working class of today. A lot of hatred had been stored up through the years.

I saw Gordon and Kay Wellesley again—those kind friends who had saved my bacon the first time I was in London—and they had me to their house for dinner. My dinner companion was a minute red-head named Lennie, who was singing the lead in a West End production of a Puccini opera. I was immensely taken with her and saw her almost every night after that for as long as I was in London. Our romance progressed to the point where she agreed to receive me at her apartment one night after her performance. She lived right off Hyde Park Gate, and she was to leave the downstairs door unlocked.

Unfortunately, I was having a problem with a fat arm. When I was first inducted into the Army, I was given those three-in-one shots: tetanus, typhus and cholera, I believe. Anyway, before the series could be finished, I went to the Aleutians. When I came back to the States, I had to start all over again. I had a couple more shots and was then rushed off to England. Upon my arrival in England, they decided to start me once more. By this time I was full of the stuff, and allergic to the shots. They touched my arm with a needle, and my arm began to swell so that it looked like the arm of a Fat Lady in the circus. Frank Capra and I shared a suite at Claridge's. I didn't want Frank to see me go out late at night with my fat arm, but I was determined to keep my assignation. So I waited until he turned in before I dressed quietly and tiptoed out.

There were no taxis to be had in London during the blackout. I had to walk from Claridge's to Hyde Park Gate. En route, an air raid started. To my distress, a new side-effect of the inoculations then manifested itself: I had to go to the bathroom. Badly. The air raid got worse, and I hurried on. I didn't want to go into Grosvenor House with my fat arm, so I walked on past it, but things were getting acute. By the time I got to the Dorchester, I really had to make up my mind whether to go in there or proceed and try to make it to my red-head's place, which wasn't far. I was sweating, it was now raining, the bombs were falling, I couldn't see a thing and the anti-aircraft guns in Hyde Park were blasting away. It was like a bad dream. The obvious thing was to go to the bathroom right there on the street during the blackout. But I couldn't bring myself to open my belt under those conditions, so I hurried on, running between seizures.

Finally I got to her place. The front door was open. I entered. I touched the little catchlock behind me and proceeded up the stairs according to instructions. There was another open door, and I went in. I could see through a dimly lighted hallway into a bedroom, and I could see red tresses upon a pillow. I didn't know the apartment, but one can always find a bathroom. When I finally got there, it was nip and tuck. I closed the door, hands shaking, clasped my belt and got my trousers half lowered . . . ! I had just asked too much.

I can't describe the ghastly thing that happened. That phrase "The shit hit the fan" comes to mind. There was a fine mist of it in the air. Everything in this lovely lady's bathroom was soiled—all the lotions, bottles, surfaces. . . . I was filthy, of course. Even my cap, which I was still wearing. It was a desecration. I sat on the toilet, surveyed the havoc and tried to keep my sanity while I figured out what to do.

First, I turned on the bath and put all my clothes in the tub. Then, stark naked, I went around with toilet paper and Kleenex and cleaned the bathroom as best I could. When the paper ran out, I used towels. In the middle of this the bathroom door opened and there she stood. She said, "What are you doing, John?" I had some lame excuse about being caught in the rain. She knew something was amiss, but, not wishing to embarrass me, she simply said, "Oh?" and closed the door. Another of life's darkest moments.

If you're alive, my dear, and read this, don't be too angry. I'm sure no one but you and I would care anymore. It was such a long time ago.

In the fall of 1943 my "vacation" in England came to an end. I received orders to proceed to Italy to document the triumphal entry of the American forces into Rome. I had met the great thriller-writer Eric Ambler at a party in London and—still acting on the principle that our two countries should combine efforts in making documentaries of the war—I suggested that he come with me, which he eagerly agreed to do. We left immediately, but found, when we arrived in Italy, that our troops were a long way from Rome.

The Italian campaign had come to a grinding halt following our initial successes, beginning at Salerno and continuing through Naples. After Casertá, north of Naples, bad weather set in, the Germans dug in their heels and the Allied attack foundered.

Naples was like a whore suffering from the beating of a brute—teeth knocked out, eyes blackened, nose broken, smelling of filth and vomit. There was an absence of soap, and even the bare legs of the girls were dirty. Cigarettes were the medium of exchange commonly employed, and anything could be had for a package. Little boys were offering their sisters and mothers for sale. At night, during the blackouts, rats appeared in packs outside the buildings and simply stood there, looking at you with red eyes, not moving. You walked around them. Fumes came out of the alleyways, down which there were establishments featuring "flesh" acts between animals and children. The men and women of Naples were a bereft, starving, desperate people who would do absolutely anything to survive. The souls of the people had been raped. It was indeed an unholy city.

One of the few times I ever had to take out my sidearm was in Naples. In a *piazza* on the outskirts of the city I came upon a riot, in the middle of which was a beleaguered military policeman with his truncheon out. The crowd was surging all around him, and everyone seemed to be fighting the nearest person at hand. The MP was hard pressed, so my driver and I went to his aid. As we got to his side, the riot reached its climax and began to quiet down. Old people in doorways were making those traditional Neapolitan gestures—hitting their chests and foreheads with their fists, then flinging their hands upward toward God.

Out of the corner of my eye I took in a surrealistic scene. A man and a woman were standing in embrace, frozen motionless in the midst of all this frantic activity. My eye went to them a couple of times, and after the riot stopped, I noticed they were still standing there, seemingly oblivious to all around them. Finally they were separated, and it was discovered that the woman had had the man's nose between her teeth. His nose was bitten through and hanging down sideways on his face. The riot had started, I found out, over an argument about cigarettes.

In Naples I bumped into the photographer Bob Capa. I had met him at a New Year's party in New York some time before the war, and had seen him off and on for years, but it was not until now that we became friends. We were walking together along a street one day when an air raid started. These raids were sporadic and not very effective, but the Italians held them in great respect; at the first sound of an air raid the streets emptied, and if you happened to be sitting in a restaurant, the waiters simply disappeared. When this raid started, Bob and I pulled into a doorway to escape the shell fragments raining down from our own anti-aircraft fire.

There was a great deal of typhus in Naples then, and a rumor of a cholera plague. The diseases were eventually contained, but many died at the outset. The dead were buried in small prefabricated coffins, all of a size. Traditional Italian Baroque hearses were kept in service by the city —great ebony affairs drawn by a span of black horses, all plumed and bedecked. From the doorway Bob and I saw one of these hearses come careening around the corner at top speed. The driver was standing up, whipping the horses to a gallop over the cobblestones. He wore a tricorne hat, breeches, silk hose and buckled shoes. The air-raid sirens were wailing, the guns were booming, and just as the hearse passed us, the back doors flew open and it began to eject coffins. The coffins burst open as they hit the cobblestones, and the street was littered with corpses, slowly unfolding from their cramped positions. It was grotesquely funny. What could we do but laugh?

Our headquarters in Caserta was a large palace of four or five stories, centered on an enormous quadrangle that must have been a hundred yards across. In front of the palace there were a number of long reflecting pools. Tiny reconnaissance planes with pontoons used to land on these pools, which were no more than twenty or thirty feet wide. The palace was crowded with Army troops, and we of the Pictorial Service—including my immediate commanding officer, Colonel Gillette—all slept in one large room in our bedrolls. That was endurable—but Eric Ambler's snoring was not.

Eric snored louder than any man I've ever heard. It was devastating. His snores echoed down the halls and out into the quad. There were twenty-five or thirty men all sleeping in the same room, and the next morning they all rose of one accord—nobody having slept a wink all night—and looked at me. I knew I had to get Eric out of there—fast.

I was assigned a combat camera crew of six men . . . and Eric. A short while later new orders arrived. We were to proceed to the front and make a picture that would explain to American audiences why U.S. forces in Italy were no longer advancing.

By early December 1943 our forces had moved into position before the Liri Valley, located some sixty miles northwest of Naples and some forty miles southeast of Rome. My unit was attached to the 143rd Infantry Regiment of the 36th Texas Infantry Division. The 143rd had been bloodied on D-Day at Salerno, was the first to enter Naples, the first to cross the Volturno and the first to do battle in the Liri Valley.

Highway 6, the only major artery to Rome, ran through the Liri Valley. At the entrance to the valley stood the little village of San Pietro, which was to be one of the most fiercely contested landmarks of the Italian campaign. The 143rd was facing four enemy battalions, dug into a line of connecting trenches and strong points before San Pietro and extending across the valley from one hill mass to another. One more German battalion was defending the high ground northwest of San Pietro: all approaches to these positions were heavily mined and crisscrossed with barbed wire and booby traps. Experienced field officers said the German position was impregnable to frontal assault. Nevertheless it was a command for a frontal assault that was passed down to the officers and men of the 143rd. The decision was a costly one.

The night before the attack our artillery threw everything we had at the Germans, but, judging from what followed, to little effect. The Germans were well dug in, and their strong points were immune to all but direct hits. Within two hundred yards the attack was slowed as our troops encountered barbed wire, heavy automatic fire and anti-personnel mines. Then came mortar and artillery fire: the enemy had excellent observation from Mount Lungo overlooking our attack, and casualties were extremely high. Many men gave their lives trying to jump the barbed wire, reach strong points and throw hand grenades through the narrow firing slits. The attack never got more than six hundred yards past the line of departure.

We subsequently launched two more frontal assaults against San Pietro.

Both were repulsed with heavy losses. The Germans threw up a wall of automatic weapon, mortar and artillery fire, both along the ridges and over the approaches to San Pietro. From the volunteer patrols that tried to push ahead and reach enemy positions, nobody ever came back alive.

Then it was decided to attack San Pietro with tanks. This was a most ill-conceived plan, undoubtedly devised by someone back of the lines who didn't know the first damned thing about the terrain around the village. Sixteen tanks were ordered to attack from the east, along a narrow dirt road full of hairpin turns and under direct enemy observation. It was just possible for two small cars to squeeze past each other on this road—but there was certainly no room to maneuver a tank. The right side of the road was a mountainside, and the other side was a drop-off down the mountain. Once committed, the tanks couldn't turn around.

The Germans let the tanks get within a few hundred yards of the town before destroying the rearmost two with anti-tank guns concealed behind the rubble. Three more tanks hit mines on the road and were abandoned. Artillery and anti-tank guns then proceeded to pick off the others one by one. Only four tanks were able to return to the bivouac area.

We could see the tanks burning and exploding, and men running and trying to hide. After it was over, we crept forward and photographed the disastrous results. It wasn't pretty. There was a boot here—with the foot and part of a leg still in it—a burned torso there, and other parts of what had been living human bodies scattered about. These shots were in the original uncut version of the film.

Previous to our first attack I had interviewed—on camera—a number of men who were to take part in the battle. Some of the things they said were quite eloquent: they were fighting for what the future might hold for them, their country and the world.

Later you saw these same men dead. Before placing the bodies in coffins for burial, the procedure was to lay them in a row in their bedrolls, make positive identification—where possible—then cover them. At that point it was necessary to lift the body up, and I had my cameras so placed that the faces of the dead came right to the lens. In the uncut version I had their living voices speaking over their dead faces about their hopes for the future.

Considering the emotional effect it would have on the families of these men, and also how American audiences of the time might react to it, we later decided not to include this material. The present generation might be up to it; it's become inured to almost anything.

The military stalemate was finally broken when Mount Lungo fell to our troops on December 16. Mount Lungo proved to have been the key in the enemy plan of defense. Even as it fell, there were signs that the Germans were preparing to pull back.

We had previously learned that we could expect a counterattack by the Germans to cover a withdrawal. Our intelligence reported that they had already evacuated the village of San Pietro. I made for the town immediately with two other officers and my crew; we wanted to be on hand as soon as our occupation began so that we could film the entire proceedings.

We moved up through the area of attacks and counterattacks, and I have never seen so many dead as on that day. It had rained during the night. We saw machine-gun emplacements, guns and equipment clean and glistening, with ammunition shining in the early-morning sunlight, while all around were the dead. I remember remarking to someone that we had seen more dead that day than living.

We finally got to the outskirts of town. San Pietro was only a couple of hundred yards above us, and a little way ahead we could see the road connecting the highway with the town. We debated whether to climb the hill to the village or go on to the road. The road might still be in the hands of the enemy, even though the Germans had pulled out of the village. On the other hand, the hill was undoubtedly mined. While we were trying to decide what to do, a machine gun opened up on us from above. We dove for cover behind a retaining wall, and luckily none of us was hit. Intelligence was wrong: the Germans obviously still held San Pietro. We lay there trying to figure what the hell to do to get out of there. Then the Germans sent in some mortar shells. This fortunately created enough dust and smoke to block the view of the machine-gunner above, and we were able to run for it, one by one.

It wasn't long after this that the Germans did in fact withdraw from San Pietro. My crew and I—along with Eric and another officer—were the first into the village, and we were able to photograph advance patrols of the American troops entering. As a bonus, we were also able to get on film Italian men, women and children as they came down from the hillside caves where they had been living during the battle. There were no young men among them; they had long since been taken away to make war elsewhere.

We hadn't been there long when the enemy started shelling the town, then sent in bombers. Only small advance patrols of our troops were then in San Pietro, but the Germans must have thought we were there in force. The American artillery made the same mistake and thought the

Germans were still there, so they opened up, too, and also sent in bombers. Both sides were throwing everything they had at the village now, and the ground literally jumped and heaved. The inhabitants ran back to their caves, and we, in some haste, did likewise.

Inside a cave I glanced over at my cameraman, and his whole body was shaking. He saw me looking at him and said, "I'll be all right, Captain. I do this sometimes, but I always get over it. Don't worry about me, Captain. I'll be all right."

But his shaking didn't stop. There was a let-up in the bombardment after a while, and we looked out. Both the Germans and the Americans had raised their shelling from the town to the surrounding country. I knew that something had to be done about my cameraman, so I said, "Come on, Sergeant, let's get a shot outside."

We went outside and I had him do a pan shot. He was still shaking, so I had him do it again. This time it was much better. Then I had him do it a third time and he was as steady as a rock—a full 360-degree pan of an encircling ring of artillery fire.

In the cave where we had taken refuge with some of the villagers there was a little girl of seven or eight who sat on my knee. She kept running her hand over my cheeks, smoothing my face. I wondered at this, and later figured out that she had not seen a shaven man for as long as she could remember. There were only old men in the village, and they all had stubble on their cheeks.

After a time we saw the smoke drifting away, and, looking down, we could see the Germans counterattacking on the floor of the valley. We knew they wouldn't just be going forward down there, but that there would be a flanking movement as well. It was high time we got the hell out of San Pietro—which we did. We had come in by jeep this time, squeezing past the disabled tanks on the road, and we went back the same way, with our tails between our legs. Eric and I were in one jeep, with a lieutenant driving. Our crew had preceded us and were out of sight. As we passed the tanks, we noticed a command car—one of ours—coming toward us. Suddenly the car stopped and stood, silhouetted, some fifty yards away. We knew that the road was under direct enemy observation, so we shouted to them to keep moving. A moment later the command car—which was filled with men—received a direct hit from an .88 shell. It disintegrated. As we drove past, there wasn't even a sign of it. It had simply disintegrated.

We drove on down the road and came to a metal bridge constructed of two "I" beams spanning a gully. The beams were spaced to accommodate the wheelbase of trucks easily, but the narrower wheelbase of the jeep caused the tires to run up on the inside raised edges of the beams on either side. The lieutenant driving our jeep got one wheel up on this raised edge—and the jeep stalled.

"Jesus, Lieutenant!" I said. "Didn't you just see what happened to that command car? Get us the hell out of here!"

The lieutenant turned to me and said, "How'd you like to drive, Captain?"

At this, Eric Ambler turned to the driver and with casual, measured accent said, "Really, Lieutenant . . . this is most precarious. We should get off this bridge as quickly as possible."

The jeep kept stalling, and I just knew we'd had it. The Germans had that road zeroed in so they could hit a dime, and it seemed to me they had a lot more time to nail us than they had had with the command car. Finally the lieutenant got the car moving again, and we passed around a bend and out of observation. I forgave my cameraman for shaking in the cave.

Eric Ambler was one of the coolest men I've ever seen under fire. "Insouciant" is the word for Eric. I'd look around when things started jumping and heaving under an artillery barrage, and Eric would be flicking dust off a boot. Except for his snoring, he was a good man to have around.

On the 17th of December the Germans pulled out of the San Pietro area for good, and the village was ours for the taking. When we came back, I looked for and finally found the little girl from the cave. I had understood that she was an orphan, and I had considered adopting her. I was happy to learn that I had made a mistake. When I found her again, she was well and happy, and with her parents.

What a welcome the people of San Pietro gave us! Whole cheeses and bottles of wine appeared from God knows where—for the village had been stripped by the Germans. Looking around at the rubble, I couldn't help wondering that the inhabitants could find anything to celebrate.

But the Italians have an innate gaiety, an ability to laugh at themselves at dark moments. I remember going through the narrow streets of Mignano after we had taken it. The kids had already picked up choice words from our troops, and they ran alongside our jeep shouting, "Fuck the Germans!" Our driver, who had a timely sense of humor, said, "Fuck the Americans!" The kids couldn't believe we were saying this about ourselves. They looked confounded and said, "No, no! Fuck the Germans!" Again the driver shouted, "No! Fuck the Americans!" And then one of the kids got it. He grinned and said, "Fuck the Italianos!" and everybody roared with laughter.

During the San Pietro operation we were, for a time, holed up in the tiny village of Prata. We got to know the owner of the wine shop, Pietro, and his wife and four children. Pietro was about four and a half feet tall with a huge mustache that must have been a foot across. We would turn over our rations to his wife, and she'd use them to prepare a meal for all of us. Their contribution was pasta and wine from their small stores. I made more than one attempt to pay Pietro for their kindness, but he refused.

Prata nestled into the hills in such a way that artillery shells went over it rather than into it, but it had no such protection from aircraft. Pietro's wife was wounded once during an air raid, and one of their little boys threw himself over her body to protect her. We spent Christmas there, and I made a recording of Pietro's children singing Italian Christmas songs to the accompaniment of the big guns booming in the background.

I especially learned great respect for the Italian farmer. On reconnaissance flights you could see the farmers beginning to plow as soon as we took land from the Germans. Beyond our lines nothing was cultivated. Sometimes you would see them plowing an area that was under artillery fire, trudging behind their white oxen, and sometimes pulling the plow themselves. The fields had been mined, and the farmers knew they were mined. Every day casualties were brought into the field hospital. But nothing deterred them. The land had to be plowed.

It was about this time that I heard that Bogie and Mayo were in Naples, making a tour for the troops. The news of his arrival received more attention than the Russian counter-offensive. I returned to Naples to see them, and we had a grand reunion. The first thing Bogie said to me was, "John, you sonofabitch! Leaving me tied to a chair!" He wasn't about to forget *Across the Pacific*.

Bogie had already managed to get himself into hot water in Naples. He loved to drink and to play the roughneck. Actually, I don't think I ever saw Bogie drunk. It was always half acting, but he loved the whole scene. On this occasion he threw a party in his room for a large group of enlisted men, and it got out of hand. A general across the hall came to the room and objected to the noise, and Bogie answered appropriately with something like "Go fuck yourself!" Bogie was shortly shipped out of Italy.

After we took San Pietro, the fighting continued on up the Liri Valley to Cassino. The attempts to take Cassino were disastrous. We had managed to cross the Rapido River, but had been driven back with heavy casualties. By this time the 36th Texas Infantry was pretty well demolished. The 143rd Regiment alone required 1,100 replacements after the Battle of San Pietro, and it was now composed almost entirely of green recruits.

I remember standing by the side of a road with a West Point major who had gone over the Rapido and back with one wave. His right hand was wrapped in a bloody temporary bandage, and I later discovered that half of it was gone. As his troops passed us in straggling groups, they saluted. And the major, dead weary, straightened up each time and came to a full salute, with hand snapping back against his helmet. After witnessing that, I never gave a sloppy salute again.

The morale of our troops was very high, even though there was ample cause for bitterness. At Monte Cassino, as at San Pietro, frontal assault after frontal assault was ordered, even when it was apparent that this method of attack was hopeless—useless. Finally orders were given to bomb the 1,400-year-old Benedictine monastery.

The monastery sat up high on the mountain, and it was obviously an excellent observation post for the Germans. But apparently it didn't occur to anyone that the whole mountain could serve in the same way. The bombing was nevertheless ordered—wave after wave of bombers dropped tons upon tons of blockbusters. It must have been something to be under, although I don't think there were many Germans in the building itself. Not only bombs but artillery, too, pounded the hell out of it. The monastery was completely destroyed. The result was that the rubble gave the defenders greater protection than had the building itself. I don't mean to sound over-sentimental about an ancient monument, but all we succeeded in doing was to destroy Monte Cassino needlessly along with its library—one of the greatest in the world, and absolutely irreplaceable. All for nothing. After the bombing the 36th attacked again, and was again repulsed. This came as no surprise to those who were doing the fighting. I went back to Caserta for a break.

I had been up forward under the heat for several weeks, and one's instinct for self-preservation is considerably sharpened under those conditions. Your reflexes also become quick and automatic. A jeep turned a corner, tires squealing, and I hit the dirt. It sounded just like an .88 shell coming in. I got up, shamefaced, brushed myself off and said to myself, "Christ! I mustn't let that happen again." Another jeep turned the corner, and I hit the dirt a second time.

While at Caserta I was invited to a party in Naples by members of the U.S. Rangers, who were celebrating their forthcoming departure to establish a beachhead at Anzio. The party was held in what had been a night-

club on a hill overlooking the bay. There was a rotunda with a balcony
overlooking the main floor, and from the ceiling, several stories high,
hung an enormous crystal-lustered chandelier. The Rangers were fit, wild
and ready to go. After a few drinks, games were in order, and one of the
games focused on the chandelier. The better athletes among them began
to take running jumps, grabbing hold of the chandelier and swinging.
That was the cue for everyone to throw plates at the swinger, who would
hold on until he was hit in the head by a plate. There were always a
couple of men unconscious on the floor underneath the chandelier.

Fights were going on all over the place. Heavy blackout curtains were
hung in such a way as to circle the room a few feet inside the windows,
so there was a walk space behind the curtains. In an opening in the curtains there suddenly appeared a face, as in a sideshow at a state fair. But
instead of throwing a baseball at it, one of the Rangers walked over and hit
the face. The face disappeared. Then it appeared again. Presently somebody else went over and hit the face. This happened time after time. The
face got worse and worse, but it kept reappearing. Finally the eyes were
closed, the nose was broken and there were no teeth in the face, but it
kept coming back.

The grand finale was when the chandelier came down. I swear to God
this thing must have weighed half a ton, maybe more. Some of those
underneath it on the floor must have been killed. I didn't stay to find
out.

The next day the Rangers started for Anzio. How the secret was kept
from the Germans I'll never know, because it was certainly no secret in
Naples. As the Rangers moved in convoy to load onto the transports, kids
ran alongside yelling, "So long, Anzio! Goodbye, Anzio!" But the Germans were taken completely by surprise. In the meantime I headed back
for the front.

The main strategy behind the Anzio landings was to pull German
troops at Cassino up to Anzio. This had worked before, particularly in
the Sicilian campaign. This time it didn't work. The Germans refused to
budge from Cassino, and after the initial successful landing at Anzio by
the Rangers we failed to follow up and drive for Rome, as we might well
have done. As a matter of fact, we had motorcyclists in the environs of
Rome who turned around and came back. I suspect that if we had continued in our attack from Anzio, we might have wrapped the Italian
campaign up then and there—or at least done a lot better than we did by
just standing still and letting the Germans regroup and consolidate their
position. If Patton had been in charge of the operation, we would have

taken Rome some months earlier than we did. But he wasn't and we didn't. The Germans held at Anzio and they maintained their position at Cassino, and we were stalemated on two fronts. Monte Cassino finally fell in late May 1944 to Polish Resistance troops who crossed those towering mountains and took the defenders from the rear. Then the German retreat began, and when it started, it was precipitous.

But before this, while we were still south of the Rapido, I received orders to return to the United States. I had everything I needed to put together the film about San Pietro, so I headed back, first to Naples, then Oran, and stopped over for a short stay in London. In London I met Willy Wyler, and we went to Claridge's for lunch and traded war stories. With Willy was a young, thin, freckle-faced English actress who, though she had lived through the worst days of the blitz in London, was blithe, happy and laughing. Her name was Deborah Kerr. Then it was back again to Astoria to put the picture of San Pietro together.

Astoria had its own set of rules. A Colonel Barret was now in charge, and he was a long-suffering man. He had been the chief lab technician in Washington during pre-war days in the Signal Corps. The Colonel was hardly equipped to contend with the personalities which the accident of war had deposited at Astoria, but he did his level best.

Rey Scott was there. He, too, had been in Italy, but not with my unit. Astoria was not Rey's cup of tea. He had been living in cellars and tents for years and he felt ill at ease in these more civilized surroundings.

Finally it got to him. Rey was standing duty one night as the Officer of the Day when he proceeded to get drunk. He made the rounds three times during the night with his entourage, and each time he called Colonel Barret at home, which was, of course, unheard of unless there was a dire emergency. The first time he said, "Colonel Barret? Captain Scott reporting. Twelve o'clock and 'aall's weell!' " Before the astonished Colonel could reply, Rey hung up on him. Exactly three hours later he called again. "Colonel Barret? Captain Scott reporting. Three o'clock and 'aaaalll's weeellll!' " The Colonel was furious by now. When Rey called the third time and started shooting off his .45, it was the last straw. The Colonel got Rey's sergeant on the line and ordered that Captain Scott be placed under arrest. It was a bad scene. Rey's .45 had had live rounds when he fired it, and the charges were quite serious. It couldn't be hushed up because there were too many witnesses.

Colonel Barret had some idea of Rey's military background, and I filled him in on points he didn't know. The simple fact was that Rey was beginning to show wear and tear; he had had too much. He was sent to

Mason General Hospital, Brentwood, Long Island, for rest and psychiatric examination. Presently he was recommended for an honorable discharge, and in due time that's what happened.

I lost track of Rey for some years after that. Then one day I received a call from him asking me to be best man at his wedding. I was on location shooting a picture and I just couldn't make it. That's the last time I heard from Rey until a few months ago when he called me while I was in Macon, Georgia, making a film. I was surprised to discover that one of my favorite men on earth was still alive. It defies all the odds.

10 A number of high-ranking Army officers, including a three-star general, were present at the first showing of *The Battle of San Pietro*. About three quarters of the way through the picture the general got up and left the projection room. It was naturally assumed that he was displeased with what he saw, and it was incumbent upon the rest to show their displeasure also. But, of course, they had to do so by rank, according to protocol. It wouldn't do for a lieutenant colonel to go stalking out before a brigadier general. The general was followed about a minute later by the next-ranking officer, and then one by one they filed out, with the low man on the totem pole bringing up the rear. I shook my head and thought, "What a bunch of assholes! There goes *San Pietro*."

Sure enough, by the time I got back to my desk, furious complaints had started coming in. The War Department wanted no part of the film. I was told by one of its spokesmen that it was "anti-war." I pompously replied that if I ever made a picture that was pro-war, I hoped someone would take me out and shoot me. The guy looked at me as if he were considering just that.

The film was classified SECRET and filed away, to ensure that it would not be viewed by enlisted men. The Army argued that the film would be demoralizing to men who were going into combat for the first time.

Yet *San Pietro* gained a certain amount of notoriety within the military establishment, and perhaps for that reason General of the Army George C. Marshall asked to see it. His official comment upon viewing the film was that "this picture should be seen by every American soldier in training. It will not discourage but rather will prepare them for the initial shock of combat." With that the whole scene changed. The sheep fell into line. Everyone praised the picture. I was decorated and promoted to major.

Life in New York was in sharp contrast to my existence of the past several months. That world of the fighting in Italy—some of the worst of the war—and the world of New York City had nothing in common.

Every now and then my astonishing good fortune hit me: to be alive instead of dead. For months I had been living in a dead man's world. I had never before seen dead in numbers, and for someone raised in conventional America—taught to abhor violence and believe that killing was a mortal sin—it was deeply shocking. But I felt I had adjusted. I remember saying to myself one day in Italy that I was really seasoned at last, a proper soldier. That same night I woke up calling out to my mother. We don't really know what goes on beneath the surface.

In New York I was staying at the St. Regis Hotel. I couldn't sleep. I'd wake up in the middle of the night, toss and turn for a while and then usually get up, put on my clothes and go out for a walk or a drink. There was a "brown-out" in New York, and the papers reported an outbreak of muggings in Central Park. In my walks I'd find myself strolling through the park with a .45 pistol in my waistband, secretly hopeful that some hapless bastard would try to jump me. Suddenly it all came together for me. Emotionally I was still in Italy in a combat zone. I couldn't sleep because there were no guns going. I'd been living for months with the sound of artillery in the background, all night long, every night. In Italy, when the guns stopped, you'd wake up and listen. Here, I was missing them in my sleep. I was suffering a mild form of anxiety neurosis.

It was in this state of mind that I fell in love with Marietta Fitzgerald. After living with violence and death for months on end, falling in love was almost a biological requirement. This is not to say I wouldn't have fallen in love with Marietta whenever I might have met her and whatever the circumstances: I would have. She was the most beautiful and desirable woman I had ever known.

She was born a Peabody. Her grandfather was Endicott Peabody, the founder of Groton. Her father was an Episcopalian bishop. She was married to Desmond Fitzgerald, a former Wall Street attorney now a commissioned officer serving in the Far East. They had one child, Frances, then about five years old.

I learned in due time, not from Marietta but from others, that her marriage was unhappy and that she and Desmond were about to separate when he went into the Army. In any case, Marietta had no intention of falling in love herself; it was against every rule of conduct in her Puritan background. But the day came when she had to admit that the unthinkable had happened. I do not believe that she was swayed by the strength of my emotion. She was not one to be led into doing something against her will. There was something of the lioness in Marietta.

That summer was a time of enchantment. I've always loved New York in the summer. It stops being a great city and becomes a small town. Voices are heard—rising and falling—along the avenues. The sound of the human voice is seldom heard in New York at any time other than mid-summer. I'd have moments of wonder at my good fortune: here I was alive with the most desirable woman in creation at my side. It seemed she floated. Her heels didn't clack on the pavement.

I would steal glances at her. The slope of her neck from shoulder to ear; the angle of her jaw, as though drawn by Piero della Francesca. I can still call up those images. Now and then one appears that I'd quite forgotten. In a dream, usually. Yes, after more than thirty years, I still dream about that time in New York.

I had Dad meet Marietta. They became friends instantly. He was deeply impressed by her but felt concern over what the future held for us. He asked me what was going to happen when Desmond came home. "Why, we'll tell him how we feel about each other and he'll give Marietta a divorce and we'll get married." "I hope it works out that way," Dad said.

Toward the end of the summer Marietta took Frankie and went for the yearly holiday with her parents. I was desolated by her absence. A good part of the time I stayed at the hospital, where I had a room and an office. Otherwise I spent it in the company of Pauline Potter.

I had dined with the John Barry Ryans one night, and Pauline had been a guest also. I saw her home afterward. She wanted to walk. We'd only gone a block or two when it began to rain. She asked me if I minded getting wet and I said I didn't. The rain came down harder and harder. Her hair, which she wore up in an old-fashioned bun, came undone and fell loose and dripping around her shoulders. We came to Jim Glennon's and I suggested we have a brandy.

Thereafter Pauline and I regularly stopped by to have a drink with Jim when we were out together. There was no idea of romance between Pauline and me; she was simply the closest woman friend I've ever had. And whether it was sheer accident or the fact that I was unconsciously seeking out relationships of value during this period, here again (as with Marietta) was a friendship that was to last a lifetime.

Pauline's taste in everything was superb. She had a house on 70th Street when we first met, three stories with two rooms on each floor. There was an atmosphere of bare-to-nakedness about the place—no rugs on the floor, and very little furniture, but each article was perfection.

Pauline had been born into a Baltimore family that had social status but little wealth. She was raised in France and spoke French before she spoke

English. She was now designing dresses for Hattie Carnegie. Taken separately, her features were not beautiful—a small, receding chin, mouse-colored hair—but she gave the impression of being a great beauty. In fact, she *was* a great beauty. She had large, heavily hooded gray eyes, was slender and tall, walked with the Grecian bend and wore clothes with an elegance I've seldom seen approached. Her voice was lovely, with tones like a clarinet, beautifully modulated. She alone didn't listen to it.

She had the ability to bring out the intelligent best in people. She guided conversations with rare grace and delicacy, and she was quick to conceal another's awkwardness of expression. It was flattering to be listened to as Pauline listened. Before long you were surpassing yourself—thinking more lucidly, speaking more eloquently, using words you had forgotten you knew, and saying exactly what you wanted to say.

In 1954, Pauline married Baron Philippe de Rothschild of the famous banking family: a poet, sportsman, author and patron of the arts, as well, of course, as being the proprietor of the great Château Mouton-Rothschild. The story is that Pauline won his heart the moment they were introduced, when she said, "Philippe de Rothschild? The poet?" It was a happy and satisfying marriage that lasted for more than twenty years.

My last documentary film for the Army was *Let There Be Light*, and its purpose was to show how men who suffered mental damage in the service should not be written off but could be helped by psychiatric treatment.

I visited a number of Army hospitals during the research phase, and finally settled on Mason General Hospital on Long Island as the best place to make the picture. It was the biggest in the East, and the officers and doctors there were most sympathetic and willing. Beyond a superficial acquaintance with the ideas of Freud, Jung and Adler, I was completely uninformed regarding the new science of psychiatry. But the doctors were always there to answer my questions. Particularly helpful was Colonel Benjamin Simon, who guided my reading and often illustrated some conceptual point with a living example. I would sit with Colonel Simon, observing patients in the receiving room. He would hazard preliminary diagnoses from their general appearance. I was skeptical at first of this mild talent and made notes to check against as therapy proceeded. Invariably, he was correct. Posture, expression and gestures had told him the particular form of the patient's illness.

The hospital admitted two groups of seventy-five patients each week, and the goal was to restore these men physically, mentally and emotionally within six to eight weeks, to the point where they could be returned to civilian life in as good condition—or almost as good—as when they came into the Army. There was no pretense at effecting complete or lasting cures, which can only be achieved by deep analysis, for the underlying cause of a neurosis usually dates back to childhood.

When the patients arrived, they were in various conditions of emotional distress. Some had tics; some were paralyzed; one in ten was psychotic. Most of them fell into the general designation of "anxiety neurosis." I decided that the best way to make the film was to follow one group through from the day of their arrival until their discharge. We set up our cameras in the receiving room, which was specially lighted for the occasion, and we started filming as the patients filed in. The receiving officer told them that they were being photographed and that their treatment would be followed by the cameras. It mattered to them not at all. Each man was deep into his own pain and oblivious to everything else.

Set-ups had been made to film the individual doctor-patient interviews, too. The cameras ran continually, one on the patient, one on the doctor. We shot thousands of feet of film—most of which couldn't be used in the picture—just to be sure of getting the extraordinary and completely unpredictable exchanges that sometimes occurred. As the men began to recover, they accepted the cameras as an integral part of their treatment. The doctors even noticed that the cameras seemed to have a stimulating effect, and that the patients being filmed showed greater progress than those in the other groups.

The things one saw happen were seemingly miraculous. Men who couldn't walk were given back the use of their legs, and men who couldn't talk were given back their voices. Of course, these inabilities were hysterical symptoms; and it was necessary to monitor their relief carefully. Conceivably, a patient given back the use of his legs might go to a window and jump out—or another yet more serious symptom might appear in the place of the first.

In psychotic cases—schizophrenics and catatonics—shock therapy was regularly used. I knew we couldn't use it in the film; it had no place in what we were doing. But I thought it was something that should be photographed for the record. Shock therapy then was much more severe than it is today. The patient used to arch his body so violently from the shock that five people were needed to hold him so he wouldn't break his back. At the same moment he would utter a sound—a kind of primal scream—that was absolutely unnerving.

There is no question that Mason General could be unsettling. Many of the psychotics there believed that they were the Messiah, or at least under the direct instructions of the Deity. I had been given a passkey which enabled me to enter any section of the hospital, and Charlie Kaufman, who collaborated with me on the script, suggested sardonically that one midnight I make a tour of the more violent wards with boxes of matches and straight-edged razors, passing them out to the patients saying: "This is God. Now go you and do that which remains to be done. . . ." Thereafter Charlie always prefaced his letters to me: "Dear G.o.d."

Colonel Simon was an expert hypnotist. Only a couple of others in the hospital were good at it, and none was as expert as he. Simon used no devices such as pendulums or prisms; he stood face to face with the subject and spoke in short, measured sentences. Often he would hypnotize a patient in less than a minute; two or three minutes was a long time. I watched him carefully and learned his technique. When I felt I had the rhythm of it, I asked him to let me try. It was actually quite simple. My subject was a good one, and he went under quickly. I got to be quite skillful, and in time they began to call on me to put a patient under when Simon was busy elsewhere. Having done so, I would then turn the patient over to a doctor for interrogation. Many cases had all the suspense of a thriller.

I recall one of a young cello-player. He had been in the Army only a short time. His father had died when he was an infant, and the boy had been raised by a mother who worked as a cleaning woman to give him a musical education. He had a deep affection for his mother, and a great sense of responsibility to her for all that she had done for him. I was present when this patient's story came out under narcosynthesis, step by step in response to questioning.

He had been in New York on leave, visiting his mother, and now his leave was up and he was going back to camp. Going down the stairs of Grand Central Station was the last thing he remembered. Apparently he had fainted. But there were no abrasions, no evidence of concussion. It was a classic case of amnesia.

Under narcosynthesis he began to recall everything, with a sense of continuity. He remembered getting up from the steps where he had fallen, and walking away down the street, but he had no conception of who or where he was. Eventually he was picked up by an ensign in the U.S. Navy and taken to a hotel. The ensign undressed him, got undressed himself and attempted to assault him sexually. Apparently the kid fought back and knocked the ensign out. Then, not knowing which clothes to put on, he mistakenly dressed in the ensign's uniform and left. He wandered the streets for a couple of days, and finally passed a nightclub on 52nd Street, where he heard an orchestra playing. There was a cello in the orchestra. He went in. The boy somehow knew that he, too, could play the cello and asked if he might try. They let him, probably because he was in uniform, and it was discovered that he was very good indeed. The club management assumed he was on leave—and hired him on the spot to fill in on the cello. And that's where he was picked up a week later, still in the ensign's uniform, happily playing the cello and living on the handouts they gave him.

Very gently this young man was brought back to awareness of who he was. His mother was notified, and I saw their reunion. Sometime after the war I saw this same young man on television. He was playing the cello in Toscanini's NBC Symphony Orchestra.

Altogether, the time at Mason General affected me almost like a religious experience. It made me begin to realize that the primary ingredient in psychological health is love: the ability to give love and to receive it. Kaufman and I wrote the script as the picture was shot, which, I think, is the ideal way to make a documentary. It was finished, cut together and made into a picture, with my father doing the narration. But again the War Department chose not to release it.

The reason given was that it violated the privacy of the patients involved. I don't think that was the real reason. The men who were in the picture—the patients whose recoveries we had witnessed—were proud of what they saw of themselves on the screen. As a matter of form, we had asked them to sign releases, and they were happy to do so. We pointed this out to the War Department, but when asked to produce these releases, we discovered that they had mysteriously disappeared. One day they were in the files at Astoria, and the next day they were gone. We then pointed out that, though the film indeed represented a deeply personal investigation into the innermost lives of these men, nothing was disclosed which might cause them to be ashamed. We proposed asking them individually to write letters of clearance, but the War Department said no. The authorities had made up their minds.

I think it boils down to the fact that they wanted to maintain the "warrior" myth, which said that our American soldiers went to war and came back all the stronger for the experience, standing tall and proud for having served their country well. Only a few weaklings fell by the wayside. Everyone was a hero, and had medals and ribbons to prove it. They might die, or they might be wounded, but their spirit remained unbroken.

When speaking of the War Department I say "they," because in that

bureaucratic morass it is impossible to pin down responsibility. I had
asked and received permission from Army Public Relations to have a
showing of *Let There Be Light* at the Museum of Modern Art in New
York, but the afternoon of the showing—a few minutes before it was to
go on the screen—two military policemen arrived and demanded the
print. Of course it was given up. Archer Winsten commented about this
in the *New York Post*:

> The Army sent an armed guard to take away John Huston's film about
> psychoneurotics . . . *Let There be Light*. . . . No reasons given. No argu-
> ments. That is the last anyone has seen of it. . . . One explanation is that the
> Army, having shrunk to its unleavened core of pre-war top executives, is
> re-embarking upon a do-nothing, say-nothing, think-nothing policy. . . .
> There is consolation in the fact that the picture will not be lost, that officials
> all retire or die sooner or later, and that waivers eventually become unneces-
> sary. Some future audience is guaranteed not only a beautiful film experi-
> ence, but also the certainty that their generation has better sense than
> ours. . . .

Winsten's faith in future generations has so far proven unwarranted. In
1970—twenty-four years after *Let There Be Light* was finished—the
Archives of American Films in Washington, D.C., prepared a showing of
all my documentaries. The Archives is a government agency, but even so,
it was refused a print.

To this day I don't know who the opponents of this picture were, or
are, but they have certainly been unflinching in their determination that
it shall not be seen. The same mentality was at work here as at the first
showing of *San Pietro*. Unfortunately, there was no George C. Marshall
around to save this one.

The two atomic bombs were dropped on Japan, and the war ended. I
went to Fort Monmouth and received my discharge. I'd prepared for that
day. My New York tailor had three suits ready for me. After four years
in uniform it was like dressing for a costume party. One night, at a bar,
a middle-aged drunk wanted to know why a young man like me wasn't
in the Army.

Word came to Marietta that Desmond was on his way home—the
dreaded moment was at hand. Marietta said she wished to tell him about
us alone and in her own time. I didn't hear from her for three days after
Desmond arrived; then she came to my hotel. I could see that she'd been
through an ordeal: her face was drawn and her eyes swollen. Desmond

had agreed to give her a divorce but only on condition that she see an analyst and undergo therapy before starting proceedings. I protested that that might take years. She said she wouldn't let it. I said I wanted to see Desmond myself. Marietta answered that he did not want to see me. That was understandable.

Marietta started her analysis, and I went to the Coast to sit it out. I was not to telephone her apartment. She would call me and tell me each time when she'd call next. I lived from one call to another. Sometimes she'd be late calling and I'd sweat blood, waiting. It was a time of frustration for me. Never was there any reassurance from her, nor did she utter those three all-important words. I gathered that she had made a promise not to commit herself in any way during this period of her analysis. The weeks became months. I became more and more certain that it was all over between us: under analysis she would discover that her feeling for me was an aberration and go back to her husband. I was going to lose her.

I met a pretty girl at a dinner party at Sir Charles Mendl's and met her again on a weekend cruise David and Jennifer gave some friends on a sailing yacht. She had played Scarlett O'Hara's younger sister in David's *Gone with the Wind*. Her name was Evelyn Keyes. She was young and vivacious and companionable. As an antidote to my depression I took her out to dinner a few times. One night at Romanoff's she leaned across the table and said, out of the blue, "John, why don't we get married?"

I had had cocktails before dinner, wine with dinner, and I was now into the brandy.

"Hell, Evelyn, we hardly know each other."

"Do you know of a better way for us to get to know each other?"

She had a point there.

I said, "All right. Why not? When?"

"Right now. Tonight. Let's go to Las Vegas."

I called Mike Romanoff over and asked what he thought about the idea. Mike was all for it. I had another drink, and suddenly heard myself saying, "Okay, let's do it!" Mike then rushed home to get a wedding band someone had lost in his swimming pool, and I called the stunt pilot Paul Mantz and chartered a plane.

By four o'clock that morning Evelyn and I were standing in front of a justice of the peace in Las Vegas. We were married, with Paul Mantz and a taxi driver as witnesses. We got back to Los Angeles just after sunrise and took separate taxis at the airport. She went to Columbia, where she was working in *Johnny O'Clock*, and I went on to Warners. Only then, sitting alone in the cab, did the utter damned absurdity of what I had done flood over me. How could I have done such a thing to Marietta? How could I have done such a thing to Evelyn? I thought briefly about getting an annulment. But then I thought, "What the hell? Maybe the best thing is just to try and make it work. What have I got to lose?"

My marriage to Evelyn was broadcast on the radio that same day, and I received a call from Pauline, who knew all about my relationship with Marietta.

"Oh, John! Is it true?"

"Yes."

"Is there anything you want me to tell Marietta?"

"No—nothing."

A few weeks later I heard that Marietta had completed her sessions with the analyst and had come to the decision that her marriage to Desmond had no future. She was getting a divorce.

The Communist witch-hunt during the late 1940s and early 1950s was a wretched period in this country's history, truly a national shame. The "Red Menace" hanging over Hollywood—and eventually over the entire country—gave rise to a miasma of fear, hysteria and guilt. There was a Communist under every bed, and everyone seemed eager to drag him out. It was brother against brother, friend against friend. Innocent people were hustled off to jail. Many lost their jobs—even their lives—simply because they believed in and exercised what they knew to be their Constitutional privileges: freedom of speech and political affiliation. In my estimation, Communism was as nothing compared to the evil done by the witch-hunters. They were the real enemies of this country. And what made it so bizarre, so unbelievable, was the fact that the worst offenders against all that this country stands for were members of a committee of the Congress of the United States, who had sworn an oath to protect and defend the Constitution. These men operated under the banner and protection of what was called the House Un-American Activities Committee—HUAC.

11

HUAC, which had been a little-recognized back-street operation since 1938, was launched into national prominence in 1948 with its successful prosecution of the Hiss case. This committee, under the direction of such men as Chairman J. Parnell Thomas and general counsel Robert Stripling, and staffed by ambitious young Congressmen like Richard Nixon, was given an awesome weapon in 1947 which it thereafter wielded with terrifying results. That weapon—provided by President Truman, Attorney General Tom Clark and J. Edgar Hoover—was the so-called Attorney General's List, a checklist of organizations which held supposed totalitarian, fascist, Communist or "any other subversive views." This list, originally compiled as an internal guide for use in screening Federal employees, later became the backbone of a "national loyalty program" and, along with a variety of other lists, was used by HUAC in its interrogation of witnesses. Beginning in 1950, when Senator Joseph McCarthy jumped on the bandwagon, these lists were used in a most wanton manner by the Senate as well, bringing the "witch-hunts" into full swing.

But the witch-hunts really started in 1947, when HUAC selected the
Hollywood film community as its first major target. There is no doubt in
my mind that the Communists were out to proselytize in Hollywood, to
win converts. But there is also no doubt in my mind that this activity in
no way posed a threat to national security. The Communists I knew were
liberals and idealists, and would have been appalled at the idea of trying
to overthrow the United States government. At that time no one knew
about the Gulag Archipelago and Stalin's mass murders. These "students"
of Marxism held meetings, with twenty or thirty people attending, in private homes. I went to such meetings two or three times, simply out of
curiosity. There would be a leader who directed the study sessions. The
students would recite their lessons from *Das Kapital* or from the text-
books and pamphlets which the Party provided them. Sometimes there
would be a fund-raising event, at which Paul Robeson or someone else
would sing. I wasn't revolted. On the contrary, I found it all very childish.
I marveled at the innocence of these good but simple people who actually
believed that this was a way of improving the social condition of mankind.

But a few years later HUAC didn't see it that way. HUAC was
convinced—along with J. Edgar Hoover—that there was a Communist
"fifth column" subverting the film community. They had rounded up the
names of a number of people they considered suspicious—Bob Rossen,
John Wexley, Lester Cole, Dalton Trumbo, Clifford Odets, among others
—and proposed to "clean house." I knew a number of these guys and
liked them, as people and for the work they did. I had no interest at all in
their private political beliefs.

The first warning of what was in the air came when a group of Congressmen came out to Los Angeles to conduct political interviews in the
motion-picture industry. They invited people to come and testify *in camera* as to what they knew about the machinations of the Communists.
Most of the studio heads complied.

I remember talking to Jack Warner about it after he had been interviewed. I said, "What sort of questions did they ask you?"

"They wanted to know the names of people I thought might be Communists out here."

"What did you say?"

"Well . . . I told them the names of a few."

"You did?"

"Yeah . . . I guess I shouldn't have, should I?"

I told him I thought he'd made a mistake.

Jack looked distraught. "I guess I'm a squealer, huh?"

A general atmosphere of hysteria and guilt swept through the industry as the investigations continued. In an effort to save their own careers, people flocked to become "friendly" witnesses by providing names of people they thought *might* be Communists—or, in other words, people that they were personally willing to blacklist.

A friend of mine, Philip Dunne, a very good writer at 20th Century-Fox, was having lunch with Willy Wyler and me one day. We agreed the handwriting was on the wall. Just before this, Lewis "Milly" Milestone— the director of *All Quiet on the Western Front* and *Two Arabian Knights*, among other great films—had been accused by Sam Wood of being a Communist. Sam Wood was a director of considerable reputation himself, but a rabid anti-Communist. One can best describe his attitude by recalling that on his deathbed he made a will stating that his daughter was to receive most of his estate—providing she didn't prove to be a Communist. I suspect Sam was slightly deranged.

I was vice-president of the Screen Directors Guild then, and at a board meeting I made a motion that we send a telegram to the House Un-American Activities Committee setting forth our disagreement with Wood's opinion. George Stevens was the president of the Guild, and he took a strong position on the subject, too.

That was the quiet before the thunderstorm, just a little sheet lightning in the air. When we saw that it wasn't going to blow over, we started talking to others, and eventually put together a group called the Committee for the First Amendment. Besides myself, Philip Dunne and Willy Wyler, this group included such prominent figures as Edward G. Robinson, Burt Lancaster, Gene Kelly, Humphrey Bogart, Billy Wilder and Judy Garland. Hollywood was righteously angry. People from the right, left and middle began raising their voices. In the name of our committee, we bought space in the trade papers—the best place in Hollywood to make our opinions visible—and issued a lengthy statement of principle. It deplored the Congressional investigation, predicted that it would endanger the jobs and livelihood of many loyal Americans, cause anguish to others and throw the motion-picture industry as a whole into disrepute. Then it pointed out how the Committee was in violation of the Bill of Rights and suggested that the charges that were being made were in fact equivalent to criminal accusations—yet the accused were being denied the right of trial. We stated our opposition to Communism, but argued that mass hysteria was no way to fight it, because hysteria of the kind encouraged by the Committee's action could destroy everything—

our industry and even the country. Finally, we invited other Hollywood people to join us in our stand. It was a good, strong statement.

Our position was greeted with unanimous enthusiasm in Hollywood, but HUAC was not deterred. In the course of the Hollywood investigations the Committee sent the infamous subpoenas to the Hollywood Ten. There were more than ten of them, but the label stuck, and when they went to Washington, D.C., to appear before the Committee, it was like lambs being led to the slaughter. We began receiving calls from the attorneys representing them—Bartley Crum was one—pleading with us to take some positive action on their behalf.

So a representative group of us decided to go to Washington and attend the hearings. We weren't sure what we would be able to do, but at least we could demonstrate our support.

I was dining one evening at the Wilshire Brown Derby when Howard Hughes phoned me and said, "John, I understand you are planning a trip to Washington, and I just want you to know that you can use one of my airplanes. Not for nothing, because, by law, I have to charge you something, but you can have it at the minimum rate allowable . . . and it will be all to yourselves." So that's what we did. In this group besides myself and Evelyn were Phil Dunne, Bogie and Betty, Ira Gershwin, Gene Kelly, Danny Kaye, Sterling Hayden, John Garfield, June Havoc, Jane Wyatt, Paul Henreid, Larry Adler, Richard Conte and a few others.

Our plane stopped a couple of times en route to Washington, and we were met each time by sympathetic reporters. We got the feeling that the country was with us, that the national temper resembled ours—indignant and disapproving of what was going on.

It took us quite a while to get to Washington, and we were bushed when we arrived. But there was an immediate press conference at our hotel. The press was good to us. The questions were of a generous disposition, and Phil Dunne and I answered for the others. Phil is a serious student of the Constitution, and a most articulate man. He had coached me in the fine points of our case, which was a good one. We had not come to attack anyone. We were not there to defend the Hollywood Ten. We were there because we felt that the Constitution of the United States—and especially the Bill of Rights—was being abused, and we were petitioning for redress of grievances. We were certain that these men were being tried unconstitutionally, not by a court of law for a crime but by the Congress (whose job was to make laws, not enforce them), for exercising freedom of speech and freedom of political beliefs.

The Committee hearings were two days away. The next night Phil and

I were asked to attend a meeting of those who had been subpoenaed, along with their attorneys. We were asked not to bring anyone else. On the way to the meeting I said, "You know, Phil, what I think they should do is to gather on the steps of the Capitol before going in to testify and tell the press exactly what they are. If they are Communists or not. We certainly don't know, and neither does anyone else. Then, after they have made a public statement, they should go before the Committee and refuse to testify on the grounds that the proceedings are unconstitutional." Phil thought for a while and agreed that it was a good idea.

We sat in on the meeting, and presently I made this proposal. It was greeted by stony silence. Most of the subpoenaed men looked at Bartley Crum. He appeared embarrassed, as did the other attorneys. Bartley stuttered a bit and said that it was a good idea, but it would be impossible because it would put them in a weakened position in court later. They had agreed among themselves to bring suits against the motion-picture companies in cases where individuals had been discharged or temporarily retired under suspicion of being Communist. I said, "Don't you think this is a much larger issue than whatever damages might be collected as the result of suits?" That went unanswered. Phil and I left the meeting feeling uneasy. Not that my idea had been all that good; it was rather that the response to it had been weak and shifty.

The next day we attended the proceedings as a group—the Committee for the First Amendment in protest. One after another, the defendants were questioned. They gave their names, addresses, then used the other questions as a point of departure for making statements, never answering the questions but talking all around them. Then came the big one: "Are you now, or have you ever been, a member of the Communist Party?" They would not give a direct answer. Parnell Thomas pounded his gavel, and the witness invariably raised his voice. Parnell Thomas pounded harder, and the witness was usually shouting by the time he was declared in contempt. One after another, they were knocked down. It was a sorry performance. You felt your skin crawl and your stomach turn. I disapproved of what was being done to the Ten, but I also disapproved of their response. They had lost a chance to defend a most important principle. It struck me as a case of thoroughly bad generalship.

Before this spectacle, the attitude of the press had been extremely sympathetic. Now it changed. The reporting about our committee in Washington, for us until that moment, was now against us. There were even some outright misquotes and misrepresentations. Various unions and other groups nevertheless sent us telegrams of support.

We had gone to Washington together, but we returned separately. On his way home Bogie was met by friends in Chicago who urged him to withdraw from our committee. He then made a public statement to the effect that he had been "ill advised" to go on this trip. Columnist George Sokolsky picked this up and wrote: "Mr. Bogart said he was ill advised. We would like to know who advised him. . . ." Phil and I sent Sokolsky a telegram saying *we* had advised him. Sokolsky reported this in his column, asking, "Who are Huston and Dunne? What is their connection with the Communist Party?"

The next thing I read about myself was by Frank Conniff, an anti-left columnist for the Hearst papers. I think Conniff was trying to fill the boots of Westbrook Pegler. He wrote that "there is very good evidence that John Huston is the brains of the Communist Party in the West!" After that I was expecting a subpoena, but they had enough sense not to throw one on me. Though I knew some of the men among the Ten, it was in no way connected with politics. I had a good war record and nothing to fear from any investigation. I had allowed my name to be used by organizations espousing principles in which I believed, and some of these were later accused of being Communist front organizations, but I had no ties to any group or organization that was to my knowledge affiliated with the Communist Party. I would have been delighted if they had subpoenaed me.

Following this trial, our Committee for the First Amendment began being described as a Communist front organization. The fact that it wasn't, and that I *knew* it wasn't, cut no ice. It later became known as *the* Communist front organization.

The thing that was most disappointing to me was the submissiveness of the American people. No voice of authority was raised in protest. J. Parnell Thomas was eventually found guilty of payroll padding and taking kickbacks, and was sentenced to prison. But very few people seemed shocked that this man—sent to jail as a common felon—had previously railroaded a number of good and decent people into prison for the "crime" of defending principles in which they believed. With Parnell gone, the way was clear for Joseph McCarthy to take the center stage. From that moment things could only get worse.

People were required to take oaths of allegiance in order to keep their jobs. This seemed to me both childish and insulting, as well as an extremely dangerous precedent. Obviously, any Communist would take the oath immediately. At a general meeting of the Screen Directors Guild a Machiavellian character named Leo McCarey—an Irish director of sophisticated comedy—proposed that the question of whether to take the oath or not be decided by a show of hands, rather than by secret ballot, so that no one would dare oppose it. I looked on in amazement as everyone in the room except Billy Wilder and me raised their hands in an affirmative vote. Even Willy Wyler, who was sitting out of my sight, went along. Billy was sitting next to me, and he took his cue from my action. When the negative vote was called for, I raised my hand, and Billy hesitantly followed suit. I doubt if he knew why, but he could tell he was in deep trouble from the muted roar that followed. I am sure it was one of the bravest things that Billy, as a naturalized German, had ever done. There were 150 to 200 directors at this meeting, and here Billy and I sat alone with our hands raised in protest against the loyalty oath. I felt like turning the table over on that bunch of assholes! It was a long time before I attended another Guild meeting, and when I did, it was a different story.

A sickness permeated the country. Nobody came to the defense of those being persecuted for personal beliefs guaranteed under our most sacred charter, the Constitution of the United States. A few refused to join the rabble, but even they, for the most part, sat back passively instead of fighting the tide of hysteria. I remember L. B. Mayer coming up to me early on, while the witch-hunts were at their peak, and telling me that he thought Joe McCarthy was one of the greatest men of our time. Then he looked at me speculatively. "John," he said, "you've done documentaries. . . . How about doing one that is a tribute to McCarthy?"

"L.B., you're out of your God-damned mind!" I just laughed and walked away.

Following the release of *We Were Strangers* in May 1949, I was immediately accused by the *Hollywood Reporter* of being a Red propagandist. The paper minced no words in calling it "a shameful handbook of Marxian dialectic . . . and the heaviest dish of Red theory ever served to audiences outside the Soviet Union. . . ." A week later the *Daily Worker* condemned the picture as "capitalistic propaganda." I was able to laugh the whole thing off as utter nonsense.

But it was no laughing matter. Careers had been ruined for less than this. In 1952 both José Ferrer and I ran head-on into trouble after bringing *Moulin Rouge* back from Paris for its premiere in Los Angeles. Joe had a reputation of being far left, but he was in fact no more a Communist than my grandmother. Nevertheless, when we opened in Los Angeles, some splinter groups from the American Legion—inspired, no doubt, by Hedda Hopper's constantly raking me over the coals in her column—paraded in front of the theater with placards declaring that José Ferrer and John Huston were Communists. I must say it took the edge off the festivities.

I was passing through New York on my way back to Europe to write the script of *Beat the Devil* when I got word through the New York representative of Columbia Pictures that Sokolsky—and an unofficial group of which he was kingpin—would like to meet with me. I accepted. Sokolsky's group was composed of other journalists, two labor representatives, somebody who I later discovered was from the State Department, anonymous members of the FBI and various others. The meeting was held in Sokolsky's house. I suppose I was on the carpet, but they didn't give me that impression at all. Am I being naïve even now? They asked me questions, but didn't ask me to name names. They wanted to know about the Committee for the First Amendment, and seemed genuinely interested in finding out if it actually did have Communist connections. I had gone quite prepared to fight my way out of the joint, but I was pleasantly surprised. I saw no need to take a defensive or belligerent posture, but merely answered their questions as honestly as I could.

Some of the questions, however, were absurd. They wanted to know about Salka Viertel, Peter's mother. I told them that she was one of the most generous, hospitable and civilized persons I knew, a kind of universal mother. Salka's "left-wing" activities had consisted mainly of making her home in Santa Monica a gathering place for European intellectuals such as Thomas Mann, Bertolt Brecht and Aldous Huxley, and for young American writers such as James Agee and Norman Mailer. This had earned her a place on the blacklist.

They asked me what I thought about Chaplin, and the question of Einstein even came up. You couldn't call them inquisitors, but it amazed me to hear them speak of Einstein as they did. They finally agreed that he was not a Communist, but rather "a misguided liberal." They looked on him as childish for his beliefs and statements, which seemed to me rather presumptuous on their part.

As for my own beliefs, I assured them that I was opposed to international Communism and all that Russia stands for, but that I mainly didn't care for dictators or bullies. "I don't like being afraid," I said, "or seeing other people be afraid. What I really like are horses, strong drink and women."

Later I read in Sokolsky's column a description of our meeting, followed by his statement that he felt assured I was a good American. Of course I was relieved to hear that!

There were very few who failed to succumb to the general fear. Several of the Ten who started out bravely had second thoughts and gave "evidence," naming names. It was even rumored that they were making deals among themselves: "You name me, and I'll name you." This sort of moral rot extended deep into the theater and television, and for me it was sad to see people for whom I had high regard, people of integrity, yielding to this obscene game of blackmail. What they did is understandable, I suppose, but hard to accept. It is difficult to say how one would behave under that kind of pressure. Fortunately, there was never any question of my having to find out.

I was away for most of this time. In 1951 I had gone to Africa to make *The African Queen*, and after that to Paris for *Moulin Rouge*. I felt no great desire to return to the United States. It had—temporarily at least—stopped being my country, and I was just as happy to stay clear of it. The anti-Communist hysteria certainly played a role in my move to Ireland shortly afterward. When I had been in Ireland a short time, I was delighted to learn that the Irish had an extremely low opinion of McCarthy and what he was doing. This further endeared them to me, but when I tried to get an American Associated Press man to relay this information to his bureau, he didn't dare to do it.

To this day you sense shame in those people who knuckled under to the witch-hunters. Sterling Hayden was one of the few among them who didn't try to excuse himself, or to justify his actions. At one time he had been an actual card-carrying Communist, but, under the pressure of the Red Scare, he changed his mind and decided that Communism was a danger to this country. He proceeded to name names—including that of his best friend. As a result, this man went to prison and later died. Knowing Sterling, I'm sure he believed he was doing the right thing at the time. But when the full significance of his act was brought home to him, he was stricken with remorse. He openly declared that he was ashamed of himself for what he had done, wrote a book which told about the episode and dedicated it to his friend. Sterling is one of the few actors I know who continued to grow over the years. I always felt great sympathy with him for this failure to live up to his own idea of himself. But even from this experience he learned and grew. There is a kingliness about Sterling now.

B. Traven's novel *Treasure of the Sierra Madre* was to be my next picture for Warner Brothers, when war was declared. Henry Blanke got them

12 to hold it for me during my time in the Army—one more thing I have to thank him for. Traven was a mysterious figure. He had cut himself off from society and was living somewhere in the wilds of Mexico. His New York publishers, Alfred A. Knopf, once sent an emissary down to locate him but, though a meeting was arranged, the elusive author never showed up.

Traven had written fan letters over the years to Lupita Tovar, a Mexican actress known as the Mary Pickford of Mexico, and at one time asked her to meet him in Acapulco. Traven instructed her to go to a certain bench on a public beach, where he would join her. Lupita kept the appointment; Traven didn't. She subsequently received a letter from him describing her actions on the bench, so she knew that he had been watching.

My friend and agent Paul Kohner later married Lupita Tovar, and also began to correspond with Traven—through a post-office box in Acapulco. Eventually he became Traven's agent. In one letter to Kohner, dated August 29, 1940, Traven talked about *The Bridge in the Jungle* as a movie script, and responded to Paul's suggestion that he might like to come to Hollywood for a while and get the feel of things:

> . . . More than one director and producer has been crazy about "The Bridge." The first one, if I remember right, was Mr. Luís Trenker who wanted to make that picture because he believed it to come out great. Now fact is that the story gives a director with lots of imagination a very wide margin into any direction. . . . I'll think it over as to what might be done in giving the screen writer more food to work with. And you are right, the best thing would be to make the picture at the same time, on the same locations, and, save a few exceptions, with the same actors in English and in Spanish. If I were to make it myself I would use very little talk, nearly none. . . . I would bring in the greatest amount of sound, any sound possible . . . from the jungle permanently awake, and sounds from the river

in all shades ever imagined, and all these sounds should blend in the most perfect manner with the voices of the people and the tunes from musical instruments and they should blend into a symphony of the deepest mysteries forever counterbalancing birth and death, creation and destruction, growing and decaying. The plot of the story should be of little consequence. The picture should, in a way, be no picture at all as we have come to accept pictures. It should be an entirely new kind of symphony . . . so strong that the audience even imagines to smell the exotic perfumes of the jungle and the cheap soap which the women used when bathing. . . .

I don't know whether I could write a picture. I have never tried to. Anyway, no man knows what he can do until he tried and was kicked off a dozen times before he finally succeeded. Quite a number of books I wrote never reached a printer's shop and were burned before they could harm any publisher or reader. . . .

And suppose I would come to Hollywood, what could I do there? I can act. Everybody can act, even Pauline [*sic*] Goddard. All you need is a director who can coach. . . . I can write. Books and stories. If I could afford two or three secretaries I could write a new book or a new picture every twenty days. Two hundred stories I could write at one sitting if must be. . . .

[But] I've heard of many well-known writers who were called to Hollywood under fixed contracts with their salaries ranging from three hundred to two thousand a week. . . . But once given an office and seated there they seemed entirely out of place . . . months without one stroke of work to do apart from collecting their salary every week until they got sick of it. . . . I know of only one well-known writer who made good in Hollywood, Ben Hecht.

[In Hollywood] everybody is thinking of money only and new contracts, nobody is thinking of doing something extraordinarily great. Nevertheless, I know new pictures will come. The next to come will be pictures in which the plot is superseded by the idea, by the basic argument which led up to the plot, and the plot will be used merely to make visible the tendency the writer had in mind and wanted to drive home. In music this has been done, or at least tried, since Haydn. It is left to great directors in Hollywood to do the same in pictures what was done long ago by Beethoven and Mozart, and also by Verdi and Rossini. . . .

About his "mystery," Traven had this to say in a letter to Herbert Kline, in care of Paul Kohner, dated October 11, 1941:

. . . please, cut out that goddamn mysterious if you mention my name or my work. There is no mystery about me, truly, not even a dot of a mystery. I am such a plain mug that any time a captain of a tramp will sign me on as a

stoker and never even think that I might have some intelligence enough to
be a fair A.B. All my mystery is that I hate columnists, feature writers,
sobsisters, reviewers who don't know anything about the book they talk
about. There is no greater joy and satisfaction for me as to be unknown as
a writer if meeting somebody or going places. Only this way I can be myself
and have no obligation to act up. Only this way I can say what I really wish
to say without being reminded by some high-stuffed or high-brow that a
writer of such a great reputation shouldn't talk so silly. If this attitude of
mine is called mystery . . . I wonder what one expects of somebody who is
really a mystery. . . . Over there in Hollywood every man who can write
four lines with only one mistake in spelling calls the [sic] Greta Garbo the
Mystery woman. What is so mysterious about her? Everybody knows
everything about her, even the name and birth dates of her great-grand-
parents and the interior decoration of the rooms she slept in while on a trip
in Italy with Leopold the Great. . . .

After purchasing *Treasure of the Sierra Madre*, Warners made a proposal
to Traven through Paul Kohner that he come immediately to Hollywood
for discussions about the script. On November 17, 1941, Traven replied
to this request as follows:

> . . . I wouldn't come immediately for two reasons. The first is this. Huston
> is actually deep in the Bette Davis picture. A picture starring Bette is always
> a very important one and Huston will have to concentrate entirely on that
> picture and will have no thoughts for any other picture until this is
> finished. . . .
> The second reason . . . is this. I am living for twenty years practically
> permanently in the tropics and in parts which are not the healthiest. If I
> would change climate rapidly during this time of the year I might arrive
> there and fall sick the second day and then be laid up perhaps for weeks
> with a terrific cold or with some tropical fever which may be latent and
> stay latent here but which might develop rapidly on changing climate with-
> out due care. . . .
> Now, Warners might say that they would take a chance on both these
> reasons. Okay. Anyway, I think I can make them a better proposition.
> Huston, or anybody who is going to direct the picture will have to come
> down to Mexico by all means before the picture is actually made, because
> you must not forget that the whole picture has to be built against a Mexican
> background or else the story wouldn't be possible. So I suggest that the
> Warners, who are ready to pay my traveling expenses for coming up there,
> spend these expenses on Huston and let him come down here as soon as he
> has finished the Bette picture . . . he would get into entirely new surround-
> ings, almost into a new world, he would obtain the atmosphere, get the feel,

the sound, the ins and outs, the way things are done, said, thought, and managed down here. All that would be of immense value to him when preparing the scripts. . . .

We would work together as fast as is convenient, and I think that in seven or eight days we could have the first draft. . . .

As soon as this first draft is done he would return back home, only more slowly. . . . This trip should occupy us the remaining twenty-four or twenty-two days of my contract. I would go with him to Durango, a very important location for the picture. From Durango we would cross the Sierra Madre. . . . He will come home now with the picture all done in his mind, he will have the perfect idea of the whole background, useful to him not only in this picture but just as well in other pictures based on books of mine. . . .

Twenty days after Traven wrote this letter the Japanese bombed Pearl Harbor. In 1946 I wrote to Traven concerning the picture. We exchanged several letters, and I began to form an image of the man based on his writing style, which suggested to me a person who, in spite of his elusiveness, was unguarded in his manner. During this same period I read a very lengthy and most discursive script by him based on *The Bridge in the Jungle*. I found it fascinating.

I wrote the script of *Treasure* and sent Traven a copy. He sent me a reply that ran twenty pages or more, filled with detailed suggestions concerning set construction, lighting and so forth. I was still most anxious to meet the man. I secured a tentative promise from him to meet with me at the Hotel Bamer in Mexico City, made the trip down and waited. He didn't show up.

One morning almost a week after my arrival I woke shortly after daybreak to discover a man standing at the foot of my bed. He took out a card which read:

HAL CROVES.

TRANSLATOR, ACAPULCO AND SAN ANTONIO.

Then he produced a letter from B. Traven, which I read while I was still in bed. It said that he, Traven, was ill and unable to come, but that Hal Croves was his great friend and knew as much about Traven's work as he himself did, and was authorized to answer any questions I might want to ask. Whatever advice Croves gave me would be just as good as if it came from Traven himself. So I arranged to see Croves later in the day.

During that meeting we talked about the script in great detail. He'd read it carefully and approved it completely. Croves had a slight accent. It didn't sound German to me, but certainly European. I thought he might very well be Traven, but out of delicacy I didn't ask. On the other hand, Croves gave an impression quite unlike the one I had formed of Traven from reading his scripts and correspondence. Croves was very tight and guarded in his manner of speaking. He was nothing at all as I had imagined Traven, and after two meetings I decided that this surely was not he.

Croves was a small, thin man with a long nose. His eyes were quite blue and close together, and he had graying blond hair. His trousers were peg-topped, he wore a big hat and had a handkerchief tied around his neck, inside the shirt collar. He had a kind of boxback jacket on, and was wearing wide suspenders. All in all, he looked as though he were country-born and -bred, unfamiliar with the ways of the city. Croves went off to Acapulco after our meetings, and a few days later I joined him there along with my wife, Evelyn, and Paulette Goddard. In Acapulco he was dressed in the same clothes, minus the jacket.

Since we were in Acapulco, I decided to go marlin-fishing. I had never caught a marlin. I'd hooked one once off Catalina and lost him when the leader broke. But I was committed from that moment; the thrill of that first strike never left me. I had read all the literature on marlin-fishing, from Zane Grey to Hemingway's *Esquire* articles, and every time I had a holiday I went deep-sea fishing, from California to Cuba. I knew all there was to know about marlin-fishing out of books, but I had never had the luck to tie into another one.

I asked Hal Croves if he knew anything about marlin-fishing, and he said that he did. So I chartered a boat and Evelyn, Croves and I went out for marlin. We fished for hours without a strike. Then Croves hooked one. The fish broke water and danced on its tail for fifty yards. I swear it was the biggest God-damned marlin I have ever seen. It was half again the size of anything I've since caught, and I've caught them up to 500 pounds. It was immediately apparent that Croves didn't know the first thing about fishing. He panicked, the line got snarled, and he dropped the rod. The marlin was gone. I gave serious thought to throwing Croves overboard.

On the return trip Evelyn and I each caught a sailfish—pretty dull fishing compared with marlin, but Evelyn insisted that the three of us pose with our catch when we got back to the dock. As the photographer snapped the picture, Croves turned his face away from the camera. I had the distinct impression this was done for my benefit. It was to make me think he wished to keep his existence a secret from the outer world. The implication, of course, was that he was B. Traven.

I wasn't particularly concerned about his identity. I was more interested in the fact that the man obviously knew Traven's work—and Mexico—well and could be a help to us as an advisor. He agreed to this, and I returned to Hollywood to start production.

The Treasure of the Sierra Madre was one of the first American films made entirely on location outside the United States. Henry Blanke went to bat for this plan and convinced Jack Warner that it was workable and economically feasible. Warner gave the go-ahead, and I then made an 8,000-mile scouting trip through Mexico with my art director, John Hughes, and the Mexican production manager, Luis Sanchez Tello. We settled on the mountain country surrounding the village of Jungapeo, near San José Purua, as our home base.

We began shooting the pre-production material in Tampico. This consisted of shots using Bogie's double and various views of Tampico for background material. We had been shooting in Tampico for about a week when I came down the stairs of the hotel where the company was staying— intending to go right on out to the set—and found the entire crew sitting disconsolately in the lobby. Orders had come from authorities in Mexico City to discontinue all shooting immediately. It seemed that the Tampico newspaper had published an article stating we had taken pictures which were a discredit to Mexico. It went on to say that the local Mexican populace had risen in righteous indignation and threatened us, going so far as to throw stones at our camera crew. There wasn't a word of truth in any of this. On the contrary, the people of Tampico had been extremely friendly, and we had received nothing but cooperation from the mayor on down. Everything had been so harmonious that we couldn't, in our innocence, understand what this was all about. We soon found out when you wanted to do anything in Tampico, it was a regular procedure to visit the editor of the newspaper and pay him a *mordida*. We had failed to do this. Hints may have been dropped, but they were either disregarded or passed over the heads of our liaison people.

We had a large investment in the picture already. Since we planned to film the entire picture in Mexico, Warner Brothers made immediate representations through the State Department. Meanwhile I'd received a call from my old friend Miguel Covarrubias asking what this was all about. I told him there was absolutely no truth to the allegations in the paper. He said, "I was sure of that, but I just wanted to hear it from you. Diego and I will go see the President." So he and Diego Rivera—also an old friend— went to see the President of Mexico, who in turn sent out a representative. He conducted an investigation and then gave his permission to resume shooting. This was the beginning of what became regular proce-

dure on the part of the Mexican government. Having a government representative with a foreign picture company on location is now common
procedure all over the world.

The editor who had written the false stories about us was shot dead
some two or three weeks later. Not for what he'd done to us, however.
He was caught in the wrong bed by a jealous husband.

We returned to Mexico in April 1947 with the three stars—Bogart,
Tim Holt, and my dad—picked up the Mexican crew and started the
principal photography at Jungapeo. Hal Croves was there with us from
the beginning of the filming. I never questioned him about his identity.
I respected his reticence. Others were less discreet. He always shook his
head and refused to answer them.

The Mexican crew was wonderful, attacking their work with a wild
energy. They moved large cacti around as though they were potted palms,
to serve as foreground pieces. They carried cameras and heavy supplies
over mountains and through jungle, always in the best of spirits. Mexican
Indians came down from the hills, some to be used as extras but many
just to watch the filming. It was explained to them that when the command
"Silencio!" was given, they must all be completely quiet. During the next
take it was so silent you could hear the humming of insects. I looked around
afterward and saw that most of the Indians had their hands over their
mouths.

Among the Mexican boys who ran beer and cold drinks to the company was a smiling little kid named Pablo. He was always on hand,
willing and eager to do anything asked of him. One night there was a
tropical downpour, and as I was going into the hotel, I noticed a face
looking out at me from underneath a truck. It was Pablo. I called him
over, took him into the hotel and put him on the sofa in my room. We
had breakfast together the next morning, and from that time on there was
no shaking him. I discovered that he was a homeless orphan, so when it
came time to leave Mexico, there was nothing to do but adopt him and
bring him back with me.

When we arrived in Los Angeles, Evelyn met me at the airport and I
introduced her to our new son. Her immediate reaction was shock. She
put on a good face, however, and tried thenceforth to be a good mother.
Pablo was educated in the United States and eventually married a lovely
Irish girl who bore him three children. Then his life turned sour. He
deserted his family, returned to Mexico City and became a used-car
dealer. Perhaps I should have left him in Jungapeo.

A young Mexican doctor was with us on location, for whom I developed a great admiration. When we'd go into a town, he'd pass the word that a *médico* was present; soon there would be a long line of the sick and injured patiently waiting for his attention, and he gave his attention to all. He removed tumors and performed all manner of surgery. I remember one of his patients was a young man who had been terribly burned around the throat. Scar tissue had formed in such a way that his chin had fused against his chest and he couldn't turn his head. The doctor performed a skin graft, removing skin from the man's thigh, and for the first time since he was a child the man was able to raise and turn his head. The electricians in the company often ran the big generator at night so the doctor could have lights for an operation. When it was not available, he'd use Coleman lanterns, hand-held by assistants, as he operated on a patient lying on a tabletop out in the open.

To express in their own Latin *macho* way their love and admiration for this man, the Mexican crew took his trousers off one day and painted his balls with mercurochrome. This ritual became a symbol of high esteem. My turn came presently, and eventually they got around to Hal Croves. He fought with such ferocity that the crew gave up immediately. Everyone was stunned by the way Croves reacted. You could see that he considered the ritual a direct assault on his dignity. From then on he was left pretty much alone.

By this time I was certain that Hal Croves was not B. Traven. After I left Mexico and the picture came out, the question of his identity became a matter of public controversy. Everyone was talking about the B. Traven mystery. In 1948 a Mexican magazine sent two reporters to shadow Croves in an attempt to ascertain the facts. They found him keeping a small store on the edge of the jungle near Acapulco. They watched his store until Croves left to go into town, then they broke in and rifled his desk. In the desk were several manuscripts by B. Traven and evidence that Croves had another name: Traven Torsvan. Hal Croves and Traven were apparently the same man, after all. Subsequent investigations have uncovered evidence of yet a fourth name: Ret Marut, an anti-war anarchist writer who disappeared from Germany in 1922. In 1923 B. Traven appeared in Mexico, and various experts have testified from examining the writing style of these two men that there is little doubt that they are one and the same.

Other published research has since argued that this strange character went by several names, and that Croves was Traven. Croves died in 1969, some years after marrying his assistant, Rosa Elena Lujan. A month after his death his widow confirmed that B. Traven had been Ret Marut. This may be, but I still have my doubts that Croves and Traven were the same man. I believe that B. Traven was two or more persons who worked in collaboration. Many have questioned how Ret Marut could have left Germany in 1922, and three and a half years later offered three novels to the world which did not deal at all with German social and political affairs—his specialty—but, instead, probed the experiences of an American, Gerard Gales, in western Europe, at sea and in Mexico: *The Death Ship, The Cotton Pickers* and *The Bridge in the Jungle.* Hal Croves could certainly have had those experiences, but hardly Ret Marut.

I met Hal Croves' stepdaughter in Mexico after Croves died. We talked about him at some length. I was amazed at her description of the man: urbane, sociable, impeccably dressed; of an eminence in Mexico City. She recalled dinners in the Croves household as formal occasions even when there were no guests present. All of this bears little resemblance to the reticent little man who stood at the foot of my bed years ago in Mexico City with his wide suspenders and "country boy" clothes. A complete transformation? An attempt to live up to his—or someone else's—image of a famous author? Interesting speculation.

For the role of Gold Hat, the bandit leader in the script, I chose a part-time Mexican actor by the name of Alfonso Bedoya. One of the two other Mexican bandits we hired had actually been a bandit. These two Mexicans took an immediate dislike to Bedoya and harassed him continually. Bedoya was terrified of them, although they were half his size. They ganged up on him during any kind of a melee, in or out of the film, and Bedoya invariably came out with a bloody nose or a black eye, to say nothing of a wounded ego. In a way, Bedoya asked for it. He was given to posturing. An American girl jumped out of a hotel window in Mexico City during the filming. Bedoya had never laid eyes on the girl, but he put on a black armband and stood around the local bars pretending that he was in mourning. He wanted people to think she had committed suicide because of him.

It was very hard to understand Bedoya's speech, and I had to work with him closely on each scene. "Horseback" always seemed to come out "whore's back," for example. His was a bravura performance, but sometimes he just couldn't manage the English; the words wouldn't come. When this happened, he'd try to make up for his incapacity with gestures, which became progressively more pronounced and violent. Often he became so engrossed he wouldn't even hear me say, "Cut!"

Bogie turned to me one day and said, "John, are you right about this? I have my doubts."

"I'm right, Bogie."

It did turn out to be right. Bedoya got several good parts after *Treasure* and actually had quite a vogue. Then he began to drink heavily, which I suspect was the main cause of his death a few years later.

It was during the filming of this picture that Bogie and I had our one and only quarrel. Bogie was very eager to get his boat, the *Santana*, into a race to Honolulu. The race was soon to be run, so he was always trying to pin me down to a finish date. I refused to let Bogie's race schedule interfere with my picture, and told him so. Bogie sulked and became progressively less cooperative.

One day I was shooting a dialogue scene between Bogie, Tim Holt and Dad. I thought Dad could be better, so I asked them to do the scene again. Bogie asked, "Why?"

I didn't want to explain why.

"It has nothing to do with you, Bogie."

"Well, I don't see why you want to do it again. I thought it was good."

"Please! Just do it!"

Bogie grumblingly did it again, and this time it came out all right. But that evening at the dinner table he started in on me again about the race. Suddenly I'd had as much as I could take. Bogie leaned across the table toward me to make a point, and I reached out and took his nose between my first two fingers and closed them into a fist. There was silence at the table.

Finally Betty Bogart couldn't stand it. "John," she said, "you're hurting him."

"Yes, I know. I mean to." I gave one more twist, and let go.

Bogie came to me later and said, "John, for heaven's sake, what are we doing? Let things be with us as they have always been."

And of course they were.

One of the reasons I'd wanted to do this picture so much was that I saw the role of the old sourdough, Howard, as being perfect for Dad. I called him as soon as I got the go-ahead on the picture.

"Dad, they're going to ask you to take this part in *Treasure*. I want you to take it. You'll be great. And Dad . . . I want you to take your teeth out for this role."

"Christ! Do I have to do that?"

I told him that I thought old Howard should be wise, sly and toothless. He agreed, but without any great enthusiasm.

There were scenes in which Dad had to speak Spanish. He didn't know the language, so I had a Mexican record his lines, and Dad memorized them. In the picture he spoke Spanish like a native. It was certainly the finest performance in any picture I ever made. *Theatre Arts*, at that time the Bible of the drama, called it the finest performance ever given on the American screen. I agreed and was immensely proud and pleased when Dad won the Academy Award as Best Supporting Actor. *Treasure* is one of the few pictures I don't turn the dial away from when I come across it on television. When he does that dance of triumph before the mountain, cackling out insults at his compadres, the goose flesh comes out and my hair stands up: a tribute to greatness that has happened, with me, in the presence of Chaliapin, the Italian thoroughbred Ribot, Jack Dempsey in his prime, and Manolete.

The day after he did that dance a cable came that Alec Huston was dead. We stopped work, went back to the hotel and Dad and I spent the rest of the day and most of the night talking about Alec. Before leaving the East the last time, I'd gone up to Canada to pay my respects. Alec was living in Orangeville, near Toronto, in a little frame house with his wife, Phoeme, and daughter, Margaret. He'd had a heart attack and was failing generally. His jaw looked extra big because his neck had shrunk. We sat in the parlor with the two women. They made drinks for us—there was hardly enough whiskey in Alec's glass to color the soda. Presently he said, "All right, John. Let's you and me go upstairs to my studio."

He had to sit down and back up the stairs with a stop every third step. As soon as we got into his studio he closed the door, turned to me eagerly and said, "Well, John, tell me about it!"

I thought perhaps he meant about the war. Not at all. He wanted to hear about my fight with Errol Flynn, blow by blow. I told him and, after that, he wanted to know about the girls I'd been to bed with. Then he brought out his latest paintings. They showed no improvement whatever. One was a portrait of Dad as *The Bad Man*, which he gave to me. I still have it.

It wasn't until just recently that I heard from my cousin, Margaret, about something that happened in his very last days. Alec was in bed then, never to get up again, and they all knew it. One afternoon there was a ring at the front door, and Phoeme left the bedroom to answer it. She returned shortly with the information that Alec had a visitor, a second cousin from Toronto. Alec said, "I won't see her."

"Why not?"

"Because she's a bore."

"Alec, she's come all the way from Toronto to see you. You can't refuse."

"Yes, I can. These are my last few hours of life, and I'm not going to spend any of them being bored. My time is far too precious."

Phoeme began to cry. "Alec, you've got to see her!"

"I don't have to see her! The last thing I want to do is to see this woman. Tell her I'm dead!"

"I can't tell her that! If that were true, I would have told her so when she came to the door."

"Tell her I died during the time it took you to get to the door and back."

Phoeme broke down in earnest.

Alec turned to his daughter and said, "Margaret, go tell that woman I'm dead!"

"Daddy, I can't! She'll come in!"

"Then bring her in! I'll play dead. Now do as I say. Go tell the woman I'm dead!"

"But you can't hold your breath that long."

"Try me!"

So Margaret did as she was told. Alec lay back, half closed his eyes and held his breath. The woman looked at him and she, too, burst into tears. Now all the women were crying. They left the room and the woman went on her way. Phoeme came back in and Alec opened his eyes and grinned. He died a few days later.

I had decided that my next film, *Key Largo*, was to be my last for Warner Brothers. Not only was I put out by Jack Warner's refusal to permit **13** me to direct O'Neill's *A Moon for the Misbegotten* back in 1946, but I was dissatisfied with the studio in general. The complexion of the place was changing. Its great innovative period was in decline, if not over. Hal Wallis was gone, and Henry Blanke had his hands tied by the studio. He had become one of the highest-paid producers in Hollywood, and when his option came up, Warners pressured him to take a drop in salary. He refused, and they proceeded to make life miserable for him. He was not only my mentor but a dear friend, and it distressed me to see him put up with petty harassment simply for the sake of money. A great indignity was done him, but he compounded it by refusing to leave the studio. It was in this mood and unfortunate set of circumstances that I started work on *Key Largo*.

Jerry Wald was the producer. He put Richard Brooks with me to help with the screenplay, and we went down to the Keys—my first visit there—and wrote it on the spot. Evelyn and Dick's wife, Harriet, accompanied us. We arrived out of season and there weren't any suitable places to stay, but we finally discovered a small hotel which looked attractive, and persuaded the owners to open the place for us before the season started. We had no sooner settled down to work than they moved in a dice table, a roulette wheel and a blackjack table. Thereafter, when Dick and I weren't writing, I was gambling.

I was in a bad streak and lost more than I could afford to, so one day I told the owner to give me another thousand in checks, but that was it. "From now on," I said, "no more." He gave me the checks and I promptly proceeded to lose them.

I went back to him, "Okay, forget what I said. Give me another thousand."

"I can't do that! When you set your limit, that's it!"

I got angry. He was entirely right and I was entirely wrong, but I got sore at him and hardly spoke to him from that time on. I behaved very badly about the whole thing.

But being refused any more credit was a blessing in disguise. I went back to work on the script in earnest.

We were in the dining room the night before we were to leave, and the owner and his wife were entertaining guests at a nearby table. I overheard the owner say something about the Immaculate Conception, and I pointed at this like a bird dog.

"Do you know what that phrase 'Immaculate Conception' means?"

The owner turned to me. "Why, it means that Mary had Jesus without—you know—without being touched by a man."

"You don't know what you're talking about." I was being deliberately offensive. "The Immaculate Conception has nothing to do with the birth of Christ."

The owner huffed and snorted and argued. When he ran down, I said, "I'll bet you five hundred dollars you're wrong."

He accepted, and we went in and called the Monsignor in Florida City. It was late at night, but the Monsignor came to the phone, listened to the argument and said, "The Immaculate Conception has nothing to do with the birth of Christ. It refers to the fact that Mary was born without Original Sin." Then he went on to tell us when the dogma was proclaimed.

The owner paid off the $500 bet, and with this stake I returned to the dice table and won back almost everything I had lost. Dick, who was also well down at this point, followed my action and won back most of his losses as well.

As Brooks and I wrote it, *Key Largo* had a stronger dramatic line than Maxwell Anderson's original 1930s play, and we brought it up to date. The high hopes and idealism of the Roosevelt years were slipping away, and the underworld—as represented by Edward G. Robinson and his hoods—was once again on the move, taking advantage of social apathy. We made this the theme of the film.

Robinson accepted the part of the gangster Johnny Rocco with some reluctance. He had never cared for the gangster image. It was as though he had actually been a gangster himself and was eager to reform—perhaps this state of mind is one reason he was prompted to collect fine art. I think *Key Largo* is best remembered by most people for the introductory scene, with Eddie in the bathtub, cigar in mouth. He looked like a crustacean with its shell off.

Since the major part of the action in *Key Largo* took place in a resort hotel, we were able to do most of the shooting in the Warner Brothers studio. A few mood shots were done in Florida. It was nominated that year for Best Picture, and Claire Trevor got the Oscar for Best Supporting Actress. There were fine performances by Bogie, Lauren Bacall and Lionel Barrymore. I especially liked working with Lionel. He told me one day that he ascribed his brother John's sad finish to the fact that John once brought back a totem pole from an Alaskan holiday and put it up in his garden. Up to that point John could do no wrong. But after that his luck turned. Lionel attributed this entirely to the totem pole. John had handled this holy object casually and thereby angered some Eskimo god.

It was around this time that I first got to know Billy Pearson. We might never have met except for a crazy horse and the fact that I collect pre-Columbian art.

I had a good little string of horses in California. Liz Whitney started me off with a mare named No Bargain, who wasn't quite up to Liz's standards because of a pigeon toe. Liz practically gave me the animal, and I was happy to get a mare of such quality. No Bargain was out of Caledonia by Omaha, good breeding, and she had a fairly good racing record. It was thought she would have been an even better performer except for the pigeon toe. No Bargain was a speed horse, and I bred her to another speed horse in California, Lassiter, which accounted for the filly Bargain Lass. Everything I got out of No Bargain was a winner.

I had always owned a horse whenever circumstances permitted, but this was my first venture into thoroughbred stock. Before long, my horses started going to the post. I bought other mares and kept adding to my string. I got nominations to the best sires in California, including Alabi and Khaled. I had one winner after another. I didn't know how lucky I was.

I have, on various occasions, put down some fairly good bets. I don't think the rate of my pulse ever increased radically when I had a few thousands on a horse's nose, even when I could ill afford it. But to see babies of yours, born in your stable, enter the starting gate decked out in your colors is quite another matter. I never seem to be able to hold them in my binoculars. They have a way of jumping out of the picture with every heartbeat.

Bargain Lass was one of these, and a very fast little filly. She had been a pet in the yard, but something happened to her in training. She went to pieces at the starting gate, rearing up and falling backward. None of the good jockeys wanted to ride her. She was fast, but there was that danger at the gate.

Then, one day, I was watching the morning workouts at Santa Anita when a little man came up to me.

"I think I could steal a race for you on that Bargain Lass."

I recognized him as Billy Pearson, one of the leading jockeys in the country. "You mean you want to ride her?"

"Sure, I'll ride her . . . but I do have conditions."

We went to have breakfast at the racetrack restaurant and discussed the deal. Billy said, "Now, when I win on Bargain Lass, I'd like my cut in pre-Columbian."

I could see that Billy had done his homework on me. I agreed to the terms.

Five days later I entered Bargain Lass in a race. In the gate Billy wrapped her tail over the back bar to keep her from flipping over, got her clear and won the race easily. He went right to the lead about five lengths, then took hold of her and kept that distance. He came in three and a half lengths ahead in a six-furlong race, which is a hell of a big lead and in a good time for that period in California racing. I paid Billy off in pre-Columbian art, and from then on he rode all of my mounts. Billy became a bosom pal. We ran a lot of horses and pulled quite a few capers together. Although we've slowed down a little, we do to this day. There's only one Billy . . . thank God!

Billy Pearson has an eye for art. He was in a hospital once, recovering from a bad fall, when somehow an illustrated book about early American furniture came to his hand. He read this book, got interested, obtained more books on American furniture and, when he got out of the hospital, began to visit museums and talk to collectors. Then he started his own collection and became an expert on the subject. In the process, he also became an expert on things like weathervanes, ship figureheads and carved duck decoys. His interest in these fields served as a bridge into the art world.

Billy got into pre-Columbian art when he went down to Mexico to ride. He depended on his eye, bought a few pieces which turned out to be authentic, and eventually developed an important collection. He has some superb pieces of Olmec and Chinesco. Of course, nobody can be a real expert in more than one or two fields of art but Billy's overall knowledge is truly amazing. In the late 1950s he won the top prize on *The $64,000 Question*, a TV quiz show; he was so popular that the show staged a special series on art with Billy and Vincent Price as the only contestants. Billy won again. When the scandals over quiz show rigging later caused *The $64,000 Question* to be canceled, Billy was called to Washington to testify in the congressional investigation. His interrogator, a senator, expressed doubt at the ability of an ex-jockey to answer difficult questions about art.

"Try me," Billy said.

"What?" the senator responded.

"You try me." Pearson was quickly excused from the proceedings.

Billy never finished high school but he reads prodigiously and remembers. He is knowledgeable about primitive art, especially African, pre-Columbian and Northwest Coast Indian art. He is an expert in Navajo blankets and pictographs on deerskin. I would take Billy's opinion in some areas over anyone else's.

Beyond that, Billy is one of the most entertaining persons alive. He has a gift of being able to go beyond the limits of acceptable behavior and yet never lose his membership in polite society. He loves to drink, loves to talk and is full of stories. His accounts of our experiences together are infinitely better than what really happened. They always contain a seed of truth, but sometimes I have difficulty in discovering it.

Anyone except Billy would be banished—or murdered—for some of the things he has done. Instead, he is cherished. The best example of this I recall was during the filming of *The Life and Times of Judge Roy Bean*, in which I had Billy play the part of a little miner. A bad man had shot the miner in the heel years before and thereafter he walked with a limp. Ava Gardner played Lillie Langtry, and the scene was her arrival in Langtry, Texas, named after her by Judge Roy Bean, by then long departed. There were only two people left in town: the head of the Judge's vigilantes, who now kept the museum, and this little crippled miner played by Billy Pearson.

The scene was beautifully staged. The period train pulls into the station and there is a glimpse of this perfect beauty through the train window. Billy is at the bottom of the steps to help her down. He puts up his hand. She takes it, and they walk up the street toward the museum with the camera preceding them. I was delighted. The train had stopped precisely where it should have. Miss Gardner was at her most graceful and elegant. Suddenly Billy, teetering in his ancient makeup and shaking with simulated age, turns to Ava and says, "How'd you like an old man to go down on you, Miss Langtry?"

These were the first words Billy had ever spoken to Ava Gardner. She walked on a few steps and then just broke up. Cut! Back to scratch. Only Billy could have got away with it.

As a rule, jockeys are thought to possess information which can make you a millionaire overnight. They don't; damned few jockeys end up as millionaires. The top jockeys get their choice of the horses they want to ride, and they like to ride winners. Their choice of mounts should tell you which horse they think will win. But once in a while they get a tip at the last moment on a long shot. I never asked Billy for information, but one time he gave me an unsolicited tip on a horse. After the race he came around and asked how I'd done.

"Christ, Billy, I didn't pay any attention to you. I bet on another horse."

He looked at me as though I were crazy—which I was. But, as a result of this experience, all my acquisitive instincts were stirred up and I was always ready and waiting for another tip from Billy.

I used to get to the track well before the first race so I could sit in the box, look at the form and have confabs. Billy usually dropped by my box before going to the dressing room. One morning I was late. I didn't get there until the horses were in the parade. I put my glasses on the procession and I saw Billy turn and look right at me. Then he nodded. I took all the money I had on me and chucked it on his mount, noting with satisfaction that the odds were very long. The race was run, and Billy's horse came in last. I had a pocketful of $100 tickets. I took them out, creased them, stacked them into a pile and made a bonfire. This was Billy's only race that day. I was warming my hands over the fire when he walked up.

"What's going on, John?"

"What the hell do you *think's* going on? These are the tickets on your horse."

"You bet on that dog?"

"Sure! You gave me the nod."

"Hell, John, I was just saying good morning!"

Actually, it is very seldom that there is a "shoo-in," as they say. The races are observed so closely and carefully that it is almost impossible to get away with anything. Only once did I have direct knowledge of a real fix. It occurred at Pomona.

A friend, who for obvious reasons must be nameless, had some horses. One day he came to me.

"John, there's going to be a killing. I'd like to borrow some money from you, and I'll put you on it, too."

He began to tell me what the set-up was at Pomona, which is known as a "getaway" track. At the end of the season the jocks, the owners and the trainers try to get even at Pomona. And if it calls for a bit of conniving, well, that's not beyond them. In this instance it was known not to a select few but to practically everyone except the general public. There was a long shot in this race, and the jocks had all agreed to shoo-in this long shot. This man owned the favorite, but, for sure, that favorite wasn't going to win. I cut him short and said, "Look, I'll lend you the money, but I don't want to hear anything more about it."

I wrote him a check and made a note to myself to stay away from Pomona.

The race was run, and I was conspicuous by my absence. The entire field tried to fall behind this long shot, pulling the heads off their mounts, and the long shot just got slower and slower. It turned out to be the slowest-run race in the history of the Pomona racetrack. This horse had never been in front of anything in his life, and he wasn't about to start now. Getting behind him took a bit of doing. The race got so slow it was beginning to be obvious. Then, about a furlong from home, the long shot broke down. My friend's horse won the race, and he had to go to a hospital. He had hocked everything he had, and had borrowed from everyone he knew. He paid everybody back in due time, but it was an unhappy afternoon for him.

I had another filly named Lady Bruce, which I owned with Virginia Bruce. Virginia had been married to Jack Gilbert, and after his death she inherited a number of horses—about which she knew nothing. She said to me, "John, will you take them? We'll go partners."

I did, and Lady Bruce was among these animals. She was then a foal.

When we put her into training as a yearling, we saw pretty soon that Lady Bruce was very fast. We sent her to be schooled under a trainer I didn't know, someone Virginia had recommended. The horse developed into a grand-looking mare. There was no doubt that she was going to win races. But just before she was ready to start, she developed splints—bony excrescences in the shins of the forelegs. She got over them (the condition is not permanent), but it kept her from running at Hollywood Park. Later I heard she was being shipped down to Del Mar for a race. I went out to Hollywood Park to see her and talk to the trainer. They had already left. But somebody remembered that her forelegs were wrapped in bandages.

"What? Was she hurt?"

"I don't know."

I smelled something funny, so I took my groom and we flew down to Del Mar. I found Lady Bruce in her stall, and she had bandages on. The trainer wasn't there. I took the bandages off and discovered that she had popped osselets—little bony knobs in her pasterns. I took the horse by the halter and led her over to another trainer I knew and asked him to keep her until I could take her away. Osselets are serious, yet her trainer was actually going to race the horse. He might have won the race and been able to collect a good bet, but it would have ruined Lady Bruce. I left a note for the trainer and another for the Racing Board saying what I had found and why I had taken the animal away. I never heard from the trainer again. I sent Lady Bruce to a veterinary hospital for salt-water treatments, and she was laid off for several months.

Lady Bruce, now a three-year-old, returned in good shape right at the turn of the season, and Billy Pearson and I put her in a seven-furlong race. She ran well ahead of the field at six furlongs, then she faded and came in fourth. But she ran the race in good time, and I knew—and so did Billy— that she would win at six furlongs. So we lay back until we got her the right race and company. It was a six-furlong event at Santa Anita. Billy said, "We've got it made, John!"

I was short of cash, as usual, but I drew out all I had in the bank, borrowed $2,000 from Anatole Litvak and another $2,000 from Willy Wyler. It added up to quite a few thousand dollars. I gave it all to Evelyn and sent her to the track with explicit instructions about how to place the bets. There was a little tout there who acted as a legman for me, and I told Evelyn to give him a thousand or so to bet for her, other friends a thousand or so each, and to make some bets herself, but not all at one window, so she wouldn't attract too much attention. I couldn't attend the track because I was in the middle of shooting *Key Largo*, but I felt that Evelyn was more than competent to handle the assignment.

I suspected that the favorite—a horse named Dry—would have been able to take Lady Bruce in seven furlongs, but I knew beyond any doubt that she would beat him out in six. This was Dry's debut. His owners, a South American named Luro and his trainer, Grillo, had paid $20,000 for him as a yearling, which was a lot of money in those days. I was so confident that I advised my friends to get their money down on Lady Bruce to win. A lot of my co-workers on *Key Largo* went out and made bets with the bookies around Burbank, then we all got together and listened to the race results on the radio.

Sure enough, Billy Pearson brought Lady Bruce home a winner, and she paid $26.80 for $2.00. Dry came in second.

I could scarcely contain myself. This was perhaps the greatest news I'd ever received. One minute I'd been scraping the bottom of the barrel, and the next minute—thanks to this marvelous animal—I was rolling in dough. The fish were jumping and the cotton was high. I could now shed the nagging debts that interfered with my life style. It was the beginning of a new era. I decided to celebrate that evening at Chasen's Restaurant in Los Angeles with some friends.

Half an hour later Art Fellows called me.

"John, something terrible has happened. We thought you should know about it as soon as possible. Brace yourself."

"What's this all about? What happened?"

"Evelyn didn't bet the money."

"What? What do you mean she didn't bet the money? How could she not have?"

"Well . . . you know Luro and Grillo?"

"Of course. For God's sake, go on!"

"John, Evelyn didn't sit in your box. She sat with Luro and Grillo. She was about to make the bets like you told her, and they talked her out of it. They were sure that Dry was going to win the race, so Evelyn placed only a token bet of a hundred bucks on Lady Bruce. I'm sorry, John. . . . So's Evelyn. She feels terrible about this. She's afraid to talk to you. What should she do?"

I was in a state of shock, but I said, "Tell her it's all right, Art. And have her meet me at Chasen's."

I finished shooting for the day, had a drink or two in my dressing room, composed myself and went to Chasen's. By this time Billy Pearson had heard what had happened, and he met me there. At first I suspected it might be a joke. What convinced me that it wasn't was the fact that you can't make telephone calls from the track, so Art had left the track to call me. I said to myself, "John, here's your chance to show a little class, it's only money." (Actually, it was so damned much money that it made me sick to think about it.) I told myself, "Never mind, John. Play it to the best of your ability, according to what you think a gentleman should do."

I waited for Evelyn. She didn't show up. Then I got a call from her. I said, "Evelyn, why aren't you here?"

"Oh, John, I was just afraid to come—afraid of what you would say to me."

"What is there to say, Evelyn? These things happen."

"Aren't you furious? Don't you hate me?"

"Of course not, my dear, of course not. It's only . . . money."

"But, John, I want to tell you what happened. Let me explain. I sat with Luro and Grillo in their box, and they had this horse named—"

"Yes, I know. Dry. I know all about it. Fine, Evelyn, forget it. Forget it entirely, and just come on over here and—"

"But, John, they said that Lady Bruce didn't have a chance!"

"Yes, honey, I know. Now, look. It's happened. I can imagine exactly how it happened. I understand this entirely. Anyone can make a mistake.

Now, you just hush up and come on over and join me. Let's never say another thing about—"

"But, John, please! Let me explain. Dry was the odds-on favorite. That was a lot of money, and they assured me Dry couldn't possibly lose this race!"

I said, "You bitch! You dismal, wretched, silly bitch!"

And there went my whole image of myself. There went Gentleman John. Evelyn did come to Chasen's, but by the time she got there I was so drunk I didn't even recognize her.

I must say Evelyn tried to make our marriage work, but the cards were stacked against her. She was allergic to most animals. The ranch in the Valley was just made for horses and dogs, and I had quite a few of both. As a matter of fact, I also had cats, monkeys, parakeets, pigs, goats and a burro named Socrates.

Evelyn had a riding habit, and she'd go out with me and sit on a gentle horse, but presently her eyes would swell and she'd have trouble breathing. I think she wanted to be around animals—at least at first—but some fault in her chemistry made it impossible. Ultimately she came to view the entire animal kingdom as her antagonist and, I fear, myself an antagonist by association.

A couple of my experiences with horses in Evelyn's presence convinced her that I was quite mad as well. One Saturday night we were having dinner with Billy Pearson and his wife, Queta. I'd drunk my dinner rather than eaten it, and I had a sudden inspiration to go out to the Valley, where I had some horses at the stables of an Italian trainer named Nino Pepitone. Billy had never jumped, so I said, "Come on, Billy, I'll lead you over the jumps!"

It was the middle of the night, but we all went out and beat on Nino's door. He took a very dim view of what we were about to do, especially since it was pitch dark, but he saddled my horse, and while he was saddling Billy's mount, I got up and started off. Nino said to me later that he heard the horse go into a gallop, and presently there was the sound as of a collision between a railroad engine and a bus. The horse came back riderless, then in due course I appeared in a beat-up condition. I had run into a parked car. Billy stared at me a moment, then shook his head and walked away. That ended the midnight steeplechase. Billy never had understood why anybody got up on a horse who wasn't paid to do so.

The worst fall I ever had was during this period in California. The Uplifters, a riding group in the Riviera Country Club, had a course which they had made into a steeplechase, and they were talking up a race that I really wanted to ride in. The problem was that I didn't have a horse that qualified, so I began to scout around for one. I heard about a horse who'd run unsuccessfully on the flat, but looked as if he had the makings of a chaser. I went to see the animal someplace out in the Valley and took him over some sticks. He could jump, all right, so I bought him.

I vanned the horse out to the Riviera, where I was to meet my groom, Charlie Lord. He was late, and Evelyn and I had a breakfast appointment at the beach, so I decided to go ahead and work the animal alone. In any circumstances this would have been an unwise decision. There are many things a helper can do when you are working a horse over the jumps. If he balks, the helper can shoo him on, or even touch the animal with a long lash if necessary. If the horse is really stubborn, you and your assistant can send him over on a lunge a few times riderless before trying it mounted. But I was impatient, and I tried it alone. The steeple jumps were big hedges, and the horse didn't like them at all. He refused one. I turned him away, then sent him at it again, using my whip. Again he refused. I tried a third time, this time using my whip for all it was worth. I think the horse decided I was trying to kill him. Suddenly he took hold of the bit and bolted blindly toward Sunset Boulevard. He was rank as they come. I couldn't begin to turn his head.

It was a Saturday morning, there was a lot of traffic on the Boulevard, moving fast, and I knew if we got up there we would both be killed. I tried everything in the book. I took a slow, long pressure on the reins and then let go all at once. He stumbled a bit, but he wouldn't slow down. I leaned out of the saddle and hit him on the nose with the side of my fist. Nothing worked.

A fence enclosed the steeple course, and beyond that a picket fence was the last obstacle before the highway. By this time I was leaning out of the saddle at a forty-five-degree angle, with both hands pulling hard on the reins. The horse continued at a gallop. I couldn't do a damned thing. He went over the course fence and headed for the picket fence. Now he was moving half sideways, crabwise. He hit the picket fence, got his two off legs on one side of the fence, his near legs on the other, and somersaulted, taking me with him, knocking out pickets as we rolled.

When we came to a halt, I couldn't move. By this time Charlie Lord and a few other people had arrived, and they sent for an ambulance. After five or ten minutes I got my breath back, smoked a cigarette and got up. I thought I was uninjured, and sent the ambulance away. The fact is I was just numb from shock. Abiding by the old rule that you mustn't let a balky horse get away with it, I said, "Come on. I'm going to get that so-and-so over at least one jump!"

With the help of the others, whipping his flanks, I got him over a fence. I jumped one more for good measure and then got off. By now I wasn't feeling well at all. We got into the car and started off to keep our breakfast date, but on the way I said, "Evelyn, I don't really feel like going to the beach. Let's turn around and go home."

About halfway to the house I started bleeding from the mouth. Evelyn stopped and called the doctor, who met us at his office. X-rays showed three broken ribs and a cracked vertebra. The doctor wrapped me so tightly I could hardly breathe, put me to bed and told me to lie flat on my back. In two days I had pneumonia. I couldn't cough because of the bandages. I was laid up for a couple of weeks, but I don't think I ever really got over it.

Between pictures, during this period, I did a lot of shooting. I had been in love with guns ever since my mother bought me my first .22 when I was a boy in Arizona. I taught myself to be quite expert with a rifle, but I never had much opportunity to do game shooting. Evelyn often accompanied me. We went deerhunting in the Sawtooth Mountains in Idaho. When I wasn't going for bigger game, I availed myself of every opportunity for bird-shooting.

One time Billy Pearson and I went out to a dove-shoot on a place owned by Morgan Maree, my business manager, in Antelope Valley. We all took our stands, and the birds came in high and fast. It was a very good shoot. In the late afternoon we each had a sack of birds, and we loaded into the pickup and drove back to the house, where the birds were then laid out on the game table and counted.

My bag was opened, and the first bird to come out was a yellow-throated thrush. I said, "Christ! How could that have happened?" The next bird was a yellow-throated thrush also, and the next, and the next. The other guys appeared embarrassed and tried not to look at me. I couldn't understand it. I thought, "Am I going blind? How could I mistake a thrush for a dove?" I went over each shot in my mind and tried to recall each bird as I had recovered it and put it in my sack. I was dumbfounded. "Surely I'd have noticed if I'd killed a thrush! Surely!" I told myself. But the evidence was there. My bag contained only two or three doves. All the rest were yellow-throated thrushes.

One takes these things very seriously. I stayed a little apart from the festivities that night. The others had a great party, drinking Jack Daniel's old-fashioneds, but I couldn't get in the mood to join them. I had a few drinks, but by myself. I liked shooting very much, but I decided it was time I gave it up. My mood wasn't helped by occasional remarks, mostly from Billy Pearson, such as: "John, come out and look at the *yellow moon!*"

True to my word, I stopped shooting entirely. It wasn't until a year or so later that Morgan Maree told me what had really happened: Billy Pearson had shot those thrushes and exchanged them for the doves in my bag.

In 1948, having completed *Key Largo*, I was approached by Sam Spiegel at a cocktail party with the idea that we go into partnership and start our own film company.

14 My contract with Warners was about to expire, and I had made up my mind not to stay there. "If you can come up with the money," I told Sam, "you've got yourself a partner." Sam negotiated a loan, and the next thing I knew we were in business as Horizon Pictures.

Sam and I were both eager to get the company going, so, hurriedly, prematurely, we decided upon *We Were Strangers* as our first picture. This was a long short story from a book called *Rough Sketch*, by Robert Sylvester. A New York columnist suggested in print that I make the story into a picture. Sam and I both saw the item, read the story and thought, "Why not?" It wasn't a very good choice, and it wasn't a very good picture.

We acquired the property, and Sam went about looking for a major studio to finance the making of the film. Finally he arranged for us to make our pitch to Metro-Goldwyn-Mayer. Every so often L. B. Mayer would call together the various heads of his departments, along with the producers at Metro, and they would discuss policy, procedure, and, on occasion, sit and listen to ideas that were advanced—such as ours to do *We Were Strangers* with them. This gave a democratic air to proceedings at MGM, but of course L.B.'s was the last word, if not the only word.

It so happened that the night before this scheduled meeting Bogie gave a riotous anniversary party at his house, during which I proceeded to get as drunk as I've ever been in my life. When I say riotous party, by the way, I don't mean orgiastic. I mean we played football in the living room.

I was much too drunk to drive, so I slept overnight at Bogie's place. I woke up around ten o'clock to the ringing of the telephone and heard Bogie saying, "Yes, Sam, he's here."

Sam had been calling all over town for me since nine o'clock.

"John, for Christ's sake, get over here immediately! We've got to make that meeting!"

I had a hangover that only a bullet could cure. I was in such a daze I couldn't even focus on my own hand.

"Sam, it's hopeless! We've got to call it off."

"We can't! John, do you realize how important this is? It's a great dispensation on their part to hear us at all!"

"Okay, Sam. I'll come out to your place and we'll talk."

Bogie's man drove me to Sam's house, where I shaved, showered and put on a shirt and tie belonging to Sam.

Sam Spiegel was about five feet nine inches tall, but he insisted I also wear one of his sportcoats. Naturally the cuffs were halfway to my elbows. I had to wear my dress trousers with a ribbon down the leg, and my patent-leather shoes. Decked out like this, I was supposed to give a convincing pitch for our project!

"Sam, I can't do it! It's impossible! I don't even remember what the hell the story's about!"

Sam said, "All right, John, but we have to make an appearance, at least." So off we went.

Upon our arrival at Metro, we were ushered into a large room, and I was introduced to various people with familiar names but whom I hadn't met before. Everyone was cordial and polite but not effusive, for we were, after all, petitioners. We had waited about five minutes when L. B. Mayer entered briskly, shook our hands and called the meeting to order. We sat down at a long board table, and everything was conducted formally: direct and to the point. Then Sam Spiegel got up and told the story of the picture we wanted to make. It was one of the finest demonstrations of pure animal courage I've ever witnessed. He just made it up as he went along, and as I sat listening to it, his rendition was so good that it actually seemed to make sense. After he finished, L.B. said they would think about our proposal, and the meeting was adjourned. Eddie Mannix asked us if we'd care to stay for lunch. Sam declined with considerable courtesy, and the two of us went back to his house, where he gave me a drink to calm my jitters.

We were sure we had blown it, but we were wrong. Metro liked the idea and eventually approved the project. In the meantime, however, Sam had received a better offer from Columbia, and we decided to go with them. I heard through the grapevine that the wheels at Metro had found the story Sam told quite interesting, but were dubious about Sam himself.

Sam had a reputation for being something of a rogue, and the MGM bosses, with their snobbish pretensions, found him to be wanting as a member of their club. I, on the other hand, was their kind of gentleman. I don't suppose I had said anything but "How do you do?" and "Goodbye," but this was interpreted as gentlemanly reserve. Metro was so impressed, in fact, that it began negotiations with Paul Kohner and arranged a two-picture contract for me to follow *We Were Strangers*.

Peter Viertel and I wrote the script for *We Were Strangers*. This was the first time I worked with Peter, whom I'd known since he was a boy. His mother, Salka Viertel, was a dear friend whose home I often visited. It served as a kind of salon in Hollywood for the intellectual community, and a refreshing haven from the day-to-day hoop-la of the movie world.

The story was about the attempted assassination of a Cuban dictator and his close associates by revolutionary forces. The leads were well played by John Garfield, Jennifer Jones and Pedro Armendariz, but the actors were not enough to carry the film. Essentially, *We Were Strangers* was pretty frail material.

Jennifer Jones looked for direction in every move she made. I would say, "Sit over there, Jennifer." She would say, "How?" At first I was confounded, but I discovered that Jennifer wanted to be told when and how to sit, stand or walk across a room. She put herself completely in the hands of the director, more than any other actress I've ever worked with. And she was not an automaton. Jennifer took what you gave her and made it distinctly her own.

I had been warned about Harry Cohn, the head of Columbia, who had a reputation for being a bully and a vulgarian. My experience with him was exactly the opposite. He couldn't have been more decent or more thoughtful. Others who knew him better may laugh, but I am only being honest when I say that I found Harry Cohn to be an extremely well-mannered man.

I went down to Cuba to scout locations for the second-unit material we were to shoot there, and Evelyn, Peter Viertel and his wife, Gige, accompanied me. At this time, through Peter, I met Ernest Hemingway. There was something close to a father-son relationship between Peter and Hemingway. Papa read all of Peter's material, analyzed and criticized it. On one occasion he even offered to write a book with Peter.

Shortly after our arrival in Havana we drove out to the Hemingways at their *finca* in the nearby village of San Francisco. I was a great admirer of Hemingway's work, but that first meeting was anything but easy. I realize now that we were simply feeling each other out. Papa was always suspicious of people at first. Peter told me afterward that Papa questioned him about me in great detail.

Even so, he was the good host. He invited us out on his boat, the *Pilar*, the following day. We saw a log bobbing around in a little bay where we were anchored. Papa picked up his .22 rifle and began shooting at the log. He was a good shot, and hit it three out of five times. I'm a good shot, but I missed it five out of five times. Papa said, "John, just think to yourself, 'If I don't hit it this time, I will never fuck again!'" With my next shot the log jumped clear out of the water.

It was mid-summer and hot—Cuban hot. We were sitting under the canopy having a cool drink when Mary saw something move on top of a little hill behind the first sand dunes on the beach. We looked closer and realized it was the head of a very large iguana. Papa picked up the .22 and fired, and the iguana jumped into the air. It had clearly been hit, and Papa declared his intention of going after it. Mary protested, "No, Papa. You wait here and let the boys get it." So Papa waited on the boat, and Peter and I swam in to pick up the iguana. We couldn't find it. There were rocks all around. We searched behind these and all over the surrounding area, but there was no sign of the iguana, other than a few drops of blood proving he had been hit. After thirty or forty minutes we gave up and swam back to the boat. Hemingway would have none of this. A hunter must collect his game. He rose and picked up his gun; he would have a look for himself. Mary couldn't dissuade him.

We were anchored, as I said, in quite shallow water, and at one point you could actually walk in to the shore, but only by a circular route which took you clear around the little cove. Papa elected to walk in. It must have taken him twenty minutes to get to the place where the iguana had been shot. We were sitting on the boat watching, and, finally, there he was. His strategy was to walk in a big circle around where he knew the iguana had been hit, making the circle smaller and smaller each time around, so that he covered every inch of ground. His figure appeared and disappeared behind dunes, and he kept this up for over two hours under that blazing sun. But he found the iguana. He heard a hiss when he passed a rock, and there it was, down in a crevice. Papa put a bullet through its brain and brought it back. I have never seen such persistence and determination.

At Hemingway's *finca* a few days after this we were talking about boxing. Earlier Peter had mentioned to me that Papa didn't see how I could be all that good. I was too light for my height. This rankled me. The gloves were there, and I said, "Let's put them on, Papa." I didn't mean this as a challenge. I just wanted to see how Papa handled himself, to see what kind of fighter he was and how he moved.

Papa replied, "I understand you're a good boxer, John. With those long arms you might just stand off and keep jabbing me in the nose, mightn't you? Maybe cut me up?"

"I wouldn't dream of doing that, Papa."

Mary pleaded with us not to box, and Peter chimed in, too. But by now Papa had his back up.

"All right, John, let's give it a try."

Papa went into the bathroom to throw cold water on his face, and Peter went with him. Peter later told me that while in the bathroom Papa said, "I'm going to cool him!"

While they were gone, Mary turned to me. "John, Papa's been ill. He's not supposed to exert himself. So please, for God's sake, don't box with him!" That was the first I had heard of Papa's illness. Mary told me that was why he had waded ashore when he went to find the iguana. When Papa came back out, I begged off. By reputation Papa liked to throw that Sunday punch, so perhaps it was just as well.

I was down in Cuba a second time for pre-production work—"keys" for back projection to be used in process shots—and I saw more of Papa. We began to feel easy with each other. Out in his boat again one day we talked about writing.

Hemingway said that nothing was as rewarding to him as the act of writing itself, when the words took wing; when the hand followed the thought, and the thought soared, the pen tracing its flight. My only thrill in writing comes after I've written something, put it away and then on re-reading it later find it still holds water . . . a feeling largely of relief. But I said to myself, "Well, this is Hemingway speaking. I suppose writing *is* a joy for him."

A couple of days later, on the deck of the small boat, we were talking about things we found hateful to do. As I recall, for Papa this was dancing . . . being on a dance floor with a partner. Papa said, "Christ, I'd rather write than dance!" I heard this with some satisfaction.

I think Papa's illness during this period was hysterical in nature. He was identifying himself with the character of the Colonel in *Across the River and into the Trees*, which he was then writing. Of course the figure of the Colonel was Hemingway. It became embarrassing at times because it was so obvious that Papa's descriptions of his hero were based upon his idea of himself. You could see through these descriptions, and as the hero in the book was living his last hours, it was incumbent upon Papa that he also be ill to the point of death. He was living the part, like an actor.

Another time Papa and I were talking about things that had happened to us during the war. Whatever I had said must have been highly complimentary to myself, for Papa remarked, "John, we don't just introduce a subject, do we? I mean like Chauncey Depew at a banquet . . . then come on with our story subtly? We just brag outright, don't we? Like fucking heroes of fucking yore!"

Bob Capa and Papa had been friends since their days in Spain during the Civil War, but during World War II their friendship suddenly ended. There was a good deal of speculation as to why. Some thought the rift between them was because Bob had made a derogatory remark about Mary and had advised Papa against marrying her. Capa denied this, and told me the real reason.

Papa and Bob were on their way to Paris and in a hurry to get there before it fell. The Germans were in full retreat, but there were still pockets of resistance along the route they were taking. Papa suggested a shortcut, but Bob objected to it because the enemy was rumored to be holding a position there that they would have to pass through. The way Hemingway put it to Capa amounted to a dare: "Well, Bob, will you come with me or not?" They'd been traveling one close behind the other. Bob answered: "Sure I'll come, but not with you. I'll follow a hundred yards behind you." So Papa started out in his car and Capa followed in his jeep. They rounded a curve and suddenly came face to face with a German Tiger tank a little above them on a hill. The tank immediately fired at them. The shell hit the road in front of Papa's car and ricocheted overhead without exploding. Since Capa was some distance behind, he had a better view of the overall scene than Papa did, and he saw the tank spin around and retreat, disappearing over the brow of the hill. Convinced the danger was past, he sped to Papa's car, stopped, whipped out his camera and took a photograph of Papa, who was head-down in a ditch with his ass sticking up in the air. When Papa looked up and saw Bob standing there with his camera, he said, "Give me that film, Bob." Bob wouldn't do it, and they stopped being friends as of that moment. Bob told me the story while Hemingway was alive, and I am certain it is true. Anybody in his right mind would hit the dirt under those circumstances, head-first or any other way.

I went out with Papa on his boat a number of times, and we spent a few evenings together in Havana. Occasionally he came to lunch with me when we were filming in the city. One afternoon I witnessed a side of Hemingway seldom if ever mentioned, a peculiar act of kindness on his part. A young Cuban who hung around the bar of the Hotel Nacional was a strident racist. His prejudice was tantamount to an obsession, and he'd grab you by the lapel to get your attention and launch into a diatribe against the blacks. He was thoroughly offensive. One day I told him so, and he turned to Papa for support. I noticed that Papa was strangely complacent. He merely smiled and nodded. Finally, when I could speak to Papa, I muttered, "I'm going to kick that sonofabitch in the ass!" Hemingway said, "John, don't you understand? He's a black." I looked at the man closely, and I saw that Papa was right. The man was indeed a black. He was trying to "pass," and Papa was being very gentle with him.

After our time in Cuba I saw Mary and Papa on several occasions, usually in Paris or London. Once I thought of making a picture based on three Hemingway short stories. I figured I would direct one, Willy Wyler the second and some other director the third. Mary and Papa had been on a visit to Spain, and Paul Kohner and I met them in St. Jean-de-Luz, France, to discuss the project. We came in on an all-night train and had breakfast with them the following morning in their room. Just as Hemingway hated the idea of being somebody's copy, he also hated to be photographed. But Paul is a camera nut, and, sure enough, during breakfast out came Paul's camera and he started clicking away. I sensed Papa's uneasiness and tried unsuccessfully to get Paul's attention. Hemingway said nothing. We finished breakfast and went out into the street.

During our walk Paul ran ahead of us, taking photographs. I still hadn't been able to get him aside and say, "For Christ's sake, stop!" Even I found it objectionable. I was expecting Papa to explode any minute. Hemingway said nothing. Then Paul smiled and said, "John, would you take one of me with Mr. Hemingway?" I looked at Papa. He nodded. I took a couple of pictures. Hemingway actually put his arm around Paul. I was astounded. I had never seen him so friendly with a stranger—usually he was on guard and taciturn with someone who was new to him, but that day he was ever so pleasant. Paul is a family man and very proud of his daughter. While discussing her he told Hemingway how much she admired his work. Suddenly Papa disappeared for a moment, then came back with one of his books, glowingly inscribed to Paul's daughter. He had ducked into a bookstore and bought a copy. On the way back to Paris I was still scratching my head about this. I said to Paul, "I've never seen anything like the hit you made with Papa. I've never known him to behave like this with anybody."

Later I discovered from Peter Viertel what had happened. Papa had thought that Paul was my principal. We were going to make a movie, and Paul was the money man. I had him down there, and it was Papa's obligation—as a favor to me—to help me plant the hook. Sometime later, when Paul was acting pompous, I leveled about his instant popularity with Hemingway.

Evelyn and I had been having our problems for some time, compounded by my involvement with animals. I must hand it to Evelyn—she tried to live at the ranch, but her allergies made it unendurable for her. When I was in Europe one time, she decided to get an apartment for us in the city, which she intended as a surprise for me upon my return. At the airport she said she had something special to show me. We had discussed her taking a place in town, so I sensed what was coming. Even so, I wasn't prepared for what I saw. The place was the Shoreham Apartments, an exclusive complex above Sunset Boulevard. It was built by Mitch Leisen, a movie director and interior decorator. Paulette Goddard and Burgess Meredith had the apartment right above Evelyn's.

I couldn't believe the place. The decor was white on white—white throw rugs, with white pillows on top of them, and white satin curtains at the windows. The bedroom had a long dark glass counter covered with exotic emollients, lotions, perfumes—from France to the Far East. Evelyn had brought in some works of art from the ranch, but, other than those, all the appointments were pure Mitch Leisen. Evelyn was very proud of it, and most happy that *we* were now going to live here, rather than in the Valley. I professed to be happy with her choice. I didn't tell her about *my* allergies.

At the completion of *We Were Strangers* there was the usual grand party, and Jennifer—who played the role of China (pronounced "Cheena") in the picture—gave me a chimpanzee named China. China was taken out of her cage for the presentation ceremony. She came to me immediately and threw her arms around me. We adored each other at first sight. This was around three o'clock in the morning. Art Fellows and I put China back in her cage and drove her to the new apartment. Evelyn was asleep in the bedroom when we arrived. I couldn't bear to see China in a cage, so we let her out. She was right in the middle of having a wonderful romp when Evelyn heard us and came to the bedroom door. "What is that?" she asked. I introduced them formally. "God, John! What are you going to do with her? She can't stay here tonight!"

"But, Evelyn," I said, "where else? I can't take her all the way out to the Valley at this hour."

I then tried putting China back into her cage. She didn't want to go, so finally I played a dirty trick on her. I bounced her up and down a few times, which she adored, and on the last of the bounces I threw her into the cage. But China, who had tasted liberty, decided to have no part of this. She put the palms of her hands on one side of the cage and the soles of her feet on the other and pushed. The cage had iron bars, but it just came apart at the seams. There was no keeping China in her cage that night; there was no cage. Art Fellows chose this moment to depart quietly.

My next tack was to put China in the bathroom with the door shut. This enraged her. She gave a scream you could have heard in downtown L.A. Clearly, I had become her father, lover and soul partner, and she had no intention of being separated from me. I said, "Evelyn, China has to sleep with us."

"Not with me!" snorted Evelyn.

She shut the bedroom door on China and me and promptly went upstairs to Paulette's apartment, where she spent the rest of the night.

China and I then went to bed, and she put her arms around me like a new wife. During the remainder of the night I heard banging, crashing and ripping noises, and I'd call out to China in the darkness. Each time I called her she came quickly back and dutifully put her arms around me. This happened through the night, and I never fully awakened until morning. Then it was to a scene of desolation. The dark glass counter was shattered. The perfumes and unguents were pools on the rug. The curtains had apparently been used as trapezes—they were ripped from the walls and shredded. And over all there was chimp shit, even in the open drawers. The stench was overpowering. I couldn't believe what one chimpanzee had been able to do in a single night. Thank God there were no works of art in the bedroom.

I was lying in bed smoking a cigarette and contemplating the awful scene when the door opened. It was Evelyn, back from Paulette's. She took one look—a very long look—then let out a wail, slammed the door and was away again. I lay there with China in my arms and thought about it. It made no sense to punish the ape. So I had another cigarette.

Again the door opened. It was Evelyn, wearing another face. She was now playing the role of a good sport; she was rising to the occasion. Suddenly the humor of the entire situation struck me, and I started laughing. I couldn't help it. Evelyn stared at me dumbfounded for a minute, then she too laughed—indulgently. "Come on, John. Let's have breakfast."

"Fine, Evelyn. I'll take a shower and be right in."

When I went in to shower, I closed the door on China, and the screaming started again. I knew this was going to go on indefinitely, so I opened the door. China was doing a mad-ape dance of rage. So distracted was she that for a time she didn't recognize me. I finally managed to calm her, and took her into the shower with me. She imitated my every movement, lathering herself under the arms and rinsing as I rinsed. After our shower I toweled her down and came out to breakfast. Evelyn, who was now inured to anything and everything, began to flatter and cuddle China. It was drawing-room comedy—a scene between wife and mistress written by Noel Coward. It looked as though they might become friends—until Evelyn decided that China should have breakfast in the kitchen with the maid. Evelyn took her by the hand. China pulled back. When Evelyn tugged at her, China bit her hand to the bone. Their budding friendship was over. I called the doctor. Evelyn's hand had to be cauterized.

It was plain that there was no keeping China in the apartment. I told Evelyn that I couldn't stay there any longer. "China can't be separated from me," I said, "so I'm just going to have to stay out at the ranch with her."

Evelyn said, "John, I think it's about time you made a choice . . . China or me."

I said, "Evelyn, dear, you're making it ever so difficult. . . . "

China and I moved back to the ranch, which was better, but she was still a constant problem. She wouldn't let me out of her sight. Finally I had to go to Europe and the decision was forced upon me. I put China in a small zoo down in the Valley. When I returned, I went to see her often. One Sunday afternoon she was kept behind in the chimpanzee house to visit with me when the other chimps were let out. She was glad enough to see me, but when the greetings were over she ran off to the window to watch her own kind giving their afternoon performance. China didn't really need me anymore either.

In the meantime Ricki Soma was an increasingly frequent visitor at the ranch. After meeting again at David Selznick's, we began seeing a good deal of each other. One thing led to another, and on February 10, 1950, I obtained a Mexican divorce from Evelyn Keyes. On February 11, Ricki and I were married at La Paz in Baja California.

My divorce from Evelyn was a financial disaster. My attorney was hardly a connoisseur of the finer things of life. He put very little value on our collection of paintings and objets d'art. Unfortunately I left the matter of the divorce entirely in his hands and just signed whatever documents he handed me. Later I discovered that I had given Evelyn not only all the cash I had and the real estate we owned, but also every last painting and half of my pre-Columbian art collection.

Some time later I met Evelyn at a cocktail party and I told her I thought the pre-Columbian collection should not be separated but under one roof. I prevailed upon her to flip a coin to see which of us got the other half. She won.

Because I was deeply in debt following *We Were Strangers*, Paul Kohner arranged a loan of $150,000 for me from Metro-Goldwyn-Mayer as part of my two-picture contract with them. It seemed like salvation at the time, but I didn't realize how unprofitable it was going to be. Paying off that loan, coupled with taxes on my salary, was like the story of the frog jumping down the stick. It turned out that as I made more and more, I wound up with less and less.

15

This was my first experience with Metro-Goldwyn-Mayer, and I must say I was impressed. Each studio had its own ambience, but Metro prided itself on being best in everything. The place had a near-languid air of elegance. The offices were handsomely furnished, befitting the dignity of Metro executives. The publicity department made sure that only the glories of Metro got into the press. In fact, they kept the press in line with bribes and threats. Those who went along with the Metro program received Christmas presents and scoops. Those who didn't received neither. The studio wielded considerable power in the city and the state. Whoever worked for Metro was treated accordingly, which added to the illusion of the studio's reputation for excellence in all things—including, of course, its pictures. Each department head was reputedly the best in his field, as was each MGM producer. There was a roster of more than fifty stars at Metro, gods and goddesses all, from the Marx Brothers to Greta Garbo. The mythology of glamour, I swear, originated with Metro. The studio felt that the image of a star was as important off the screen as on. Meetings were held to decide such things as off-screen wardrobe for the female stars, including furs, and what cars the male stars would drive. One never heard of an actor being put on suspension. Metro was all one big, happy family. There was an air of superiority to the place that was impressive . . . yet slightly absurd.

All of this was on the surface, of course. It was a patriarchal system, and the image of the father was supplied by L. B. Mayer. Mayer had solidified his position after a power struggle with Irving Thalberg. Thalberg had been the prince of motion pictures, a boy genius who left an indelible mark upon the motion-picture industry. His approach to film-making was different from that of other producers. His name never appeared on the screen. His whole role, it seemed, was to educate and uplift the motion-picture public. He was enormously successful—so much so that he began to threaten the rule of L. B. Mayer. That was his undoing. Thalberg went on a trip to Europe. When he left, he was virtually in control of Metro. When he came back, he was just another Metro producer. L.B. had taken over completely. From then on, there was no prince at Metro, just the king and his liege lords.

Second in command at the studio was Eddie Mannix, the MGM vice-president, a bull of a man known for his terrible rages. I believe he found his way into pictures from being a bouncer in a New Jersey amusement park. Mannix was known as the minister without portfolio—a description he never understood.

The first picture I worked on at Metro was *Quo Vadis*, with Arthur Hornblow. Considerable research had been done for this film by a classics scholar named Hugh Gray, who happened to be in the research department. He might just as well have been an Oxford don. He was an exceptionally cultivated man with a delightful personality. I requested that he collaborate with me. We wrote about half the script, and I thought it was quite good, but it wasn't what L. B. Mayer wanted. Mayer was after a De Mille-like religious epic. Gray and I were writing a modern treatment about Nero and his fanatical determination to eliminate the Christians in much the same manner as his historic counterpart and fellow madman, Adolf Hitler, tried to destroy the Jews two thousand years later.

Arthur Hornblow, who was quite prepared to do the picture L.B. wanted, had reservations when he heard what Gray and I were doing. But as we went along, he fell in more and more with our concept until finally he was defending it like a champion.

One day I got a call from L.B. "John, would you come over to my house on Sunday? Come over and have breakfast with me." This was quite unlike L.B., and Arthur Hornblow was most eager to hear why I had been summoned. I went. By this time L.B. had read some of our material, and it wasn't what he wanted. He told me a story about how during some picture with Jeanette MacDonald and Nelson Eddy he had instructed Jeanette MacDonald how to sing "Oh, Sweet Mystery of Life" by singing the Jewish "Eli, Eli" for her. She was so moved, he said, that she wept. Yes, wept! She who had the reputation of pissing icewater!

He sang the same song for me by way of demonstration. Then he said that if I could make *Quo Vadis* into that kind of picture, he would crawl

to me on his knees and kiss my hands . . . which he then proceeded to do.
I sat there and thought, "This is not happening to me. I've nothing to do
with any of this!" L.B. pressed me for an answer. I told him I wasn't at all
sure I could give him what he wanted. He said, "You can only try! Try,
John! Try!"

I left the house in a cold sweat and went straight to Arthur's. I told him
I was sure they'd never buy our version of the picture. But Arthur said,
"Well, let's not give up yet. Maybe we can convince them."

Pre-production began. First, we made tests of Peter Ustinov for Nero,
Greg Peck for the male lead and Elizabeth Taylor for the female lead.
Then Arthur and I went to Paris to cast. I'd grown to like Arthur very
much, and we worked well together.

I stayed at the Ritz in Paris, where I had a calendar of appointments to
interview hopeful actresses for the film. They were scheduled to come up
to my hotel suite at half-hour intervals. After a couple of days I noticed
the staff at the Ritz looking at me with considerable respect. More and
still more young ladies appeared and the bows got deeper and deeper.
Then I figured it out: they didn't know I was casting a picture.

We returned to Los Angeles, where Metro saw the tests and approved
them. The picture was due to start in Rome in July, but the production
was not sufficiently advanced to enable us to get in ahead of the rainy
season. Then Gregory Peck got an eye infection, and Metro decided to
put it off for a year. At this point Arthur decided he didn't want to do
the picture anyway. There had been some criticism of him because the
production was not on schedule, and he resented this. He asked to be
relieved of the picture, and I said, "In that case, I'll do the same."

From there on, it was out of our hands. L.B. assigned producer Sam
Zimbalist and director Mervyn LeRoy, and got the story he had wanted
all along. It was another dreadful spectacle, catering to the audience L.B.
thought was there. L.B. was right; the audience *was* there.

Upon resigning from *Quo Vadis*, Arthur and I asked to do W. B.
Burnett's *The Asphalt Jungle*. I consulted with Burnett several times
during the writing of the script, and he approved the final draft, which I
wrote with Ben Maddow.

My old friend Sam Jaffe played the master criminal who plans the
caper in the movie, and for it he received the Cannes Award for the Best
Performance of the Year. The picture as a whole was beautifully cast.
Sterling Hayden was the central character, the bad-luck hood Dix Hand-
ley, and Louis Calhern was the gang's crooked lawyer. One of the lines
which Calhern speaks expresses the theme of the film: "Crime is only a

left-handed form of human endeavor." That's the tone of the film. There were a number of virtuoso performances in *The Asphalt Jungle*, and it was, of course, where Marilyn Monroe got her start. *The Asphalt Jungle* became the model for a number of films of this genre.

Gottfried Reinhardt, Wolfgang's younger brother, was a producer at MGM. We talked about doing a film together. I suggested Stephen Crane's *Red Badge of Courage*. He liked the idea and, together, we proposed it to Dore Schary. Schary had been installed recently as vice-president in charge of production. This was supposed to be with L.B.'s blessing, but everyone knew L.B. had also "been like a father" to Thalberg.

Schary, too, was taken with the idea—so I wrote a script. The script went the rounds of the studio—a regular procedure—and finally reached L.B.'s desk. L.B. didn't like anything about it. It didn't jibe with his notions of "entertainment." What was and what wasn't entertainment had been the basic quarrel between Thalberg and L.B. Now, years later, the same threat was being introduced by Dore Schary. L.B. said, "No!" Schary said, "Yes!" L.B.'s word had been law until that moment. Now his authority was being challenged. In this manner, a comparatively small picture with a moderate budget became a *cause célèbre*. Pictures on this scale were normally approved and put into production without comment. But *Red Badge* became the occasion for a bitter debate. Whoever prevailed would control the studio, and the loser would be relegated to limbo.

The decision rested, finally, with a little man behind a desk in New York, Nicholas Schenck, the president of Loew's, Inc. L.B. had all the kudos—and the biggest salary of anybody in the United States—but it was Nick Schenck who had the last word at Metro. Schenck was known as The General, but there was nothing flamboyant about him. His name seldom appeared in *Variety* or the *Reporter*—only in the *Wall Street Journal*. He had a reputation of having blood of hyperborean temperature. He scared people to death. Dore Schary, determined to do *Red Badge*, took his argument to the General.

I thought this was carrying things too far, and I had no desire to see anyone's head roll, so I went to see L. B. Mayer.

"L.B., if you feel this strongly against the picture, why, let's just forget the whole thing."

"John Huston, I'm ashamed of you! Do you believe in this picture? Have you any reason for wanting to make it other than the fact that you believe in it?"

"No."

"Then stick by your guns! Never let me hear you talk like this again! I don't like this picture. I don't think it will make money. I don't want to make it, and I will continue to do everything in my power to keep you from making it. But you—you should do everything in your power to make it!"

The issue was settled when Schenck gave Schary the go-ahead to make *The Red Badge of Courage.* Dore Schary was in; L. B. Mayer was out. I suspect the whole thing was set up in advance by Schenck. Mayer had toppled Thalberg, and now it was his turn to go. He had become too powerful. *Red Badge* went into production, and a short while later L.B. left the studio—to retirement and oblivion.

While I was still in the process of preparing the script, Lillian Ross approached me with the proposal that she write the "history" of the *Red Badge* film production from beginning to end. Lillian had previously written a short piece about me in the "Talk of the Town" section in *The New Yorker.* I liked everything I'd read of hers, and agreed.

Lillian did a masterful job. Her reportage first appeared as a series of articles in *The New Yorker* and later in book form under the title *Picture: A Story About Hollywood.* It was not flattering. She cut any number of "famous" people down to size—including me—in clear, concise portraits. Hollywood readers waited in line at the newsstands for the next issue of *The New Yorker,* eager to see who would be done in next, frequently discovering to their dismay that they were themselves the targets.

Lillian has an uncanny ability to remember word-for-word what was said in a conversation. There is nothing particularly striking about her appearance. She is a nice-looking little creature, gentle, quiet and unobtrusive. People forget after a while that she's present, and express themselves with complete freedom. Lillian was present during the shooting of the entire film. We became great friends, and are to this day.

L. B. Mayer was right when he said he didn't think *Red Badge* would make money, and there is more than a touch of irony in that. It brings up the question of "right" and "wrong" as opposed to the quest for truth. It was well received critically when it was released, but audiences rejected it out of hand.

Audiences are an enigma. There have been technical and scientific experiments aimed at analyzing the reaction of audiences, including measurements of heartbeats, skin temperatures and so forth. Not one of these experiments explains why an audience tends to react as though it had one body and mind. When in an accepting mood, in sympathy with the picture and caught up in its rhythm, an audience may display, as a group, a degree of perceptiveness and sensitivity beyond that of any individual member. Once caught up this way, an audience will grasp and react to the subtlest kind of humor. It's as though the members of an audience have a collective sensibility.

By the same token, they can be absolutely monolithic in their resistance to what is on the screen. They can put up a barrier so solid that they don't hear what the picture is saying. That happened to *The Red Badge of Courage*. During the preview you could actually feel the audience stiffen against the film. That's an experience I don't look forward to reliving, and when it happened, I knew the picture had no future.

I had made what I thought was a good picture. In fact, in its original version it was a *very* good picture, but audiences were not prepared to accept it. The scene to which they objected most was the one I happened to think the best: the death of the Tall Soldier with the Boy and the Tattered Soldier looking on. It's a strange death. The Tall Soldier has climbed a hill to meet it. He warns the others to stand away from him as death comes closer and closer. When he finally falls, it's like a tree falling.

The Tattered Soldier, followed by the Boy, descends the hill. He is garrulous and repetitive. He walks in circles, then drops to his knees. He, too, is mortally wounded, and doesn't know it. The scene is an anticlimax, as in the novel, but all the more shocking for being unexpected. It was, in fact, too shocking. It backfired. It was during this scene, beautifully acted by Royal Dano, that the preview audience began to walk out.

I went to Africa for *The African Queen* before *Red Badge* came out, and Gottfried Reinhardt worked with Dore Schary trying to cut the film to make it more acceptable. They put in some narration, cut (among others) the scene of the Tattered Soldier's death and shortened the picture considerably. It was never a long picture, but they cut it to sixty-nine minutes, which is too short for a proper feature. It was released in that version, however, playing second feature on Metro bills. There was no serious attempt to release it abroad.

An English critic happened to see a print of *Red Badge* running as a second feature in a suburban theater in London. He took it upon himself to call the other London critics together, and they had a private showing in MGM's London projection room. Then each critic wrote a column demanding that the film be given a West End showing. Metro didn't want to waste theater time on it, but this was too strong a protest for them to buck, so *Red Badge* opened in the London West End. Nobody went. It was no more acceptable in Britain than it had been in the United States.

Now, more than two decades later, this film is accepted by audiences and hailed by many as an American film classic. It is a truism to say that these changes in audience taste never occur overnight, but they certainly do occur. Today *Red Badge* is always mentioned as being among my best pictures. I received a cable from Metro when I was doing *The Man Who Would Be King* in 1975, asking if by any chance I had a print of the original *Red Badge*. They wanted to release it in its original form. I didn't have a print. It doesn't exist. However, after seeing *Red Badge* in the cut version, I instructed Paul Kohner to include in all of my future contracts a stipulation that I receive a sixteen-millimeter print of the first cut of any film I made.

On April 6, 1950, I arranged a birthday party for my father at Romanoff's in Los Angeles. He had plans for a movie and had flown in a couple of days before, checking into the Beverly Hills Hotel, where he was to meet the caretaker of his place in Running Springs. On the night of his birthday Dad wasn't feeling well. He asked me to express his regrets to the guests.

16

I was worried, because this was most unlike my father. I met the others at Romanoff's, made Dad's apologies and immediately drove back to the hotel. Dad was in pain when I returned. It was so intense that he almost fainted. When the doctors arrived and examined him, they expressed the opinion that it was perhaps a kidney stone. It seemed to be that kind of pain, very acute and lasting a minute or so—passing, then recurring.

Dad said something about having seen a doctor in New York, so the Los Angeles doctors called the New York man, who said that he suspected an aneurysm of the aorta. The two physicians conferred, then gave Dad something to reduce the pain and left, saying that they would be back in the morning. It seemed to them better to leave him where he was than to move him to a hospital. I had a room right across the hall. The caretaker and one of the hotel porters slept in the room with Dad. In the middle of the night I heard a rapping on my door. It was the caretaker. He said, "John, your father is unconscious." I called the doctors again, and they both came right away. Dad never regained consciousness, except perhaps dimly; once he opened his eyes briefly, seemed to recognize me and squeezed my hand ever so slightly. Then he slipped out of his life as gracefully as he had lived it.

My father and I were as close as a father and son can be. He was my companion and friend. Dad neither corrected nor criticized me when I was a child, but I always knew when I did something that displeased him; a vertical line appeared on his forehead. When I saw this, I knew that I had really done wrong. I much preferred to see Dad laughing, so I tried hard not to make that line appear.

Dad loved to laugh, and when he did, tears soon came to his eyes.

Absurdities delighted him. We used to play a game in which I would try to make him laugh, and when I had succeeded or failed, he would try to make *me* laugh. It could be a very bitter game. When you are doing something that you think excruciatingly funny and your audience doesn't respond . . . well, steel enters your soul. But these games always ended by our collapsing upon each other in laughter.

I think the happiest period in Dad's life was his last years, in the house near Running Springs. I remember once playing the laughing game with him there. We had failed to make each other laugh three or four times, and now it was his turn again. He disappeared into his room for a few minutes, then returned stark naked except for six neckties, one around his neck, one around each wrist and ankle. There was one more necktie. I laughed.

The house at Running Springs was usually snowed in during the winter. It was high in the mountains, and I swear you could see for a hundred miles. It had a great living room some sixty or seventy feet long, and a huge swimming pool. There was a high place where Dad kept a telescope, and he used to go up and look at the stars. He made no attempt to study astronomy seriously. He just knew the names of many of the stars and planets, and liked to look at them. It gave him some kind of peace.

Dad had none of the hard edges associated with most "personalities." He always let the next man have the best of it. He made no effort to come out the winner in a transaction or personal relationship. His forbearance was endless. I don't think I ever saw him in a temper. I never heard him raise his voice in anger. I never heard him take others to task, either to their faces or in their absence. It was very much live-and-let-live. He might express an opinion, but never twice in the same company. I could tell if he disagreed with someone, but the person with whom he disagreed seldom, if ever, knew. When he gambled—which was rarely—one felt he did it for the love of the game only. He liked playing bridge or poker, but the amounts won or lost were unimportant to him.

People often turned to my father for advice and instruction. They knew that whatever he told them would be without self-interest. He had an inborn politeness and respect for others. He made no attempt to win anyone over. And he was not unduly impressed by great names. The few people he thoroughly admired included Franklin D. Roosevelt, Eugene O'Neill, Bernard Baruch, Jed Harris, Loyal Davis. He responded to quality.

I never heard my father express a belief or a disbelief in religion, but I also never heard him utter an oath or an obscenity. He'd say, "Damn!" but never "God damn!"

Dad used to help individuals, which I would discover only by accident. And he helped them constructively, not just by giving them money. Here's an example.

He said to me once, "John, you ought to have an answering service."

"What's that?"

"Well, it's something new," said Dad, and went on to explain how an answering service worked.

I said, "Why would I need that? There's always a servant here to answer the phone."

"Yeah . . . but they might not get it straight."

"Look, Dad, it sounds like a good idea, but I really don't think I want an answering service."

I thought that would be the end of that, but a couple more times Dad brought the subject up. I was puzzled why he was pressing me to get an answering service. Years after his death I learned why. I met a woman who told me that she had once worked with Dad in a play and later come to Hollywood to have a shot at movies. She wasn't very successful, and Dad had encouraged her to try to do something else. He suggested a telephone-answering service, set her up in it—the first in Los Angeles—and it proved to be very successful. Finally I understood. Dad had been hustling business for this old girl.

Dad became friends with Toscanini and used to go to the NBC Symphony rehearsals with him. He once told me that if he could have been anything other than an actor, it would have been a symphony orchestra conductor. He made a joke of it, but he knew classical music well, as did most of my family. He loved jazz, and he had a fine, keen ear. Although Dad introduced "September Song" to the world in *Knickerbocker Holiday*, he didn't sing it; he spoke it. He couldn't be called a singer by any stretch of the imagination.

Walter had natural rhythm and masculine grace in everything he did. He took tennis lessons from the professional at the Beverly Hills Hotel, and it wasn't long before he was beating the pro. He'd been a fine hockey-player with the Toronto team. He was a good golfer, shooting in the low eighties. He shot pool well. He hadn't ridden a horse until he made a Western picture, but then he became a good horseman. He worked well with his hands, and his hobby was cabinet-making. Like his father, he made fine furniture.

After *Mr. Pitt*, in 1924, Dad appeared in a number of hit plays during the next ten years: *The Barker, Kongo, Desire under the Elms* and *Dodsworth*, to mention but a few. He also made a number of movies: *Gentlemen of the Press, The Virginian, The Bad Man, A House Divided,*

Law and Order, Rain and *American Madness* are among those that come immediately to mind.

But that wasn't enough. It had been his dream all of his life—and that of his sister Margaret—to perform Shakespeare on the stage. Finally, in 1934, he got his chance. He and Nan Sunderland went to Central City, Colorado, and did *Othello*. Nan played Desdemona. I didn't go out to see the performance, but I watched them often during rehearsals before they left New York. I thought it was the best thing Dad had ever done. Margaret helped him. I don't think he ever worked so hard at anything as he did at *Othello*. The Central City production was an enormous success, and Robert Edmond Jones agreed to stage and direct it in New York.

I went to a performance in Philadelphia prior to its coming to New York, and I was made uneasy by what I saw. The theater was very big. Jones' sets were superb, as were the costumes. Every scene was a delight to the eye. You couldn't fault the production. Indeed, its very magnificence was one of the things that disturbed me; it seemed to diminish the performances. One came away with a sense more of spectacle rather than drama. There seemed to be a screen between the actors and the audience. The magic that had happened when I had seen the play in hotel rooms and rehearsal halls, close up, just wasn't there in this large theater.

The play opened in New York in January 1937, at the New Amsterdam Theatre. After the final curtain there was an ovation, but I had come to distrust Broadway applause. Dad's friends and supporters assured him, after the play, that it was a success . . . but I had my doubts. Still hoping for the best, I stayed up all night waiting for the papers, but when they came out, the reviews were not good.

I knew this meant more to my father than anything he had ever done, so, very early in the morning, I took the papers to the Waldorf Towers, where he was staying. I went up to his room, and just as I was about to knock, I heard laughter from inside. "Well," I thought, "he won't be laughing when he sees these!" I was glad that at least I would be on hand when he read them. As I entered, I saw the papers strewn over the floor. He was laughing at the reviews! He was laughing at himself! All those years of work and planning that had gone into his *Othello* . . . . down the drain! This was to have been his definitive performance. The joke was on him. Pretty soon he had me laughing, too.

Walter Huston was the complete actor. He couldn't have been anything else, nor did he want to be anything else. Vaudeville, theater, finally motion pictures. His real love, however, was playing to a live audience. He once wrote:

Marietta Fitzgerald,
late 1940s

JH with Evelyn
Keyes, his third wife,
at the time of their
marriage in 1945

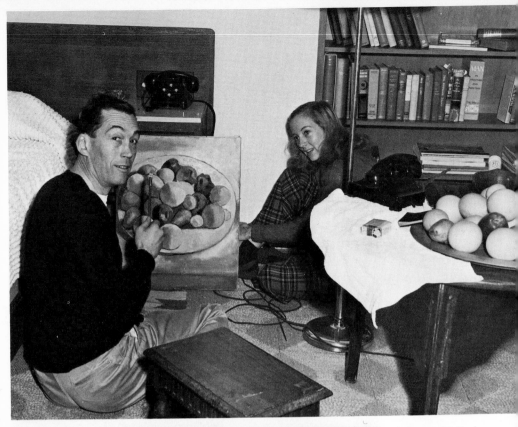

At home with Evelyn,
late 1940s

JH with Suzanne Flon in h[
dressing room on the openi[
night of Jean Anouilh's pla[
The Lark, in which she star[
Paris, 1953 (*Jean F. Clair*)

With Elaine Steinbeck, Rome, 1954
(*David Seymour, Magnum*)

Ricki Soma Huston,
JH's fourth wife
© *Philippe Halsman*

Ricki with Anjelica,
Courtown, Ireland, 1953
(*Geoffrey Keating*)

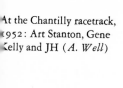

At the Chantilly racetrack,
1952: Art Stanton, Gene
Kelly and JH (*A. Well*)

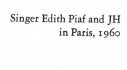

Singer Edith Piaf and JH
in Paris, 1960

JH is supported by associate producer Kevin McClory, left, and
Truman Capote during the filming of *Beat the Devil*, 1953
(*Courtesy Kevin McClory*)

With John Wayne in Japan,
casting *The Barbarian
and the Geisha*, 1957

In Africa making
The Roots of Heaven.
The women above are
spectators, not cast members.
At left, JH directs
Juliette Greco

During the production of
The Misfits in 1960. At left, JH
and Gladys Hill teach Marilyn
Monroe how to gamble. Left
below, JH goes over the script
for *The Misfits* with Gladys Hill
and, below, watches a scene in
progress (*Eve Arnold*)

Billy Pearson
tries out Izzy,
his mount for t[
great Virginia
City camel race
(*Pete Breinig,
San Francisco
Chronicle*)

JH, at left, draws a bead
during a tiger hunt in
Assam, 1955

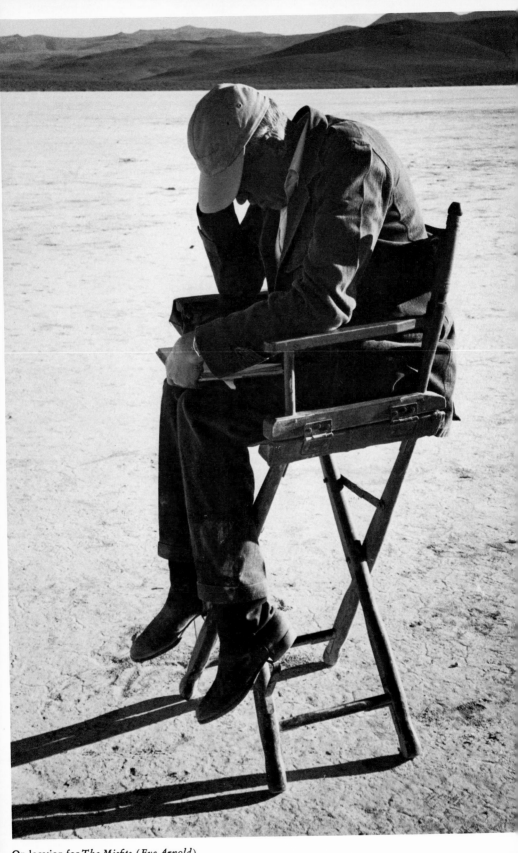

On location for *The Misfits* (*Eve Arnold*)

Only through playing to a live audience, and playing a part time after time, whittling it, shaping it, smoothing it, can perfection be attained. In motion pictures all too often, an actor is given so little time to prepare for a part that he must resort to tricks. Tricks to a good actor are a cheap device . . . he may fool others with them, but he can't fool himself.

I think it goes further than that. Leonardo da Vinci said that an artist should "paint as if in the presence of God.'" I think that's what a true actor does—subconsciously. He is playing to God . . . a surrogate God . . . a live audience . . . faceless, numberless, therefore infinite. He can play to this "God" and win instant approval—as he merits it. I suspect that's what actors really mean when they say they prefer the theater to film-making, where there is no applause, only the approval of the director.

Further, playing directly to an audience brings out the childlike magic in an actor, that ability to make believe with such enthusiasm and commitment that he actually becomes another person in another world. Dad had that gift of being able to transform himself. Suddenly he would be a Russian archduke or a bush-league baseball-player. He didn't study being these things. It would just be there, magically. Where it came from no one knew.

Now Dad was gone. There was no one else with whom I would laugh in the same way or share the same freedom. Dad's lifelong friend, the neurosurgeon, Loyal Davis, came out from Chicago to be present at the autopsy. An aneurysm of the aorta was, in fact, the cause of death. Within a few years vascular surgeons mastered the technique of dealing with an aneurysm. I myself am living proof, having recently undergone a successful operation for exactly the same thing—but, for Dad, this surgical procedure came a few years too late.

The memorial service for my father was held in the Academy Award Theatre in Hollywood. Spencer Tracy, his old friend, delivered the tribute.

When Walter Huston died, in the eighth hour of his sixty-sixth year, it was without a prolonged illness. The night before, he celebrated his birthday, chatted with friends. He told them about a new, low-slung car he was getting. Apparently it was a sort of dignified hot-rod, and his eyes lit up when he talked about it. Then, without much warning or stalling, Walter Huston died in the shank of that morning, and prompted the remark: "He was too big a man to get sick, he just died." That's about the sum of Walter Huston. Professionally he's easy to rate. He was the best. There were no long-winded arguments in Broadway cafés. Walter Huston just happened to be the best, that's all. Two Americans have won the Nobel prize for literature. It's no accident that when you mention Sinclair Lewis or Eugene O'Neill you think of Walter Huston. He helped them tell their stories better than anyone else. He gave more color to their lines, he gave more drive to their action. He turned guts into a good word. . . .

Actually there's nothing odd about being the top man in a profession . . . somebody has to be. But there is something odd if the top man happens to be the nicest . . . and Walter Huston was just about that. Now, on occasions like this, it is customary to say a man was kind. However, in most cases it's necessary to search out an example to support the claim. In the case of Walter Huston all you have to do is sort the events of the last week . . . or a thousand other weeks. Because all the days we knew him, Walter Huston had a gentle mind, and he had the only thing that makes such a virtue endurable . . . he had the strength to quietly oppose the things that were wrong.

I suppose most people remember Dad for the dance he did in *Treasure* or, perhaps, for "September Song." I remember another dance one day in early spring. Nan Sunderland, Dad, Dorothy and I had gone on a picnic. Wild flowers were scattered in profusion over the hillsides. We stopped the car and sat down together in a brilliant field of them, exclaiming over the beauty of the newly opened blossoms. Suddenly Dad leaned over and pounded a flower into the ground with his fist. There were millions of them, but it seemed a terrible act of desecration. Dad pounded some more flowers with his fist, then jumped up and went at them with his feet, prancing about, stamping on flowers. It was shocking! Panic, in a real sense, was in the air. Dad—the Great God Pan!—was at it again. Appalled, Nan asked what he was doing.

"I'm stopping the spring!" Dad said.

While I was finishing *The Red Badge of Courage*, Sam Spiegel and I talked a lot about the next film for Horizon. Our prime choice was *The African Queen*. Columbia had bought the rights years before from C. S. Forester, planning to make a film starring Elsa Lanchester and Charles Laughton. For some reason they didn't make it. Then Warners bought the property from Columbia for Bette Davis. They, too, never followed through.

17

Warners were willing to sell the rights to Horizon for $50,000. Sam and I together had nothing like this amount. We debated whether I should make another picture first, aiming to pick up enough cash for a down payment, with Sam to add whatever he could manage to scrape up. Then Spiegel had an inspiration. He went to Sound Services, Inc., and asked them for the full amount we needed. Sound Services, a company that supplied sound equipment to studios, wasn't in the habit of making loans, but Sam was desperate, trying anybody and everybody. I believe he told them that, in addition to repaying the loan, he would use their equipment on location, give them credit in titles, and I don't know what not. Miraculously, they agreed, gave Sam the money, and the rights to *The African Queen* were ours.

Katharine Hepburn and Humphrey Bogart agreed to play the leads. On the basis of their names, Spiegel arranged for a loan for the American budget from the Walter E. Heller Co. of Chicago. He then made a deal with Romulus Films, Ltd., London—John and Jimmy Woolf—for the sterling required. We were going to shoot in sterling areas. For this they got the European distribution rights. United Artists were the distributors in the United States.

While Sam was busy selling, cajoling, pleading and charming our backers, Ricki and I were living in Malibu, waiting for our first child. Walter Anthony—named after his two grandfathers—was born on April 16, 1950. Ricki wore her long, dark hair parted in the middle; when she took our blond son in her arms, she looked like a Quattrocento madonna.

I had been single-minded about *The African Queen*—and I was equally single-minded about who I was to write the screenplay with: James Agee.

James Agee was a poet, novelist and the best motion-picture critic this country has ever had. He wrote for *The Nation, Time, Fortune* and *Life*. All his books—*Let Us Now Praise Famous Men, The Morning Watch* and *A Death in the Family*—have become classics.

I had read everything of Agee's as it was published. During the war he reviewed *The Battle of San Pietro* for *Time*, and his piece was so sensitive and perceptive that I sent him a note of appreciation, the one and only time I have ever addressed myself to a critic. I met him after the war when he did an article about me for *Life*.

Agee was over six feet, heavy of torso, with big, strong hands, a pale face, brown hair, blue eyes and a mouth from which a number of teeth were missing. I remember that every time he laughed he would put his hand up furtively to cover his mouth. When I got to know him better, I tried to convince him to go to a dentist. He'd say he would, but never did, even though I made appointments for him.

Jim's clothes were always unpressed; as far as I know, he had only one tie, and his shoes were never polished. He loved to talk—and I felt he often gave people credit for being more interesting and intelligent than they really were because of his way of reading deep meanings into commonplace remarks.

While Jim was writing the *Life* article, I was still married to Evelyn Keyes. Evelyn, Gilbert Roland and I decided to go on a shooting trip to Idaho, and we took Jim along. We chose a place in the Bitterroot Mountains run by a bush pilot named Ben Bennett. It was so remote and so hard to get to that, so far as I know, no other plane ever ventured in there.

Agee had never been in the Western wilderness before. He loved it. He didn't want to shoot a gun, to kill anything, but on the other hand he didn't want to miss anything either. He went on every outing. Evenings, we would sit around and play poker or listen to Ben's stories about his days as an Alaskan bush pilot. Agee liked to listen, and I doubt he ever forgot anything.

It was during this trip that he shyly confessed to me that he wanted to write for pictures. So, a year or so later, when it was time to start on *The African Queen*, I phoned him in New York and said, "How about it?" He agreed, came to Los Angeles, and we went to a resort hotel outside Santa Barbara and started to work.

The place in Santa Barbara was run rather like a club. There were individual bungalows, a good restaurant, a pool, tennis courts and stables. Only my immediate family and a few friends knew where we were. We didn't want to be disturbed or distracted, and, once settled in, we rarely left the premises.

I thought this an opportunity to live the good life and get into shape, so I proposed to Jim that we follow a stiff regimen of work and exercise. We decided to play one or two sets of tennis each morning before breakfast, and at least two sets each afternoon after work. We swam a couple of times a day, avoided nighttime activities and cocktail parties, and, so far as I knew, Jim, like me, hit the sack before ten p.m.

David Selznick and Jennifer Jones appeared on the scene a few weeks after we arrived. They met Jim and liked him instantly. We had dinner with them a few times, but always excused ourselves at an early hour. We were determined not to break our schedule.

Jim was a willing collaborator. We quickly worked out a routine. We'd discuss a sequence, then block it out and write alternate scenes. Then we would exchange scenes and rework each other's material. This method was all right, except Jim got too far ahead. I marveled at the volume of material he was turning out. Then I discovered that he was not going to bed at ten p.m., but working deep into the night. I said, "Jesus, Jim . . . that's a hell of a work load!" He assured me there was no problem—his normal work hours were at night. I didn't argue with him. It seemed to me likely that without pressure and deadlines he would gradually give up the old routine for the new. He just needed time to adjust.

Billy Pearson phoned me one morning. A pre-Columbian collection had turned up that he wanted me to see. I flew up to San Francisco, admired the pieces—there were some fine Colima figures—and was having a pleasant break visiting with Billy and his wife when Jennifer phoned to say that Jim had had a heart attack. I took the first plane back.

When I arrived at the club, David was waiting for me. He told me that it had been touch-and-go for a while and Jim was now under sedation. He was being constantly attended, of course. The doctors were leaving him in his room for the time being, because they didn't dare to move him to a hospital. It was that bad.

When I went to see Jim the next day, he was awake and, of all things, conscience-stricken. He felt he had let me down, and began to apologize for being sick. I put a finger to my lips, enjoining silence. Then I assured him there was no problem. The collaboration would continue when he was able to work. The ending wasn't written yet, but I would write a temporary one and send him the script for his approval. When the doctors said he was out of danger, he could join me in Africa and we would wind things up. This seemed to pacify him.

One of the doctors asked me about Jim's way of life. I told him that Jim was a chain smoker and a bottle-a-day man. The doctor said if he kept on that way he wouldn't have long to live. He would have to give up smoking and drinking and be moderate in all things, including the hours he worked.

When Jim was told this he said, "I don't intend to change my way of life." And, sure enough, a few days later when we were alone, he asked me for a cigarette.

"Hell, Jim, you owe it to the doctor to follow his orders. He's a professional, like you, and his reputation is at stake. Do you want to kill yourself and embarrass him?"

He didn't ask me again.

When Jim had his heart attack, our screenplay was not quite finished. I wrote a rather slapdash ending, planning to re-do it, and then flew to England with Sam.

It was about a year and a half before I saw Jim again. We met at "21." He greeted me with a drink in hand—his fingers yellow-stained as ever. He hadn't slowed down. In 1955 he had another heart attack, and that one killed him.

Jim Agee was a Poet of Truth—a man who cared nothing for his appearance, only his integrity. This he guarded as something more precious than his life. He carried this love of truth to the point of obsession. In *Let Us Now Praise Famous Men* his description of objects in a room is detailed to the point of being an homage to truth. For one fraction of eternity those objects existed in a given arrangement within a circumscribed area; that was truth. Truth was worth telling.

C. S. Forester had told me that he had never been satisfied with the way *The African Queen* ended. He had written two different endings for the novel; one was used in the American edition, the other in the English. Neither one, he felt, was satisfactory. I thought the film should have a happy ending. Since Agee's health never permitted him to come to Africa, I asked Peter Viertel to work on the final scenes with me. He and Gige joined us in Entebbe before we started shooting, and together we wrote my ending—the ending that we later filmed.

Sam Spiegel, Wilfred Shingleton—our art director—and I had flown from London to Kenya to pick locations. I had never been in Africa before. In Nairobi we hired the Noon and Pierce Air Charter Service, and Alec Noon, one of the owners, and John "Hank" Hankins were our pilots from that time on.

There were little clearings in the Congo forest that had been made during the war to serve as emergency landing strips; many of them had never been used. We got permission to land on these strips.

At first Sam, Wilfred and I concentrated on looking at places from the air—mostly following rivers. We followed the coast to Mombasa, flew down over Tanganyika, then went to Entebbe and Stanleyville. Sam didn't care much for this kind of action and went back to London. Wilfred and I continued: Northern Rhodesia, the Congo, Uganda. When we saw a likely spot, we'd find the strip nearest a river, land and then go exploring by launch or pirogue. Wilfred and I enjoyed ourselves, but no more, I think, than Hank Hankins did. It was the kind of flying he liked best. Hank had eyes like binoculars. I swear he could pick out the elephant with the best set of tusks in a herd before I could see the herd. He could see things that even the black hunters couldn't.

During this first "recce" we made a trip on the Congo in a pirogue that must have been fifty feet long. It had fifty paddlers, and boasted a Devil Dancer in the bow inspiring the crew, who were all chanting. In those days everything was done to song. There was always a drummer in a pirogue, no matter what its size, who announced our approach to villages along the river, and the drums on shore beat incessantly in reply.

Late one afternoon Alec Noon, Shingleton, and I found ourselves in a village in the Belgian Congo called Ponthierville and were taken to the home of the local commissioner. The house was imposing, a handsome one-story building with a wide veranda and several big, cool rooms. Everything was screened and the windows were shuttered as well.

We waited a couple of hours on the veranda before the commissioner showed up. He arrived in an enclosed litter slung between two poles with four bearers carrying him. He welcomed us and gave us a whiskey, and we talked. He had been away holding court in various villages throughout his remote domain. He was a young man, and it was obvious from his manner that he enjoyed his position of power and authority.

Time passed. I expected him to invite us in for dinner and was surprised when he didn't. Finally I asked if there was a place where we could spend the night.

"Of course," replied the commissioner, and instructed one of his servants to take us to our sleeping quarters, which I assumed were nearby.

Our guide led us away through the jungle. We must have walked at least half an hour. We were completely lost by the time we arrived at a little hut just as darkness fell. We went inside to inspect the place and decided at once that we couldn't stay there. It had apparently been a one-cell prison. There were bars on the windows, no screens and a dirt floor.

The roof was falling in. I turned to look for our guide—he was gone. We were alone in the middle of the jungle, in the dark, with no possible means of finding our way out.

In that jungle you couldn't stand still for a moment or the ants would crawl up your legs and bite you, so we had to stay inside. There was an old car seat on the floor, and that was the only "bed." We had a deck of cards, a flashlight and a couple of bottles of whiskey between us—so we found a board, placed it over a keg, and Alec Noon and I sat up all night playing two-handed poker. Wilfred lay down on the car seat.

As the night deepened, the insects swarmed in. There was no defense against them. Without the two bottles of whiskey to help us through the night, I believe we would have gone out of our minds.

In the morning we looked at ourselves. Alec and I were both badly bitten, but I less so than Alec. We looked at Shingleton, who had finally slept for a couple of hours. Wilfred's entire body was covered with bites. There were bites on top of bites. He became so ill he had to be sent to a hospital in Nairobi, where he remained for weeks. By the time our guide returned for us and led us back to the house, the commissioner had departed. I'm afraid that if I had been able to lay my hands on the man, I would have strangled him.

I went back to London and finished casting. Katie Hepburn was there and I saw her briefly. Then I returned to Africa, still scouting for locations. I never went back to England until *The African Queen* was finished.

Jinja is on the Uganda shore of Lake Victoria Nyanza. One of the branches of the Nile begins there. The town is a main terminal of the Kenya-Uganda Railroad. The superintendent of the yards put us into the care of "Mr. Wilson," a thoroughly trustworthy man who would show us whatever we wished to see.

When Mr. Wilson was introduced, he put out his hand and took off his hat, both at the same time. His mother was a Ugandan and his father an Englishman—an English consul, I was later informed. Mr. Wilson might have been wearing his father's clothes by the cut of his suit, complete with waistcoat, with the bottom button left correctly unbuttoned. He carried an umbrella. He was freshly shaven and smelled of eau de cologne. Unlike most Africans, the whites of his eyes were very clear. With him was a boy about ten years old who was immaculately clean, dressed in English style, with knee-high white stockings. The boy's shirt was freshly pressed and starched, and he wore a tie.

Mr. Wilson took us upriver in a power launch, and on the way he pointed out his house, a bungalow standing about a hundred yards back from the river. It had a well-tended lawn in front, and there were tin cans with blooming flowers on the windowsills. Mr. Wilson asked us to stop for tea. I thanked him and said we'd like to do that very much, but on our way back.

Nothing we saw at this location was right for the picture. The terrain was too open, the river too wide. We needed close jungle and a narrow river where we could work at close range.

On our way back we stopped at Mr. Wilson's for tea. The house was spotlessly clean and meticulously appointed. Mrs. Wilson welcomed us with a lovely smile.

There were many photographs of the family about. I asked Mr. Wilson about the children: three sons and a daughter. The daughter taught in a school nearby. Her pupils were mostly children of railroad employees. There was a picture of her with a number of little girls dressed in bloomers and middy blouses.

One son was an elephant hunter for the railroad, among a number of hunters employed to destroy those animals who got in the habit of knocking down bridges or telephone lines. While Mr. Wilson was telling me about his children, I noticed a large leopard skin on one wall and said that I would like to shoot a leopard. Mr. Wilson didn't answer for a moment. Then he said, "Oh, yes. There are many leopard about."

There was one son unaccounted for. I looked at his photograph. It had been taken when he was about the same age as the young boy who had been with us all day. I pointed to it and asked, "What does this son do?"

"That son is dead. He was killed some years ago."

"How did that happen?"

Mr. Wilson stared at me for some time, then said quietly: "He was killed by a leopard."

He told me the story. An American sportsman appeared on the scene one day with his gunbearer and asked Mr. Wilson to guide him on a hunt for leopard. He had filled his bag with four of the five species of big game classified as dangerous: rhino, elephant, buffalo and lion. He had not yet killed the fifth: a leopard. Mr. Wilson agreed to go with him.

At that time in Africa, blacks—even those of mixed blood—were not allowed to own rifles other than muzzle-loaders. Since Mr. Wilson considered himself an Englishman, he would not submit to the indignity of carrying a muzzle-loader—so he carried nothing. Accompanied by his son, then about eleven years old, Mr. Wilson led the hunter and his gunbearer into the forest.

The leopard is one of the most dangerous of all big-game animals because you never know what he will do—especially if he is wounded. A lion will retire when shot. He will usually retire two or three times before making his ultimate charge—but with a leopard you have no idea. He may turn tail and you'll never see him again, or he may just come at you. A hunter should feel absolutely certain he's going to kill before squeezing off that first shot at a leopard.

Shortly after entering the forest, they came upon a leopard. Mr. Wilson, his son and the gunbearer saw it and signaled the hunter. He couldn't see it until it started to move away—and he fired at the animal in motion. The leopard was knocked over by the impact of the bullet. He rolled, got to his feet and sprang into the bush.

As the leopard ran, the hunter plunged right after him. Mr. Wilson called out, "Wait!"—but the hunter went right ahead as though he hadn't heard.

When a dangerous animal is hit, you should give him time to stiffen up. Then you follow his spoor.

They hadn't proceeded fifty yards when the leopard charged. The hunter raised his rifle, squeezed the trigger. Nothing happened. The gun didn't fire.

A lion will attack one person in a group and then run on. A leopard often takes a swipe at everybody, as this one did. He slashed the hunter, Mr. Wilson, the gunbearer, and ran off with the boy. He just took him in his mouth and ran off with him.

Mr. Wilson grabbed the gun from the hunter and inspected it. It was still on safety. The man had simply lost his head. He had been repeatedly squeezing the trigger with the gun on safety.

They immediately set off in pursuit, and a short way up the trail they found the body of Mr. Wilson's son. Mr. Wilson told the others to carry his son home. He then went after the leopard and killed him. And this was the leopard skin on the wall, the only skin in the house. I gave up any idea of shooting a leopard.

Butiaba was a railroad terminal on the shores of Lake Albert in Uganda. It was there that Wilfred found the hull for *The African Queen*. He put her in a shop, and local carpenters started putting her together.

By this time we had chosen our locations. The first was to be on the Ruiki River and the second near Butiaba; we would finish the film at Murchison Falls. Construction had begun on the first two sites, and I had time off.

Hank Hankins flew me to the Congo side of Lake Albert, where there was a camp run by a Polish chap and his sister. It consisted of a little bar and some huts in which travelers waiting to cross the lake could sleep. I told them I wanted to shoot an elephant. I didn't want to go on a proper safari, but just by myself with an experienced black hunter. I was given their best man. His name was Mascota. He was wearing a Turkish fez and a pair of khaki shorts, which put him several notches above his fellows. His face had the deepest tribal cicatrices I have ever seen. One expected a savage behind the savage mask, but he was one of the most intelligent and endearing men I have ever known. We were together almost constantly for about three weeks. We would go off for four or five days at a time, sleeping out. We were almost that long tracking one old bull elephant whom in the end I never got a shot at.

There are hunting signals you must learn in Africa. It is often imperative that there be no conversation at all, and a minimum of movement. Raising the upper lip to expose your teeth, as in a grin—but it is not a grin—signifies the presence of game. Moving one hand slowly up and down, palm downward, means, "Don't move." Thrusting one shoulder forward means, "Move."

One day we were near a little glade in the forest, and Mascota put on a show for me. He gave the "Presence of game" signal, and then the "Don't move" signal. I froze. Mascota then moved forward on his belly like a snake, crossed the glade some ten or twelve yards and reached up with both hands to move the vines apart so I could see. There, within inches of his hand, was an elephant's leg. He was right under it. Then he squirmed back and whispered, "It was only a cow."

I didn't kill an elephant while I was with Mascota. I've never killed an elephant, although I surely tried. I never got a shot at one whose trophies were worth the crime. No, not crime—sin. I wouldn't dream of shooting an elephant today—in fact, I've given up all shooting with a rifle—but at that time the pursuit of big game was very important to me.

I rejoined the construction gang at the Ruiki location, not far from Ponthierville. The Ruiki is one of the small tributaries that feed into the Congo. A narrow winding river with trees and heavy vines arching overhead, it was ideal for our purposes.

We were building a compound boasting a restaurant, bar and one-room bungalows with verandas. Shooting here had to be completed within thirty days. Everything was made out of palm leaves and raffia from the surrounding jungle. As this vegetable matter decays, it becomes attractive to soldier ants. Trenches were dug around the camp and filled with kerosene which we could set afire in case of an attack. According to the natives, soldier ants are supposed to be fiendishly clever. The story is that they will bide their time until all the ants in an attacking force are in position to strike. Then, as if on signal, they will all bite their assigned prey simultaneously. I can't verify this from experience, thank God, but I do know that whenever they come, they eat everything in sight, even paper off walls. If a goat is tethered, they will leave only his bones. They can destroy a village as effectively as a fire can, and if they launch a serious attack, there is really no defense. You just have to get out.

King Paul, the black chief of the area, was most helpful to us while we were building the compound and throughout our stay. He was a big, wonderful-looking fellow, and we used him in the picture. The leopard skin he wore in the film wasn't a costume. It was his own regalia worn on occasions of state.

There were eight to ten of us in this first group. We didn't have our commissary set up yet, so we contracted with a black hunter to shoot for the pot. I went out with him several times. He only had a muzzle-loader, and he couldn't hit anything unless he was right on top of it. Game was scarce, and I wondered how in the hell he could manage to shoot enough meat for the pot, which was kept going constantly. The pot consisted of an indiscriminate sort of stew comprised of monkey, forest pig, deer and you-name-it. Eventually someone did.

One afternoon a group of soldiers marched into camp and arrested our black hunter. We weren't told why. They refused to tell us. But finally King Paul confided to me that villagers had been disappearing mysteriously. It seems that when the hunter couldn't find game for the pot, he got the meat in the simplest possible way. I must say I couldn't tell the difference in the taste. The black hunter was executed a few days later. I was thankful that the "long pig" was served before the main group arrived. Only a few of us were privileged to dine so exclusively.

In the middle of the compound there was a big galvanized tub in which someone had placed a baby crocodile. Each time you crossed the compound square, you had to remember that the croc was there, because he always came out charging, snapping away at your legs. From time to time there would be a cry of anguish and the curses of someone trying to pry the croc's jaws from his ankle.

The natives held dances in their compound. We often went over in the evenings to watch them. We provided the beer, and King Paul did the honors, passing out a bottle to each man, after which the festivities intensified. Night after night I lay awake in my hammock listening to the sound of the drums and the singing, and quite fell under the spell of the place.

The *African Queen* arrived. She had been transported from Butiaba to the Congo side, and then by lorry to the Ruiki, thence to the location under her own power.

Final dates and arrangements were completed. Palm thatching was cut green and put on the structures to be used in the picture. Katie and the Bogarts arrived with the remainder of the cast, crew and Sam Spiegel. Ricki had hoped to leave Tony with her parents and come out for a visit, but she was pregnant again, so, of course, that was out of the question.

Very early in the morning on the first day of shooting, a very excited native came to my hut. I took him to King Paul, who translated his message into French for me. It seemed that there was a herd of elephants in the area which had trampled through a nearby plantation and some native huts. They knew I had guns, so they came to me. If we acted quickly, we could catch up with the herd. One of the elephants was described as a big-tusker, and I thought this was my chance to get a trophy at last.

The company was just getting up. I went to the dining room and asked for someone to go along with me. I wanted another gun, and also some-one who could operate a camera. After a little talk among themselves it was decided that the best man for the job would be the boom boy, Kevin McClory. They assured me McClory would be good as a back-up man, and he had a camera. The regular still-cameraman wanted no part of this.

Kevin McClory was sent for. I didn't know him except by sight. He was a good-looking young man with a pronounced stammer. Kevin agreed to go, and we sat out in a small pirogue with three natives, heading downstream. We took a fork in the river and, when this side stream became too narrow, left the pirogue and proceeded on foot. Finally we got to a place where there were very high grasses and a coffee-and-banana plantation. We passed the huts the elephants had knocked over, and there were signs of a considerable herd. We hurried on, and as we passed from elephant grass to thick forest to elephant grass and marshes, the tracker went first. I followed with a Rigby .470 express rifle. Then came the other two natives. Kevin brought up the rear. The country through which we were passing was populated with little red buffalo. They are very fast and very mean, sometimes attacking without provocation. I explained this to Kevin, and cautioned him to glance behind occasionally. This made more of an impression on him than I had intended, because I looked around a short time later and saw that he was walking backward. He had my light rifle, and it was at the ready. I could tell by now that

Kevin had doubts about this venture. The one thing that kept him going —he told me later—was his confidence in my knowledge of forest ways.

Eventually we got close. We came to a stretch of open country just in time to see the elephants go into a large, shallow lake, ford it and enter some forest land on the other side. The lake was too big to walk around, and there wasn't enough time to build a raft. I had a motion-picture company waiting for me a few miles away, and it was the first day of shooting—which is very important in establishing the whole morale and tenor of such an enterprise as ours—so we had to give up and turn back.

In the midst of all this Kevin asked me how many elephants I had killed.

"Well, actually, none," I confessed.

Most of the hunting lore I had been expounding to Kevin came directly from *Big Game and Big Game Rifles*, by Pondoro Taylor, a famous white hunter in Africa at one time. To hear Kevin tell the story later—with a stammer which makes it funnier—the whole undertaking suddenly took on a different aspect. Now he didn't know whether to turn his back on me or on the red buffalo.

At the Ruiki site we had what must certainly have been the strangest flotilla African waterways had ever seen. The *African Queen* would furnish the power to pull four rafts—we hoped. On the first raft—and this was my idea—we built a replica of the *Queen*. That raft itself became our stage. We could put cameras and equipment on it and move around, photographing Katie and Bogie in the mock-up with as much facility as we'd have had on a studio floor. The second raft carried all of the equipment, lights and props. The third was for the generator. The fourth was Katie's, equipped with a privy, a full-length mirror and a private dressing room. This turned out to be one too many for the little *Queen* to tow, so we had to drop Katie's raft. Katie had to use the jungle toilet like the rest of us. Her full-length mirror got broken very quickly; those two halves were broken again, and finally she was reduced to using hand-held pieces of mirror while she did her makeup.

When Katie first joined us, she was a little skeptical about the whole operation. She looked on me as a young, inexperienced director, and I could sense her reserve. I think Katie viewed most people with considerable suspicion until they proved themselves. More important to the film, however, was the fact that her performance just wasn't right.

It had been—in my estimation—surely part of "Rosie's" upbringing never to be rude to an inferior unless he deserved a proper reprimand. "Charlie Alnutt" was doing nothing, in his own eyes, to offend her. He was just being himself. With this a gentlewoman could have no quarrel. But Rosie was behaving toward Charlie with no pretense of politeness. Indeed, she was treating him with open hostility. I made suggestions, but Katie ignored them. In fact, whatever I told her, she did just the opposite.

By the third day I had still made no headway with her and we were about to get into scenes that were critical. So that evening I sent Katie a note, asking if we could have a talk at her place after dinner. I didn't have to ask, of course, but I wanted to introduce a certain note of formality to the occasion.

Katie sent back immediate agreement to my request, and I joined her that evening, sitting out on her veranda. She said, "Yes, John? What is it you want to talk about?"

I said, "Katie, I don't want this to become a discussion. Please listen to what I've got to say without comment and, after I'm all through, decide whether or not I'm right."

Katie nodded. "Very well."

I told her that her interpretation of Rosie was doing harm to the picture as well as hurting the character. That her behavior toward Charlie put her on a level with him, whereas she should consider Charlie so far beneath her that she treats him as a lady treats a servant. This, rather than rudeness, would put a real distance between them.

"A lady?" Katie said as if I weren't aware that I happened to be addressing the real article. "What lady? Have you a particular lady in mind, John?"

I thought for a while. "Eleanor Roosevelt. Let her be your model. Good night, Katie."

It worked; she understood what I was after. From that moment she was perfect.

About two weeks after we started filming, the soldier ants made a foray against the camp—not a serious all-out attack, but one rather exploratory in nature. Everyone ran out to fight them, and we lit the kerosene in the ditches encircling the camp. All this noise awakened Katie, who thought it was a drunken revel. She came out and told everyone off.

"What's the meaning of this? We have work to do tomorrow. You should all be in bed . . . and you should be ashamed of yourselves!"

But when she discovered it was an invasion, she pitched right in and led the fight against the ants—the Jeanne d'Arc of Ruiki.

Both Bogie and I teased Katie unmercifully at the beginning. She thought we were rascals, scamps, rogues. We did everything we could to support this belief. We pretended to get roaring drunk. We even wrote dirty words in soap on her mirror. But eventually she saw through our antics and learned to trust us as friends.

We had a guard posted on the *African Queen*, and he was instructed to watch it closely and not let anyone steal anything. One morning we came out and discovered that the *Queen* had sunk during the night.

"Why didn't you tell us?" I asked the guard.

He shrugged. "There was nothing to tell." He pointed down to where she rested on the bottom of the river. "She's right there. Nobody stole anything!"

A little later that same day I was talking to Sam Spiegel by radio. He asked, "How's everything?"

"Everything's just fine, except for one item. The *African Queen* sank last night."

There was a period of silence . . . then Sam laughed. "I thought you said the *African Queen* sank."

"That's right."

"Oy!"

We got her up eventually by sheer manpower, patched the holes in her, and she continued to function.

We used to go a considerable distance up the Ruiki and then turn around and do most of our shooting while drifting downstream. The first day we were attacked by black wasps from the forest. Almost everyone was bitten. On the way back that evening, at the same spot, the wasps saw us and went for us again. They were fighter pilots attacking an invasion fleet. The next morning they hit us again—but not so hard—and on the return trip we were hardly molested. Apparently they were getting used to us. From the third day on, they paid no attention at all.

Not quite half of the shooting was done on the Ruiki. We finished on schedule, before the soldier ants came back, and then moved on to the location near Butiaba. The script called for the German East African settlement, in which Brother Samuel (Robert Morley) and his sister, Rosie, ran a mission, to be burned by the Germans. The village which we built for the express purpose of burning it had no inhabitants, of course, so we contracted with a local king to furnish us with villagers during the filming. A small hitch developed: no one turned up on the day filming was to begin, which baffled us until we found that word had circulated suggesting that anyone coming ran a risk of being eaten. Cannibalism was still a reality in that area. I had to drive over and give the king my word that his people would be safe. Even so, a couple of volunteers had to check us out first.

Diarrhea was rife at the Butiaba site. There were three to four persons waiting at all times to get into our portable outdoor toilet. One day Kevin McClory came out of it headlong with his pants down around his ankles, shouting, "Black mamba! Black mamba!" He had been sitting there when he looked up and saw a black cylinder moving above his head. The black mamba is one of the few really aggressive snakes around, and quite deadly. We all got a glimpse of it as it slid down out of the toilet into the elephant grass. It was a mamba all right. I have never seen a snake move so fast. Black mambas are known to move in pairs. From that moment all symptoms of diarrhea in camp disappeared.

After a week or so in Butiaba we moved on to Murchison Falls to complete the film. The last leg of this trip was accomplished on a big paddleboat, the *Isle of Murchison*.

It was a wild and lovely trip, through miles and miles of papyrus reeds. Upon arrival, we lived on the paddleboat, constructed another mock-up of the *African Queen* on a raft and commenced filming again.

I used to go out in the early morning, sometimes in the late afternoon after work, to shoot deer, pig and other game for the pot. Katie shook her head over this.

She endured it in silence as long as she could, then said, "Oh, John! You seem to be a sensitive person. How can you shoot anything as beautiful as these creatures? Are you a murderer at heart?"

"Katie, there's no explaining it. You'd have to go and see for yourself to understand."

"All right, I will!"

So Katie went with me, and from one hour to the next her attitude changed. She became Diana incarnate. Not that she herself wanted to kill anything; that would be overdoing it. But she did carry my light rifle. She used to come and wake me up in the early morning so we would have an hour's shooting before the day's work began.

One time I got us into a hell of a jam. We were with a self-styled "white hunter" (he put this down as his profession when he registered at the hotel in Stanleyville) about whom I had my doubts. He was just a little too ornamental to be the real thing. Anyway, he came with us one day when we went out after elephant.

We found a herd and tracked it for some time. I kept checking the wind drift: I wanted to be sure we stayed downwind. Presently we entered some very heavy foliage and were slowly working our way through it when I heard an elephant's stomach rumble. The sound came from only a few feet away. A few moments later I heard it again—this time on the other side of us—and realized that I had accidentally worked us right into the middle of a herd of elephants. The thing to do in such a situation is to retrace your steps as quietly as possible, getting clear of the herd. We started to do this, but the elephants picked up our scent, panicked and, trumpeting, began to crash through the jungle all around us like big locomotives. One came bearing down on us. Our white hunter broke and hightailed it. It was an extremely dangerous situation, but I knew that Katie's and my best chance was to remain immobile. An elephant can see you better if you are moving, and if he notices you, he is apt to pick you up and toss you away.

I looked around to see how Katie was taking this. She was carrying a little Manlicher rifle—a peashooter capable of putting out an elephant's eye but nothing more. There she was, one heel to the ground, her little rifle up, and her jaw line clean. She was as game as could be. I was carrying the Rigby .470 express rifle, but I don't mind admitting that I didn't feel safe even with that. I was severely shaken. All I could think about was the fact that I had got a woman—my star—into such a situation. It was unforgivable. The herd finally dispersed, and we started home. Looking somewhat sheepish, the white hunter reappeared. It was sheer luck that each of us was in one piece.

On the way back to camp Katie was walking ahead of me on the trail when I saw her stop, lean her rifle against a tree and raise her eight-millimeter movie camera to photograph something ahead on the trail. I hurried to catch up with her, and discovered that she was walking toward the biggest wild boar I had ever seen. It must have weighed 400 pounds, and its tusks were enormous. I said, ever so quietly, "Stop, Katie!" But she kept right on advancing until her camera ran down and she paused to rewind. By this time we were so close I was afraid to shoot the boar because, even with a bullet in his heart, one of these animals can maintain a charge. I was sure he was going to attack—and I was actually squeezing the trigger. At that instant his family ran across an open space in the trail behind him. He turned to look at them, looked back at us and suddenly veered away into the bush to join his family. That was a day on the hunt with Katie. She was delighted with the pictures she got. I was nearly prostrate.

I remember the many nights I sat with Katie on the top deck of the paddleboat and watched the eyes of the hippos in the water all around us; every eye seemed to be staring in our direction. And we talked. We talked about anything and everything. But there was never an idea of romance—Spencer Tracy was the only man in Katie's life.

Angela Allen was my script girl. Not only was she an expert at her job, she could work under duress and never turn a hair. We were out one day in a little flat-bottomed boat just below Murchison Falls. The crocs there were the biggest that I have seen anywhere. One great-grandfather of a croc must have been over thirty feet long. As we floated downriver on the boat, we could see the crocks sliding down the banks and into the water ahead of us, and hippos submerged as we approached. Suddenly we bumped into something. The boat began to rise slowly until it was completely out of the water. We were on a hippo's back! Luck was with us and we didn't tip over—the water was filled with crocs who would have liked nothing better—but simply rose slowly on the hippo's back, as on an elevator, and descended the same way. Angie didn't bat an eye. She continued to add to her notes, and I don't think she missed a comma.

Africa continued to enchant me. One day we were on the raft quite close to shore, shooting scenes on the mock-up of the *Queen*, when a big family of baboons came out of the forest to watch. The little ones went up into the trees, but the older ones came right down to the bank, only a few yards away. One old fellow sat on a log and crossed his legs. Presently we went back to work, and they watched a scene being played. When it was over, I asked Katie and Bogie if they liked playing to a live audience. Every afternoon for the next three days the baboons came out to watch us. It was as if they were in a theater watching a play. The old fellow always went to his place on the log. We talked about what they might do when we left off shooting for the day. I could imagine them coming aboard the raft and reenacting the scene they'd watched: Bogie and Katie, including the embrace.

Bogie didn't care for Africa. Unlike Katie, he didn't look on this as an adventure. He never went out with me on a hunt. He preferred to sit in camp, drink in hand, and tell stories. I suspect he would never have gone to such a place as Africa with anyone else but me. With Bogie, it wasn't so much where you acted but how you acted, and he'd just as soon have been at home. He liked the London or Paris night-life scene, but when it came to acting, he saw no reason why it couldn't be done in comfort in the studio.

Bogie didn't particularly care for the Charlie Alnutt role when he started, but I slowly got him into it, showing him by expression and gesture what I thought Alnutt should be like. He first imitated me, then all at once he got under the skin of that wretched, sleazy, absurd, brave little man. He realized he was on to something new and good. He said to me, "John, don't let me lose it. Watch me. Don't let me lose it." And, of course, he was superb in the part. He fully deserved the Academy Award that it brought him.

We had a lot of sickness at the Murchison Falls location. I did the rounds every morning and made sure that everyone took paludrine pills, and the kitchen was inspected constantly, but nevertheless people became ill. We finally discovered that the filters in the water system were not working properly. We then had bottled water brought in by railroad from Nairobi, but the sickness continued. It turned out that the water in the bottles was just as contaminated as the river water. Bogie and I never got sick, possibly because we always drank scotch with our water.

One afternoon I was working on a scene with Katie and Bogie when a runner carrying a message from Butiaba appeared. It had taken him three days to reach us; we had no other means of communication with the outside world. He handed me an envelope and I glanced at the cable inside. It was from California. Ricki had had a daughter; both she and the baby were fine. I stuck the paper silently in my pocket and went on with the scene. As I had expected, Katie couldn't stand it. "John," she finally blurted, "for heaven's sake, tell us!" And I did.

All in all, for a film where everything we needed had to be flown in or shipped in laboriously overland, things went quite smoothly. We lacked luxuries, but we had basic comforts, and we ate well—thanks largely to Betty Bogart, who took over the kitchen. I have feelings of special tenderness toward the *Queen* and all the people involved in it. It was with some regret that I wrapped up operations at the Murchison site and headed back for Entebbe—and civilization.

From Paris I returned to London, was reunited with Ricki and Tony and held the infant Anjelica in my arms for the first time. We took a flat in Grosvenor Square, and I went about finishing the post-production work on *The African Queen*.

18

Jimmy Woolf gave me a copy of Pierre La Mure's *Moulin Rouge*, a highly romanticized novel about Toulouse-Lautrec. After I read the book, I had an idea for the end that made me want to make a picture of it. I imagined Lautrec on his deathbed in the château at Toulouse, his mother and father watching the priest administer extreme unction. He smiles and his eyes open. He is hallucinating: the shades from his beloved *Moulin Rouge* enter the room, come there to bid farewell to their departing friend. The music of the can-can starts and Lautrec breathes his last. It would be a truly happy ending.

Sam Spiegel and I hadn't been too happy with each other during the shooting of the *Queen*, and I didn't feel like starting another picture with him right away. Under my contract with Horizon, I was allowed to make every other picture an outside one. So I told the Woolf brothers I would prefer to both produce and direct *Moulin Rouge*. They agreed, and Jimmy Woolf and I flew to New York to acquire the film rights to the book, negotiate a deal with United Artists and put José Ferrer under contract. Those things accomplished, I went to look for a suitable domicile in France, a place near Paris where Ricki and the children would be comfortable and where I could write and maybe get up on a horse's back now and then. I found it in Chantilly—a small villa owned by the La Rochefoucaulds—and we moved in.

Tony Veiller, my favorite American screenwriter, and I had worked together on *The Killers* and had also collaborated on the British-American documentary during the war. I was still under contract to Warners when Tony and I wrote *The Killers* for Mark Hellinger. I was sure that Warners wouldn't make a fuss about it, but I didn't take screenplay credit on it because of my commitment to them. The screenplay was nominated for an Academy Award. Our efforts had proved so rewarding that I asked

United Artists to make a deal with Tony to come and work with me on the screenplay of *Moulin Rouge*. He and his wife and their two kids moved into a hotel not too far away. I cannot remember a more agreeable summer. Early mornings I'd ride either along one of the myriad bridle paths in the forest of Chantilly or go out to the meadows and watch the sets of thoroughbreds working in the streamers of ground mist. It was a lovely way to begin the day.

In writing the screenplay, Veiller and I kept with La Mure's sentimentalized version of Lautrec's life; his attachment to a prostitute was a concession to the times. The censors of the early fifties wouldn't have allowed Toulouse-Lautrec's real life to be made into a picture.

My constant worry while we were writing *Moulin Rouge* was money: I had none. My financial affairs were in a proper mess. My divorce from Evelyn two years before had left me strapped. She'd got everything: ranch, livestock, paintings, works of art—and, on top of that, alimony. I had other debts as well, among them the $150,000 that Metro had loaned me. For *The African Queen* I was to receive living expenses and a nominal salary that would enable me to satisfy my creditors. Although the various backers put funds at Horizon's disposal, I never saw a penny of them. For over eighteen months there was no cash flow into my account. Now everything I was being paid for *Moulin Rouge* over and above our living expenses went toward back alimony and other indebtedness. However, *The African Queen* was now in release, and proceeds from it would soon be forthcoming. At least, this is what I was told.

Billy Pearson was racing his way around the world. He sailed on a cruise ship from Los Angeles, stopped off in Hawaii to ride in a few races. He rode in Tokyo for the Emperor of Japan and in Bangkok for the King of Siam. I got cards and cables occasionally, and eventually Billy arrived in Paris.

He announced that he wanted to ride in France. One of my good friends in Paris was Laudy Lawrence, who was a partner with Aly Khan in a stud farm. I asked Laudy if we could do anything to arrange this and found out Billy wasn't at all welcome: French jockeys didn't want an American riding on French turf. Thanks to Laudy, however, Billy was invited to work some horses at Chantilly for the Marquis de Courtois, a very fine sportsman who owned a small but select stable.

Two days before the workout Billy came down with a severe case of influenza. The morning he was to ride, Tony and I helped him get dressed. He'd been delirious most of the night. I was against him going through with it, but he insisted. We drove to the meadows. The Courtois contingent was waiting. Billy sprang out of the car and put on an incredible show of good health and bonhomie for Courtois, his trainer and all present. Then Billy was put up on a filly named Pomerey II. Out of the gate, Billy broke first and came in well ahead of the heat. He did it a second time and a third time on other mounts and made a fine impression, after which we returned home and Billy lapsed back into his delirium.

That exhibition made Billy with Courtois, thanks to whom he became the first American to ride in France for something like forty years. It was clear from his first race that the French jocks were more interested in keeping Billy from winning than in winning themselves.

Billy was invited to ride for other stables, and the harassment continued. Then one afternoon he said, "John, they're out to murder me! Paul Blanc tried to put me into the rail that last race." This was serious—running him into the rail is about the worst thing one jockey can do to another. It's a good way to kill somebody. I was outraged, and, like the fight manager who says to his boy, "They can't do that to us," I said, "Let's show them, Billy!" The next week Billy was to ride Pomerey II for Courtois in the Grand Prix de Saint James. He'd gotten his education in Mexico as a bug rider, and anything goes down there. We agreed that in the Prix de Saint James he was to cut loose and make devout Christians of the other jocks.

I then collected my friends from the American colony in Paris: Gene Kelly, Irwin Shaw, Art Buchwald, John Steinbeck, Anatole Litvak, Bob Capa and others. We brought along reinforcements from among bellboys at the Lancaster Hotel and waiters from restaurants that I frequented. We all pledged to defend Billy from the French crowd if it turned on him. I think there was even a plan for setting fire to the grandstands as a diversionary tactic if things really got out of hand. Luckily, that wasn't necessary. Billy did it in style. He came out cutting and kicking. He used leg locks, he jerked bridles, he slammed into horses that got anywhere near him, knocking them off stride. He stirrup-hooked a couple and slashed at others with his whip. Billy committed every foul in the book and others never seen before in the entire history of French racing. The objection gong began to toll almost as soon as the horses came out of the gate. There were twelve horses in the race. Six finished with riders on their backs; Billy had picked off the other six one by one.

He won the race, of course, and our defense group had gathered in the winner's circle to welcome him. We kept between Billy and the crowd, which was shaking its fists and spitting at him. Naturally, Billy was disqualified. He was whisked from the winner's circle to the stewards' room, where he was asked to explain his actions. The stewards knew, of course, the background to the occasion, and they bent over backward to be just. The other jockeys were brought in to testify, and among them was Paul Blanc, who had a whip burn across his eyes and the bridge of his nose. He said that Billy had struck him with his whip as they were passing behind Le Petit Bois, where the horses disappear from view of the stands for several long moments. Billy flatly denied it. "How could he," the stewards asked, "in the face of such evidence."

"I not only deny it—I can prove it's false!" He asked permission to take off his silks. Billy is wired with platinum from his breastbone through his shoulder and down to his right elbow—repair work after a bad fall some years earlier. As Blanc told it, the blow had been delivered by Billy's right hand slashing horizontally at eye level.

"I can't raise my arm over a forty-five-degree angle. I couldn't have hit him that way!" Billy protested.

A French doctor confirmed Billy's claim, which was fortunate because he could have been barred from racing for life. Instead, he was ruled off the course for three days and fined a few thousand francs. I remember asking Billy afterward whether it was really true that he couldn't raise his arm. "Shit!" he declared, and then threw the most beautiful raking backhand you could possibly imagine.

Three days later Billy rode Ilu, a Courtois stake horse, at St. Cloud. Before the race Billy asked Courtois if there were any instructions. Courtois smiled, "Yes, Beel. *Revanche!*" Billy rode a beautiful race. He lay so far back I thought he could never make up the ground, but he knew exactly what he was doing and won the race by half a length. He gave his share of the purse to the French Jockeys' Guild. Within a month he was elected its Honorary President in perpetuity. Both the jockeys and the French public were won over and Billy Pearson was the toast of Paris.

Roger Poincelet was then the leading rider in France, and he and Billy had become good friends. At the morning works at Chantilly one day I saw Poincelet on a striking two-year-old I'd never seen before. The name of the horse was Thunderhead II, and when I saw the way he moved, I was deeply impressed. Poincelet told Billy that Thunderhead II was entered in the Two Thousand Guineas, the first of the three great English classics, and he further assured Billy that Thunderhead II was going to win that race. I decided to put some early money on the horse, called Ladbroke's, my bookie in London, and made a bet. He was 30 to 1—a big price. Then, every time I had a cocktail too many or whenever the spirit moved me, I called up and made another bet. Finally I had a very big bet going. I didn't have any money, but the race was still several weeks away and I figured that the first returns from *The African Queen* would be coming in at any moment and I would have enough to pay off my debt if we lost.

Thunderhead II had his first outing at Longchamps. He ran in good company, although the race wasn't a classic, and won in a canter. This reassured me.

Ricki and I went to London the day of the race and drove down to the course at Newmarket, where Billy met us. Billy had come over in the cargo plane with Poincelet and Thunderhead II. Right away Billy said, "I've got another horse for us, John." I had only £30 or £40 in my pocket—or, for that matter, to my name—and I bet it on Billy's horse. The horse won, at very good odds, so we now had a few hundred pounds in cash, which we promptly put down on Thunderhead II at track odds.

The time came for the race, and Billy and Ricki and I went into the stands to watch it. There's a long stretch at Newmarket when you look at the horses coming toward you head-on and through the binoculars it's terribly hard to tell who's ahead. The horses seem to be floating, as in the long lens of a camera. I couldn't even locate Thunderhead II. Ricki was yelling, urging our horse on. Billy got impatient and grabbed the binoculars from me. He couldn't see the horse either. I had a sinking sensation in the pit of my stomach. But Thunderhead II was in fact so far ahead of the field that we had missed him entirely. He was at least eight lengths out front, and he finished that way.

Billy and I collected our winnings at the track, and the three of us sat down on a little lawn outside the jocks' and trainers' stands to celebrate with anyone who cared to stop and have a drink out of our champagne bottles. After a couple of other races I looked over at the paddock some fifty yards away and saw the horses that were going to run in the last race. Among them I spotted a colt that looked good to me. I liked the way he carried himself. I didn't know his name, but I could see his number, and I asked Billy to go over and make a bet on this horse. He put down a good one, and I'll be damned if this horse didn't come in, too! We just couldn't lose, that day.

The big bet I had put down through Ladbroke's—several thousand pounds at thirty to one—was brought to me at Claridge's in London in a black fiber case full of £5 notes. They even left the case. That impressed me the most. It was a lot of money: the biggest bet I have ever won.

Before we collected our bets on this race, the Pearsons and the Hustons

had been flat broke, but now we proceeded to live high off the hog.
Queta Pearson came over from Pasadena. We took suites at Claridge's.
There were dinner parties every night. Ricki and Queta proceeded to
buy out Asprey's and appear in outfits from the finest fashion houses;
expensive gifts arrived for the children and their nurse. It was illegal in
England at that time to take more than £10 out of the country, so Billy
and I, in addition to ordering shoes and boots from Maxwell's, and suits
and riding clothes from the tailors Tautz, invested in Benin bronzes and
other *objets d'art*.

No money arrived from *The African Queen*. No money ever arrived
from *The African Queen*. It was promised. It didn't come in. Excuses
would be made. More promises. I phoned Bogie to ask him how he was
faring. He told me that certain discrepancies had been discovered in
Horizon's books by his business manager, Morgan Maree. Bogie's share of
the picture was not in order. He was owed a goodly amount, and if it was
not paid immediately, Bogie would be suing Horizon. Maree was in London and would come to Paris the following week. Bogie strongly recommended that we get together and that I be guided by Maree's counsel.

That's how I met Morgan, who was to be my friend and business
manager for many years. Maree filled me in on a few of the deals Sam had
made—all in his favor, naturally—and advised me to disassociate myself
from Horizon and its shenanigans without delay. It was the best-inten-
tioned, worst advice I ever accepted. I got out of my contract with
Horizon. No more partnership. No more share of the possible profits.

The African Queen was one of the most successful pictures I ever
made—and Sam got all the money. My leaving Horizon is one of the
"what if's" of my career. What if I had waited? How much would I have
made? Actually, I know: a more than comfortable sum. It might have
changed my life.

While Billy had been clawing his way to the top of the heap and
Thunderhead II had been the recipient of many acts of faith on my part
and I was signing away a fortune, life on the motion-picture level went
on in its prescribed manner: Tony Veiller and I finished the screenplay;
Paul Sheriff built sets; Elsa Schiaparelli designed costumes; and I completed casting. We were almost ready to go.

I was going to try to use color on the screen as Lautrec had used it in
his paintings. Our idea was to flatten the color, render it in planes of solid
hues, do away with the highlights and the illusion of third dimension
which modeling introduced. I hired *Life* photographer Eliot Elisofon to
experiment with the use of this sort of color in still photography, and he

and Oswald Morris, the cameraman, attempted to obtain with the motion-picture camera the effects we had in stills.

Before shooting began, we made our final color tests. For interiors we used a filter that up until then had been employed only outside to simulate fog—and we added to that effect by actually lying in smoke so that scenes took on a flat monochromatic quality.

The result was so striking that the Technicolor studios wanted nothing to do with it. They told us to shoot in the conventional way, that they would create our special effects in their lab. We told them to go ahead and show us. We shot some film in the standard method, and they worked on it. It wasn't what we were after. We then declared our intention of doing it our way. Technicolor wrote to Romulus and United Artists, disclaiming all responsibility. But both Romulus and United Artists backed us up, and we proceeded.

It turned out that this unique use of color was the best thing about the film. It was the first picture that succeeded in dominating the color instead of being dominated by it. This was the first western film since Robert Edmond Jones' *Becky Sharp* to have a "palette," so to speak. The Japanese had done some interesting experimental work in *The Gates of Hell* but they were the only ones beside Jones and ourselves who had tried to render film color in something other than the garish hues of bad billboards.

On several occasions during the shooting of *Moulin Rouge* I did close-ups of "Lautrec's hand" drawing a scene going on in the background. The actual hand was that of the artist Marcel Vertès, who had survived the hard years after World War I in Paris by making very credible forgeries of Lautrec before establishing a reputation for his own work. He sketched with such speed that he could complete a drawing of an entire ongoing scene in the time it took us to shoot it.

Today it is virtually impossible to get permission to shoot in Paris, but at that time the authorities were ever so agreeable. They were helpful even to the point of blocking off some 45,000 square feet in front of the Deux Magots on the Left Bank for one full Saturday afternoon in order to create a realistic scene out of the Gay Nineties. We cleared the area of cars, buses, motorcycles and pedestrians, and introduced horse-drawn carriages and other period paraphernalia. On the right of the square was a five-way intersection, on which some thirty gendarmes blocked traffic for hours. You can't imagine the outrage of the French motorists. They blew their horns in unison. The noise was so deafening that the actors couldn't hear each other at all. They had to read lips in order to pick up their cues and know when to start speaking. The dialogue was dubbed in later. And, once stopped, the motorists—with Gallic logic—refused to start again. The jam was colossal.

Demonstrations of French individualism were a constant problem during shooting. A Frenchman coming home after work with his brief case in one hand and a market basket in the other would walk right through a lighted street where actors were playing a scene. Signs and a three-bell warning meant nothing to him. He, by God, was doing as he had been doing for the last twenty years, and nor wind nor weather nor film-makers was going to stop or detour him. You might just as well have tried to stop a Sherman tank. He was going home!

I remember one scene in which Toulouse-Lautrec was walking along the street at night. He walked toward the camera, then passed by and disappeared in the darkness. For the close-ups we used José, and for the long shots we used a real dwarf. The real dwarf would disappear briefly behind a barrel or some object and José would emerge in a close-up, so that you couldn't see his legs. All this in one shot. It was most effective. In the course of this scene there was an encounter with the prostitute, played by Colette Marchand. As the dialogue began, however, hammering started on a nearby fire escape. It turned out to be a French woman declaring war on us, making it impossible to record the dialogue. Our French assistants tried to reason with the woman, but to no avail. She wanted to be paid to stop. We would have been delighted to pay her off, but had we done so, every fire escape in the area would have erupted. The police were called in, but there was nothing they could do. "Someone is hitting a fire escape, Monsieur? So what? It is her own fire escape!" The Gallic code of individualism tolerated this sort of thing. We had to stop shooting. Only when one of the French assistants uncovered the district fortune-teller, whom he paid to visit the woman and tell her to desist hitting her fire escape or bad luck would pursue her forever and ever, was the solution finally found.

Later I discovered that on the same night we were being secretly observed by Picasso. He was very interested in the picture and had rented some rooms in a little hotel overlooking the street to watch the action. I understand that he later used to do imitations of José Ferrer walking on his knees.

One night in Paris—I think it was Bastille Day—José gave a little dinner party at the Tour d'Eiffel. The guests included Aly Khan, Zsa Zsa Gabor, Bob Capa and his fiancée, Suzanne Flon and myself. José had taken great pains about the menu and the wines. Aly Khan left the table briefly during the meal, and when José went to pay the bill, he was informed that it had been taken care of by Aly. José took great exception to this and told Aly off in very certain terms. Aly retired, deeply embarrassed. Somebody at the next table who had witnessed this commented that it served that "nigger" Aly Khan right. I took exception to *this*. Anyway, the party turned into a shambles, not at all the happy affair that José had planned. Then things got worse.

I took Suzanne Flon home in a taxi, and we stopped outside her apartment building in Montparnasse to say good night. Suddenly the taxi door flew open and someone jumped inside and began beating the living bejesus out of me. I'd had too much to drink, and it took me a few moments to get my wits together, but I finally got a knee into his groin. The man then scrambled out of the car and ran shouting into the apartment building. I got out of the cab and followed him. Suzanne came after me, crying, "Go, John, for God's sake, go!"

We were standing in the dimly lighted courtyard when the man came running down the stairs with a gun in his hand. He stopped at the bottom of the stairs and aimed the pistol at my heart. Suzanne screamed. He pulled the trigger. I heard the click, but the gun didn't fire. At this point the taxi driver and a passing stranger flung themselves between the man and myself. My assailant then ran back up the stairs, and I was prevented from following him. Suzanne kept pleading with me to go. I was dragged back to the cab and shoved in, and before the door could catch in the lock, the taxi burned rubber getting out of there.

I was cut up pretty badly and wore dark glasses the following morning, but they didn't conceal the damage. We were shooting in the Place Vendôme just outside the Ritz, where the company had rented a suite for the principals in lieu of dressing rooms. Suzanne and I went up to the suite. She was still quite distressed. She told me the man's name; he lived on the floor below her. He had been of great help to her and her family during the war. She was grateful to him and felt protective toward him, but his jealousy and possessiveness were an increasing problem to her. She pleaded with me to forget it—but I wasn't about to let it pass.

There was a tough, capable ex-boxer on the film who acted as a general bodyguard and troubleshooter. He used to give me rubdowns. I said to him, "I want you to come with me this evening. We've got a job to do."

That night we went to the man's apartment. I knocked on the door. The man opened it a crack, and I leaned into it hard, driving him back into the room. My friend had instructions to stay out of things unless a gun was produced, so he stood back while we went at it. The fellow wasn't very good, and after taking a few blows, he stopped trying to defend himself and began to cry. I was too furious to care about that, but my friend grabbed me and held my arms.

Then came such a pathetic story that I began to cool down. He had known Suzanne for many years. He knew what he had done was terrible, but it was an act of someone driven mad by jealousy. After he finished, I said, "Where's your gun? Get your gun." The man went into the bedroom and came back with a .22 pistol. I took the bullets from the gun and asked him if he had any more ammunition. He said he didn't. About then there was a knock on the door. It was the gendarmes, summoned by neighbors who had heard the row. The man had a bloody nose, but he convinced the police that there had been no quarrel and that we had just been roughhousing. As soon as the police departed, I gave the man back his gun and we left. Later I looked at the bullets I had taken from the pistol. One of them had an indentation on the rim where it had been struck by the firing pin. I had assumed, when I heard the click, that the gun was unloaded. This proved that it had indeed been loaded. At that range, pointed directly at my heart, even a .22 bullet would have killed me. I got angry all over again, and threw the bullets into the Seine.

The day after, word came that the poor, jealous wretch had shot himself and was in a hospital. He had aimed for his heart, but the bullet apparently had struck a rib and lodged just below the heart. The next piece of news was that the man had escaped from the hospital. I could just imagine him planning to take somebody along if he had to go, so I posted various people to keep an eye open for anyone answering to his description. We would be leaving Paris in just a day or two, and I didn't want any of this to get into the papers. No one knew what had happened except Suzanne, myself, the ex-boxer and Bob Capa, and I wanted to keep it that way. When we finally left Paris, I put Bob in charge of the cover-up. I was still glancing back over my shoulder even as I was boarding the airplane.

Eliot Elisofon was a supreme egotist. He made no bones about it: he was the greatest photographer alive. With Eliot, you didn't know where innocence left off and egotism began. I liked him enormously and found him quite unbearable.

When we were in London, putting the finishing touches on *Moulin Rouge*, Eliot told me about taking a very young English actress into the darkroom to show her some color transparencies of herself. I mentioned this to José, and he and I decided to compose a letter to Eliot from the girl's "mother." Joe wrote out the letter in longhand and addressed it to the Manager of the Studio. The "mother" stated, in essence, that a Mr. Elisofon had taken her daughter into a darkroom and made indecent advances. The girl was under age, and this was tantamount to rape. She intended to proceed against the studio. They would be hearing from her solicitor.

When Eliot came in the next day, he was informed that the chief of security wished to see him. Everyone was in on this, and when Eliot went to see the chief of security, the manager of the studio was also there with this letter. They both assured Eliot that they didn't put any stock in these charges, but nevertheless they would like to hear from him exactly what had occurred.

"Absolutely nothing!" exclaimed Eliot. "I just let her in to see some pictures of herself. The pictures were very flattering, and the girl was delighted with them. I can't understand what her mother is talking about." They said they believed him and he left, reassured.

Eliot was booked to go back to New York with his wife and child a few days later. The following day we arranged to have him called into the manager's office again, where he was told that the incident had gotten a little out of hand. It seemed that the Home Office had been informed, and was it true that he intended to leave England in a few days? He did. Did the departure have anything to do with the incident with the girl?

"No! Absolutely not! I purchased those tickets weeks ago!"

"Well, unfortunately, it appears that you are running out on an unpleasant episode. Is it not possible for you to delay taking passage for a week, say?"

"Quite impossible! I have business engagements in New York. Besides —my God! What would my wife think? I'd have to tell her the reason for the delay."

"Is there any cause for you to think your wife wouldn't believe you?"

"Of course not, my wife has every confidence in me, but it would be ...uh...awkward...."

And so it went. The manager agreed to talk with the Home Office and inform them of Eliot's circumstances.

Eliot was called back later that day and told that the Home Office was of the opinion that if he left the country before this was cleared up, he would be leaving under a cloud and might have difficulty coming back to England again. Alarmed, Eliot went to Jack Clayton, the production manager for *Moulin Rouge*.

"Eliot, have you told John?"

"Lord, no! I don't want him to hear about this!"

"Well, I think you should tell John. In fact, you *must* tell John."

Convinced at last that he had no choice, Eliot came to see me, but by this time the shooting was finished for the day and I had left. Jack said, "Well, make sure you see John the first thing in the morning."

When Eliot showed up the following morning, he had only one day left before getting on the boat. I had everyone on the set coached: when Eliot approached me, they were to take me away from him, create emergencies, anything. I wasn't to be allowed time to talk with him. Eliot came up to me immediately and said, "John, I've got to talk to you."

"Of course, Eliot, what's the . . . Oh! Excuse me. Yes, Jack, what's the problem?"

I went back to Eliot, but someone else came running up and took me away again. I watched Eliot out of the corner of my eye, and each time he started to sidle up to me I got terribly busy with something else. During lunch I was called away for a conference. I saw Eliot shaking his head as if to say, "No! This can't be happening to me!" The shaking of the head became more pronounced as the day wore on, and he began muttering to himself.

By the end of the shooting day Eliot still hadn't had a chance to talk to me, so he followed me into the projection room. Now the head-shaking had become habitual. Whereas before it had been a doleful negation, it was now a series of short, rapid jerks. It had, in fact, become a tic. He sat right beside me while I looked at the rushes. He couldn't talk to me then, but right afterward he said: "John, I've got to talk to you! Got to! Got to!"

"Why, of course, Eliot." We went over to Jack Clayton's office where Eliot proceeded to tell me the whole story from beginning to end.

When he was through, I nodded. "All right, Eliot, level with me. What *did* happen in the darkroom?"

"As God is my judge, nothing! I promise you, nothing!"

"Eliot, we've all done things we aren't proud of. When you tell me the truth of this matter, why, I'll make a confession to you about something I'm ashamed of also."

"But, John, nothing happened! I'll swear to Christ! Nothing! Nothing!" and he got down on his knees and swore it on the life of his wife and child. Well, I'd been trying to hold myself in, and so had Jack. If I'd been just a little better person, compassion would have flooded through me rather than mirth. But I wasn't, and it didn't. I began to laugh, and so did Jack.

Eliot looked up at us, and I know what he saw were two imps from Hades laughing at his torment. For this I'll surely cook in hell for a few extra eons. And then comprehension began to show in Eliot's eyes. When I saw understanding dawn, I backed off a few steps and got a desk between us. I didn't know what might happen when full realization hit him.

But I need not have worried. Suddenly Eliot smiled. It was like the sun coming up. He said, "It's a joke! It's a joke!" He had been delivered from a terrible dream, and he felt nothing but gratitude. He jumped to his feet. "It's a joke! I'll buy the drinks. I'll buy drinks for everybody!" I wished he had punched me instead.

In 1951, just before starting work on *The African Queen*, I went to Ireland for the first time on an invitation from Lady Oonagh Oranmore and

19 Browne, one of the three Guinness sisters. The sisters, Oonagh, Eloise and Eileen, are all witches—lovely ones to be sure, but witches nonetheless. They are all transparent-skinned, with pale hair and light blue eyes. You can very nearly see through them. They are quite capable of changing swinish folk into real swine before your very eyes, and turning them back again without their even knowing it. Or changing people's shoes—left shoe to right foot and vice versa—so that they become awkward and stumble about. Or putting the wrong words into the mouths of pretentious persons, so that everyone, including the victims, is appalled at the nonsense they talk. These strange talents are not uncommon among the Irish, especially among Irish women. There's a magic and a mystery about Irish women, but they also possess a down-to-earth approach to life that is most refreshing. No one would argue that a woman was equal in all respects to men—there is little furor over women's rights in Ireland—but, unlike the American male, an Irishman makes no major decision without consulting his wife. She is his equal in all decisions that are important to their lives.

The woman in an Irish house is usually the one who extends the hospitality. She, rather than the man, does the talking. This is true not only in the case of great Irish ladies such as Oonagh and her sisters, but throughout the life of Ireland, in whatever social stratum. If you go into a thatched-roof cottage, you will be royally received—by the woman. The man usually stands by, nodding and smiling.

The occasion of my first visit to Ireland was a hunt ball in the Gresham Hotel in Dublin. I had been to English hunt balls—restrained and correct affairs, for the most part. An Irish hunt ball has an air of abandon. Music is faster, spirits run higher. The Galway Blazer Hunt staged this particular event, and before the night was over I fully expected someone to get killed. It would certainly have been in the highest tradition of that renowned hunt. The Galway Blazers got their name after a ball which was such a triumph that, instead of merely throwing their champagne glasses into the fireplace, they touched off the house.

As this evening wore on, the young bucks started a game of follow-the-leader. The leader jumped over a large buffet table filling the center of the room, and some thirty revelers followed him. A waiter undertook to defend the table, swinging a champagne bucket as each jumper came flying through the air. This only made the game more attractive. Finally the waiters moved the table against the wall, and the procession turned its attention elsewhere. It went up the stairs to a balcony above the dance floor, where the leader jumped off, head first, and piled up unconscious. His followers came after him, one after another, until the floor was littered with young men with broken bones and heads.

After the ball I was taken with other weekend guests to Lugalla, Oonagh's place in County Wicklow, a shooting lodge her grandfather had built. The night was dark and I couldn't see much during the drive, but I had an impression of water-soaked hills, trickling springs and racing clouds, and finally of a long descent down a steep, narrow road through big trees. The house had an excellent butler named Patrick Cummins, who showed me up to a lovely room with a four-poster bed. On a table beside the bed was a copy of a book by Claude Cockburn, another house-guest, whom I'd known in my pre-war days. The name of the book was *Beat the Devil*, written under the *nom de plume* James Helvick. It was the only book in my room. I later discovered other copies of Claude's book strategically placed about the house.

The next morning at dawn I went to the window and looked out upon a scene I have never forgotten. Through pines and yews in the garden I saw, across a running stream, a field of marigolds and beyond the field—surprisingly—a white sandy beach bordering a black lake. I learned later that the sand had been brought in from some beach on the Irish Sea. Above the lake was a mountain of black rock rising precipitously, and on its crest—like a shawl over a piano—a profusion of purple heather. I was to go back to Lugalla many times, but I'll never forget that first impression. I was Ireland's own from that moment.

Oonagh had married and then divorced an acquaintance of mine who bears my favorite name: Lord Dominick Oranmore and Browne. After the divorce they remained friends. I went to the home of each for visits, and Oonagh often came to visit me wherever I was making a picture.

Through Oonagh I made another great Irish friend, Norah Fitzgerald. Norah was a marvelous-looking woman, very tall and somewhat reminiscent of Garbo. She was the acknowledged queen of Dublin as its premier wine merchant—the proprietor of Fitzgerald and Sons. Norah was good at her business, like her father before her. She owned racehorses, and sponsored many charities. Because of all her charity work, the Dublin police extended certain privileges to Norah. If they found her Mercedes parked in the middle of the street, they did not tow it away, as they would anyone else's, but simply stood by it until she came back. Norah drove like a fiend; she regularly wrecked two cars each year—always Mercedes. I used to send her ritual cables just before Christmas: "Be careful driving over the holidays. We don't want to lose you!"

Norah liked to stand on her head at extraordinary times. You never knew when this was going to happen, and it was always a shock to look up and see Norah upside down, dress around her neck, bare from bra to pink panties to stocking tops. No one would have dreamed of remarking disparagingly on her behavior. Norah was a lady: she just happened to be completely independent in her thought and conduct.

Norah's father had been a character in his own right. Once, in England, he had expressed an opinion that called forth the comment: "I smell an Irishman."

So Mr. Fitzgerald had shot the man's nose off.

I had hunted the fox in the States, in England and on the Continent, but Irish hunting came as a new and joyful experience. It had little of the formality of the other hunts. You heard laughter and shouting as the hunt went on; there was a festive feeling about it all. Everyone was in high spirits.

I rode with the Kildare Fox Hounds, the Meath and the Ward Union. I grew to love the hunt so much that in 1953 I brought Ricki and the children over to Ireland and we leased a country house near Kilcock, in County Kildare, called Courtown. Courtown was a big house, located on some 300 acres of very productive land, and staffed by a fine group of servants, several of whom came to work for me after the place was sold some years later. It was owned by Captain Drummond, who was head of the Drummond Banks in Scotland and London. Captain Drummond told me over the telephone what he wanted for the house, and I said I thought that the figure was quite reasonable. This astounded him. He was so pleased that he threw in, as part of the lease, all the farm produce we could use: eggs, milk, fruits and vegetables in season.

Captain Drummond was a tall, spare, sinister figure, balding, with a hawk nose, a military mustache and a deep gash on his forehead—a wound from the First World War—at the base of which there was an exposed vein. When the Captain became angry or disturbed, this vein would pulse hugely. One could observe this phenomenon at will. You had only to mention the name Churchill. The Captain had quite decided opinions. Did I know that Churchill and Roosevelt had plotted the death of General Patton? Did I know that Patton was killed on their orders? When I professed incredulity, he supplied me with detail upon detail in a clipped Sandhurst accent which brooked no opposition.

One of Captain Drummond's decided opinions had gotten him into serious trouble during the Battle of Britain. He had made a pronouncement in the Cavalry Club in London: "There's a great deal to be said in Hitler's favor!" The trouble was that the floor of the club was at that very moment rocking from falling German bombs. Although this was considered a treasonous statement, the British didn't want to put the good Captain into prison. It was not just because of his record in World War I and his eminence in the financial world; he was also a friend of the Royal Family and had even taught the Prince of Wales to ride. He was, however, sent to the Isle of Man and kept virtually a prisoner there until the end of the war. His hatred of Churchill stemmed from this experience, for it was Churchill, of course, who was responsible for his detention. Captain Drummond was out of a very old English book.

The Kildare Hounds hunted three times a week—Tuesday, Thursday and Saturday. Courtown was in the middle of Tuesday country. I went to the meets with Norah Fitzgerald and with Betty O'Kelly, who was later to become my estate manager. Her father, Bernard O'Kelly, had been president of the Royal Dublin Society a year or so before and had been a great fox-hunting man until a fall had forced him to give it up. He was the estate agent for Courtown and other important properties.

The lives of most of my neighbors revolved around the hunt. It was much more than a casual sport; it was a way of life. In fox-hunting you follow the hounds, usually twenty couple, or forty hounds. There is a bitch pack and a dog pack, hunted separately. These animals are carefully bred, and there are as many breeds of hounds as there are of horses. The Huntsman "casts" the hounds into a covert, or thick growth, where the fox lives. The night before the hunt, paid locals stop up the existing burrows so that the fox cannot "go to ground." When it gets too hot in the covert for the fox, he will break and run for another covert, which may be close by or many miles away. The fox is allowed to break clean before the hounds are put on his trail, and the hunters follow the hounds, jumping whatever obstacles may lie in their way.

A "check" occurs when the hounds lose the scent. The hunt must stop and wait for them to pick it up again. The speed of the hunt depends largely upon the scent and the obstacles encountered. If it's good, and the fox is running well, the chase can be fast and furious. You jump things that neither you nor the horse would ever dream of taking on in cold blood. "Throw your heart over the wall and follow it," they say. You may cover up to a twenty-mile point in a single hunt, although it is usually much less than that. I have, however, gone at a hard gallop for more than two hours.

The countryside can vary greatly from county to county, and its character determines the kind of obstacles the hunter will encounter. Galway has dry stone fences bordering small fields, and sometimes there are jumps every fifty yards or so. One visitor counted over 400 jumps on a single Galway hunt. The Meath has big ditches, and Limerick and Cork have large banks called doubles, which can be very high and formidable. The horses gather themselves like cats, spring upward and clamber to the top. They must then spring outward and hit the ground running to lessen the impact. The braver the animal, the bigger the leap. Very often a horse trained for Galway is no good in Limerick, and vice versa. The Galway horse does not know the Irish doubles, and the Limerick horse doesn't fly his fences. The Galway hunt is perhaps faster than the Limerick or the Cork because most of the jumping is in stride: you spend almost as much time in the air as on the ground.

Fox-hunting is in fact an anachronism, with Ireland almost the last holdout. As a sport it has come under fire, during the last decade especially. It is a blood sport, to be sure, for without attempting to kill the fox there would be little point to the hunt. But no one is there simply to see the fox killed. More often than not, the fox gets clean away.

The fox-hunt is paradoxically the main reason that there are any foxes alive in England and Ireland. The fox is not a nice fellow—he often kills not only for food but out of sheer, wanton blood-lust. He will enter a henyard, take one chicken for his meal and then kill everything in sight. There are sporting farmers who themselves hunt, but, by and large, if foxes were left to the farmer, he'd shoot or poison them one and all.

The fox-hunt is financed by yearly contributions from the members and a "cap fee" paid by visitors. The members must be invited to join, and they put up the necessary money and vote on the business of the hunt. In Ireland today the Master of the Hunt may be either someone chosen from the membership or a paid professional who serves as Huntsman as well as Master. In the latter case he is provided with a place to live and a stipend with which to run the hunt.

The Huntsman is usually a hired professional. His is a demanding, full-time occupation. In addition to supervising the stables, he must provide for the care and feeding of the hounds and oversee the kennels. The Huntsman knows each hound by name and character, and it is amazing how he can call certain hounds by name out of a pack of forty and they will respond from half a mile away. When the fox goes to ground, it is the duty of the Huntsman to dig him out or send a terrier down to get him.

The Whippers-In keep the hounds together, among other duties. Hounds are always straying off; the pack will divide; or a hound will get sore and stop—so after a hunt there are usually lost hounds which have to be collected.

The Field Master keeps the members of the hunt in line. There are certain acts which are strictly forbidden. You must not, of course, let your horse ride over the hounds. You must be careful not to "head the fox"—that is, turn the fox away from the line he has taken. The Huntsman and the Master always have priority—in that order. If there's room for only one person at a time to jump an obstacle—as is often the case—the Huntsman and the Master get the first crack at it, and the members follow as they can.

The rules on a hunt are simple, but they are rigidly enforced. The protocol and the dress have, for the most part, a practical purpose. The black silk top hat is reinforced: it's a helmet. The velvet-visored cap, also reinforced, is worn by the Master, hunt servants and children. Other members may wear it only if given permission to do so. The original reason for the "stock" was that it could be taken off and used for a bandage. The red-and-black colors worn by the hunters are chosen for their visibility—if someone falls and can't get out of the way, you and your horse can see him more clearly and more easily avoid riding over him. The rules about clothing are strict except in the case of local farmers; they may wear whatever they wish. They may also hunt without having to pay, whereas a guest must pay unless he is there at the invitation of the Master or a member of the Master's family.

Hunts may last from ten minutes to two hours or more and are often more hazardous for the hunters than for the hunted. Once Morgan Maree came to visit me in Kildare. He was a good horseman, had bought himself all the proper gear and was eager to go. I suggested that he come along and watch a hunt first. He did, and on this particular day casualties occurred one after another. People were carried off the field on gates. Ned Cash, a former tinker, the father of four jockeys and a lion in the hunting field, fell over a stone fence and cut his head open. He tied it up with a horse bandage, but the blood soaked through and dripped down over his eyes, forcing him to put another bandage over the first. He had a great turban by then, and I'll never forget the wild figure he cut when the bandage came undone. There were three or four yards of bloody horse bandage streaming behind him, and Ned was still going furiously. There was also one broken collarbone, a broken shoulder and even a broken neck.

It was one of my lucky days, and I didn't have a fall. When I came home that evening, Morgan was sitting by the fire in the study. So far as I was concerned, it had been a great day. I'd forgotten about the casualties by this time, as one is apt to do. I got a drink and joined Morgan by the fire.

"Well, Morgan, how did you like it? What do you think of the hunt?"

"Think of it? I think you're all crazy! You're all out of your minds, and I wouldn't dream of having anything to do with it!"

After that we couldn't even get Morgan on a horse for a gallop around the fields.

But not all my memories of Irish hunting are of disasters. There was a little train that ran from Dublin to Galway, and one day during a check next to the railroad tracks we heard its whistle in the distance. The hounds were on the tracks, and the Whips were frantically trying to collect them. The Field Master, Peter Patrick, Lord Hemphill, saw that there was some danger, so he rode hard back up the tracks and stopped the train. We got the hounds off the tracks and running again, and the hunt resumed. As the train passed by slowly, handkerchiefs fluttered out the windows. Peter Patrick doffed his high hat and made a sweeping bow to the train, which whistled in response. It could have happened only in Ireland.

Another time there were two coverts very close together across the road from a convent. The fox kept running back and forth between them. A group of novices came out to see what was going on. Suddenly the Mother Superior appeared and bore down on the novices like a thundercloud. At that moment the fox broke cover and ran in front of her. There is a sound you make when you see the fox. Not a clear "yoicks" (pronounced "hikes") but rather a bestial-sounding half-cry, half-growl. Mother Superior stopped in her tracks and gave this savage call. The Reverend Mother had apparently come from hunting stock.

By and large, the Irish are the best horsemen in the world, with the possible exception of the Afghans. The horse is the symbol of Ireland.

Many Irishmen divide their lives into periods when they had certain horses. When a man lives out seven or eight horses, he's led a long life. Long after they are able to hunt, you will see grandfathers or grandmothers—usually grandmothers—turning up at a hunt meeting mounted, with grandchildren beside them on ponies. So the child gets to know the form even before he is able to talk.

Christabel, Lady Ampthill, rode to hounds sidesaddle well into her seventies, resplendent in blue velvet jacket and divided skirt, high hat and veil. A number of women ride sidesaddle—it's actually a firmer seat than astride. Lady Ampthill had one of those very rare accidents: she got her foot caught in the stirrup and was dragged. The horse headed for a five-foot stone fence. Betty O'Kelly raced to the horse's head and stopped it a yard or two before it *and* Lady Ampthill went over. Lady Ampthill said, "I suppose I should thank you, my dear—but. my, it would have been a lovely way to go, wouldn't it?"

An old doctor would come out for the meeting of the Kildare hunt, maybe take a few fences, then go off home. One day while they were casting the hounds I congratulated the doctor on his horse's appearance. It was an old horse, but his hooves were polished, his mane was braided and he was beautifully turned out.

The doctor replied: "Huston, would you like to know how old this horse is?"

"Yes, I would."

"You won't tell anybody? In case I want to sell him or something?"

"I won't breathe it to a soul."

"Well, the horse is fifteen years old!"

"That's remarkable. He looks just marvelous, Doctor. It's a tribute to the care you've given him."

The doctor stared at me for a moment. Then he said: "Would you like to know how old *I* am, Huston?"

"Well—I'd like to, yes."

"Now, you won't tell anyone? You'll have to give me your word on this, for it's not good for a doctor to be too old."

"All right, Doctor, you have my solemn promise."

"I'm seventy-six!"

"That's wonderful, Doctor. That's just wonderful, the way you look— it is certainly the good life you've led."

The hounds were then away. We came to the first check and again the doctor and I were together. He looked at me speculatively for a while.

"Huston—I made the horse a few years younger than he is. I told you fifteen, didn't I?"

"Yes, that's what you said, Doctor."

"Well—the horse is twenty—and I'm eighty!"

Ricki wanted to hunt, but I was dead set against it. She had no aptitude as a rider. She had good balance and coordination from her training as a ballet dancer, but she couldn't get the hang of the horse. Ricki had been to riding school in the United States, and had received instruction from an Italian teacher. Again in France, at Chantilly, she had good private schooling. But she got nowhere. Finally, in Ireland, as a last resort, I undertook the task myself. I've always been against a member of the family teaching other members of the family to ride, because you must be very authoritarian, and the necessity all too often leads to recriminations, injured feelings and curses or tears. My tutoring was a complete failure. God, Ricki would fall! I told her, "Honey, you're just not meant to get on a horse's back."

But Ricki persisted. She undertook on her own to go to Colonel Joe Dudgeon, a very fine teacher and one of the great horsemen of the world. And where everyone else had failed, Colonel Dudgeon brought it all together. Ricki learned to sit on a horse's back at the walk, trot and gallop.

The idea of her hunting never entered my mind. But I went away to do a picture and when I got back that's what had happened. To prove it she had a broken front tooth and a permanent bump on her forehead. I tried to persuade her to give it up but if she heard me, she didn't let on. She took fall after fall. Once when her horse refused at a fence and I saw her go flying head over heels, I said to myself, "That was the mother of my children."

But she survived and, finally, there came the great day when Ricki didn't have a fall. Her courage had paid off in the long run and she was elated. It was late afternoon and Betty O'Kelly, Ricki and I were riding home together through a barnyard which was deep in muck. I glanced over my shoulder and saw Ricki's horse pawing the ground. I knew he was going to lie down and roll, and I yelled, "Ricki! Give him the whip!" She didn't do it fast enough, and the horse went down with her. The muck was so deep that Ricki just disappeared. She came up so covered with the stuff that she had to wipe her eyes to see. It was like a Mack Sennett comedy. She had been immaculate, and now she was mud and manure from head to toe. I started to laugh and couldn't stop. I was never forgiven.

20 From Courtown I used to drive out to Galway, Limerick and Cork with my horse in a trailer, for short tours of hunting. On one of these hunts—in Galway—we were crossing a field and I saw a house in the distance behind a ruined tower. I asked about it, and was told that its name was St. Clerans.

Some months later Ricki went out to stay with Derek Trench and his wife, Pat, for the Galway Race Meeting. Only in Dublin do you go to a hotel. Everyone knows everyone else in Ireland, and wherever you go you're someone's guest. The Old South in the United States must have been something like that. If you want to bring your horse for the hunt, both you and your horse are put up.

When Ricki came back, she mentioned having seen a beautiful old place named St. Clerans that was now vacant and for sale. I went right down to get a good look at it. St. Clerans was located near Galway City between Loughrea and Craughwell in Ireland's western coastal region. The house was in utter disrepair. The roof was leaking and the flooring gone, but the stonework was beautiful and the proportions were classic. It was a fine example of a Georgian manor house. The estate itself consisted of 100 Irish acres (about 110 U.S. acres), and the setting was extraordinary. There was an enormous vegetable garden and a great walled tree garden. Irish captains of sailing ships used to bring back trees from around the world, and at St. Clerans one of them had created a tree garden full of exotic species, bordered by flowers. I fell in love with the place instantly and decided to buy it.

St. Clerans was then owned by the Land Commission, and we purchased it at an auction. It cost very little to buy, but a small fortune and the better part of two years to restore.

The estate was in two sections, with the manor house to the fore. You walked down a gravel path through the trees and across a trout stream to get to the other section, where there were a thirteenth-century tower, the groom's quarters, stables and a lovely little steward's cottage. This cottage was the first building to be redone, and became Ricki's domain. It was here that she raised the children. Even after the big house was restored she still preferred the little house and spent most of her time there with the nurse, Tony and Anjelica. In this section, above the garages and stables, there were two spacious lofts, one of which I used for my studio. My assistant, Gladys Hill, lived in the other.

Gladys came to work for me in 1960. She had been Sam Spiegel's secretary, and in 1945, when I was doing some writing for Sam and Orson Welles on *The Stranger*, Sam sent Gladys out to Tarzana to work with me. According to Sam, she had no equal. He simply turned his life over to her—at least that part which bore scrutiny. After a few days of having quiet, reserved Gladys around I had to agree that Sam was absolutely right about her. She was a secretary nonpareil.

Gladys was fascinated by the paintings—by Soutine, Klee, Gris—and sculptures in the Tarzana house. She was particularly interested in the pre-Columbian art. I learned later that she wanted to know about various regions and styles. Following that brief initiation she started reading about Mexican art, visited the museums and dealers, bought a few small pieces and became quite knowledgeable. She left Sam in 1952 to marry an electrical engineer. They made their home in Mexico and began collecting. She developed an exceptional eye. To this day I'd take her word on West Coast material over that of anyone I know.

She and her husband were divorced, and in the fall of 1959 Gladys returned to Los Angeles. She took a temporary job with an independent producer who sent me a script, and with it was a note from Gladys telling me what she was doing. I happened to be without a secretary, so I sent her a cable: "Since you like to travel and since your job is temporary, why not come to Ireland and work for me forever and ever?"

Gladys accepted immediately and in a few weeks arrived at St. Clerans and took over my life, including the parts that don't bear scrutiny. She knows more about me than I know about myself—legally, medically and financially. She's weathered two of my marriages and various liaisons without being on the outs with anybody. Gladys manages to stay on good terms with whomever I happen to be involved.

I recognized early on that Gladys had a fine literary sense, and I learned to respect her judgment concerning scripts. Her criticisms, suggestions and contributions to the many screenplays I worked on had to be, in all fairness, recognized. Today she's my collaborator. She could now go on her own as a screenwriter. As a matter of fact, she's had an Academy Award nomination for one of her scripts.

Billy Pearson calls Gladys Hill "The Iron Maiden." It's true she's a model of rectitude—in all departments moral and ethical save one: smuggling. Here she's to be counted as one of the world's great criminals. She has no truck with nonsense like false backings and hidden compartments: those ploys are far beneath her. With Gladys it's entirely a matter of psychology. She knows she looks like the last person in the world to be carrying contraband. This knowledge is her sole armor in dealing with customs officials. She almost always hastens to open her bags. I've seen her proudly display an entire row of cardboard cartons tied with schoolgirl knots. She will start with them and wear the officials out, fumbling with knots, opening boxes, showing them dictionaries, files, manuscripts, office supplies—insisting, as well, on opening her typewriter case with every appearance of willingness to take out the machine for their examination. I once heard an official exclaiming disbelievingly, "*More* papers?" after which he chalked every single carton and suitcase in order to get rid of Miss Hill. On rare occasions, when there's a mob of people and mountains of luggage, she may ask blandly if it's really necessary—but it's said with her fingers on a combination lock or poised over a knot. It's more a matter of psychology than anything else. Gladys doesn't feel like a smuggler. She walks in virtue, so to speak. On that single occasion in Cairo when it was a conflict of wills between her antagonist and herself, he simply quailed before virtue. He couldn't believe she was a criminal.

Many of the art objects with which I filled St. Clerans arrived there as the direct result of Miss Hill's prowess as a smuggler.

Even before the restoration of St. Clerans was finished I began to collect things wherever I went around the world. From Japan I had an entire Japanese bath, with shoji doors and mats, sent over and installed. The bath accommodated up to six bathers, and was wonderful for after hunting. I saw a Kenzo screen in Japan which had a flowering stump with a bird on it—beautifully simple—and I asked a printmaker to reproduce it, which he did by means of the largest woodblocks ever made in Japan. We compared them with the original, and they were exact copies. You couldn't tell the difference except that the prints were signed by the maker. We used them for wallpaper in the dining room. In the drawing room there were silk curtains especially woven from an ancient Chinese pattern.

St. Clerans had three stories. The main entrance was on the second floor. The lower floor had a stone-and-concrete moat—a surround—that permitted full windows and plenty of light. It was here that I had the Japanese bath. I also installed a gallery for pre-Columbian art. There was an office for the estate manager, a storeroom, the wine cellar, an apartment for members of the staff and a lovely room we called the TV room. We only visited the TV room to see world soccer, horseracing, boxing matches, events we'd watch in groups, betting fiercely with one another.

The front part of the main floor had been added in 1820. There was a spacious entrance hall paved in Galway marble—a marble with the imprint of oyster and other fossil shells and plants—white against black. I put that in. The dining room and the drawing room were long and wide, identical in size, with bow windows. There was a large inner hall with a bar and the main staircase. The study was on one side of the inner hallway and the kitchen on the other. Off the kitchen were the pantry, the staff room and maids' rooms.

In the third-floor hallway two Chinese porcelain drum-stools flanked the Red Sitting Room—so-called from the color of its silk wallcoverings—in which there were beautiful Venetian cupboards. There were Chinese porcelain; Etruscan, Magna Grecia and Arrezzo ceramics; and paintings by Juan Gris and Morris Graves. Also on this floor was the Gray Room—a woman's bedroom, muted in color. In it there were Japanese screens and a collection of Japanese "fan paintings"—paintings made to be copied on fans. On the wall of the Gray Room, above the headboard (a Mexican colonial altarpiece), hung a fourteenth-century Sicilian carved wooden crucifix.

Another bedroom (there were five on this floor, all told) was called the Napoleon Room because of its canopied Empire bed. A Bhutan Room contained bronzes and fabrics from that little-known country. The fourth bedroom was the Gold Room—again because of its color—furnished with a charming old Irish bed of brass and painted porcelain, Georgian wardrobe and Georgian sofa table.

My room had a big, canopied four-poster Florentine matrimonial bed, carved with doves and flowers, two Louis XIV leather chairs with brass studs, a thirteenth-century Greek ikon and a chest of drawers which had originally been used for vestments in a French cathedral. All of the bedrooms were large, and all had fireplaces. Even the bathrooms had fireplaces.

I had old tiles imported from Mexico for the kitchen and all the bathrooms. The library-study featured mostly primitive art—African, Sepik River—and a few pieces of pre-Columbian. There were no paintings in the dining room—only the Japanese woodblocks. The table was a thirteen-foot mahogany Georgian three-pod, with chairs of the same period.

The drawing room was predominantly Louis XV, punctuated by artifacts: a Greek marble horse's head, Japanese screens from the Momoyama period, a Gandhara head, Egyptian eighteenth-dynasty pieces and a "Water Lily" painting by Monet.

I like to mix good art. The fact that pieces are not of the same period and culture doesn't mean that they will not go together. On the contrary, I think it is very interesting to mix periods, races and cultures. The very contrasts tend to show off the various pieces to better advantage.

As the years rolled by, we kept adding and changing. Gottfried Reinhardt gave me a Meissen chandelier from his father's castle in Salzburg; Ricki found a great marble-topped French table; Giacomo Manzu made me a gift of one of his bronze chairs with vegetables and . . . the list is too long!

The main entrance to the manor house was flanked by medieval stone lions I'd found in County Cork; in the courtyard there was a cast-iron figure of Punchinello which I discovered in the Paris Flea Market. St. Clerans has been described as one of the most beautiful homes in the world. For me, it was all of that and more.

I remember with nostalgia the lovely countryside, the horses and the people—those wonderful Irish people who were my neighbors. I had a constant stream of visitors with famous names—motion-picture stars, writers, musicians and painters—but my neighbors seldom had any idea who these people were. When they did, they were not in the least impressed. For them the only truly important thing in the world was the hunt. Hunting was enough.

Betty O'Kelly, small, fair, blue-eyed—another Irish witch—ran St. Clerans inside and out. When she wasn't hunting, she spent her daytime hours supervising the stables, arranging the breedings of the thoroughbred mares, getting them to the various stud farms and back again with their foals at their sides, buying calves, selling bullocks, consulting the staff as to the needs of the house and somehow still had time for her special love, the flower garden.

As a summertime occupation Betty and I—often accompanied by Ricki and Gladys—would drive through the back roads of Galway, Clare, Cork and Limerick looking for horses to buy. The best hunters result from the breeding of thoroughbreds to Irish draft mares or to mares half draft, half thoroughbred. Government-owned stallions were sent around the country to cover those mares. There was no stud fee. Once the colt or filly was born, the farmer had the keep of it until it was three years old, when it might be sold as a prospective hunter. It was usually a losing gamble for a farmer to raise a horse—he'd do better with three or four bullocks—but occasionally he got something worth the time and effort.

On our drives through the countryside Betty and I would spot horses in the distance, climb dry stone fences and cross fields to get a closer view. We came across some superb animals this way. We bought a number of them for under £200 that Betty and my groom, Paddy Lynch, broke, trained and sold. Among these animals, two won prizes at the Dublin Horse Show (a First middleweight hunter and a Reserve heavyweight hunter), and two went on to the Olympics.

Tommy Kelly, our vet, was a tiny man in his eighties who handled big, strong hunters with ease. I never saw a horse win the battle with Tommy. He was known throughout the British Isles. The British Bloodstock Agency wanted him to be its Head Veterinarian, but he refused. He loved Galway, the place where he was born, and wanted to be there and nowhere else. Tommy was out in his pickup day in and day out, starting at dawn. He would sometimes work with an animal the whole night through, and it made no difference whether it was a blood horse or a cow or a sheep. As Tommy once said, "A cow can be just as important to a poor farmer as a Derby candidate is to a bloodstock man."

Tommy was called to St. Clerans at least two or three times a month, and he dropped by on his own perhaps twice a week to look at the livestock and make sure everything was all right. He was paid once a year. I remember getting Tommy's first bill: £75! It wasn't enough that we owed him ten times that amount. I told Betty to see that it was taken care of, but she said, no, that that would offend Tommy.

Our medical doctor from nearby Loughrea, Dr. Martyn Dyar, was of the same cut as Tommy Kelly. Gladys once sent him an amount in excess of his very moderate bill, and he called her on it. She covered her tracks by saying the excess was intended as a donation to the Home for the Aged, of which he was the guiding light.

Dyar had taken over an old building in Loughrea, still remembered as "The Workhouse" from famine times when paupers were sent to it. It had become an Old People's Home, but its fearful reputation persisted. It was said that once you were in, you never came out alive. Under Dr. Dyar, it changed; you could hardly imagine old people in a happier environment. The nuns there took care of them as if they were their own fathers or mothers. The place and its inmates were kept spotless. Those who were able to go out on the town, could. They were even given small amounts of money to bet on the races, buy a "jar" or two or have tea in the town. There were no recriminations if anyone came back after-drink-taken. None of the usual institutional restrictions were laid on them. I know of no other country which supports such an establishment. I'm not sure even Ireland has another like it.

Dyar was an affable man. After a visit he'd have his drink and hold forth with jokes for twenty minutes or so before continuing his rounds. His office was in his home in Loughrea, and it was a clutter. There were stacks of medical manuscripts and books piled around a Bunsen burner, a microscope, a glass instrument case and a sink. But he was a very fine doctor. Two or three serious illnesses and as many hunting accidents occurred at St. Clerans while he was in attendance, and his diagnosis and treatment invariably proved correct.

Martin Tierney, from Loughrea, worked briefly at St. Clerans. He lived to shoot and fish. I used to take him out with Tony, and whenever we were talking about dapping on a lake when the mayflies were hatching or making plans to shoot snipe in frost-rimmed fields, Martin would, like a good dog, begin to tremble with excitement. Work as a houseman wasn't for him, so he emigrated to the United States, were he had relatives in Boston.

Martin arrived in Boston when a sportsmen's convention and show was under way. He talked to shooters and fishermen and, being fresh from Ireland, he was listened to. At the fly-casting exhibition Martin watched for a time and then remarked: "Tony Huston can cast as well as that!"

"Who's Tony Huston?"

"John Huston's son in Ireland. He can cast better than your fly-casters can cast, and he's only twelve years old!"

There were some good fly-casters present, and Martin's remarks ruffled a few feathers. He was invited to take a rod and cast a fly himself. Martin was of course an expert, and he dropped the fly lightly dead center of the ring. The spectators applauded, and Martin said, "Ah, that's nothin' compared with what Tony Huston can do—and he's only twelve years old!"

I once had a broken knee from a fall out hunting and entered the Regional Hospital in Galway. It was run by the Blue Sisters, a nursing order, and I recommend them to anyone thinking of breaking a leg, arm or neck. They had no false modesty. They'd give me a bath, washing the upper and lower portions of my body, then hand me a wet cloth and say, "There now. You do the middle part yourself!" In the evening, after the visitors had gone and just before lights out, one of the Sisters would come around and say, "Mr. Huston, would you like a little nightcap? It will help you to go to sleep." So I'd have my nightcap. She'd go, and a few minutes later another Sister would come in. "Would you like to have a little nightcap, Mr. Huston?" I never went to sleep sober. Sometimes I'd have four or five nightcaps.

Ireland is ninety-six percent Catholic. I wanted it known immediately that I had no orthodox religion, so I announced right off the bat that I was an atheist. And I had the feeling they were particularly nice to me. "He's a good fellow who's surely going to hell, so why not make things as pleasant as possible for him—temporarily?" They certainly did that.

In 1964 I became an Irish citizen. Shortly afterward my newfound countrymen tied the knot in the bow by awarding me the honorary title of Doctor of Literature at Trinity University in Dublin. Although my artistic contributions to the world were extolled, the occasion was also tinged with a bit of Irish provincialism: "Recently—and this is a particular reason for us to rejoice—[Huston] has become an Irish citizen and lives in Galway, where, they say, the local foxes have learned to fear his prowess as a hunter. . . . Lots of people can write, direct and act in films, but few can sit well an Irish hunter."

After a year or so of riding with the Galway Blazers, I was approached one day by the Master of the Hunt, Paddy Pickersgill, and Derek Trench. Paddy's part of the financial burden of the hunt had become too heavy for him to carry. They asked me if I would consent to be the Joint Master. I told them there were other members better qualified than myself and offered to increase my contribution to the hunt if that was the major problem. But they insisted. I subsequently spent ten years with the Galway Blazers as Joint Master. They were ten of the best years of my life.

I've had four great hunters in my lifetime, and three of them were in Ireland: Naso, Daisy Belle and Frisco. Naso was a powerhouse, about sixteen-three, enormously strong and with a great leap. The biggest jump I've ever taken was on Naso's back. He was determined to take it; I wasn't. I just went along for the ride. Naso took a bit of a hold. When the hounds were running, he was an animal of very strong opinions. He knew just where he wanted to go, and it was hell trying to make him go anywhere else. That wasn't all bad, for rarely did he make a mistake and jump where he shouldn't. He'd take on jumps of a size that were sometimes startling, but if you had faith, he'd usually see you through.

It's a pretty good piece of advice when things are desperate with you and your horse to throw your reins away and take a handful of mane. Leave it up to the horse. Give him as much freedom as you possibly can, and there's a good likelihood of him getting you out of trouble.

I rode Naso once in a steeplechase I'll never forget. The first steeplechase ever was supposed to have taken place in the eighteenth century in County Limerick. A Colonel Savage said to a Captain Slaughter, "Sir, I'll race you to that steeple!"

"Point to Point" then meant from the spire of one church to another. The steeplechase I speak of was over a five-mile course at a place called Buttevant. Each hunt in Ireland sent three riders as entrants, and Tim Durant, Betty O'Kelly and I represented the Kildare Hounds.

Lining up for the start, there were over seventy horses gathered more or less shoulder to shoulder. I had the devil of a time with Naso. He was being a menace. Naso didn't give a damn about protocol. He didn't want to just go through the other horses, he wanted to go right over them! So I had to circle him once and let the field string out after the start. But then we made up ground until after a couple of miles I was lying fourth and hadn't yet let Naso extend himself. A little lunatic named Pat Hogan was in the lead, two fields ahead of me; Betty was one field ahead of me; and another rider and I were in the same field, with him a little ahead.

I saw Pat Hogan stop his horse. Then he disappeared. I knew he had run into something up ahead, but I didn't know what. It was supposed to be against the rules to walk or ride this course beforehand, but that ruling had been dropped before the race. We hadn't known about this change in time to take advantage of it, but obviously Pat Hogan had.

Where Pat had stopped his horse, Betty and the other rider disappeared going all-out. Pat had been reining in because he knew what was ahead, but the other two didn't have time to stop their horses. I tried to turn Naso. It was no use. He had taken hold of his bit and wasn't about to slow down. Next thing we were in the air headed for a steep, stone-faced embankment overlooking a road. Naso saw what awaited us, and he turned in mid-flight, unseating me. I hit the embankment hard and had the breath knocked out of me, but I wasn't hurt. When I got to my knees, I saw the other rider trying to pull Betty off the road before the rest of the field came on. Betty was unconscious. The man was having a hard time of it. He turned to me and said, "Ah, Huston, me tail's broke!" So it was—he had a fractured coccyx. Together we pulled Betty out of the way. Luckily, the riders behind us realized that the place was a trap and reined their horses in. Of course Pat Hogan went on to win the race.

I always rode with a snaffle, never with a double rein. Most Irish horses are ridden with a snaffle bit because there are many surprises in a hunting field and you don't want to risk hurting your horse's mouth as you can with a bar or curb bit. But this had its drawbacks with Naso. You exerted whatever influence you could, but a snaffle bit wasn't especially effective with him. After Naso it was always a luxury to ride Daisy Belle and be able to choose which way you wanted to go.

Daisy Belle, sixteen-two, had a beautiful mouth. With her, all that was required was a touch of the reins and she knew exactly what you wanted to do, and did it for you.

I remember a jump she once made over a very narrow gate with wire on top. The jump was over six feet, and I had my doubts about it, but as we approached the gate, I felt a surge of power in her and her certainty that she was going to clear it. And she did. No other horse behind me even tried it. The hunt took a turn and we came back the same way, and she did it again. Daisy Belle liked vertical rather than horizontal jumps. She didn't like the ditches. She'd go over them, but with little enthusiasm. With Naso it didn't matter. It was all the same with him, up or across. Anything.

Frisco was the last horse I had in Ireland. He was about sixteen hands, not strongly built, but a horse of great courage and consistency. He never had the leap that Naso had, but point him at something and he'd have a crack at it. He never refused. His attitude was: "If you're game, I am, so hang on!"

We photographed a fox-hunt for *The List of Adrian Messenger*, and it took some doing. It is all but impossible to photograph a real hunt, for there is no way of knowing which way the fox will run. We had to lay down an aniseed scent over a predetermined course. Although I was Joint Master of the Galway Blazers, I was voted down in the matter of using the Galway Blazer hounds. The members didn't want the stigma attached to having our hounds follow a drag rather than a real fox, even though it was for a motion picture. The Dublin Harriers were not as sensitive about this. Their Master, Michael O'Brien (in his eighties today and still going strong), and the members of his hunt agreed to be in the film and to let us use their pack.

My twelve-year-old son, Tony, played the part of a young peer whose life was being plotted against. His death was to look like an accident in the hunt. He had a beautiful little gray—Connemara with a lot of Arab in him. The two of them were a perfect match.

There was one particularly hairy jump, I recall, and, rather than risk Tony before it was all perfectly set up, they had a professional take a horse over. He fell and continued to fall. Tony said, "Let me try it." We all held out breath, but Tony took his pony over effortlessly.

A child can very often do things with a horse that an adult can't. This is particularly true of little girls. If you have a problem animal, put him into the company of a bunch of little girls who like horses. They'll accomplish miracles. Pretty soon they'll be sliding down his neck, walking around under his belly and climbing all over him. And he'll let them—a horse that you wouldn't have gotten within an arm's length of before. I wouldn't recommend trying this with a confirmed outlaw, but, for most horses, little girls are the greatest trainers in the world.

Each year, on the 20th of December, Paddy the groom, Brian the handy man and Johnny the second gardener would bring in a tree—a big, tall

21 tree that took up one whole corner of the inner hall and rose up through the stairwell to the floor above. The children and Betty decorated it, and all the gifts were piled beneath it.

Christmas Eve we had a party for the staff and neighboring farmers—usually about twenty adults and twice as many children. The children were scrubbed to a high gloss, and they, their parents, other friends and ourselves waited together for Santa. Soon we'd hear his sleigh bells jingling; then there would be a hammering on the big front door, the sound echoing around the entrance hall. The kids' faces would be either absolutely drained of color—livid white—or a pulsating red.

Betty would open the door. Santa, in traditional costume, would come into the house and go to the tree. The one question that was never raised, never uttered and, I believe, never considered by the children was: How did the presents get *inside* the house before Santa arrived in his sleigh, and how did he know they were there?

Santa's assistant, Betty, would hand him a gift and whisper a name, which Santa would repeat at the top of his voice. As their names were called and they were given their presents with Santa's praises ringing in their ears, each recipient said, "Thank you, Santa" in exactly the same strangled voice. One voice would have served for all.

When all the gifts had been distributed to children and adults alike, Paddy Lynch would ask for three cheers for Mr. Huston—Hip! Hip! Hooray!—a touching moment for the squire. Then we would drift into the kitchen, where food and drink awaited, and enjoy ourselves. There was singing, recitations of poetry, dancing, and tales of the old days by such as our gardener, Odie Spellman, retired at age eighty-five. It was grand.

Our regular Santa was a neighbor, Tommy Holland. One year he was sick, and, after much convincing, our guest John Steinbeck agreed to fill in. He docilely accepted the ministrations of Anjelica and her friend Joan

Buck as they adjusted his raiment and stuck on his white beard and eyebrows with spirit gum. He was a great Santa, although he claimed to have spat cotton each time his prompter gave him a name to say.

Christmas morning we would assemble between ten and eleven in our best robes and slippers. No presents could be touched until we all were together. Creagh would serve champagne as we opened our gifts, sitting on the floor or on the hall benches or having a good view of the proceedings from the stairs.

About 12:30 the County arrived. The same people came at almost the same time every year, bringing with them their children and their guests: Ann and Peter Patrick Hemphill, Maria and Edmond Mahony, Anita Leslie and Bill King, Pat and Derek Trench, Eileen and Tommy Kelly, Bea and Dick Lovett, Ellie and Fifi French. We toasted one another, and tree presents were exchanged.

At three o'clock Creagh would announce dinner. Christmas dinner was never for less than fourteen. The Creaghs, Margaret McCarty, Mary Bodkin and Paddy Coyne did everything to perfection: Irish linen, Georgian silver, old Waterford glass, hothouse flowers and, naturally, fruit cakes and plum pudding made in October and carefully mellowed with brandy.

Boxing Day, December 26, was a grand hunt event throughout Ireland. The Galway Blazers had a lawn meet at St. Clerans. When we returned at the end of the day, the house was full: musicians with tin whistles and accordions, fiddles, sometimes a brass instrument and always a singer or two. Anjelica, Mary Lynch and little Karen Creagh joined in the Irish dances. Karen was to win over 300 medals in Irish dancing competitions as she was growing up, and even at six she was outstanding.

"Wren Boys" wandered through. These were little boys from the neighborhood, always masked and in outlandish attire. You would be careful not to recognize them as they sang, danced, recited or put on some kind of dialogue. When they had done their turn and been given a few coins, they dashed for the front door to repeat the performance elsewhere.

Elaine and John Steinbeck were among our regular Christmas guests at St. Clerans. John had a low, deep voice that came out of his chest. Although it wasn't loud, you could almost feel the vibration. John never took over a conversation or held forth, but often his remarks were memorable. One day someone remarked that Seamus, my Irish wolfhound, was the biggest damned wolfhound he'd ever seen. Steinbeck said, "Yes, and he packs flat, too!" John was one of the least vain men I've ever known. He told me he didn't think he merited the Nobel Prize. It was one of the few things I disagreed with him on—that and his support of Lyndon Johnson. But his appraisals of people and things were so honest you couldn't quarrel with them; you could only differ.

John became fascinated by the story of Daly, our resident ghost. Some two hundred years earlier a man by that name was accused of shooting at the gamekeeper of St. Clerans. The gamekeeper was also a bailiff. For an Irishman to fire a gun at such a functionary was punishable by death.

Daly's defense was that he was such a good shot that if he had wanted to kill the bailiff, he wouldn't have missed. He insisted he was innocent.

The judge, a Burke who owned St. Clerans, pronounced sentence on Daly: he was to hang.

The gallows was about a mile away from St. Clerans on top of a small hill. The ladies in the Burke family secretly watched the execution from two windows of an upstairs bedroom on the south side. After the hanging, the windows were blocked up so there was no view of the hanging ground from the house, and they remained so until I bought St. Clerans. In restoring the house, I had them opened up again despite the locals' warnings that if I did so, Daly's ghost would surely come into the place— and that's how we inherited him.

After Daly's death his mother pronounced a widow's curse upon the Burkes. "No Burke will ever die peaceable in his bed again," she said, "and no rooks will ever again nest at St. Clerans." I understand that Burkes tended to meet violent deaths to the end of their tenure there, and although there are rookeries all around St. Clerans, the birds never build nests on the estate proper. Whether this is after the fact or not I don't know. I do know that grass never grows on the spot where the gallows stood.

You could often hear our ghost walking in the hallways. Doors and windows opened and shut with nobody near them, and on two occasions when I was in residence in St. Clerans, people saw Daly. He was always in knee breeches and had on a long, full-sleeved shirt. I, like others, can say that I've heard Daly, but who knows for certain how to distinguish such sounds from the creaks and groans of a big house?

John Steinbeck wanted to pursue the story of Daly, and made inquiries of a priest in Loughrea who was an authority. The priest corroborated one part of the story we had heard: that, after Daly's hanging, another man had on his deathbed confessed to having shot at the bailiff. Yes, Daly was innocent. But the priest advised John against writing anything on the subject. The sad episode had occurred only two centuries before, and it was too soon, the priest said, to bring the matter up again.

The Irish believe deeply in ghosts, for sound reasons. They also believe in the Banshee—who wails to foretell a death—and in hosts of the Little People. A Fairy Circle is the enclosure made by a circle of yew trees, deliberately planted to grow in this manner. The fear of and respect for these places goes back to Druidical times, perhaps even earlier. The design of the new airport at Dublin had to be changed because one of the runways would have cut through a Fairy Circle and the workmen would neither enter it nor permit its destruction. I am by no means certain that there is any connection between the Irish respect for the supernatural and their love for strong drink, but I've sometimes thought there might be.

When I first went to Ireland, you could be sure that if ever you entered a shop or a place of business in town, you'd be offered a drink. I remarked one day that the only place I hadn't been offered a drink was the bank. And I'll be damned if the very next time I wasn't called back to the bank manager's office for a jar.

Yet for all the drinking you don't see many drunks around. The rowdy Irish boozer is oftener seen on New York's Third Avenue than in the Old Country. Which is not to say that the lads on their bicycles weaving home from the country pub at night always view the world with the clear eye of sobriety. I recall one who fell off, landing in a thorn tree. His story was that he had been attacked by two otters. One otter knocked him off his bicycle, and then the other ran at him before he could recover.

St. Clerans was a wonderful haven. When I came back from a trip abroad and entered that atmosphere, it was a world apart. The style of life was charming. People dressed for dinner—women in long gowns, men in black ties or even formal attire for members of the hunt: scarlet tailcoats with white silk lapels. It was as beautiful and as fantastic as a masquerade. We ate dinner by the light of fifty candles, and in the winter the hearth was always going. This was a life style that had existed for hundreds of years, but by the time I moved to Ireland it was already a dying tradition.

Witness Dunsandle. Bose Daly, the inheritor and master, would mount his horse from the front steps, then, returning from the hunt, would dismount onto the same steps. Legend had it that his foot never touched the earth. Daly came back from the war, having distinguished himself, and resumed his duties as Master of the Galway Blazers.

The house itself was one of the most beautiful in all Ireland, and Daly lived a life steeped in tradition and circumstance. Like a king he was. Then he made the mistake of falling in love with an English actress and divorced his wife of many years. From then on it was steps down for Daly. The entire community took his action amiss. The Bishop wouldn't bless the hounds, farmers refused him permission to ride over their lands, the number of fox-hunters dwindled to a handful and Daly was generally shunned by his neighbors and former friends.

Finally he left Dunsandle, which then went to ruin. It shouldn't have been allowed to happen, but the place was eventually torn down. At last report—about the time I moved to St. Clerans—Daly had married his actress and was living down in Cork in modest circumstances. I understand he was reduced to watching golf matches on television.

Then there was Derek Trench. Derek and his wife, Pat, were perhaps our most constant visitors at St. Clerans. They lived about twenty miles away in an enormous Victorian manor house called Woodlawn—built on a grand scale, like Buckingham Palace. It possessed some 600 acres, with a lake, streams, "pleasure grounds," gardens, hothouses and all the accouterments of a great estate.

Derek was an ex-Guardsman whose family had been in Ireland since the twelfth century on one side and the fifteenth century on the other. He was Anglo-Irish, very brave and able in the hunting field and quite "Old English" in his mannerisms, with a Guardsman's accent of the sort designed not to be understood by the lower class.

Then Derek began to feel the money pinch. When I moved to Ireland, the cost of a household staff was so low that it tempted you to indulge yourself, which Derek and I and others did. Then inflation began. Costs rose and kept rising. Anyone on a fixed income was in trouble. Not that Ireland became more expensive than other countries, but it became, year by year, *as* expensive. Many of us found ourselves sadly overcommitted— huge estates with large staffs, expensive grounds to maintain, stables and entertainment on a lavish scale. The only way one could afford it, finally, was to have sufficient land suitable for farming, or some other way of making the estate pay for itself. Few did. They were more concerned with the hunt than with learning modern farming and—ignoring the danger signals—waited until too late to make the necessary changes.

Derek and Pat started by closing down most of the main house—a structure of some sixty rooms—and converting a few rooms into an apartment with a small kitchen. One by one, they let the servants go, keeping only an old woman who had been with the family since Derek was a child. Then they sold all but half a dozen horses. Taxes continued to mount, and Derek was eventually forced to sell Woodlawn to the Land

Commission. I thought it was with the understanding that he and Pat would be allowed to live there for the rest of their lives.

My turn came. I had spent eighteen glorious years in St. Clerans, but at last I had to give it up. The decision was forced upon me. It became so expensive to run that I had to stay away and work in order to maintain it. I had little time to enjoy the house or the hunt; some years I only made it back for Christmas.

If I had purchased a place with enough land for farming, I could have survived, but at the time I bought St. Clerans the salaries of employees were inconsiderable and I felt no need for that kind of insurance. Even when salaries doubled, the cost was acceptable, but when they quadrupled, I began to feel it. I cut down the staff from sixteen to twelve, but from then on it was money up the spout. So one sad day I sold it all—the house and almost everything in it, except for a few works of art. I sometimes feel that I sold a little bit of my soul when I let St. Clerans go.

One of the hardest things for me was parting with the staff. The Creaghs and Paddy Lynch had been with me almost twenty years, and they were marvelous people. When I broke up the establishment, I helped the Creaghs and the nurse, Kathleen Shine, to purchase homes, and Paddy Lynch to buy into a pub. They would all be in comfortable circumstances, but I hated to see that idyllic existence we shared disappear.

I put Gladys Hill in complete charge of closing St. Clerans. She made the decisions about what was to be sold at auction, what to be sold to dealers, what to be stored. To this day I don't know any of the details. I don't want to know.

I remember how I'd look out in the mornings at the foals being led into the fields with their dams. Then, like beautiful little watches, they'd unwind and you'd see that opening run. It was special. Everyone felt it.

After I sold St. Clerans I heard that Derek's and Pat's tenure under the Land Commission had been a short one and that they had moved into the steward's quarters of a Victorian castle called Lough Coutra. The next time I was in Ireland I went down to Galway to see them. They had a little apartment in pleasant surroundings, and I assumed that all of their difficulties were resolved—they seemed well off and happy. It was summer. The horses were turned out and there was no hunting, but I was sure that when the season opened Pat and Derek would be back in the saddle.

When the season came around, Derek didn't have a horse. He had sold them all. On opening day he stocked his van with oysters and champagne and followed the hunt, sharing this repast with the riders when they went from covert to covert.

Then Derek went home and took his gun out to the fields to shoot pheasant. It got later and later, and finally his dog—a chocolate-colored Labrador retriever—came home alone. Pat went out and found him: Derek had had an accident. His going was a long step toward the end of an era.

Claude Cockburn's ploy of leaving his "James Helvick" novel, *Beat the Devil*, on my nightstand at Oonagh's home had worked. I thought I saw a picture in the book.

22 Claude, a friend of many years, had been a roving correspondent for the London *Times* in the 1930s and his byline was one of the best known in Europe. He quit the *Times* to start a political tip sheet called *The Week*, which was read by important newspaper people everywhere. When World War II was declared, security measures caused many of Claude's sources to dry up. He retired to County Limerick in Ireland, where he and his wife had property. Claude was running short on cash when he wrote *Beat the Devil* as a potboiler. If he'd signed his own name to it, it might have been a success; as it was, he badly needed the money that a motion-picture sale would give him.

I called Bogie, who then had a film company with Morgan Maree, and told him about the book. He bought it on my say for $10,000, which made Claude very happy.

Some time later Morgan Maree telephoned me from the States. "What about this book? When are we going to make a film of it?"

I told him I hadn't given it any thought.

"John—you got Bogie to buy the damned thing!"

I said I'd see what I could do. I didn't want to write the screenplay myself, so I gave it to Peter Viertel and Tony Veiller. They wrote a script which wasn't very good, then washed their hands of it. Before the script was finished, the picture was cast. Jennifer Jones and Peter Lorre had already been hired, and we were about ready to roll. When I arrived in Italy, I still didn't have a script or a scriptwriter. But it just so happened that Truman Capote was in Rome. I hardly knew Truman, although we had met. I told him that I needed help badly, and asked if he would give me a hand. Fortunately, he agreed, because we probably could never have made the picture without him.

We weren't going to have a chance to start writing until we reached Ravello, the little town south of Naples where we were going to shoot. I knew it was going to be nip-and-tuck. The money for the film was being put up by a conglomerate of backers that included Roberto Haggiag, the Woolf brothers and Bogart himself.

In Rome I told Bogie that we were in a desperate situation. "We haven't got a script, and I don't know what the hell is going to come of this," I said. "It may be a disaster. In fact, it's got all the earmarks of a disaster."

Bogie was not known to be profligate with a buck, but he turned to me with that crooked grin of his. "Why, John, I'm surprised at you. Hell, it's only money!"

That stiffened my back. You can't argue with somebody like that, so we went ahead to do the best we could.

When we were ready to leave Rome, Roberto Haggiag provided Bogie and me with a Mercedes and driver. The car was a fine machine, but I had my doubts about the driver. We were on our way to Naples when the road branched, one fork going to Monte Cassino and the other to Naples. The driver couldn't make up his mind which road to take, so he went straight ahead, right over an island, through a heavy stone wall and into a ditch. I was up front, so I had a chance to brace myself, but Bogie was asleep on the back seat. When we came to a stop, I looked back to see how he was. He was lying on the floor. "Bogie, are you all right?" I asked. Somewhat groggily, he pulled himself up so he could look over the back of my seat. "Chrith, no! Somethin'th happen t' my tongue!" He stuck his tongue out. A piece of it was split over into a flap like a little trapdoor. Moreover, all his front teeth—actually a full bridge—had been knocked out. When I realized he wasn't seriously hurt, I couldn't help laughing. Bogie glared at me. "John, you thun-of-a-bith! You dirty, no-good thun-of-a-bith!" Figures soon approached out of the darkness, chattering excitedly in Italian. There was a garage nearby, to which our damaged vehicle was towed. We rented another car to continue our journey. The driver was unhurt and, thank God, chastened.

We called ahead and arrangements were made for Bogie to go directly to a hospital in Naples. A doctor stitched his tongue, and a new bridge was ordered from his dentist in California. Waiting for Bogie's teeth delayed things for a week or so and gave Truman and me a chance to work on the script.

Jack Clayton, now a fine director, was the production manager, and he was in our conspiracy to stall for time. We didn't want the company to know that the script wasn't ready, so Jack announced that I didn't want the actors to see their lines until just before we shot a scene. He explained that I was experimenting with a new technique, trying to encourage a more spontaneous approach to the material. But, in spite of his fast talk, the picture caught up with us.

There was a section written by Viertel and Veiller that just didn't work. I knew it was going to take time to fix it. In a desperate delaying action, I went down and staged a scene so elaborately that the carpenters had to remove "wild" walls and make all sorts of alterations. I figured it would take the crew at least half a day to get ready to shoot, plus rehearsal time. While they were preparing the set, Truman and I went upstairs and wrote an entire new scene. That's how close it was.

Truman Capote was remarkable. I remember finding him one evening with his face swollen and lopsided—he had an impacted wisdom tooth. Although in considerable pain, he was still working. We called an ambulance. Truman asked for his purple Balmain shawl, one that Jennifer had given him. We wrapped him in it and saw him off. That same night new pages of script arrived from the hospital! Truman was all courage.

One night there was arm wrestling. Bogie and Truman were engaged, and it almost became a fight. It did, in fact, turn into a wrestling match. And Truman took Bogie! He pinned Bogie's shoulders to the floor and held him there. Truman's epicene comportment was downright deceptive: he was remarkably strong and had pit bulldog in him.

David Selznick visited the set from time to time. He had no connection with the picture except that his wife, Jennifer Jones, was in it. It didn't matter: when she signed a contract, David started his memorandums.

Throughout *Beat the Devil* I would get memorandums from him, mostly by cable, concerning production and recommendations for scenes, and on and on, ad infinitum. David numbered the pages of his cables. Some ran ten to twelve pages—or more. One day, after receiving a particularly long cable from David, I sent him a cable back. Page one answered various points he had made. I then omitted page two and jumped to page three. From then on I answered anything he asked me by replying: "Refer page two my cable X date." I understand this drove him right up the wall. It was rough on the cable company, too, because David was out to find page two.

The town of Ravello is high up in the mountains behind Sorrento. An old city, reputed to have been a pirates' lair, it is famous for a grand villa that overlooks the sea where Greta Garbo and Stokowski stayed during their much-publicized romantic holiday. A good deal of the picture was shot at this villa.

The surrounding mountains are terraced and planted with grapes and fruit trees, very carefully laid out so that when the fruit trees are bare, the grapes get the sun. Some of the best wine in Italy is made in Ravello— a white and a rosé.

Every evening, and sometimes all Saturday night into Sunday morning, poker was played by members of the cast and crew. When Truman and I weren't working on the script, we were sitting in on the poker game. I'm afraid Bogie and I rather dominated the table. Bob Capa, who was there to take promotion shots, and Truman were our main victims. Their services on the picture came pretty cheap because we regularly won back whatever salaries were paid them.

One night during a game the fumes got to me. I got up, fixed myself a martini and strolled out onto the terrace, marveling at my surroundings. Below me, the bay with the sodium lights on the fishing boats was making constellations to rival those above. Suddenly through my reverie, I realized I was falling, glass in hand. Luckily a tree broke my fall and I dropped through it to the ground.

As we figured it out later, it had been a fall of some forty feet but, miraculously, I was quite unhurt. The cliff from which I'd fallen was almost perpendicular, and there was no way of getting back up without assistance. I called for help and presently was rescued. I made myself another martini and returned to my place at the table.

There was a general air of gaiety and lightheartedness throughout the picture. The book is about a young English couple's adventures with a group of ridiculous thieves. Everyone in it is an eccentric. The book is funny, but the humor in the script was broadened further and the absurdities were accentuated. Jack Clayton, Truman and I would look at the rushes and wonder whether others would think it as funny as we did. They didn't.

Beat the Devil was ahead of its time. Its off-the-wall humor left viewers bewildered and confused. A few critics hailed it as a little masterpiece . . . but they were all European. There was not an American among them. But slowly, despite its early reception, the picture began to attract audiences, particularly in university towns. Now it has a cult following. *Beat the Devil* has done well over the years. I only wish Bogie could have been around to see this happen.

It was the last picture I made with Bogie. I was working on *Moby Dick* in 1956 when I heard that he had had an operation on his throat. It was then thought that he was going to recover with no problems.

Some time later, at the St. Regis Hotel in New York, I was about to return to Ireland. Downstairs, ready to check out, I was told there was a call for me. I took it in the lobby. The call was from Betty Bogart and Morgan Maree. Betty said, "John, brace yourself. We know that you're leaving, but I wanted to tell you myself. Bogie is going to die. We don't know how soon—maybe some months from now—but the cancer is terminal. I'd like you to write the eulogy so that in case you're not here when he dies, it can be read by someone else." I could hardly speak. It was a great shock. When I got to Courtown, I tried to write something, but found it absolutely impossible.

I did get back to the States before Bogie died, and every evening we would gather at his house—just a few of his very close friends. He was losing weight steadily. The cords of his neck stood out, and his eyes were enormous in his gaunt face. Betty decided not to tell Bogie the truth of his condition. I'm not sure whether that was the correct choice, but we went along. One night Betty, Bogie's doctor, Morgan Maree and I were all sitting around in his living room when Bogie said, "Look, give me the lowdown. You aren't kidding me, are you?" I took a deep breath and held it. The doctor finally assured Bogie that it was the treatments he had undergone that were making him feel badly and lose weight. Now that he was off the treatments, he should improve rapidly. Then we all chimed in compounding the falsehood. He seemed to accept it.

When I spoke a few words of farewell at Bogie's funeral on January 17, 1957, I described these last days.

> Bogie's hospitality went far beyond food and drink. He fed a guest's spirit as well as his body, plied him with good will until he was drunk in the heart as well as in the legs. This tradition continued until the last hour he was able to sit upright. Let me tell you with what effort it was extended through the last days.
>
> He would lie on his couch upstairs at five o'clock, to be shaved and groomed and dressed in gray flannels and scarlet smoking jacket. When he was no longer able to walk, his emaciated body would be lifted into a wheelchair and pushed to a dumbwaiter on the second-floor landing. The top of the dumbwaiter had been removed to give him headroom. His nurses would help him in, and, sitting on a little stool, he would be lowered down to the kitchen, where another transfer would be made and, again by wheelchair, he'd be transported through the house into the library and his chair. And there he would be, sherry glass in one hand and cigarette in the other, at five thirty when the guests started to arrive. They were limited now to those who had known him best and longest, and they stayed, two and three at a time, for a half hour or so until about eight o'clock, which was the time for him to go back upstairs by the same route he had descended. No one who sat in his presence during those final weeks will ever forget. It

was a unique display of sheer animal courage. After the first visit—that visit was spent getting over the initial shock—one quickened to the grandeur of it, expanded and felt strangely elated, proud to be there, proud to be his friend, the friend of such a brave man. . . .

My last words said, I believe, what we all felt about Bogie: "We have no reason to feel any sorrow for him—only for ourselves for having lost him. He is quite irreplaceable. There will never be another like him." More than twenty years later I am more convinced than ever that this is true.

Moby Dick was the most difficult picture I ever made. I lost so many battles during it that I even began to suspect that my assistant director was plotting against me. Then I realized that it was only God. God had a perfectly good reason. Ahab saw the White Whale as a mask worn by the Deity, and he saw the Deity as a malignant force. It was God's pleasure to torment and torture man. Ahab didn't deny God, he simply looked on him as a murderer—a thought that is utterly blasphemous: "Is Ahab Ahab? Is it I, God, or who, that lifts this arm? . . . Where do murderers go? . . . Who's to doom, when the judge himself is dragged to the bar?"

23

The picture, like the book, is a blasphemy, so I suppose we can just lay it to God's defending Himself when He sent those awful winds and waves against us.

I've heard people say they have read *Moby Dick* as a child. This brands them instantly as liars. They may have read schoolroom versions of it, but no one who isn't at least in his late teens—and very mature for his age— could contend with those pages. Translating a work of this scope into a screenplay was a staggering proposition. Looking back now, I wonder if it is possible to do justice to *Moby Dick* on film.

I had read a number of short stories by Ray Bradbury, and saw something of Melville's elusive quality in his work. Ray had indicated that he would like to collaborate with me, so when it came time to do the screenplay, I asked him to join me in Ireland.

Ray is the best argument I know of for those who believe that Hal Croves was B. Traven. Highly original in his writing, from the idea itself to the very turn of a sentence, in casual intercourse Ray spoke entirely in clichés and platitudes. This man, who sent people on exploratory flights to the distant stars, was terrified of airplanes. You could hardly coax him into a car. I remember driving into Dublin one morning with Ray. We had a careful driver, who was proceeding at a moderate speed. I was in the front seat. I murmured just loud enough for Ray to hear, "You're taking it a little too fast, driver. Slow down." Ray immediately said, "Yes, slow down, for God's sake!" The driver looked at me with a confused expression. I winked. He caught on and slowed down. We were now doing about twenty miles an hour on an open highway. "For Chrissake, man! Do you want to kill us all?" I exclaimed. Ray was now practically crying. When we got down to ten miles an hour, Ray was still begging the driver to slow down.

Before we started filming, to assist us in fabricating the models I asked that a series of drawings be made of all the scenes involving whales—from the normal hunt and harpooning to sighting the Great White Whale to the final chase and death of Ahab. These drawings would help us decide which scenes would be shot in the studio, cyclorama, tanks, or open sea and would illustrate how we would cut from the model to "live action" involving actors on full-size vessels.

That's how I first saw the work of a young sketch artist named Stephen Grimes who was doing animation for the Disney studio in London. I immediately recognized a superior draftsman, and put him on the job.

Steve was a painfully shy young man in his early twenties, with red hair and a pale English complexion. If you addressed him directly, a great blush spread over his face. It's a good thing he could draw, because he could hardly speak. He's better now, but you still must tune your ear to hear what he's saying. He thinks he's shouting. I once paid a visit to the Grimes household and discovered that the entire family communicated in voices that were hardly audible. You could see their lips move, but nothing seemed to be coming out. They heard one another perfectly, but no one outside the family circle was aware that a conversation was taking place. I used to think I was going deaf when I was with Steve.

Steve and I have since worked on many pictures together. He is such a fine artist that I'd hoped he would give himself seriously to painting after he served his time as an art director. Apparently he couldn't afford to do that. Not only did he have a wife and several children, but, despite his shyness, he acquired liaisons as he went along. Wherever we happened to be, he fell passionately in love with someone. As a rule, the women he loved were separated from their husbands and had children already, so that Steve—who is highly responsible—felt called upon to take care of them. When they moved into the background of his life, he went on taking care of them, so he had a list of responsibilities the length of a Chinese scroll. His women were all sizes, shapes and nationalities and all, as a rule, attractive.

Rockwell Kent once did some interesting illustrations for a limited edition of *Moby Dick*. There was one in particular—his drawing of

Queequeg—that looked very much like my old friend Count Friedrich Ledebur. We tested several people, but none of them had that massive presence, the combination of fierce primitivism and kindness, that I wanted this character to have. So I prevailed on Friedrich to make a test. He is some six feet four inches, slim, yet hard-muscled, and he was just the right age. His makeup was elaborate. His head was shaved and a topknot of hair fastened to his bald pate. His eyes were blue, so dark contact lenses had to be made for him. His face was tatooed as described by Melville. The aquiline countenance of this Austrian aristocrat transformed beautifully into that of the savage.

Our pre-production work was done in Madeira, where Portuguese whalers still hunt from open longboats just as they did generations ago. After that we shot a number of interiors in the Shepperton studios outside London, including Ishmael's first night at the inn, and Father Mapple's sermon—a virtuoso performance by Orson Welles. Orson's performance was so nearly flawless as to make me optimistic about the rest of the shooting. I should not have been.

We had constructed several whales, from giant models to models only a few feet long. De Havilland Aircraft Company did some work on an electronic model. None of the mechnical whales proved to be satisfactory. They moved all right on their supports in the workshop, but when they were placed in the water, their behavior changed radically. Most of them went straight to the bottom.

For the model work we built a tank with a concrete cyclorama at the ABC studios outside London. It was well enough executed, but the choice of location was unfortunate. At a very early hour in the afternoon the sun moved behind some trees on property adjoining the studio lot and threw shadows on the cyclorama. The people who owned the property quite properly refused to cut the trees, but those shadows reduced our shooting time to a few morning hours, apart from the shots we could make when the sky was overcast. The model work continued throughout the entire production, but we shot very little footage of any value against the cyclorama. Most of the filming had to be done at sea, under dreadful conditions.

Our next move was to Fishguard in Wales to get the White Whale scenes, and that's when the real trouble began. That winter had the worst weather in the history of the British Isles. Two special power-rescue launches actually capsized outside the Fishguard harbor. The catalogue of misadventures was unbelievable.

What difficulties Nature had in store for us were compounded by the

fact that the ABC studios in London—through whom we were working
—kept trying to save money by taking shortcuts. They were working in
collaboration with the principals in the United States—Elliot Hyman, the
Mirisch brothers and other backers—but they were inveterately tight-
fisted, and in the process wound up spending many times the amounts
they were trying to save.

An example of this was in the outfitting of Ahab's ship, the *Pequod*, a
104-foot wooden-hulled three-master originally named the *Rylands*. It
had been launched some hundred years earlier, and when we bought it, it
was being used as a sea-going aquarium and tourist attraction at Scar-
borough on the Yorkshire coast. We had her modified, built a superstruc-
ture, added an elevated poopdeck astern and rigged her out in an English
shipyard. Then they put engines in her which—to save money—were too
small for the size and weight of the hull. Finally, instead of placing the
engines and the generators amidships, where they should have been, the
studio insisted on putting them where it cost the least—under the poopdeck. The noise was constant and inescapable.

We wanted the ship authentically square-rigged, but the art of square-
rigging had gone with the past. Although the rigging looked right
enough, there were essential weaknesses in it which accounted for the
ship being dismasted twice. All of these deficiencies, along with the bad
weather, created a nightmare of problems. The high poopdeck made us a
plaything to the winds, and we were knocked around so much as to be
almost spinning at times. We had to keep the engines running constantly
to maintain headway, and this meant we couldn't record dialogue because
of the noise. It was just one thing after another.

We had two captains for the ship during the picture. The first captain
was a little man. I used to watch him. He'd go to the helm and invariably
hit his head on the boom, after which he'd glare at the boom and everyone around him. Apparently these cracks on the head took their toll; the
man got progressively worse. He erupted in outbursts and tantrums. He
got to think of himself as master in every sense of the word, not only in
sailing the ship but also in making the picture. At that point we had to
dispense with him. We were then fortunate enough to get the best sailing
man alive: Allan Villiers, a superb big-ship sailor and the author of a
dozen great books on seamanship and sailing history. We would never
have managed without him, for it was after he took over that the really
bad weather started.

One day there was a high gale that sent us running for the harbor. But
the wind that day was from an unusual direction and blew directly into

the harbor, making it as unprotected as the open sea. Our engines were insufficient to maintain headway, so we were being towed by a tug. As we entered the harbor channel, I was appalled to see a number of ships and boats piled up on the rocks *inside*—where under normal conditions they would have been moored in calm water.

We had no sooner cleared the harbor entrance than the cable to the tugboat snapped. The wind was hitting the *Pequod* broadside, driving us toward the rocks, too. Captain Villiers put down a small motor launch and sent it to the tug to get a new line. This launch then took the line to a buoy, secured it and scuttled back to the *Pequod*, where the line was quickly secured around the mainmast. By the time all this could be accomplished, there were only a few yards of line left. Once the first line was secured, they got another line to the ship from the tug and we were safe once more. I remember Villiers' words as this was being done:

"Act quickly, gentlemen! The safety of the ship is at stake!"

The Great White Whale which we used in the ocean was about ninety feet long and constructed so that it could be towed by a tug. It was designed to submerge and surface according to the speed at which it was being towed. We had several of those models, constructed of steel and wood covered with latex. They were quite expensive—$25,000 to $30,000 each. We lost two of them. They were being pulled with nylon cables two inches thick, but the force of the waves in this bad weather was so great that when slack in a cable was suddenly taken up, the damn thing broke like a guitar string. The last whale we lost was sighted by an ocean liner, which reported it as a navigational hazard. I believe it eventually bumped into a dike on the shores of Holland.

We usually had men out in longboats when we were photographing the whale. This was risky in bad weather, and when the seas became dangerously high, we'd bring the longboats back to the ship. But it was in precisely this kind of weather that the cables would snap and the whale would begin to drift away. So we were confronted with a choice: save the men or save the whale. Besides the sums spent on vanished whales, there was the cost of not having the whales available for filming during the infrequent times when the weather abated. The seas were so high that often we couldn't go out at all, so the accumulation of lost time was dreadful.

In spite of the bad weather conditions, there were few casualties during the filming of *Moby Dick*. Leo Genn injured his back when he dropped some twenty feet into a longboat which went down when it should have been coming up. He was taken to a hospital and put in a cast, but was back on the job in a couple of weeks. We were lucky that nobody got killed.

One day off Fishguard I was out in a tug making full shots of the *Pequod*. It was windy. The sails were bellied out, but it was not a gale. It was, however, bitterly cold. There was a man in each of her three mast-heads, and finally Angela Allen said, "John, they've been up there almost two hours. That's an awfully long time in this cold." I immediately got a hailer and called them down. Just as the last man hit the deck, the three masts went. The masts were guyed together; when one went, they all went. If they had gone a moment before, or if I'd called the men down a moment later, they would have fallen to the deck some ninety feet below or been thrown overboard. Either way, we would have lost them.

Once our American producers paid us a call to find out why we were behind schedule. We were at sea when they arrived in Fishguard, and they put out in a power launch to join us on the *Pequod*. When they came alongside, there were great swells. The launch was rising and falling sickeningly. They looked up at us, their faces green and agonized. I glanced at my shipmates lining the rails, and they were all grinning wolfishly.

It was impossible to transfer from one vessel to another in seas like that, and the producers went back to shore as fast as they could. By the time we made harbor and gathered with them that night in the hotel, all their questions about delay had been answered. They offered—at considerable cost to themselves—to change the location of our remaining at-sea sequences to the Canary Islands. I must take my hat off to them: they were very game.

There were some lighthearted moments during our filming off Fishguard. Once we saw a liner headed toward us. I gave the word for everyone to lie down on deck and play dead. The liner came to within a hundred yards or so of us. We could see people rushing about on her decks, pointing at the *Pequod*. We must have looked like a ghost ship from another century. When the liner stopped and started to lower a lifeboat, we all jumped up and waved.

The harbor scenes were shot at Youghal, near Cork City. Here again, all attempts to economize turned right back upon us. For instance, they dredged the harbor at Youghal at considerable cost, and for a little more they could have gone a few feet deeper. As it was, we could take the *Pequod* in and out only at high tide—that is, during only about an hour a day. Another stalemate.

Youghal harbor was made to look like New Bedford. We painted the fronts of the houses along one street to make them look like New England clapboard. There was only one man who wouldn't agree to change the front of his property—a public house. It wasn't critical that he do so (we could easily shoot around him), but he didn't know this and he held out to get paid something extra. The people of Youghal thought he'd behaved badly and punished him by boycotting his establishment. After we'd been shooting there for a week or so, I heard that nobody was going into his bar, so I dropped by with a couple of friends. It was empty. The owner recognized me, and I said, "I'm sorry to hear what's happened to you." He shrugged. "I had it coming. I was trying to get something for nothing." Where but in Ireland would you ever hear such an admission?

After Youghal we did a bit more work in London, then went to the Canary Islands to finish the sea sequences. Since we had lost two big whales off Fishguard, we had to build another when we arrived in the Canaries, and we knew we simply couldn't afford to lose it. We had a crew of well over 100 persons in the Canaries at considerable expense; the picture had already cost half again as much as it was budgeted for. If we lost this whale, it could well mean the end of the picture. This time I'm not sure I would have gone first to save the men in the longboats.

We started shooting, and, sure enough, one day the cable snapped and the whale was once more adrift. I settled the matter of its drifting away unattended by getting into the whale. Lose the whale, lose me. I remember it was New Year's Eve, 1955. I opened the hatch, got into the whale with bottle in hand, saluted the crew, took a long pull from the bottle and said, "I'll see you next year." Then I popped inside, closing the hatch after me.

The problem was to secure the cable through a big eye on the bottom of the whale. Two men undertook to do this: a Spanish assistant director who was a champion swimmer; and Kevin McClory, who was good in the water and game as they come. The two of them dived repeatedly under the whale, trying to secure the line. Big waves were raising the whale out of the water and slamming it down again—these men were risking their lives—but they finally got the line secured and the whale was under tow again. I then emerged from the whale and went back aboard the *Pequod*.

The last shot of the picture was Ahab lashed to the back of Moby Dick by harpoon lines. This had to be done by Greg Peck himself. A stunt man could not fill in, because of the close-ups. The model—which was a section of the head and body of the White Whale—was actually a big drum, geared to revolve at a constant rate. There was a hole for Greg to put his leg through, and then he had to be quite securely fastened as the model was slowly revolved in the sea at the end of a long pier. All this time the wind machines were roaring and there were torrents of water as Greg was submerged time and again so that the "harpoon lines" would appear to be wrapping around his body, lashing him forever to his mortal enemy. The model was twenty feet in diameter, so Greg was underwater for a good long time each revolution. The danger, of course, was that the contraption might get stuck while he was underwater. We all held our breath (as I assume he did) when we started this sequence, but everything went as planned, and "Ahab" came up each time with his arm moving with the motion of the whale so it appeared to be beckoning to his shipmates.

It was perfect on the first take, and I said, "That's it!"

Greg shook his head. "Let's do it again, John, and make sure." I was certain we had it, but Greg insisted. "We can never come back for it, John. Let's do it again." So we did it again, and the second time also everything went perfectly.

When *Moby Dick* was released, I thought it was good, but a number of the critics didn't agree with me. I was cited by the Motion Picture National Board of Review for the year's best direction, and then won the New York Film Critics' Award for best direction, but some of the reviews—especially those concerning Greg's performance—were not kind, and must have affected public acceptance of the picture.

I myself felt that Peck brought a superb dignity to the role. Ahab's obsession was revealed to us through softly spoken words, a deranged, controlled intensity in thought and action, as if his soul had been transfixed by the lightning which had seared him from crown to heel. I can't imagine the "It's a mild, mild day . . ." speech being better spoken by any actor. I think the next generation will appreciate it more than the last. What many people had seen in the original Barrymore version of *Moby Dick* had led them to expect an Ahab of wild gestures and staring eyes: that wasn't Melville. The picture is now truly coming into its own, and Greg Peck is getting the applause he always deserved.

Greg is one of the nicest, straightest guys I ever knew, and there's a size to him. I conceived a great affection for him during the making of this picture—I had a chance to observe him closely and he was not found wanting in any department. After *Moby Dick* I wanted to do *Typee* with him, but it proved to be too expensive for the Mirisch brothers of Allied Artists. Then there was the notion of doing *The Bridge in the Jungle*, but the part Greg could have played in that picture was comparatively small, not a starring role. Actually, he was perfectly agreeable to the idea of taking any role I suggested, starring or otherwise. "I'll do this picture for you," he said, "and then you do one for me, both working at the same price, so that price doesn't matter. It can be nothing or half a million." In the end *The Bridge in the Jungle* didn't come off either, because Allied Artists decided against it. But the story illustrates the regard in which Greg and I held each other.

About the first thing I'd do on arriving in California would be to call Greg and arrange to get together with him. Greg and I had a number of interests in common apart from pictures: horses, primitive art—but, mostly, I simply enjoyed being with him.

One such time I visited him on a set when he was making a film. Véronique, his wife, was with him in his dressing room. I went to kiss her on the cheek, and she backed away from me a couple of steps and threw an appealing look at Greg. It was a queer, clumsy piece of behavior, and I wondered what in Christ's name possessed her. Maybe, I thought, Greg's turned jealous and told her not to kiss or let herself be kissed by anyone— and that questioning look was to ask if that order applied to me, too? I dismissed that notion as being out of character for Greg.

But from then on Greg avoided me. At first I didn't believe it. I'd call and leave messages at his house and at his office—but he never called back. Had it been almost anyone else, I'd have said, "To hell with it," but not with Greg. I valued our friendship far too much. I searched my memory for some clue to his behavior. We'd been partners in a racehorse. I called my business manager and made sure Greg hadn't got the worst of it in any way. Then I asked a good friend of Greg's if he had any idea what it was all about. He hadn't, but said he'd try to find out. He saw Greg, but Greg refused to talk.

Not long afterward I was in the recording room at Universal studios, where Greg had an office. He came in unexpectedly, saw me, acknowledged my presence by a nod, turned on his heel and left. I gave him time to get back to his office, then phoned him. After quite a long pause his secretary said he wasn't in. I knew he was, but I said I wished to see him as soon as possible. I never heard from him. I called again half an hour later, and she said he'd left the lot. I asked her if she'd given him my message, and she said she had.

Why did Véronique back away from me that time in the dressing room? Had she told Greg I'd made some kind of an advance? I was a holdover from his past besides being a very close friend, and new wives dislike such encumbrances.

Years later I met Greg on another motion-picture lot. He acted genuinely glad to see me. It was obvious that he would have liked to talk, but this time I turned away. It was far too late to start over.

Moby Dick may have been the most difficult picture—in physical terms —I ever made, but I never came closer to downright disaster than on my next two completed films, *Heaven Knows, Mr. Allison* and *The Barbarian and the Geisha*—both of which I made for Buddy Adler of 20th Century-Fox. I had known Adler when he was a lieutenant colonel in the Signal Corps at the Pentagon, and after the war he became the executive head of production at Fox. On several occasions he had asked me to make a picture for him, but I had always been occupied with something else. Following *Moby Dick*, however, Paul Kohner arranged a three-picture contract for me with Fox. Adler then sent me a script written by John Lee Mahin, who had been a star writer during the old days at Metro. The script showed considerable promise, although it was taken from a very bad novel which exploited all the obvious sexual implications of a marine and a nun cast together on a South Pacific island. For that reason I had earlier rejected it as a possibility for a film. But Mahin's approach revived my interest. He had laundered the story tastefully, and I saw how—with additional changes—it could be made into a good picture. Mahin and I went down to Ensenada, in Baja California, and wrote a new script in five or six weeks, working steadily and trading scenes back and forth. The only interruptions were when Billy Pearson came to pay us visits.

Billy and John Lee fell together like pancakes. They came into my room one morning with my secretary, Lorrie Sherwood. I remember the date was August 6, 1956, because the preceding evening I had celebrated my fiftieth birthday at a party thrown by a Mexican friend in his country house outside Ensenada. The party had been a roaring success. I didn't even remember coming back to the hotel.

When they arrived, late in the morning, I was still putting cold towels on my head, talking lightly about the party and how I'd felt the night before as compared with this morning. John Lee, Billy and Lorrie remained sober-faced. They didn't pick up on the banter. They were almost like some official delegation. Finally I asked, "What's the matter?"

Lorrie answered, "John, the boys have something to tell you. We talked about it downstairs, and I think you should know, if you don't know already."

"What do you mean? What are you talking about?"

"What do you remember doing after we came home from the party?" asked Lorrie.

"I don't remember a damn thing!"

"Well, I'm not surprised, because what happened isn't at all like you."

"What happened? What the hell are you talking about anyway?"

Then Billy and John Lee spoke up. After returning to my room, I had apparently gone downstairs, crossed the lobby and entered the restaurant —which was open all night—stark, bare-assed naked.

"Jesus Christ! It's impossible!"

"Oh, it's quite possible," said Billy. "The waiters there recognized you. They put a tablecloth around you and led you back upstairs."

"John, do you ever sleepwalk?" John Lee inquired.

"Yes, as a kid. But not since I was a kid."

The problem was compounded by the fact that there was a Los Angeles gossip columnist in the restaurant at the time. Billy said, "John, you'd better prepare yourself for what that broad is going to say about you in print." Well, I was simply astounded. I was aghast. They tried to cheer me up. Billy forced a laugh: "You know, John . . . what the hell! You've done it. It's funny . . . well . . . at least in our eyes. . . ." Everything they said just opened the wound deeper.

I phoned the desk, spoke to the manager and asked him what had happened the night before. Yes, there'd been some kind of commotion in the restaurant, but he had no details. I would have to wait until that afternoon when the night manager and staff came back on duty. I sweated blood all day. When the new shift arrived, I called the night manager. He said yes, it was all true, but . . . the hero of the story was a Los Angeles dentist. Not me. Billy and John Lee had set me up! Lorrie had known nothing about it; they had just used her as a foil. Those bastards laughed like hyenas.

Our script turned out very well, I thought. The casting was also very much to my satisfaction: Deborah Kerr and Bob Mitchum. I'd only known Bob casually, but I had great respect for his talents. This was even more of a two-person story than *The African Queen*. Bob and I talked in London, then went on to Tobago, where we were to make the picture. Tobago was a British possession, and the film was to be made jointly by Fox and an English company, with an English crew. It went smoothly indeed.

I had been told that Bob Mitchum was difficult. Nothing could have been further from the truth. He was a delight to work with, and he gave a beautiful performance. He is one of the finest actors I've ever had anything to do with. His air of casualness or, rather, his lack of pomposity is put down as a lack of seriousness, but when I say he's a fine actor, I mean an actor of the caliber of Olivier, Burton and Brando. In other words, the very best in the field. He simply walks through most of his pictures with his eyes half open because that's all that's called for, but he is in fact capable of playing *King Lear*. As for being difficult—well, here's an instance.

In one scene Bob had to crawl through the grass on his elbows like a snake—the Army crawl. I shot the scene, but it wasn't quite right, so I asked him to do it again. We did it three or four times. Finally I said, "That's it!" Bob got up and turned around, and he was blood from the neck down. He had been crawling over stinging nettles.

"Jesus Christ, Bob!" I said, and asked him why he did it.

"That's what you wanted," he answered. And that was the whole size of it. He didn't do it for effect, either. There is no playing to the gallery on Bob's part.

As I recall, Deborah was nominated for an Oscar for her performance in *Mr. Allison*. There was a scene in which she ran into a mangrove swamp, fell and spent the night unconscious—until Allison discovered her. Tobago offered what the scene called for—a swamp consisting of mud and ooze, full of snakes and queer little animals. Deborah had to lie down in this mess, and she did it without a word of complaint. It was only years later that I discovered this had been such an ordeal for her that it almost unnerved her totally. She had said nothing when we shot the scene, but she had dreams of this swamp for weeks afterward. To this day she still occasionally has them.

The near-disaster to which I referred occurred during the "bombing" of the island, which was supposed to be held by the Japanese. The scene would show Japanese soldiers running, with bombs exploding around them.

A powder man was flown in especially from the States to lay the charges. This took several days. The powder man used very large charges of dynamite so that there would be big explosions, with tons of earth thrown up in the air. There were about twenty such "bombs," each of which was wired to an individual key on a keyboard which the powder man played. Each key acted as a switch, triggering an explosion in a certain sector. Good powder men are trained to play those keyboards like Paderewski. They are remarkable: they never lose their heads and touch the wrong key. I remember a scene in *The Red Badge of Courage* in which a man accidentally fell in the middle of an area mined for explosions. The scene involved hundreds of men charging up a hill, but the powder man saw this one man fall and didn't touch the key for that particular mine. The places where the charges are laid cannot be marked clearly, since the camera might pick up the marks, so the powder man simply has to remember where each charge is laid and keep track of the action. Obviously, such a man must possess a remarkable memory, as well as the ability to see through smoke and dust.

Everyone had been rehearsed several times so no one could possibly make a mistake. The powder man, the cameraman and I, along with the main camera, were atop a forty-foot platform of fitted metal piping. Other cameras were variously located. The powder man threw the master switch, which primed the whole thing, and in just a matter of seconds we saw smoke coming up from the ground. The powder man turned to me, white-faced; all he could say was "Jesus Christ!" It was obvious to him that the rain the night before had caused short circuits in the underground wires. It was not the powder man's fault, but just one of those unpredictable things. I guessed what was happening and yelled, "Action!" At this the troops began to run. Through the loud-hailer I shouted, "Keep going! Keep going! Faster, faster!"

And then the whole damned thing went up, all at once. Not *bang! bang! bang!* like a string of bombs, but a great explosion that blinded and deafened us all. The blast rocked our platform so violently that we were almost thrown off. The camera was chained down, but it tore loose. Rocks and debris showered all around us. By some miracle, none of us was hurt and the "troops" had run clear of the blast area.

We waited for the ground to dry and did the entire thing over again. This time it went off without a hitch.

Allison is seldom referred to, but I think it was one of the best things I ever made. It was unostentatious, had very simple, clean dialogue and was built on a first-rate foundation. We escaped the cliché of the nun and the marine, and the material was treated with great delicacy of feeling. A censor came down and stayed with us during the production—a precaution taken by Fox—but there was no need for him; there was never a kiss or even an embrace. Audiences grew to love those two people.

Those involved in making pictures from beginning to end, especially on location, come to think of each separate picture as a world and a life unto itself. The actors, crew, technicians—all are caught up in the little planetary system, which one day simply comes to an end. Suddenly it's over, and you can never go back to it. Thus the picture-maker's life is subdivided into many lives. When one of those lives has been a joyous experience, as *Mr. Allison* was, I hate to see it end. Nor do I like to say goodbye; I always try to get out and away before goodbyes are in order. I despair at farewell parties. In the case of this picture, I lined up the last shot and left before the take.

I was in Paris when I received a call from Charlie Grayson and Eugene

Frenke. They wanted me to film the story of Townsend Harris as my second picture for Fox. Harris was the first American diplomat sent to Japan after Commodore Perry and his fleet forced the opening of that country in 1853. He arrived in 1856 and, according to legend, fell in love with a geisha named Okichi. She supposedly committed suicide after his departure.

Charlie had written a script and we could proceed immediately. They played on one of my weak points—I would have a chance to go to Japan, a place I had never seen. I agreed, and that's how *The Barbarian and the Geisha* got started. It might have been better if it hadn't.

Eugene Frenke is a scrawny little man who speaks English with a pronounced Russian accent and is given to obscene gestures. He is married to Anna Sten, to whom he has been faithless for, lo, these many years. Luckily, she understands and adores him, as he does her. Frenke hasn't changed one iota in appearance from the first day I set eyes on him till the present. He attributes this to a potion he imbibes twice a year in Japan. He is very active in the bedroom and on the tennis court, and, for all I know, he is ninety-nine years old. He looks and behaves at least twenty years younger than I do, and he is full of good will, good works and big ideas.

I returned to Los Angeles, and after some preliminary talks Charlie Grayson and I went to Mexico to work on the screenplay. It was fairly well constructed, but not very well written. About three months before we were to start filming, with the script still incomplete, Charlie and I went to Tokyo. I was delighted with what I saw. Jack Smith, the art director from Fox, joined us there, and we decided on major locations and interviewed some fine Japanese actors. Our primary casting concern was the role of Okichi, the Japanese girl.

Since 1957 there has been a revolution of taste and culture in Japan. Today Japanese actors and actresses undergo eye and nose operations and follow the latest hair styles and modes of the Western world. But when we were there, our corruptive influences were only beginning to be felt. The Japanese concept of feminine beauty was a short woman with a large nose. The feature most admired in a woman was the exposed nape of the neck. We looked in vain among the Japanese actresses for an Okichi who would be physically attractive to Western audiences. In our search we went to numerous geisha houses, which, contrary to Western belief, are not primarily brothels but rather places of entertainment in which skills of conversation, dancing and music play a major part. Of course sex is involved, too, but in a fairly special way. Rich customers bid for the right to deflower a young *maiko* whose training is complete. "Pillow money" for the first, second and third nights. This money is used to reimburse the house for the original sum given to the girl's parents and for her elaborate education. Once this obligation has been paid off, the girl becomes a full geisha.

On one of our first nights in Tokyo we visited a geisha house and saw there a girl more beautiful than anyone we found during several subsequent weeks of looking. Charlie Grayson reminded me of her, and I asked the Fox representatives to find out whether we could get her to make a test. They did, but it turned out that the geisha house wanted "pillow money" if we made the test. The house also inquired whether I wanted to "partake fully." I replied, "No, pay the pillow money, but let's keep her virginal." There was silence from the geisha house for a while, and the next thing we heard was that the girl had suffered an attack of appendicitis and had been sent back to her village. Apparently there was only one proper way to proceed in such a matter, and the house wasn't about to make an exception for me.

Only a few days before we left for the United States we selected the actress Eiko Ando for the part. She was tall and long-legged, unlike most Japanese, and came from the northern part of the northernmost island of Hokkaido. The Japanese, by and large, didn't approve of her. They felt she lacked distinction; her kind of beauty was not appealing to them.

After that first trip Charlie and I came back to the States and went about finishing the script—or trying to. We never did finish it to my satisfaction. I had various other writers lend Charlie a hand, but nothing good came of it. When we finally returned to Japan and began filming the picture again, I found myself shooting in the daytime and writing future scenes at night.

John Wayne was cast as Townsend Harris, the idea being that his massive frame, bluff innocence and rough edges would be an interesting contrast to the small, highly cultivated Japanese; that the physical comparison would help serve to emphasize their dissimilar viewpoints and cultures.

My second near-disaster occurred during the filming of this picture. Townsend Harris played a heroic role during a cholera epidemic. To prevent the spread of the disease, he put the torch to an infected village, then took the bodies of the cholera victims, piled them on boats and ran them out to sea to be burned, boats and all. For this latter scene we constructed a barge some forty feet long which was supposed to be full of bodies. We then set fire to it and launched it on log rollers from a beach near the village of Ito. Before the launching, a line, attached to the barge as a means of controlling it, had been run to a pier farther along the beach in the opposite direction from the village. Somehow this line got caught underneath the barge, as it rolled into the sea, and was severed. The flaming barge drifted free, trailing a long length of its mooring cable. This was fine for the moment, because we got what we had hoped for—a shot of the burning pyre moving slowly away in the darkness. But then an inshore wind caught the barge and drove it toward a number of Japanese fishing boats anchored in a small cove close to the village. We stood by helplessly, watching this huge, floating torch—burning furiously by now—drift right into the middle of those boats. All of them were powered with engines and had fuel tanks aboard. A number immediately caught fire. Ito itself was little more than a collection of paper houses stacked closely around the cove. One spark would have sent the entire village up in flames. It would have been a holocaust; hundreds of people would have perished.

The day—or, rather, the night—was saved by a Japanese sculling a little boat with an oar over the stern. He found the end of the cut cable trailing behind the barge, dived for it and then hauled it in to the nearest spot on shore, where we were waiting. We took the line and marched the barge along the shoreline back to the pier—away from town. In the meantime the villagers had rushed out to help the fishermen fight the fires on their boats, and they managed to extinguish them before they got to the gas tanks. It was that close.

Then the riots started. Some people used to think the Japanese were stoical, polite little people who never showed emotion. I know better. They went crazy. Fishermen and townspeople attacked the Japanese connected with the film company. Many were clubbed unconscious, and why no one was killed I'll never know. It would be quelled from time to time, and then it would break out all over again. Our people were just as bad as the townspeople. There would be a lull, then someone from our side would start the whole thing again by running at the villagers—or vice versa. It continued off and on for hours.

The original title of this picture was *The Townsend Harris Story*. I was in the process of shooting a scene outside Tokyo when someone handed me a clipping from a Hollywood trade paper announcing that the title had been changed by Fox to *The Barbarian and the Geisha*. I still don't like it.

The Barbarian and the Geisha turned out to be a bad picture, but it was a good picture before it became a bad picture. I've made pictures that were not good, for which I was responsible, but this was not one of them. When I brought it to Hollywood, the picture, including the music, was finished, as far as I was concerned. It was a sensitive, well-balanced work. I turned it over to the studio and hurried on to Africa to work on *The Roots of Heaven*, which had been scheduled even before I went to Japan. John Wayne apparently took over after I left. He pulled a lot of weight at Fox, so the studio went along with his demands for changes. The picture was released before I got back to France after *Roots*, and when I finally saw it, I was aghast. A number of scenes had been reshot, at Wayne's insistence, simply because he didn't like the way he looked in the original version. By the time the studio finished hacking up the picture according to Wayne's instructions, it was a complete mess. My friend Buddy Adler put up with all this. I would have taken legal steps to have my name removed from the picture, but learned that Adler was terminally ill with a brain tumor. Bringing suit under such circumstances was unthinkable.

David O. Selznick was a big man of enormous energies and appetites, with a great capacity for work and life. I liked him, and I liked his wife Irene

24 very much. Irene, the daughter of L. B. Mayer and therefore a royal princess in Hollywood, had a dark, vivid beauty. I remember her in sheathlike gowns—usually black or red— with a strand of pearls around her throat and on her wedding-ring finger a beautifully cut diamond David had given her. Irene was something of an oracle in Hollywood. There was an air of wisdom about her that led people to go to her for advice. She had a manner of speaking which contributed to that image: she spoke in so low a voice that you had to give her your undivided attention. You found yourself answering in the same hushed tones. It was like conducting secret negotiations.

Irene and David, and Irene's sister, Edie, and her husband, Bill Goetz, held separate courts in Hollywood at that time. There was no rivalry between the sisters; the composition of one group was entirely different from that of the other. The Bohemian outlook of David and Irene contrasted sharply with that of the conservative Goetzes. Sunday afternoon around the Selznick pool, followed by dinner, became a regular event. The guests were invariably an entertaining group. Those occasions were the best Hollywood had to offer.

There was something childlike about David—a spoiled child. He liked giving commands, telling others what to do and how to do it. The thing is, he knew! Who else has a record to compare with David's? *Westward Passage, Bill of Divorcement, Dinner at Eight, David Copperfield, Anna Karenina, A Tale of Two Cities, A Star is Born, Rebecca, Gone With the Wind*, to mention a few. David fell in love with Jennifer Jones. She was under contract to him and he had loaned her to Fox for her first big success, "The Song of Bernadette." He and Irene were divorced, and David married Jennifer. Irene went to New York to become the producer of *A Streetcar Named Desire*, and other fine plays. She never married again.

David's love for Jennifer was very real and touching but in it lay the seeds of the failures that marked the last years of his life. Everything he did was for Jennifer. His whole life centered upon her, to the detriment of his good judgment. David never did anything worth a damn after he married Jennifer.

I was saddened when David and Irene separated, but between the principals there was none of the conflict usual when a marriage breaks up. I saw a lot of David and Jennifer, and had no feeling of disloyalty to Irene when I attended their parties. The Sunday sessions were on with the same cast as before at their place overlooking Beverly Hills. David sometimes chartered a big sailboat for his parties. He was extravagant in whatever he did—or should I say magnificent?

When it came to publicizing or exploiting a picture, David was in a class by himself. His ideas were original—sometimes bizarre—and they worked. The scam he devised with Paul MacNamara, his longtime publicity man, to publicize *Duel in the Sun* was a classic. He obtained lists of names of bartenders in cities and towns all over the country, then hired teams of workers to sit down and write—by hand—thousands of letters, addressing each bartender by his first name:

> Hi Charlie. Well I made it. I'm out here in California finally, and it sure is everything they said it was. The sun shines just about every day. They got palm trees all right, and my sister even has a swimming pool in her back yard. I'm staying with her. We go down to the beach at a place called Santa Monica just about every Saturday or Sunday for a swim in the Pacific Ocean and sometimes downtown to take in a picture. There's sure a lot of things to see and do here. One of the things I liked best was getting to go out to one of the movie lots and actually see them making a movie. It was called *Duel in the Sun*, with Jennifer Jones. Boy is she an eyeful! It's a Western, but not like any Western you ever saw. It's got a surprise ending. They told me what it was, but said I shouldn't tell, so I won't—but it's sure going to be one of the best pictures of all times.
>
> Well Charlie, I got to go now. Say hi to all the gang there for me will you? Hope to see you soon.
>
> Your old buddy, Joe

Naturally, the bartender would show this letter to the regulars at the bar, and they would try to decide who "Joe" was. Usually they came up with two or three "Joes." Selznick followed this up with a major publicity campaign, including billboards emblazoned with a ten-foot-high sexy portrait of Jennifer Jones—Indian blouse ripped away from one shoulder. Bartenders and their patrons in every state in the Union saw the billboards and exclaimed: "Hey! That's the picture old Joe was talking about!"

Duel in the Sun was not a good movie. Even Selznick had to admit this after seeing the previews, so he came up with another idea which had never been tried before. He ordered about three times the usual number of prints made, distributed them and had the movie released simultaneously in theaters across the country, so that the picture would get its money back before word of mouth could have its ill effects. Not only did it get its money back; it made a profit.

David's brother, Myron, was the number-one agent in Hollywood. In his way, Myron was more powerful than David. He represented the biggest names in the business. Thus empowered, he took on the heads of studios—bearded the lions in their dens—and made them pay salaries in proportion to a star's box-office value. It was the beginning, though no one guessed it at the time, of the stars and their agents assuming control of the industry (or, as someone described it, the lunatics taking over the asylum). Myron was brilliant, quarrelsome, a good friend and a bad enemy. He drank heavily—unlike David—and you had the feeling that Myron didn't give a damn about anything or anybody (including himself), apart from David. The two brothers had great affection for each other, and Myron's death was a terrible blow to David.

Over the years, David had proposed doing several films with me, but most of the time I was under contract to someone else and busy elsewhere. I wasn't sure I wanted to anyway, after my experience with him during *Beat the Devil*. But after *Heaven Knows, Mr. Allison*, I was free. David suggested we do Hemingway's *A Farewell to Arms*, and the fact that Ben Hecht was writing the script reassured me considerably. I agreed to direct the picture.

Ben Hecht wrote pictures for a flat fee, with incredible speed, sometimes completing an entire script in three or four days. When he started to work, he didn't stop, other than to eat and sleep sparingly, until it was finished. There was great style, raciness and color to Ben's work; he was a screenwriter *par excellence*. But none of this applies to *A Farewell to Arms*. He had written it to David's prescription, and he was at his level worst. I know it had been agony for him; it was certainly a great disappointment to me.

From the moment I saw the script, David and I were in conflict. Through David's influence on Hecht, the Hemingway story had simply become a vehicle for the female lead—Jennifer Jones. I joined David and Ben in Italy, where we had long sessions about it. A good picture had been made of it back in the thirties, starring Gary Cooper and Helen Hayes, but in that case the screenplay had been radically different from the book. Hemingway's stories don't dramatize readily. Scenes seem to have a beginning, a middle and an end when in fact they don't. Ben Hecht put it succinctly: "That sonofabitch writes in *water!*" David's interference made the already difficult job almost impossible for Ben. Talking with him in Italy, I had the feeling he was now just trying to get out from under—to type the last page, get his money and go home.

I saw Hemingway during this period, and he was upset. He had been paid a very small amount for his rights to the novel when Paramount did the original version of *A Farewell to Arms*. The property then went to Warners and eventually to David. Presumably it was to somebody's benefit each time it changed hands—but never Papa's. He felt he was being cheated. Also, he didn't like David. There was nothing remarkable about that; except for attractive females, Papa seldom liked anyone he'd met only once. But a later incident confirmed his worst opinion about Selznick.

When he was in Cuba once, David told Peter Viertel that he would like to see Hemingway if it was convenient. A number of meetings were scheduled and canceled. Then Peter and Mary Hemingway showed up unexpectedly one day in David's hotel suite. David didn't stand up. He was—he later told me—being taught a new card game by a Cuban friend, and he was wearing only a sportshirt and undershorts. He thought it would be more rude to stand than to remain seated—but Mary didn't know this. She told Papa that David hadn't risen when she came into the room. From then on, Selznick's name was a dirty word in the Hemingway household.

The starting date was imminent. We went to the Abruzzi—the high mountains of Italy—where the opening scenes of the picture were to be shot: troop movements and battle scenes. There were a few rehearsals with Jennifer and Rock Hudson, the male lead. My differences with David continued. Sometimes an element of absurdity crept in. I told Hudson to have his hair cut short, like all enlisted men in World War I. David countermanded my instruction. He said it would take away from Hudson's romantic appeal.

One morning Art Fellows, David's production manager, called on me. He said, "John, I have a memo from David. I'm supposed to hand it to you, but, Jesus, I'm afraid to do it!"

"Is it that bad?"

"It's worse. I'm afraid if you read it, you'll walk away from the picture."

"Well, let me read it."

Art handed me a memo which ran to sixteen pages. A condensed version would go something like this:

Dear John:
 I should be less than candid with you if I didn't tell you that I am most desperately unhappy about the way things are going. It is an experience completely unique in my very long career. It is an experience that I feel is going to lead us, not to a better picture . . . but to a worse one—because it will represent neither what you think the picture should be, nor what I think it should be. . . . There have been few books ever transcribed to the screen with the studied and loving care that Ben and I gave this one. . . . Also, pardon me if I say that the trick was not achieved in *Moby Dick*. . . . Indeed, John, I hope it is clear to you . . . that I will not expect even any individual lines to be cut, altered, or transposed without my express approval; and this is one of the several purposes of my always being available. . . . I am forced to ask you, John, how many actual camera setups have you decided upon? Is it ten, twenty, fifty? . . . Maybe this is the way you have worked, John. It is not the way I have worked. . . . It is not the way I shall work on *A Farewell to Arms*. . . . Fervently as I want you to direct the picture, I would rather face the awful consequence of your not directing it than go through what I am presently going through. . . .

I didn't get halfway through this "memo" before I called my secretary. "Come on up here and help me pack!"
 My departure from the picture was deemed newsworthy, so in Rome I gave a brief conference in which I said nothing against David, only that there had been "a division of opinion." As I said these words, I remembered a story Hemingway had once told me: A matador had come back to his hotel after an afternoon of disgrace. Every pillow and every bottle in the plaza had been thrown at him. Following the fight he came into the hotel with his picador, and the hotel manager asked, "How did it go?" The matador replied, "There was a division of opinion." The picador said, "Yes, there was a division of opinion. Some wanted to shit on his father, and some wanted to shit on his mother."
 However, I did get in one good lick at the conference which more than satisfied my appetite for revenge. I said, "Regardless of our professional differences, I must express my admiration for Mr. Selznick personally. I know him to be a man of his word, and he assured me of his intention to give Mr. Hemingway the first $100,000 out of the proceeds." David had earlier agreed with me that Hemingway should get something, but this was more by far than the amount that had been intended. It would,

however, have made David seem churlish to deny my statement, and, in the absence of a denial, it amounted to a black-and-white commitment. Papa never got anything out of it, for there were no profits on the movie. It was a debacle.

I never saw the picture. It turned out to be an unhappy experience for everyone connected with it. After I left, Charlie Vidor replaced me. He telephoned and asked if I had any objection to his taking over. I assured him to the contrary and wished him all the luck in the world. But it was unpleasant for him, too. David immediately buried him in memorandums.

Apparently David had got the notion that all the people I'd brought in were against him and against the movie, which was far from the truth. One by one, he began to let them go. Ossie Morris was the first, then Steve Grimes. Finally, in a fit of anger, he pushed Art Fellows, who had been his number-one man for years. Art promptly slapped him and knocked his glasses off. That finished Art. Not long after the film was released, Charlie Vidor died.

Selznick was optimistic about the picture to the bitter end, but of course this was a dream. I'm afraid that none of the pictures David and Jennifer made together after their marriage amounted to much. One must certainly be sympathetic. There's even a kind of grandeur to the way David laid everything on the line for her.

A year or so after *Farewell to Arms* came out, I met David in the lobby of the St. Regis Hotel in New York. He smiled at me, began to put out his hand and then hesitated, as if he were afraid I might not take it. I immediately took his hand. Shortly after that I was out in California and Jennifer phoned. "John, we're giving a party. Won't you come?"

I said, "No, I won't come. I'm still mad at him. But I'll get over it one of these days. Then, if you still want me, I'll come." Not long after that, David was dead.

I must say that in his prime David O. Selznick was the best. Nobody could hold a candle to him. Not only did he make some very good pictures, but he knew what to do with them. His like simply does not exist today. I admired David, and he was my friend for many years. I wish I had gone to that party.

Even before the decision was made to do *The Barbarian and the Geisha*, two or three people had mentioned to me Romain Gary's *The Roots of Heaven*, which had won the Prix Goncourt in France. I read

25 it, liked it and got together with Gary—who was then the French consul in Los Angeles—and we talked about making it into a picture. I then spoke to Buddy Adler, and he bought the property for me. But Darryl Zanuck, who had the right to pre-empt any material acquired by Fox, took the property over my head. Then he came to me and said, "How about doing it with me?"

I'd known Darryl for a long time. He was my friend, but I had never worked with him. I was still smarting from the problems with Selznick on *A Farewell to Arms*, and was a little reluctant to work with another strong-minded producer. But I wanted to do this picture. Darryl convinced me by promising to help in every way. His only requirement was that Juliette Greco play the female lead. Greco had been a nightclub singer, and she was a friend of Simone de Beauvoir, Albert Camus and other French Existentialists. Many of her lyrics reflected the philosophy of that group. I'd seen her perform, and there was something magnetic about her. She also had the reputation of being a good actress, so I had no objection to Darryl's one requirement.

I chose a friend of mine to do the screenplay: Patrick Leigh Fermor, an excellent writer and an exceptional man altogether. Paddy is the author of some of the best travel books of this century: *Mani, Roumeli, The Traveller's Tree* and, most recently, *A Time of Gifts*. He had fought with the guerrillas in Greece during the war; capturing a German general was one of his exploits, and an English motion picture had been made about that.

I was about midway through *The Barbarian and the Geisha* when Paddy's screenplay arrived from Paris. It wasn't very good. Gary's book makes a philosophical statement of some power, but the script in my hand was for an action picture, and not a very good action picture at that. Good writers who are unfamiliar with pictures often try to popularize their material. They don't want to appear literary, so they lean over backward, too far, and they topple. That happened in this case. What was handed to me was a vehicle into which a great deal of action had been crammed, and as little thought.

The book begins with a man in a German prison camp. He is rebellious, comes into conflict with the commandant of the *stalag* and is put into solitary confinement. As time passes, he begins to hallucinate. He conjures up a vision of elephants, the only free creatures on earth . . . free of fear because of their great size and strength. He identifies with these animals and that kind of freedom. He dreams along with the elephants and in this way preserves his sanity.

After the war the man goes to Africa in quest of the freedom enjoyed by the elephants, discovers that they are being persecuted and becomes their defender. His efforts take on a symbolic significance, and great scientists, artists and politicians from all over the world come to join him. *The Roots of Heaven* was a prophetic book, anticipating the concerns of today's environmentalists.

That was the plot, but it was diminished by being told in terms of pure action. Darryl was quite high on it, and I was quite low on it, but there wasn't much I could do just then, since I had my hands full with the picture I was working on in Tokyo.

Darryl proceeded, with his usual show of energy, to set up the production. He faithfully secured all the people I'd asked for: Steve Grimes was the art director, Ossie Morris the cameraman and so on down my list of requirements. I had everything I needed to make a good picture except a good script. But we had either to proceed immediately or else to delay the film for another full year: we couldn't work during the rainy season. All the plans had been laid out in great detail by Darryl, and it would have cost us dearly to call them off. To have done so was unthinkable but in retrospect I can see that I should have. Sometimes the unthinkable is the only thing to do.

Darryl and I went to Africa together to visit the various locations Steve Grimes had selected. The Cameroons—in what was then French Equatorial Africa—is a blasted part of the world. Bone-dry deserts are studded with outcroppings of rock, with oases as widely spaced as in the Sahara. There are very primitive tribes in this area, some with pygmy blood, the men with their penises tied to their thighs with leather thongs. One wonders how they exist; for month upon month no cloud appears in the sky, which is brassy with heat. The ground is too hot to walk on barefoot, even at night.

The aide-de-camp for the production was a retired colonel named Bois-
lambert. He took charge of all our logistics—camps, kitchens and transport.
He had been a brevet general in the French Army and had marched with
General Le Clerc from Lake Chad. He was a superb sportsman and an
excellent shot. After *The Roots of Heaven*, Boislambert became the French
Ambassador to Nigeria.

The cast and crew were finally assembled, and we went to work. The
cast was first-rate: Errol Flynn, Trevor Howard, Juliette Greco, Eddie
Albert, Paul Lukas and Orson Welles. Darryl had asked me if I had any
objection to working with Errol. Of course I hadn't, because I thought he
would be very good in the role. He came in shortly after our arrival, and
we shook hands. It was our first meeting since that bloody night long ago
at Selznick's house.

The location was one of the most difficult I have ever been on. Temperatures were killing; the thermometer got up to 125° during the day,
and seldom fell below 100° at night. People started dropping right and
left. I remember looking around for my first assistant one day and finding
him on the ground. I then looked around for my second assistant and
found him on the ground, too. Both had been downed by heat prostration. One after another, members of the company fell victim to the climate
and had to be sent back to Paris. Every plane brought replacements. A
poor script and rampant sickness. Even as I made the picture I knew it
wasn't going to be any good. You kid yourself, try to buoy yourself up,
but eventually you have to face it.

Darryl had made no secret of his infatuation with Juliette Greco, but I
realized fairly soon that it was a one-sided affair. She was openly rude to
him and spoke slightingly of him behind his back—even to me, until I set
her straight. Paddy Leigh Fermor also fell in love with Juliette, but because of his high regard for Darryl he kept it a secret passion. Being Paddy,
he went to the bottle. One night he was missing, and we were worried because recently some of the local natives had been taken by lions or—equally
frightful—lion men, members of a lion cult. Bodies torn by claws had been
found. We went out with a search party, but we didn't find Paddy until
the next morning. Sure enough, he was scratched and torn, but lion men
hadn't done it. He had fallen into a thorn tree, in which he spent the night.
One hand was deeply scratched; it became infected, and pretty soon it
turned blue. For a while it looked like the whole arm might have to be
amputated. I was all for sending Paddy back to Paris, but he wouldn't
hear of it and made light of the whole thing. He banged his blue arm
around with complete abandon. Fortunately, his instinct proved right. He
responded to the antibiotics, and the infection cleared up.

When he isn't working, Trevor Howard is also known to partake, so the company had its share of drinking men. You always knew when Howard was on a bender, for you'd hear his voice raised in banter and laughter. If I could get high like Trevor, I'd remain drunk all the time. There are no "black" moments with him, and apparently he had no difficulty recovering.

Eddie Albert began to worry because he wasn't getting any word from his wife. Nobody was getting any mail, but Eddie was a family man, and it began to prey on his mind. He just couldn't accept the fact that he was in the heart of Africa, where the principal means of communication was by drum. I passed his tent one night and heard muffled sobbing. I went in and tried to comfort him, but he was utterly distracted. Shortly after that he contracted an "affliction" in his legs. He could stand; but to get to the bathroom he had to hang from a pole carried aloft by two bearers.

Errol Flynn was truly ill, but it had nothing to do with Africa. He had a vastly enlarged liver. He continued to drink, however, and he was also on drugs. He knew he was in bad shape, but he put on a great show of good spirits. He'd brought along some fine French wines, potted grouse and various delicacies from Paris—and plenty of vodka. I remember seeing Errol sitting alone night after night in the middle of the compound with a book, reading by the light of a Coleman lantern. There was always a bottle of vodka on the camp table beside him. When I went to sleep he was there, and when I'd wake up in the middle of the night I'd see him still sitting there—the book open, but Errol not reading any longer, just looking into his future, I think, of which there wasn't very much left.

The company doctor came around to see Darryl and me one day and told us he wasn't going to give Errol any more drugs. He said that if this meant he must leave, he would do so, but he felt professionally obligated to take this stand. We concurred, so Errol found himself another doctor—a French army doctor who'd been at Dien Bien Phu and was now stationed at Fort Archimbault. We discovered in short order that he was unfettered on such things as ethics.

I used to hear cats meowing at night, and I wondered why I never saw any cats. Then I discovered that the French doctor was supplying Errol not only with drugs but with girls as well. The girls came around at night and signaled their presence to Errol by meowing. He would open his door furtively and let them slip in. All these young ladies had been given bismuth treatments for venereal disease by the French doctor and pronounced eligible for Errol's delectation.

We came to a pause in shooting to change locations, and I had almost a week off. My old friend Count Friedrich Ledebur, who was there at the time, Boislambert and I decided to go on a hunt. I didn't want to take anyone else from the company, because none of them were really hunters and I didn't want my little sideshow to be ruined. But Errol smelled a rat, and said, "John, you're going on a shoot, aren't you?"

I had to admit it.

"I'm coming with you!"

"No, Errol, not on this one. It's going to be a very rough hunt."

"John, I want to. I'm asking you to do this for me as a friend."

We *were* friends by now, and you certainly can't refuse a request like that, so I said, "All right, Errol, but if you come, you have to go easy on the drink and you can't have drugs of any kind. I must have your word on that."

"It's a promise," he answered. So Errol came with us.

Though he didn't go on our long jaunts, he did go out with Boislambert's second-in-command, and he did quite well. Often we'd come back to camp from a long haul and there would be Errol, not drunk, and all excitement over his day. I thanked heaven I'd taken him. I do to this day. He said afterward that he'd not had such a good time in years.

Someone gave a mongoose to Juliette Greco, and I adopted him. What a marvelous creature he was! He would sometimes bite other people, but I could pick him up and do anything with him. He used to bring me snakes and lay them dead at my door. When we were away from the camp, he was kept in a cage in the shade of a tree. One day someone forgot to move him as the sun changed position, and when I got back to camp, I found that the poor thing had all but died of heat and exposure. I doused him with water and managed to bring him back to life, but a few days later the same damned thing happened again, and this time the mongoose died. I hated everybody for days.

Another acquisition was an eight-foot python, the gift of a local king. He was a very gentle python, and when we moved to the hotel in Bangui some months later, I took him with me. He used to wind himself around the plumbing in the bathroom. When we got ready to leave Bangui, I took him into the forest and let him go.

The hotel in Bangui was probably the worst-run hotel I have ever been in. Nothing worked properly, including the lights and the plumbing. The food was poisonous, and the service non-existent. The manager went about snarling at everybody; he had become inured to all complaints. I sized him up and decided on a tactic based on Goebbels' theory that if a falsehood is brazen enough, and repeated often enough, it will be believed.

I proceeded to compliment the manager on everything connected with the hotel. I told him it deserved a place among the great hotels in the world, along with the Ritz and Claridge's. It was admittedly smaller, but what counted was quality. He looked startled at first . . . then began preening himself. From then on I could do no wrong. It had been all but impossible to get a drink in the bar in the evening after working all day in the hot sun. Everyone complained about it—to no avail. But all I had to do was to appear. The manager would crawl over the bar, fix me a drink, then climb back and place it reverently in my hand. It was always the finest cocktail I'd ever drunk. I assured him that he shouldn't be upset by the behavior of the others; they obviously weren't accustomed to the better things in life. Darryl quite properly tagged me for the complete Judas that I was.

Errol Flynn's girlfriend joined him in Bangui. Fox had paid her transportation, and Darryl was scared to death when he learned that the girl was something like fifteen years old. It put the studio in an awkward legal position. So far as I could see, the girl had come into this world older than most people leave it. Darryl agreed, but this did little to allay his fears. Errol later took the girl to Paris, then on to the United States, where the girl's mother and a lawsuit awaited him.

The Frenchman in charge of transportation was not only very competent but also a scrupulously polite fellow who met us at the hotel each morning, greeted us with a smile and a cheery *"Bonjour!"*—opened and closed doors for us and saw us off with a salute. We were working on an island in the middle of the Ubangi River, which flows by Bangui. It is a big, wide river with a swift current, and transporting cast, crew and equipment to and from the set each day was the responsibility of this transportation man. It was a difficult matter, but he handled it very well. One morning we came out of the hotel to find the transportation man there, as usual, but there was no smile and no greeting, and he closed the car door with a slam. Darryl looked startled. I thought things were probably getting to the poor fellow—God knows his job was tough enough—and forgot about it.

There was an airstrip near Bangui which received weather information daily by radio and relayed it to us on the island via walkie-talkie. One day, shortly after the door-slamming incident, the transportation man radioed that we had to get off the island immediately because a big storm was coming up. The river would rise, he said, and engulf the island. Now, this seemed odd, since there was not a cloud in the sky. We were reluctant to move—it was quite a job getting our heavy equipment off the island on barges—and Darryl asked me what I thought. I suggested we wait for at least some sign of bad weather.

We waited, and nothing happened. The next day the transportation man called again and said even more urgently that we simply *had* to get off the island. We finally realized that the man had gone crackers. We discovered later that he'd typed up stock certificates and distributed them gratis to shopkeepers and other people he knew around town, giving them shares in a picture he was coming back to make in Bangui. He shortly became violent and had to be shipped to Paris in a strait-jacket.

We were fighting time all the way. Sickness slowed us down considerably. Altogether, there were almost a thousand sick calls, encompassing everything from heat prostration to scratches, infections and malaria. Darryl and I held up well, but upon our return to Paris he came down with the shingles. I believe I was the only one who came out undamaged. We managed to finish shooting and get out before the heavy July rains caught us.

After Bangui, most of the company went to Paris, where we would shoot the final sequences—some exteriors in the forest of Fontainebleau and a few interiors in the Boulogne studios. Meanwhile—with a skeleton crew—I went on to a wildlife experimental station called Gangia Na-bodio, hoping to get some good elephant scenes. The staff there was trying to domesticate the African elephant. The station was at the northeast corner of the Congo, right on the Sudan border, and a Commandant Lefevre was in charge. There has been much trouble in that area since, and I have heard conflicting reports about whether the place is still in existence.

Gangia Na-bodio was actually a giant natural zoo, with thirty cow elephants and their offspring, and many other kinds of animals. The animals had great freedom, and each elephant had the African equivalent of an Indian mahout to care for him. Two chimpanzees roamed the place like a couple of Katzenjammer Kids. When they did something particularly naughty, they were put in a cage, whereupon a howling ensued that could be heard for miles. There was a big giraffe with a large field to gambol in, and even a couple of Sitatonga deer—little swamp creatures, very rare, standing some eighteen inches high on legs as slender as lead pencils. One day we were lunching under a marquee and a monkey came down out of a tree. He had a cut on his hand and he was crying. He held his hand out to us. Someone got a Band-Aid and patched him up.

Among the young elephants was one who took a fancy to me and followed me everywhere. His name was Albert, but the natives couldn't

A fishing expedition with Tony at St. Clerans

The director at work. Above, with
Montgomery Clift and Susannah York
on the set of *Freud* in Munich, 1962.
At left, with Richard Harris playing
Cain, JH sprawls in place of Abel
during the filming of *The Bible* in Italy
(*Louis Goldman, Dino de Laurentis
Productions*). At right, shooting *The
Night of the Iguana* in Puerto Vallarta,
Mexico: above, a discussion with
Elizabeth Taylor, a visitor to the set, and
below, preparing for a scene with
Richard Burton (*Geoffrey Keating*)

JH acting as host for a
meeting of the Galway
Blazers at St. Clerans,
before becoming Master

nowing Tony how to shoot.
elow, a morning's bag
Agence Dalmas)

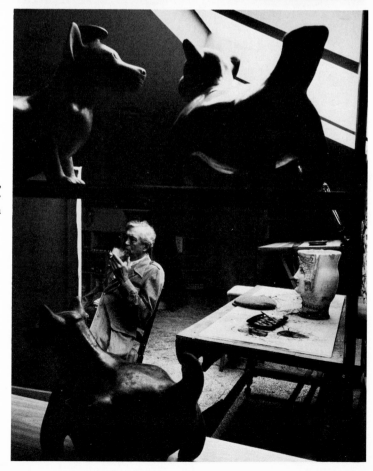

In his studio at St. Clerans,
1968, framed by a few
of his pre-Columbian
sculptures (*Dennis Stock*)

JH and gorillas at
Howletts, a private zoo near
Canterbury in England
(*Geoffrey Keating*)

Playing with one o
Kitty-kat's kittens a
St. Cleran

Exercising the Blazers' pac

The great Seamus, JH's
Irish wolfhound, who lived
to the wonderful age of 14.
JH holds Betty O'Kelly's
shih-tzu, Choo-choo (*Daily
Express, Manchester*)

With a young filly at
St. Clerans

In the dining room
St. Clerans, 196

Pauline and Philippe de
Rothschild, 1970

Life at Las Caletas. Above left, working on a script (*Glenn T. Carter*). Above, Allegra with Gladys Hill's adopted daughter, Marisol (*Joan Blake*). Left, JH and Gladys on the beach (*Cath de Longpre*), and below, JH and his Rotweiler Don Diego go for a dip (*Glenn T. Carter*). Above right, JH sits on the rocky beach near his cottage (*Bert Gore*). Below right, Maricela Hernandez and JH enroute from Puerto Vallarta to Las Caletas (*Joan Blake*).

Producer John
Foreman, JH and
stunt man during
making of *The Li[...]
and Times of Jud[...]
Roy Bean*, 1972.
Below, Sean Conn[...]
and JH on locatio[...]
in Morocco for
*The Man Who
Would Be King*,
1975

ming *Wise Blood,* 1979. Michael Fitzgerald
l his wife are at right, Benedict Fitzgerald and JH at left

A meeting with Orson Welles in Toronto, 1979
(*Courtesy Timothy Greenfield-Sanders*)

JH and his children at Tony's wedding. Tony is standing at left,
next to his half-brother, Danny. JH is flanked by Anjelica, left, and Allegra

pronounce that, so it became something like "Alouber." Alouber would come right up to the camera, sometimes knocking it over, and almost every shot we made had him in it. I played with the idea of bringing Alouber back to Ireland with me, and went so far as to ask Betty O'Kelly by cable what she thought about it. She took a very dim view of putting an African elephant in with our thoroughbreds.

I played a game with one giraffe. I would stand under him with my hat on, and he would lower his great neck slowly, nip the hat off my head and carry it as high as he could before dropping it. He loved this game, and he would continue as long as I would stand there and play it with him. I wanted to use this giraffe in a shot, so they brought him in from the pasture with a halter and a long rope. He got the line wrapped around his legs and became frantic. I went to disentangle him, but Commandant Lefevre yelled at me to keep clear. A giraffe in panic is dangerous; it can actually kill a lion with its hooves. So I walked quietly around in front of him and began talking to him. He recognized my voice, stopped struggling, then bent his head and took my hat. We played our game for a minute or two, and he calmed down so that I was able to snake the rope from around his legs.

The most important shot—that of a cow elephant rescuing her young one from a stockade—was simple enough to set up. We separated a mother from her baby and placed the youngster in a log-fenced enclosure. The old lady went racing around the stockade, picking up speed rapidly—and an elephant can move very fast—until she decided there was no alternative but to go right through the timbers after her child. She proceeded to do just that, and the result was the best shot in the picture.

I would like to go back to Gangia Na-bodio. A great river flowed by it, and there was a lovely hour just before sunset when the mahouts took their charges down to the river for their nightly bath. After they had been scrubbed down thoroughly, the elephants lay on their sides in the river and played with each other, spraying water happily. Then the cows were led up a short road and chained, and each baby elephant ran unerringly to his or her mother's side. At sunset the mahouts stood at attention by their elephants while the flag was lowered and the tattoo sounded.

Only successful pictures are made over again; I've never understood why. I've never known of an instance where the remake was as good as the original. There is no formula that enables one to re-create the unique chemistry that went into making a particular picture a success. It should be the other way around. Unsuccessful pictures—those based on good material—which for reasons of time, place or circumstance just didn't come off the first time around, are the ones that should be given a second chance. That certainly applies to *The Roots of Heaven*. I wish I could do it over again. Today. Only with Darryl. But that's impossible because he died the other day.

The Roots of Heaven completed my three-picture commitment to 20th Century-Fox. It was then that I made the mistake of agreeing to direct a Western called *The Unforgiven*. Hecht-Hill-Lancaster had come to me with the proposal. I read the script by Ben Maddow (who had worked with me on *The Asphalt Jungle*), considered the strength of the cast—Burt Lancaster, Audrey Hepburn, Audie Murphy, Charles Bickford and Lillian Gish—and decided to do it. I thought I saw in Maddow's script the potential for a more serious—and better—film than either he or Hecht-Hill-Lancaster had originally contemplated; I wanted to turn it into the story of racial intolerance in a frontier town, a comment on the real nature of community "morality." The trouble was that the producers disagreed. What they wanted was what I had unfortunately signed on to make when I accepted the job in the first place—a swashbuckler about a larger-than-life frontiersman.

26

This difference of intention did not become an issue until we were very close to shooting time, and quite mistakenly I agreed to stick it out, thus violating my own conviction that a picture-maker should undertake nothing but what he believes in—regardless. From that moment the entire picture turned sour. Everything went to hell. It was as if some celestial vengeance had been loosed upon me for infidelity to my principles.

Some of the things that happened are painful to remember. While we were shooting in Durango in Mexico, Audrey Hepburn fell off a horse and fractured a vertebra in her back. I felt responsible, having put her on a horse for the first time. No matter that she had had a good teacher, was brought on slowly, and turned out to be a natural rider. When her horse bolted and some idiot tried to stop it by throwing up his arms, her fall was on my conscience. It delayed shooting for three weeks. Then there was the near-drowning of Audie Murphy and an old friend of mine from Army days named Bill Pickens, who had gone out duck-shooting on a lake in Durango. Audie, who had a bad hip from a war wound, couldn't swim, and Bill wouldn't leave him; they both would have gone down had not the photographer Inge Morath, a championship swimmer, happened to spot them from shore through the telephoto lens of her camera. She realized they were in trouble, immediately stripped to panties and bra and swam out to them. It was about half a mile, but she reached them just in time and supported both Audie and Bill back to shore. The rescue was picked up by the newspapers and treated as though it were a publicity stunt. Nothing could have been further from the truth.

But in the end the worst of it was the picture we made. Some of my pictures I don't care for, but *The Unforgiven* is the only one I actually dislike. Despite some good performances, the overall tone is bombastic and over-inflated. Everybody in it is bigger than life. I watched it on television one night recently, and after about half a reel I had to turn the damned thing off. I couldn't bear it.

I have to admit that there is one joyful memory from that time in Mexico. Billy Pearson had come down to visit me. A new luxury golf club outside Durango was celebrating its opening with a major tournament, and an international cast of golfing celebrities was on hand for it. Billy and I thought about this, and hit upon a caper that was wild even by Billy's standards. We bought 2,000 ping-pong balls and inscribed them with the most terrible things we could think of: "Go home you Yankee sons-of-bitches!" "Fuck you dirty Mexican cabrones!" and similar sentiments. Then we rented a small airplane and dumped all 2,000 ping-pong balls on the fairway while play was under way. It was a triumph. Nobody could possibly locate a golf ball. It took days to clean up the course, the tournament was canceled and everybody was furious—especially Burt Lancaster, who was one of the tournament sponsors and took his golf quite seriously.

I saw a good deal of Pauline and Philippe de Rothschild. She had come to live in Europe, of course. I often went to Mouton, and they spent a week or two every year with me at St. Clerans.

Mouton was the most beautifully run of any house I've ever been in. It seemed to happen miraculously; except for meals, one scarcely ever saw a servant. But they were there. Your soiled linen was collected as soon as you left your room, and was waiting, washed and pressed, when you came back. I had never known sheets to feel the way Mouton sheets felt at night—so smooth and fresh against the skin. One day, passing an open door, I discovered why: two maids were ironing a bed with flat irons.

Pauline's table decorations were famous. They were her own unique expression: centerpieces of grasses, mosses, fern leaves arranged into miniature landscapes. Sometimes each piece would have an individual creation. There was no attempt at realism, no little mirrors for lakes or ponds: they were abstract compositions, perfect expressions of *shibui*—the Japanese word meaning a taste in art like the aftertaste of a persimmon, almost bitter.

One day I had a call from Philippe. He was with Pauline in Boston seeing a heart specialist. She had to be operated on. There was an eminent surgeon in New Zealand, and they were going there. Perhaps, Philippe suggested, I would like to see her before they went. I got the message and was on the next plane.

She explained the open-heart procedure to me with the help of medical charts. If she felt any anxiety, it was completely hidden. She only marveled at the artfulness of the operation.

She nearly died in New Zealand: she was in fact dead—without a heartbeat—for more than three minutes. Describing the incident afterwards, she said she left her body and came back to it. But the experience of dying had not been at all frightening: it made death lose all terror for her.

Pauline and Philippe traveled extensively after the operation, and I visited them wherever they happened to be. Pauline didn't care for exotic places. She liked things bleak, wintry, austere—Venice in the winter, Holland—a fourteenth-century castle with a dark moat in which black swans circled endlessly. Russia she found particularly to her liking and once expressed the desire to live there. Philippe would do anything that Pauline asked but this left him aghast. He said to me, "Good god! Can you imagine me, a Rothschild, living in Russia?"

A second operation became necessary. This time it was to be done in Boston. American techniques were now the equal of any. She had to be there several weeks beforehand in preparation. I was able to spend a few days with her. She had me meet her surgeon—a handsome, youngish man. She questioned me: What did I think of him? Did I like him? I was able to say with honesty that I trusted and liked him very much. My approval seemed to put her mind at rest.

I went away and came back a few days after the surgery. Philippe was distressed. Her condition was critical and worsening. Before going in to her he said, "Don't touch her, John. She doesn't like anyone to touch her—even her doctor." We went in and I spoke to her . . . and, very slowly, her hand came out to me. I hesitated—then took it. It gripped mine. Later she told me she had wanted to die and be out of her misery until that moment; from then on she felt like living. My voice was from a happier time; it offered an escape from present pain.

The last time I saw Pauline was in Santa Barbara, California. I flew up to Los Angeles and had lunch with her. She looked tired, I thought. She was on some kind of heart medication. She took long walks every day. We talked about my selling St. Clerans. It saddened her. When it was time to leave she came with me to the airport. It was a long ride from the hotel, but she insisted on seeing me off. Two days later she went out for her walk, came back into the lobby of the hotel and fell dead.

There was something elemental between Pauline and me—an affinity. Often we read each other's thoughts. It's come to me that we were supposed to be in love. If we were, it was another kind of love. Her going left a hole in my life.

In 1959, while I was home in Ireland, I got a call from Frank Taylor. He said he was interested in producing a film called *The Misfits*. Arthur Miller had written the script with a role for his wife, Marilyn Monroe. Would I like to read it? I didn't know Miller at the time, but I admired his work, and I said by all means. Frank sent it to me, and it was excellent. I called him back and told him I would very much like to make the picture.

I had met Marilyn Monroe in 1949 when I was filming *We Were Strangers*. She used to come to the set and watch the shooting. She knew Sam Spiegel. There was some talk of Columbia giving her a screen test. She was a very pretty girl, young and appealing, but so are thousands of girls in Hollywood. Such talk often leads to the casting couch rather than to the studio floor, and I suspected someone was setting her up. Something about Marilyn elicited my protectiveness, so, to forestall any hankypanky, I expressed my readiness to do a test, in color, with John Garfield playing opposite her. It would not by any means be a cheap test to make. I didn't see Marilyn around after that. She just disappeared, and I forgot about her.

I was testing for *The Asphalt Jungle* when little Johnny Hyde of the William Morris Agency called and said he had a girl just right for the part of Angela—might she read for me? Arthur Hornblow, the producer of *The Asphalt Jungle*, was with me a few days later when Johnny brought the girl around. I recognized her as the girl I'd saved from the casting couch. The scene she was to read called for Angela to be stretched out on a divan; there was no divan in my office, so Marilyn said, "I'd like to do the scene on the floor."

"Of course, my dear, any way it feels right to you."

And that's the way she did it. She kicked off her shoes, lay down on the floor and read for us. When she finished, Arthur and I looked at each other and nodded. She was Angela to a "T." I later discovered that Johnny Hyde was in love with her. Johnny was a very fine, very reliable agent, and we were friends, but Marilyn didn't get the part because of Johnny. She got it because she was damned good.

Her drama coach, a Russian woman named Natasha Lytess, appeared on the set with her. At the end of a take Marilyn would look to her for approval. The coach would nod her head. Marilyn was excellent in the film. She had been under contract to 20th Century-Fox, but they had dropped the option. When Darryl Zanuck saw *The Asphalt Jungle*, Fox picked her up again, fast. That role was the beginning for Marilyn, and she was always grateful to me. It started her on her way to fame and led—more than a decade later—to our working together in *The Misfits*, her last completed film.

We had some costume fittings with Marilyn in New York, and then Frank Taylor and I flew to Nevada to look at locations Steve Grimes wanted me to see. During the filming we lived in the Mapes Hotel in Reno, and I spent a lot of my nights in the downstairs casino.

In 1960 there was no comparing Reno and Las Vegas. Reno still had some flavor of the Old West. It hadn't yet begun catering to the two-dollar bettors, nor was its chief asset the one-armed bandit. There was mostly craps, blackjack and roulette. Every so often a high-roller would come in, put up his bundle, get the limit raised and try to break the house. I had a marvelous time losing my ass one night and winning it back the next.

I knew Marilyn's reputation for being late on the set, so before we started shooting I had the daily call changed from 9:00 a.m. to 10:00 a.m., hoping this would make things easier for her. It didn't. Clark Gable would drive out to work in his little sports car, rehearse his lines with his stand-in, then open a book. He never uttered one word of complaint, no matter what time Marilyn showed up. Arthur Miller said Marilyn was afraid that if she didn't get enough sleep she wouldn't look her best the next day; this idea amounted to an obsession, so she was taking pills to go to sleep and pills to wake up in the morning. I was very disturbed by her actions and appearance. She seemed to be in a daze half the time. When she was herself, though, she could be marvelously effective. She wasn't acting—I mean she was not pretending to an emotion. It was the real thing. She would go deep down within herself and find it and bring it up into consciousness. But maybe that's what all truly good acting consists of. It was profoundly sad to see what was happening to her. One time I talked to Arthur Miller about it. "You've got to get Marilyn off the drugs. You're her husband and the only one who can do it. If you don't, you'll feel guilty as long as you live. If she doesn't stop now, she'll be in an institution in two or three years—or dead!" I was lecturing him, little realizing that he had already done everything in his power and was at the end of his rope.

The material looked good on the screen. Marilyn was always late getting to the set, and she came later and later. Sometimes we got in only a couple of hours work a day. She was in most of the scenes, and we had to wait until she showed up before we could start shooting. Not only was Marilyn in a bad way, but it was obvious that things were bad between her and Arthur. I saw him humiliated a couple of times, not only by Marilyn but by some of her hangers-on. I think they hoped to demonstrate their loyalty to Marilyn by being impertinent to Arthur. On these occasions Arthur never changed expression. One evening I was about to drive away from the location—miles out in the desert—when I saw Arthur standing alone. Marilyn and her friends hadn't offered him a ride back; they'd just left him. If I hadn't happened to see him, he would have been stranded out there. My sympathies were more and more with him.

Marilyn continued heavily into the drugs, and finally the young doctor on location refused to give her any more, even though he feared he might lose his job by not catering to her desires. She got drugs elsewhere, however, and eventually she broke down completely and had to be sent to a hospital in Los Angeles for two weeks. The picture closed down. There were no holidays to help us, so we had to pay the entire crew for every working day lost. This added enormously to our costs—which already were staggering. The cast alone made *The Misfits* the most expensive black-and-white film—above the line—that had been made up until then: Clark Gable, Marilyn Monroe, Eli Wallach, Montgomery Clift, Thelma Ritter, Kevin McCarthy. Now the below-the-line costs were getting out of hand, primarily due to these interminable delays.

I went to see Marilyn in the hospital, and she seemed so much better that I took heart. She was bright, alert, guilty about her behavior during the picture. She knew, oh, so well what the drugs were doing to her, and she asked me if I could ever forgive her. I reassured her. When she came back to Reno, she was given a great welcome at the airport.

Marilyn had a wonderful spontaneous skill in dealing with the press, which was there on location all of the time. At the airport, before disembarking from her chartered flight, she spent three quarters of an hour preparing herself to be seen and interviewed. She had the knack of saying exactly the right thing:

"Miss Monroe, what do you wear to bed at night?"

"Chanel Number Five!"

After Marilyn's return we were all sure it would be different from here on. In a few days we knew better. Marilyn returned to her old ways as though she'd never had a break. Arthur moved to another hotel—at her request, I was told. One Sunday afternoon I visited her in her suite to get some idea of what to expect in the week ahead. She greeted me euphorically—then went into a kind of trance. She was the worst I'd ever seen her. Her hair was a tangle; her hands and feet were grubby; she was wearing only a short nightgown which wasn't any cleaner than the rest of her.

There was something very touching about her, a kind of vulnerability. When Suzanne Flon visited me on location, Marilyn admired a jet necklace she was wearing, so Suzanne took it off and gave it to her. The next day Marilyn went to Suzanne's room and gave her a diamond ring. Suzanne didn't want it, but she couldn't refuse. When we talked about Marilyn, tears came to Suzanne's eyes. She knew somehow—we all did—that something awful was going to happen to her.

I never felt Marilyn's much-publicized sexual attraction in the flesh, but on the screen it came across forcefully. But there was much more to her than that. She was appreciated as an artist in Europe long before her acceptance as anything but a sex symbol in the United States. Jean-Paul Sartre considered Marilyn Monroe the finest actress alive. He wanted her to play the leading female role in *Freud*.

We finished the picture. It had been an agonizing experience, not only for me but for everyone, including Marilyn. She started another film, was taken off it and then killed herself by accident. Too many sleeping pills—a bottle of them at hand and no one there to save her. She'd made this mistake several times before and had received emergency treatment. I'm sure she never meant to take her life.

Montgomery Clift and Marilyn were extraordinary together, particularly in a long scene—several pages—behind a saloon, against a hill of beer cans and junk automobiles. It was a love scene that wasn't a love scene, and Arthur Miller at his best, too. From what Monty did in *The Misfits*, I had every reason to have faith in him. But unfortunately he turned out to be another bad case. He was presently to suffer Marilyn's problems himself, and follow more or less in her footsteps. And I would again be an involved witness.

Clark Gable had a bad back, and in one scene, driving through the crowd, going to the rodeo, Monty kept hammering on it out of sheer exuberance. Clark said, "For God's sake, Monty! Take it easy!" Later, when Clark took off his shirt, there were black-and-blue marks on his shoulders and arms. But this made no impression on Monty, who was deep into his role, and he did it again. Finally Clark got furious. He turned on Monty. "I'm going to hang one on you, you little bastard, if you do that again!" Monty burst into tears.

One of the myths attached to *The Misfits* was that Clark Gable died of a heart attack because of over-exertion in this film. That is utter nonsense. Toward the end of the picture there was a contest between Clark and the stallion the cowboys had captured. It looked like rough work, and it was, but it was the stunt men who were thrown around, not Clark.

I got on well with Clark. I spent many hours with him in his trailer—thanks to Marilyn. He thought of himself as an actor, not a screen personality. He liked reminiscing about his early days in the theater—old-time actors' talk. I saw very soon that Clark knew exactly what he was doing. Two or three times I thought I saw ways to improve his performance. I was mistaken. Each time I had him go back to his own way. He was nonplussed by Marilyn's behavior. It was as though she'd revealed some horrid fact of life that just couldn't be accepted in his scheme of things.

Because I edit as I go along, Clark got to see the first cut of the film, and he was delighted. The picture was way over budget. It would cost about $4,000,000—and that was a lot of money in those days for a black-and-white film. Clark said, "Hell, John! If the studio is unhappy about the cost, I'll buy this picture for four million dollars. I think it's the best thing I've ever done. Now all I want is to see that kid of mine born!" That was on November 4, and he was due to become a father in February. It wasn't to be. He suffered a heart attack on November 5 and died less than two weeks later.

Because of Clark's death and the tragedy of seeing Marilyn slowly destroying herself, my memories of *The Misfits* are mostly melancholy. But there were some good moments, too. There was, for example, the Labor Day Camel Race at nearby Virginia City.

One day Ernie Anderson called me from San Francisco. "John, have you ever ridden a camel?"

"Well, I've been on a camel's back," I said. "Why do you ask?"

"Would you like to ride in a camel race against Billy Pearson?"

"Sure!"

It was some weeks away, and I always say yes if something is far enough in the future. It seems that camels had been imported into the Virginia City area in the nineteenth century as an experiment. They could carry supplies and ore across the desert much more easily and in greater quantities than horses or mules could. But somehow they never caught on. When I compare the character of a horse or a mule with that of a camel, I think I know why. Camels are vicious animals at best. A good camel driver, on awakening in the morning, and before addressing Mecca, finds himself a big stick and beats the hell out of his camel. That starts the day. I don't believe there is any such thing as a faithful camel. Besides their bad temper, I understand that camels can carry a spirochete, so that when they bite you—which is often—you may contract a disease similar to syphilis.

Anyway, a hundred years earlier there had been a great camel race in Virginia City. This was to be a commemoration of that race. But only four camels could be located, two of them from the San Francisco zoo. When the race was announced, reporters from the San Francisco *Chronicle*—which was backing Billy Pearson—went out to the zoo with Billy to inspect the camels. They got into the pen with the camels and were promptly chased out. I was to ride one of them, a five-year-old Bactrian, or two-humped camel, named Old Heenan. Billy's was a seven-year-old Arabian dromedary, or one-humped camel, named Izzy. A third entry, from Indio, California, was a fifteen-year-old female named Sheba, and I'm not ashamed to say I've forgotten what the fourth entry was called.

The two camels from San Francisco arrived in Virginia City about a week before the race. Obviously no rider had ever been on their backs, and there was too little time even to attempt to break them. I began, however, to get the germ of an idea of how I might pull this race off. Billy came down and stayed with me in the Mapes Hotel—undoubtedly to scout my strategy, but I kept a closed mouth. The other two camels were decked out in fancy accouterments, and the cowboys who rode them were dressed like Arabs. I didn't think they would give me too much trouble; it was Billy Pearson I had to beat. There were still four or five days remaining before the race, so I had the time to put my plan in motion.

The animals were stabled in an old barn at the foot of the main street in Virginia City, and that fact was at the core of my strategy. I approached the officials of the race and persuaded them to change the one-mile course from an area outside town to one that would begin at the head of the main street and terminate at the barn. I then swore my keeper to secrecy and told him that if he ever revealed what we were about to do, I would shoot him dead.

"Tonight lead my camel to the starting line, then lead him back to the barn and have feed in the manger. Do this twice tonight, and tomorrow I will give you further instructions."

The next day, after work, I called him and asked, "How did it go?"

"No problems," he replied. "I did as you said. I led him down and back and down and back again."

"Good! Now, tonight you are to lead the camel down once and lead him back. Then take him to the starting line again and let him go. Call me back and tell me what happens."

He called back and said, "I turned him loose, Mr. Huston, and he went right back to the barn!"

"Excellent. Do this every night until the race starts. By the way, did he *run* back?"

"Well," replied the keeper, "he didn't exactly run, but he kind of trotted."

"Good. Good. Now, just remember to do this every night, and tell no one!"

The day of the race came. It started with a champagne breakfast in Reno, after which we all climbed into antique autos supplied by Harrah's Club for the drive to Virginia City. Herb Caen claimed later that when my machine failed on a hill I shot it in the radiator—to keep it from being captured and burnt at the stake by the Indians. I don't believe that this is true, but I can't positively swear to the events myself. I'm afraid I was as pissed as most of the contestants and spectators. Everyone in the entire town was rollicking drunk before the end of the day.

The time came for the race, and we proceeded to "saddle up" our mounts. This became quite a contest in itself. The camels were excited by the crowds, and most uncooperative. I had a hell of a time getting a hackamore on my steed, who was trying his best to bite me, and I received a round of applause from the spectators when I finally managed it.

Billy was upset because my camel had two humps—which I could sit between—while his had only one. His attendants tried to compensate for this by winding a tennis net around his camel so he had something to hold on to. Billy was dressed in racing silks—my colors, green and white. The Indio contingent was arrayed as Bedouins. For my part, I wore English jodhpurs and a mauve shirt sporting a Faubus-for-President button.

As we prepared to mount, I told my attendants what to do. "Wait till everyone else is mounted—put me up last. As soon as my ass touches the camel, fire the starting gun and give the beast one whale of a smack across his quarters."

This they did. When the gun went off, the camel from Indio jumped straight up in the air, and I think his rider is still up there somewhere. The other import turned and bolted in the opposite direction. Billy's camel started off at an angle, scattering the crowd, jumped onto the bed of a pickup truck, cleared a Thunderbird and finally, going full tilt, disappeared into Piper's Opera House, with Billy hanging on for dear life to his tennis net.

My camel took off straight for the barn. I don't think he even knew I was on his back. A car was running alongside, loaded with photographers, and they say Old Heenan hit forty miles per hour—better than racehorse speed—which is not to be believed, of course. But he was running flat out.

As we crossed the finish line and approached the barn, I ducked to keep from being knocked off by the top beam of the doorway, then jumped clear before Old Heenan could enter his stall. Of course I won the race hands down, and Lucius Beebe presented me with the trophy. One account—I believe Herb Caen's—of a radio interview following the race went something like this:

"Mr. Huston, to what do you attribute your victory in this race?"

"I owe my splendid victory to a deep understanding of the camel. You're really living when you're up there between those humps. It has its up and downs, but so has life."

"How did you manage to mount the animal?"

"It was man against beast. Either I mounted him or he mounted me."

"And what about your chief competitor, Billy Pearson? He's quite a famous jockey. Weren't you worried about him?"

"Billy Pearson is an obvious disgrace to the camel-riding profession. He rode over parked cars, widows, orphans—in fact, there are camel-stunned babies scattered all over these historic hillsides. It is a scene of carnage, owing to Pearson's shocking disregard for life, liberty and the pursuit of happiness. He just doesn't belong up there on the hump of a camel."

"Mr. Huston, Billy Pearson claims it was a foul start."

"Perhaps so, but when you come right down to it, anything to do with camels is foul" . . . and so on.

Before the war, when Wolfgang Reinhardt and I were writing *Dr. Ehrlich's Magic Bullet* for Warners, we discussed the possibility of making a picture based on Freud's life and work. Wolfgang brought 27 the subject up again during one of his visits to St. Clerans—it would have been about midsummer in 1959. We discussed a number of approaches, and finally agreed that this should be something that breathed brimstone; Freud's descent into the unconscious should be as terrifying as Dante's descent into Hell. With this in mind, Wolfgang and I went to Paris to see Jean-Paul Sartre.

Although I had directed Sartre's play *No Exit* in New York in 1946, I hadn't met the man until 1952, while filming *Moulin Rouge* in Paris. We had subsequently seen each other a few times and, at one point, talked briefly about making his play *Lucifer* into a film. Sartre was a Communist and an anti-Freudian. Nevertheless I considered him the ideal man to write the *Freud* screenplay. He had read psychology deeply, knew Freud's works intimately and would have an objective and logical approach.

Sartre disagreed with Freud in a social sense rather than in a scientific sense. He regarded Freud's studies as valuable for what they discovered about the human mind, but of little social import because the role of the psychoanalyst was in fact so limited. I'm inclined to agree. Bored wives and problem children of the affluent make up the bulk of a top-ranking psychoanalyst's practice. Fees are exorbitant, and treatment is usually a matter of years. The movers and shakers have no time for it, and those who most need psychiatric counseling are precisely those who can't afford it.

Sartre agreed to write the screenplay for $25,000. I phoned Elliot Hyman, who had been in on *Moby Dick* and *Moulin Rouge*, and without hesitation he put up the money.

Sartre was slow getting started because he had to finish a play and a book, but he finally got down to it, and one day I received his first draft. As I recall, it ran well over 300 pages in French. Figuring a page a minute, it was more than five hours of motion picture. The story, as Sartre saw it, described the development of Freud's theory of the Oedipus Complex.

I agreed with this story line in principle, but Sartre explored in turn each wrong alley down which Freud had ventured. He related (in prodigious detail) Freud's relationships with his several surrogate fathers, at long last reaching the point where Freud turned to self-analysis and discovered that his own neurosis was based on his relationship with his real father.

It was simply too much to tell in one motion picture. We corresponded about the problem, and Sartre came to St. Clerans at the beginning of January 1960 for two weeks of long daily meetings during which we attempted to reduce the material to screenplay length.

I've never known anyone to work with the singlemindedness of Sartre. He made notes—of his own words—as he talked. There was no such thing as a conversation with him; he talked incessantly, and there was no interrupting him. You'd wait for him to catch his breath, but he wouldn't. The words came out in an absolute torrent. You might be able to catch him off guard and get in a point, but if he answered you at all—which was seldom—he would resume his monologue instantly. Sartre spoke no English, and because of the rapidity of his speech, I could barely follow even his basic thought processes. I am sure that much of what he said was brilliant. It was never, however, succinct. Everyone's face had a glazed look, even though they all spoke fluent French. It was quite a scene: Sartre himself taking notes, with both his secretary and Wolfgang's flipping pages in their steno pads as they tried to keep up, while Wolfgang and I milled about the edges. Sometimes I'd leave the room in desperation—on the verge of exhaustion from trying to follow what he was saying; the drone of his voice followed me until I was out of earshot and, when I'd return, he wouldn't even have noticed that I'd been gone.

Sartre disappeared after dinner every evening and worked up his notes of the day, which his secretary—a multilingual Arab girl—then typed in English. He started work very early in the morning, and by the time I'd get down, around 10:30 a.m., he'd be sitting there with as many as twenty-five pages in hand.

Sartre was a little barrel of a man, and as ugly as a human being can be. His face was both bloated and pitted, his teeth were yellowed and he was wall-eyed. He wore a gray suit, black shoes, white shirt, tie and vest. His appearance never changed. He'd come down in the morning in this suit, and he would still be wearing it the last thing at night. The suit always appeared to be clean, and his shirt was clean, but I never knew if he owned one gray suit or several identical gray suits.

He had a play opening in Paris, and I remember being struck by his complete lack of interest in the opening-night reception. The reviews arrived one morning—in a fat envelope—and he never even interrupted our discussion (or rather his monologue) to see what they said. When it was time for lunch, he retired for a few moments into a small room to look them over, then said nothing when he returned. I had to ask to read them to find out that they were in fact good. I gazed at this monster of imperturbability sipping his sherry—and thought about sitting up all night to find out how Dad's *Othello* had fared.

One morning he came down and his cheek was swollen. He had a bad tooth.

I said, "We'd best get you to Dublin with that."

"No, no. Let's just go in to Galway."

I didn't know any dentist in Galway, but that didn't matter to him. So we made an appointment with a local dentist and took him in. He was out in a few minutes, having had the tooth pulled. A tooth more or less made no difference in Sartre's cosmos. The physical world he left to others; his was of the mind. He was, by the way, very heavy into the pills. I think he had to be to keep going at his pace.

I showed Sartre *Let There Be Light*. He was fascinated by the hypnosis scenes, so I told him that I had learned the technique in the process of making the film, and agreed to demonstrate with the Arab girl. She was an easy subject. Then Sartre wanted to be hypnotized, but it turned out to be quite impossible. Occasionally you encounter someone like that— one other whom I found to be hypnotically impregnable was Otto Preminger.

Sartre and I talked about various shortcuts in the script, and he went back to Paris to make them. Some time later he sent me the revised version. I wasn't too surprised to discover that it was even longer than the first draft. Sartre once wrote a foreword to a book by Jean Genet that was longer than the book.

I had told Sartre not to give any thought to censorship, either in language or in the content of scenes, and he had apparently taken this to mean that complete freedom was the order of the day. He saw no reason why the picture shouldn't be eight hours long.

A few days after I received this second screenplay, Frank Taylor phoned to ask me to direct *The Misfits*. I was free to do so because *Freud* had not been sold to any studio and the only money spent on it so far was the comparatively small amount for Sartre's services.

When the *Misfits* was completed, I came back to *Freud* and had conversations with the heads of Universal about it. They agreed to do it if the problem of censorship could be overcome. They worried that the picture would be censored out of existence, and insisted that I clear the script with the Catholic Church in New York before they would proceed. The Catholic Church couldn't stop us from making the picture, but could damage its commercial prospects by forbidding the faithful to see it.

I met with two priests and one lay woman, and we discussed the script at length. Their opposition was on moral grounds: Freud's philosophy, they claimed, does not admit the existence of Good and Evil. Only a priest has the right to search into the soul of man. The very suggestion of sexuality in children was repugnant to them. I could not, of course, change *Freud* to suit such Catholic prejudice without completely destroying the picture—to say nothing of Freudianism—and the best I could hope for was a compromise. Our discussions were partly theological and scientific, but mostly pseudo-theological and pseudo-scientific. It wasn't easy, but I managed to come to enough of an understanding with them for Universal to proceed with the project. As soon as Universal gave me the green light, I returned to Ireland, where Wolfgang joined me. By this time it was plain that going on with Sartre made no sense, so at my suggestion Universal put Charlie Kaufman on salary to do a treatment. Charlie and I had worked together on the script of *Let There Be Light*, and he was familiar to some extent with the subject. I thought Charlie, Wolfgang and I would make a good team.

Unfortunately, I could see from the first pages Charlie turned in that he was intent on following the pattern of the biographical pictures Warners had done before the war (*Zola, Pasteur, Dr. Ehrlich's Magic Bullet*). The protagonist is invariably a hero, and lovable to the point of banality. This was the very opposite of the sheet lightning and sulfur I had in mind.

Charlie had been in St. Clerans only a few weeks when a personal emergency—serious illness in his family—called him back to Hollywood. I never asked him to return.

Wolfgang and I then went to work. Wolfgang's command of English wasn't very good, and he didn't know much about writing a scene, but he was exceptionally knowledgeable about Freud and about psychoanalysis in general. He spent long hours daily working with Sartre's script, cutting, trimming, synthesizing. He'd hand material to Gladys Hill from time to time, and she would type it into good English, make suggestions and turn it over to me for further editing. In this manner, it took us almost six months to write our version of *Freud*. Much of what Sartre had done was in our version—in fact, it was the backbone of it. In some scenes his dialogue was left intact.

The screenplay ran to about 190 pages, which meant a three-hour film—an hour longer than most feature films. For obvious reasons, the studio wanted me to cut it. I argued that the story couldn't be told in less time. The question was deferred. Perhaps we'd put in an intermission. In any case, we'd leave it up to the preview audiences to decide. Meanwhile I was to shoot it as written.

I wanted to know what Sartre thought about our new script. He was vacationing in Rome, so I sent him a copy by Wolfgang, thinking that they would have discussions about it. After some days Wolfgang phoned to say that Sartre wanted nothing further to do with it. He had no comments and, furthermore, wanted his name removed from the picture. I was quite surprised and disappointed by this news. I said, "Surely we're entitled to hear his comments! Doesn't he have *anything* to say about it? He has, after all, been paid in full. I think this only proper."

Wolfgang said he would relay my request to Sartre.

I have no idea what happened between Sartre and Wolfgang during their meetings in Rome, but Sartre's answer to me was a letter full of recriminations. He questioned the depth of my understanding of Freud, and suggested that I pay greater attention to Wolfgang, who knew even more about Freud than he, Sartre, and a great deal more than I, Huston. Sartre's letter divided us into two camps. He and Wolfgang against me. It had to be with Wolfgang's knowledge and approval. I was surprised and dismayed at this breach of friendship. But he really had no place in Hollywood. He and his brother, Gottfried, had been raised as princes. Their father, Max, had the greatest reputation, I suppose, that any director in the theater has ever had. When he left Austria for the United States, it was like an emperor abdicating.

Gottfried was better able to cope with that world of agents, columnists, studio heads and sycophants than Wolfgang, who lacked the common touch and was secretly appalled by the vulgarities of those around him. He was therefore appreciated only by a limited few. I remember when we worked together at Warners he was no more than tolerated, and at each option his job was in danger. Blanke defended him. Jack Warner had small regard for him.

Wolfgang was a beautifully educated, discriminating man who was quite unable to juggle his values opportunistically. When I say "unable," I mean just that. He couldn't. He lived with his wife, Lolly, and their three sons in Santa Monica for years, in a kind of retirement from Hollywood. He associated mostly with people like Christopher Isherwood, Aldous Huxley, Salka Viertel, Iris Tree and Friedrich Ledebur. They were all of the Old World. I found their company most refreshing—an oasis in Hollywood. On the other hand, I shared in the Hollywood life to some extent. Wolfgang couldn't. As a consequence he was misunderstood, distrusted and ill-used by the people who happened to be in power. A great indignity was done Wolfgang in Hollywood, and I think it embittered him. During the making of *Freud* I saw the teethmarks it had left on him. Recently I have read remarks made by Wolfgang concerning incidents that supposedly occurred during the making of the picture. They are either complete fabrications or sadly twisted versions of what really happened. It may be that when we made *Freud* Wolfgang regarded me as the personification of Hollywood—of that world he so thoroughly detested. One can only speculate.

There were still things unresolved in the script. How, for instance, to demonstrate the psychic mechanism of repression? It is one thing to understand it, but quite another to demonstrate it effectively to an audience. I finally enlisted the assistance of Dr. David Stafford-Clark, one of the leading psychiatrists in England, who arranged to spend his vacation time with me in Ireland. David was head of the Psychiatric Clinic at Guy's Hospital in London, among many other things, and was an enormous help.

He was with me in August 1961 when Montgomery Clift arrived. Monty was to play Freud. He had deteriorated to a shocking degree since I had worked with him on *The Misfits*. He was supposedly on the wagon, so no one ever saw him with a drink in his hand, but I soon discovered that each time he passed the bar he'd pick up a bottle of whatever was handy, tip it up and drink from the bottle directly, then wander off. He was also on drugs.

Monty wanted to sit in on our discussions. He had been seeing psychiatrists since 1950 and fancied himself an expert on Freud. Monty would come into the room, take off his shoes and lie down on the floor. He said it was the only way he could think. He would interrupt at the wrong moments, and his remarks were largely incomprehensible. His presence served only to delay and confuse. One day I told him we couldn't include him anymore, explained why, and shut and locked the door. Monty stood outside the door and cried. Then he turned to the bar and drank himself unconscious.

I should have dropped Monty right then, but I didn't. I thought that

when we got on the set and he had the lines he would be all right. I was
mistaken. I would rather make *The Roots of Heaven* again, with all its
hardships, than again go through a single week of what I went through
with Monty on *Freud*.

Monty never stopped drinking. On the plane from London to Munich
he refused to fasten his seatbelt. The Lufthansa attendants had to hold
him down physically and buckle him into his seat.

As soon as we started shooting, I knew I was in for big trouble. He
somehow got hold of past versions of the screenplay and, combining parts
of all the scripts, tried to rewrite scenes. He would produce pages that
were so scrawled they were quite undecipherable to me and he could
hardly read them himself. He would squint and hold them up to his eyes.
I thought that he was simply nearsighted. I'd listen to what he had to say,
then give him the scene we were set up to shoot. He'd read it and
say:

"I . . . can't . . . say . . . it . . . that . . . way. I've . . . got . . . to
. . . say . . . it . . . this . . . way."

What he produced was invariably infantile and absurd.

Finally I realized that this was primarily a stall for time. Monty was
having difficulty memorizing lines. I was surprised at this because he had
done so well during *The Misfits*, only a couple of years earlier. The
explanation is obvious, of course, in retrospect. Monty's lines in *The
Misfits* had been simple, and he had had time to study them. His lines in
Freud were quite difficult. There were many long speeches, the vocabu-
lary was scientific and unfamiliar, and included words of Freud's own
coinage. Monty's dialogue would have taxed the technique of a fine actor
at his best; and Monty was far from being at his best. His accident some
years before had done him great damage. There had been head injuries,
and there is no question in my mind that they included brain damage. His
prior brilliance now came through in fitful flashes. His petulant and obsti-
nate behavior was an attempt to hide from me and the others—and probably himself—that he was no longer able to contend. I'm sure Monty had
almost no conception of the significance of what he said in the picture—
yet he had the ability to make you believe that he did. There was a mist
between him and the rest of the world that you simply couldn't pene-
trate. It must have been agony for him during those moments when he
was fully aware. At times I saw a crucified look on his face. But if the
picture was hell for Monty, it was equally harrowing for me.

Eventually it reached the point where I had to write his lines on boards
and even—having rehearsed the secne—put the lines down on the labels

of bottles, door frames and other objects about the set so that he could move around and arrive at a spot where, on cue, the line would be there for him to read. It worked, but I was loath to do it. At that time the idea of having an actor read lines from a board was abhorrent to me. Times (and actors) have changed; I wouldn't hesitate now.

During this picture Monty was in some ways the male equivalent of Marilyn Monroe, and at about the same stage in his deterioration as she had been during *The Misfits*. Marilyn had been our first choice to do the part of Cecily in *Freud*. Her own analyst, however, advised against it. Not out of concern for Marilyn; he didn't believe a picture about Freud should be made at all because Freud's daughter Anna opposed the project. Later, after he had seen the picture, he told me that he felt he had made a mistake in this. If he had known the type of picture it was to be, he would have recommended that Marilyn do it.

The girl who did play the part of Cecily, Susannah York, was a talented but spoiled young lady, and I had difficulty with her. When we got to her part—quite far along in the shooting schedule—she came over from London. Susannah was the personification of the uninformed arrogance of youth. Shortly, under Monty's influence, she became convinced that she was entitled to scientific opinions regarding a subject of which she was woefully ignorant. She and Monty would stay up night after night rewriting Cecily-Freud scenes and present me with their proposed changes each morning. Once Susannah refused to do a scene as it was written. The production manager took her to a telephone and called her agent, who advised her to do as she was told. From then on she was obedient—but barely.

Monty collected a small group of protective converts and supporters around him who professed to be aghast at the "brutal" manner in which I was treating him. In fact I was doing everything I knew how simply to get a performance out of him, but Monty had the knack of making even the most reasonable request look like persecution. His group of protectors included Susannah, the woman who furnished the period clothing and a few other members of the company, mostly female. I could understand this. Although you often felt like strangling Monty, there was at the same time something fundamentally appealing about him. He called forth your pity and your sympathy, and you'd suddenly feel like embracing and comforting him.

Older women in particular yearned to protect Monty. Nan Sunderland, my father's widow, adored him and often went with him to concerts or the theater. She along with such women as Rosalind Russell and Myrna

Loy—all twice his age—were eager candidates for the role of Monty's surrogate mother. Monty elicited great sympathy by the little-boy way he conducted himself, seeming always on the verge of tears. He skillfully played upon this.

In spite of all these things, it was impossible not to marvel at and admire his talent. Monty's eyes would light up, and you could actually "see" an idea being born in "Freud's" mind. Monty looked intelligent. He looked as though he were having a thought. He wasn't, Christ knows.

As time went by, the situation became worse and worse and the costs due to lost time escalated enormously. I held my temper, exercised all the patience I could muster and continued to try with every trick I knew to get a performance from Monty. Nothing worked. Finally I decided I would get rough with him. I went to his dressing room, opened the door and slammed it behind me so hard that a mirror fell from the wall and shattered, showering glass shards all over the room. Monty looked up at me with a blank expression. I stared back at him—hard. I wanted him to feel my anger. Finally he said, "What are you going to do . . . kill me?" I said, "I'm seriously considering it!" Monty shrugged; it didn't make any difference.

I have read recent accounts of this incident that had me going into Monty's room and smashing chairs, breaking mirrors, tearing the couch apart. It simply didn't happen that way. But now, to Monty and his sympathizers, the charges of brutality were backed up with "facts." Monty added fuel to the fire during a mountain-climbing "dream" sequence. He was "climbing" a short length of rope, beneath which were mattresses. These were placed there for Monty's safety in case he slipped. At the end of each take he could either release his hold and drop the few feet to the mattresses or let himself down hand over hand. Instead, after each shot, when I called "Cut!" Monty proceeded to slide down the rope, holding tightly. In this way he burned his hands horribly. Why he did this I'll never understand. Perhaps he was completely disoriented. Perhaps he was desensitized by drugs. I only remember how shocked I was by the sight of his hands. Monty's defenders have charged that I did this to him deliberately, going so far as to demand take after take while blood from Monty's hands streamed onto the rope. Unthinkable nonsense! Monty, for his own reasons, was beating himself up.

My reputation for cruelty appears to stem directly from this one picture. I find this impossible to understand. That simply isn't me; it isn't the way I work. I don't even give direction when it's called for except in a quiet aside to the artist. When an actor has any doubts, it shows through, to the detriment of the performance—so I go about trying to build an ego, not to destroy it. Apart from Montgomery Clift and—through association—Susannah York, I don't think I've ever had a conflict with an artist—certainly not an important conflict, or one that persisted.

In the next-to-the-last scene in the film Freud delivers his famous lecture on the Oedipus Complex to a hostile audience and then makes his way out into the street. A small scuffle ensues, during which his silk hat is knocked off. He commands a man who has insulted him to pick it up, and the man does so. In falling off, the hat apparently brushed Monty's eye. We couldn't see a bruise or a mark of any kind, but he complained the next day that his eye had been injured. He couldn't see well, and he insisted the studio was responsible. So we had him examined, and it was discovered that Monty had severe cataracts on both eyes and was, in fact, on the verge of losing his eyesight. Before we heard any of this, I was guilty of a remark in very bad taste. I had thought Monty's insistence on seeing an eye doctor at our expense was simply another bit of malingering. The holidays were approaching, and I said, "I suppose now we'll have to get Monty a seeing-eye dog for Christmas, to lead him around the set." As it turned out, that was not so funny.

There was no reasoning with Monty. He was faced with incontrovertible evidence that the problem with his eyes was a long-standing one, but he insisted the damage had been caused by the falling silk hat, and he wanted to sue the studio. In fact, all he was legally entitled to—in the event that his claim was a just one—was $75 a week disability pay. But Monty wouldn't listen when this was explained to him. He wanted to sue. I advised him to call his agents and get them to tell him what his position was. He wouldn't do that, so I called Lew Wasserman—the head of MCA, who represented Monty—and talked with him in front of Monty, hoping that he would listen to reason from someone in whom he had confidence. Not one word sank in. Monty was impossible. I talked with Wasserman again and said, "Lew, you've got to send someone here from your organization to talk to Monty. He needs help!" Lew sent a man from the MCA office in London, but Monty paid scant attention to him either.

The poor devil was *non compos mentis* most of the time. You would forget in moments of frustration that Monty was a woefully sick man.

The construction of *Freud* scene by scene, or rather thought by thought, was predicated, as I said, upon the steps Freud took in working out the theory of the Oedipus Complex. Each step had to be very clearly demonstrated and thoroughly understood by the audience if interest was to be maintained. It was an intellectual suspense story, and no step in its logic could be removed without affecting the whole. The audience had to be educated during the course of the film, but the educational process had to remain integral to the flow of the story line. Audiences don't like to be told that they are being educated after they've paid their money to be entertained. Making clear a concept so difficult as the unconscious took some doing. Yet without an understanding of the nature of the unconscious, the story made no sense. I had hoped that the picture would send the audiences out of the theater in a state of doubt as to their own powers of conscious choice or free will, an understanding that their conscious minds played only a minor role in many of their decisions.

When the picture was finished, it was some two hours and twenty minutes long. We had a number of studio previews to invited audiences, and the picture was generally admired, but the major comment on the cards was that it was too long. There was little action to speak of, and no opportunity for release through humor. The tension built up relentlessly as the picture followed Freud's line of reasoning. I must admit that the audiences appeared to be more fatigued than enlightened.

This was considered by many to be a very daring film for its time. But the prediction about public moral outrage at the suggestion of sexuality in children, for example, was greatly exaggerated. Audiences didn't give a damn whether children thought about, were influenced by or practiced sex. They were, if anything, disappointed that there wasn't more sex in the picture, especially on an adult level. But what they wanted was "healthy" sex—the Marilyn Monroe kind of sex. I am sure some were turned off by the very suggestion that there could be anything sexual about their mothers.

I wanted the picture to be released as it was, but the reaction of the preview audiences was against me. The studio executives prevailed upon me to cut one scene because it offended their own moral concepts. The scene showed a girl under hypnosis telling, in the presence of her father, of his assault upon her. I should not have accepted this cut; the scene was very important to the story because it showed one of the false leads that put Freud onto a wrong line of country. The fact that this one incident was true led him to accept as true other similar testimonies regarding sexual assaults, whereas most of these other patients had merely imagined "relationships" with their fathers; their confessions were simply wish-fulfillments.

But the cut was made, and the picture was still too long. There were other minor cuts, bringing it to something under two hours, and audiences still complained about its length. You don't necessarily speed up slow movies by cutting scenes. If anything, it was a longer picture for the deletions, because the all-important chain of logic had been broken.

The studio decided on a rather long run in New York art theaters before giving the picture a general release. *Freud* was very successful in those theaters and played to packed audiences. But in general release it was not well received. It got a few good reviews, and psychiatrists praised it, but it was, by and large, rejected by audiences. The studio heads had put great stock in this film, thinking it would be their most important production of the year. It turned out to be anything but, disappointing both them and me grievously. They tried changing the name to *Freud: The Secret Passion*, but that didn't make any difference. Nothing helped.

I saw *Freud* again recently. There are good things in the picture. In spite of the difficulties I had had with Monty, his genius shows through, and in the end I think he gives quite an extraordinary performance.

There were exceptions. The opening scene between Freud and his mother was weak—reminiscent of the old biographical pictures. It was in fact a substitute scene, the last to be shot, and a poor replacement for one that Monty hadn't been up to. So the picture got off to a bad start. I don't think, however, that this was the reason behind the general audience rejection. I don't have any answer for that.

28 Ray Stark, head of Rastar and one of the principal shareholders in Columbia Pictures, is a small, well set-up man with light hair and blue eyes rimmed with thick blond lashes. He laughs at himself a great deal, and at the world around him, but he is relentless in his pursuit of an objective. He has excellent judgment, an appealing kind of amorality and considerable mother wit. He is a gambler, but not the kind of gambler who plays card games or shoots craps. His game is the movies. Today he is one of the most powerful figures in the film industry.

In Ray's Beverly Hills garden is one of the finest collections of sculpture in the West—Giacometti, Manzu, Marini, Lachaise, Moore. Inland from Santa Barbara he has a horse ranch with some forty horses. Unlike the moguls of yore who raised thoroughbreds but could hardly tell one from the other, Ray knows each of his horses by name, and whenever he is in residence makes a point of feeding each and every animal a giant-size carrot daily at sundown.

If something scares Ray, he doesn't back away; he goes for it. Ray knows nothing about horseback riding or high diving, but I have seen him climb onto a horse and take it over the jumps, and I have seen him dive from the highest board at a pool. He refuses to be intimidated, even by himself.

Ray has a series of gambits. I know them all by now. If he phones you and starts out dolorously—"Have you heard the terrible thing that happened?"—you know that good news is forthcoming. On the other hand, if he starts out with a sprightly joke, you know that something bad, or at least something unpleasant, is on the way. Ray is adept at throwing people off balance. He makes a practice of starting rows among people working for him, believing that out of the fires of dissension flows molten excellence. Though he appears to swing from bonhomie to a fierce enjoyment of an open row, there is a steady, calculating intellect in command, ever watchful. I have a deep affection for Ray, and when he suggested we make a film of Tennessee Williams' *The Night of the Iguana* together, I accepted with pleasure.

In the play, the Reverend Lawrence Shannon is an Episcopal clergy-man who has been locked out of his church after a scandal involving a young girl. He is finally reduced to serving as a guide to a group of schoolteachers on a cut-rate tour of Mexico—a broken man, drinking heavily and at the end of his tether. Ray and I agreed that Richard Burton was ideal for the role, with Deborah Kerr as Hannah Jelkes, the itinerant artist, and Ava Gardner doing Maxine, the keeper of the hotel where Shannon's party is stranded. We went to see them, one after another. Rich-ard, in Switzerland, promptly accepted; likewise Deborah in London. That took us to Madrid and Ava Gardner.

I had met Ava when Tony Veiller and I were working on the script of Hemingway's *The Killers*. As I watched her on that set, I was intrigued. I sensed a basic, fundamental thing about her, an earthiness bordering on the roughneck, even though she was at pains to conceal it. Some time later I met her again and tried to make a conquest. I was completely unsuccessful. No midnight swims, no weekends . . . no Huston.

During our visit with her in Madrid—some eighteen years later—the impression I had had concerning Ava's fundamental character was rein-forced. Before, she had been shy and hesitant in her delivery, having to overcome a Southern accent which prompted her to speak slowly and carefully; now she spoke freely—I might even say, with abandon. This, combined with her beauty and her maturity, made her perfect for Maxine. But Ava said she had misgivings about her ability to do the part. I knew damned well that Ava was going to do it; she did, too—but she wanted to be courted. So Ray and I stayed on in Madrid another week and played the game. I should say that we stayed for the dance. It was all as conven-tional as a minuet, but one had to go through the steps. With Ava, this took some doing. Because of my earlier strikeout, I let Ray take the lead.

The first night we went out, I left the scene around four in the morn-ing. Ray stayed on with Ava. This went on for three or four days—through most of the night spots and flamenco dance groups in Madrid—and I started leaving at midnight. Ray became more haggard and gray-faced. Ava blossomed. She was just pursuing her regular routine. When we left, poor Ray was a shattered wreck, but Ava had agreed to do the picture.

Tony Veiller agreed to work with me on the screenplay; then he and I flew down to Key West to see Tennessee Williams at his cottage there. We stayed at a nearby hotel. It was mostly a social visit, though we had some general talks about the adaptation. Tennessee's ménage consisted of an older man with whom he had been living for many years and who was now ill, a young man named Freddy, of whom Tennessee was currently enamored, and four or five black poodles, the favorite of the pack being Gigi.

Tennessee went out of his way to be a gracious host. Although it was hardly a regular activity of his, he took us fishing. His young man tried to swim around the boat, panicked and began crying for help. Someone threw him a life-preserver and hauled him aboard, where Tennessee gave him artificial respiration while the captain looked on in disbelief. I think this must have been the captain's first encounter with the gay side of life.

Back in Los Angeles we cast the other parts, among them Cyril Delevanti, a longtime bit actor in Hollywood, who played Deborah's grandfather—the world's oldest living and practicing poet. I think Cyril must have been in his eighties, and this was his first really important part. He said to me, "I hope this leads to better things." Sure enough, it did. Cyril was from that time on in demand. He was never again without an offer, and the last years of his life were happy ones.

In Los Angeles I met a Puerto Vallarta architect and entrepreneur named Guillermo Wulff, an engaging man in his forties. I was thinking about locations for *Iguana*, and Guillermo urged me to go to Mismaloya. It was only a few miles by boat from Puerto Vallarta's only pier—at Playa Los Muertos—and although Mismaloya was Indian land, Wulff said he had a lease on it and could build anything he wanted there. I knew, generally, where Mismaloya must be, having made two previous trips along that section of the coast south of Vallarta. One, as I mentioned earlier, in a dugout canoe, and the second to scout locations for *Typee*.

Guillermo's reminder struck home. I went to Puerto Vallarta to have a look.

Mismaloya was ideal. There was a long, wide, sandy beach, and a jungly-overgrown tongue of land jutted out into the sea. The view from the top of this point—clear on three sides—was spectacular. It seemed to me perfect for shooting, and for keeping the motion-picture company together. We could film most of the movie there and live there, too.

Ray came down, an agreement was reached and with Stark's blessing Guillermo began construction: living quarters and a cutting room; a large kitchen, restaurant and bar; tanks and pumps for an adequate water supply; a light-generating plant; and whatever paths and roads were required. Steve Grimes was to design and oversee construction of the single set—an old hotel.

After deciding on Mismaloya and other locations in and around Vallarta, I returned to St. Clerans with Tony Veiller to begin writing the script in earnest. I talked to Ray by telephone often, and he told me Guillermo was having problems. What we had originally had in mind was cement-slab or clay flooring, wattle walls and simple thatched roofs for the living quarters—with the conveniences of running water and electricity. Guillermo's idea was to turn Mismaloya into a club after the movie was finished, and for this he had already collected money from investors. The structures accordingly became cement-and-stone houses with red tile roofs, tile floors and expensive appointments throughout. Torn between his club and its contributors, his budget for construction from Seven Arts, plus a deadline for completion, Guillermo apparently overextended. I think he simply promised everybody more than he could deliver. In that lay the seeds of calamity.

Before we began filming, Ray and I discussed whether *The Night of the Iguana* should be in black-and-white or color. Ray wanted color; I wanted black-and-white. I thought that color—especially of sea, sky, jungle, flowers, birds, iguanas, beaches—would be distracting. Black-and-white would place the emphasis where it belonged—on the story. Ray deferred to my judgment, and we made the picture in black-and-white. Looking back now, I think I was probably wrong.

My idea of having the cast and crew live on Mismaloya worked. We were all there except for our principals, who preferred the luxury of large private houses in Puerto Vallarta. Richard and Liz rented the Casa Kimberly (which they later bought); Deborah Kerr and Peter Viertel took another house; Ava a third; Sue Lyons a fourth. Then they rented or purchased speedboats to take them back and forth to location.

We saw our rushes once or twice a week in Puerto Vallarta's main movie house. The townspeople caught on quickly. When they saw Ralph Kemplen, our editor, and Eunice Mountjoy, his assistant, going into the theater with film cans, word would spread. By the time the rest of us arrived, the front of the house would be filled with locals of all ages. For the most part, they didn't understand a word of what they were hearing, but they were delighted to recognize the places, and thoroughly enjoyed themselves. To this day they have a proprietary attitude toward *Iguana*.

The tangled web of relationships among the *Night of the Iguana* principals set something of a record. Richard Burton was accompanied by Elizabeth Taylor, who was still married to Eddie Fisher. Michael Wilding, Elizabeth's ex-husband, arrived to handle the job of publicizing Richard Burton. Peter Viertel, Deborah's second husband, had once been involved with Ava Gardner. Ava's "attendants" in the picture were two local beach boys, and they followed her everyplace she went. Of course every *macho* Mexican lover in town was after Sue Lyons, who—unfortunately for them—was being jealously guarded by both her fiancé and her mother.

There was much conjecture as to what would happen, to whom and how soon. So before starting the picture, I purchased five gold-plated derringers, which I solemnly presented to Richard, Elizabeth, Ava, Deborah and Sue. Each gun came with four golden bullets engraved with the names of the other recipients.

The press was attracted in great numbers. There were more reporters on the site than iguanas—I don't think any picture I've made has called forth as much interest. There were reporters and photographers from all over the world, and though they arrived and left in flocks, there always seemed to be at least a dozen hanging around, waiting for the great day when the derringers were pulled out and the shooting started.

They waited in vain. There were no fireworks. All the members of the cast—especially our stars—got along famously. At the end of each working day Elizabeth would call for Richard; Peter would collect Deborah; Ava, flanked by her beach boys, would water-ski back to town; and Sue would be escorted home by either her fiancé or her mother.

When we started shooting, Tennessee Williams showed up fairly regularly to look at rushes. He always arrived with his friend Freddy and his dog Gigi. Gigi kept getting sunstroke. There was one scene that had given Tony and me particular trouble in the writing. It was between Shannon and the young girl in his room at the hotel. She has been trying to seduce him, and he has been trying his best to resist her; he's already had quite enough trouble with young girls. As the scene begins, Shannon is shaving in front of a mirror on a chiffonier. Beside it is a bottle of whiskey. The door suddenly opens and again he is under attack by the teenager. He explains to her all the reasons why they should not become lovers. The dialogue was good, but the scene just didn't come alive. I showed it to Tennessee and asked him if he could help us with it. What he did is an example of his genius.

As Tennessee rewrote it, the girl comes into the room suddenly and Shannon is startled. He knocks the bottle of liquor off the chiffonier, so there is broken glass all over the floor. Explaining his position to the girl, he starts to pace the floor, and so great is his agitation that he doesn't realize he's walking barefoot on broken glass and cutting his feet. The girl watches him, then, suddenly inspired, kicks off her shoes and joins him in walking over the glass. What had been a dull scene became one of the best in the picture—frightening and funny at the same time.

Tennessee and I had several discussions in Vallarta about the ending. He had written the character Maxine with considerable affection, then, at the end, turned her into a spider woman who devoured her mate. This was done to make his point that animalism and brutality will inevitably prevail over sensitivity and breeding. For this point to make sense, it should have been a tragedy that Maxine kept the Reverend Shannon with her. But Maxine was written too well—she was too real—and in fact to be taken in by Maxine was the best thing that could happen to Shannon. I felt Tennessee had perfunctorily changed Maxine's character for his own dark purposes, as a means of expressing his own prejudice against women, and I called him on it. I argued for a happy ending. Not just because it would be popular with audiences, but because I felt the material demanded it. Tennessee didn't agree. I told Tennessee I thought his conscious and unconscious were at war. "You see women as your rivals," I said. "You don't want a woman to have a place in the love life of a man. That's why you chose to do this with the character of Maxine. You've been unjust to your own creation."

Curiously, Tennessee didn't defend himself. I was surprised, because I thought he would tell me to go to hell, and he didn't. It was as though he had no strong convictions on this point. Eventually, however, he got in the last word. Not long ago, I saw Tennessee at a luncheon party in London. It was a happy occasion. I took real pleasure in seeing him again and talking after so many years. But, as we were saying our goodbyes, he remarked: "I still don't like the finish, John!"

The heart of the picture is a long scene between Deborah and Richard. I shot it and thought it was good. Tony and Ray saw the rushes before I did and were disappointed. When I saw it, I had to agree. Deborah had shaped her performance for a theater audience, and her lines came out of the Royal Academy of Dramatic Art instead of inside herself. I pointed this out to her. We re-shot it, and the scene became what it was supposed to be: the most significant of the picture.

One day, about three quarters of the way through the filming, we were doing night work. We finished at about four o'clock in the morning, the company dispersed, and as I was walking down the hill from the "hotel" to my bungalow, I heard a crash, followed by a cry. I rushed toward the sound and saw Tommy Shaw, my assistant director, and Terry Moore, my second assistant, lying in a pile of rubble some twenty feet down the hillside from the cottage they shared. They had sat down on their balcony—which was supposed to be reinforced concrete—and it had col-lapsed. Terry was soon able to stand up, but Tommy just lay there, and we realized he was seriously hurt.

We improvised a stretcher, put him on board a fishing boat and headed for Vallarta. When we arrived at Los Muertos Beach, we found that we couldn't reach the shore because of the shelving bottom, yet the water at that point was over a man's head. But somebody immediately jumped in, and all of a sudden there were a dozen men in the surf, their heads below the water and their hands above it, carrying Tommy on his litter. I'll never forget the sight of those hands holding the stretcher above the sur-face while the men walking on the bottom brought Tommy to shore.

X rays showed that Tommy's back was broken, so we got a plane and had him flown out that same morning. It was touch-and-go for some time whether he would live or not. Only because Tommy had been a very fine athlete and was in splendid physical condition at the time of the accident did he survive.

Except for this accident—and especially in comparison to *Moby Dick* and *The Roots of Heaven*—the making of this picture was a serene experience.

Now, some sixteen years later, the site of *The Night of the Iguana* has become a ghost town. Except for the old hotel—which serves as a home for the Mexican caretaker and his family—all that remains are shells of houses and piles of rubble. The occasional tourist wanders up from Mis-maloya Beach below, but, for the most part, it is a silent and deserted place, its rough edges thankfully softened by the ever encroaching jungle. No one—other than an old man who passes there on an occasional trip between Las Caletas and Vallarta—seems to give a damn what happens to the place. He would like to see it torn down and given back to the iguanas. The old man is me of course.

I've always thought that I have a better way with animals than most people have. Perhaps this very confidence enables me to do things with animals that others with less confidence can't do. My mother had this same understanding and assurance. When Dorothy and I were living on Lafayette Street in New York in the 1920s, Mother gave me a little Capuchin monkey. I was told that if the monkey bit or misbehaved I was to flick his nose with my finger. One day he bit me, and I flicked his nose. I flicked too hard, and he had a nosebleed. He put his hand to his nose, looked at the blood on his hand and began to cry. Right then I decided I would never punish him like that again. I didn't, and he never bit me again.

The Monk became more than tame. He was so trusting that I swear he would have let me perform surgery on him. He knew that whatever I did to him was for his own good. When he first saw himself in the mirror, he touched his reflection and began to talk to it. Then he kissed it. When I brought him a toy, he always ran to the mirror to show it to the other monkey, and the other monkey would have the same toy. He would spin in front of the mirror, trying to catch the other monkey off guard. I once brought him a toy mouse that ran around on the floor, which would so excite him that he would have an erection. His little flowerlike penis would get between him and the toy, and he would slap at it, never ceasing to inspect the toy.

The Monk had fads, periods during which he would devote himself completely to some one activity. My mother was sewing one day, and he showed great interest. She laid her work aside and left the room for a moment, and when she returned, the Monk was pushing the needle back and forth through the material. After that nothing through which he could force a needle escaped his attention: clothes, curtains, even newspapers. This lasted for some weeks.

His art phase came when he saw me drawing one day. He followed the lines with his finger as I drew them. Then he himself began to draw. He held the pencil with one hand and drew a line while following it with the forefinger of his other hand. The Monk spent most of his time on my shoulder. He was sitting there one day while I was turning the pages of a book with animal pictures in it, and when he saw a close-up head of a baby monkey, he became very excited. He jumped down and reached around behind the book, feeling for the other monkey. Then he kissed the picture. He learned to leaf through the book until he found this picture; the page is smudged with his kisses. Kissing to the Monk meant friendship. When strangers came in, I would tell them to make a kissing noise at him, and the Monk would come to them. If they didn't do this, he would stay well away.

My mother went to Europe and left Dorothy and me her Pekingese. The Monk and the Peke became great friends. I used to take them out for walks, and the Monk always rode on the Peke's back. In the winter months I dressed the Monk in a little sweater and we went out in the snow for long walks.

One day a big black dog turned the street corner. The Peke and the Monk were ahead of me, and the Peke said to the Monk—in whatever language they used to communicate—"get up on that window ledge and wait for me while I take care of this big sonofabitch!" That was the only time I ever saw the Monk leave the Peke's back, but he did as he was told: he jumped up to the ledge and sat there wringing his hands as the little Peke went after the big dog. I got there in time to save the Peke's life.

The Monk used to sit on my chest and trace my eyelid with his finger. This delicate little finger would run around the very edge of the lid, just touching it, and then move on to my ears and my nose. One time he put his hand inside my shirt and felt hair. He made a new sound, a deep "Hoo! Hoo!" From that time on I was the Big Monk. The bridge had been crossed, and I was now truly his father.

When Dorothy and I moved to California in 1930, we left the Monk with my grandmother in Indiana until such time as we could get settled. I don't know exactly how it happened, but the Monk fell from a tree and accidentally hanged himself. I suspect they had a collar around his neck, attached to a chain. I said at the time that I would never have another monkey, but presently I couldn't resist, and I got another Capuchin. I shouldn't have, because he didn't begin to measure up to his predecessor. I tried a couple more times, with the same results. The difference between individual animals is every bit as great as the difference between people.

When I say I love and understand animals, that also includes snakes and birds—all species other than parrots. Parrots are undoubtedly Satan's own creatures. A parrot has, like Adam and Eve after eating the apple, the knowledge of good and evil. The cobra and the tiger act in obedience to Nature's laws and are therefore free of guilt. Not so the parrot, who is motivated by sheer, everlasting malice. There have been two parrots in my life, my mother's and my grandmother's.

My grandmother had a parrot from as far back as I can remember. I assume her parents had had it before her because parrots live forever—at least nobody ever heard of a parrot dying of old age, that is. I did everything I could to endear myself to that fiendish bird, but it wanted no part of me. It hated me as a toddler; it hated me as a teenager; and it hated me as a grown man. Years later Gram willed the parrot to a niece of hers, and, for all I know, it's still around. But Gram's parrot was gentle in comparison to my mother's. Gram's would only tear at the flesh of my hand when I went to scratch its head. Mother's bird would bite my finger to the bone— and then pry into it for the marrow.

I've observed that parrots are keenly aware of sex: they like either men or women, but never both. This parrot liked women. If a man approached its cage, its neck sleeked down, feathers closed, and the bird became reptilian in appearance. But for a woman the feathers always rose and fluffed. It loved to be caressed by a woman. One day I decided to try to fool the parrot into thinking I was a female. Mother had been to a masquerade. There was a wig on her dressing table. I put on the wig, powdered my face, forced my hands into Mother's white kid gloves as far as they would go and finished off by spraying myself with Mother's perfume. I approached the parrot's cage, speaking in a falsetto voice. The parrot's feathers fluffed out. I put my hand in the cage and the parrot cooed. Suddenly it cocked its head, looked me right in the eye and then proceeded to dismantle my finger.

I said that parrots seem to love or hate male or female, but I must qualify that. One time in Paris an antique dealer took me to his apartment to see some choice pieces. As we entered, I noticed a parrot in a cage. The man went to the cage to take the bird out, and immediately the parrot started with those dulcet, cooing sounds they make when they feel affectionate. I started to go over to the bird, and the man said, "Be careful. He'll bite!" I was surprised, because this contradicted my theory about parrots being attracted to only one sex. I mentioned this to the dealer, and he smiled. "And also *pédérastes*."

My mother was living in California when a particularly hideous murder occurred. It involved the kidnapping of a banker's little daughter for ransom. The child was eventually killed and left on a neighbor's lawn, her eyes, for some ghoulish reason, wired open. It was dreadful from every standpoint. The police knew that the murderer had been an employee of the bank, and they launched what was probably the biggest man-hunt in the history of California. The wretched man was caught, and confessed to the crime.

Shortly after his apprehension the murderer's mother arrived in California from Kansas City. My mother read in the paper that she was destitute, so she arranged for the woman to stay in her apartment in Beverly Hills during the son's arraignment. The woman was in a pitiable state, destroyed by grief. Mother came down to stay with me at the beach, leaving the parrot behind. The woman had been in the apartment about a week when Mother asked me to drop by, check the larder and see if there was anything we could do for her.

There was no answer to my knock, so I went in. Soul-wrenching sounds of weeping and sobbing were coming from the bedroom. I hesitated, thinking it was the woman—but then it struck me there was something strange about the weeping. I discovered that it was the *parrot* sobbing. And it wasn't so much an imitation of the woman's crying as it was a malicious mockery of her anguish.

One day at Calabasas in the San Fernando Valley, where I had a seventy-five-acre horse-breeding ranch, I was out in the pasture when I saw a slight movement in the grasses. I looked closer and discovered a tiny, naked, baby hummingbird, smaller than my fingernail. It had undoubtedly been blown out of its nest. I picked it up and made a house for it in a penny matchbox. Then I mixed a nectar, put it in an eyedropper and touched it to this little thing's beak. Presently it swallowed. I kept the bird in the bathroom, on a shelf of an open medicine chest. It grew and put on feathers, and eventually it was flying, hanging in the air, wings a blur, and drinking from the eyedropper.

After about two months it was a full-grown, beautifully opalescent hummingbird. It appeared to be strong and quite capable of looking after itself, so I took it outside and let it go. It circled and vanished. I went into the seed room to check supplies, and when I came back out, I saw a slight motion on a leaf above me. I put out my finger, and the hummingbird immediately came down and perched on it! I returned it to its matchbox home—into which it could still fit—and it lived there for another week. Then I took it out and let it go once more. It went like a shot, and I never saw it again.

I went from individual pets to beasts on a large scale during production of *The Bible.* We were shooting *Genesis: In the Beginning* in continuity, and although the Ark sequence was some months away, we were preparing the ground, building the sets and acquiring the animals. They were being flown in from Tripoli, Egypt, Africa, West Germany to Rome almost daily to be accommodated on the back lot of the Dino De Laurentiis studio. Every morning before beginning work, I visited the animals.

One of the elephants, Candy, loved to be scratched on the belly behind her foreleg. I'd scratch her and she would lean farther and farther toward me until there was some danger of her toppling over on me. One time I started to walk away from her, and she reached out and took my wrist with her trunk and pulled me back to her side. It was a command: "Don't stop!" I used it in the picture. Noah scratches the elephant's belly and walks away, and the elephant pulls him back to her time after time.

There was also a hippo named Beppo. I fed him daily with a bucketful of milk, and it got so that Beppo would open his mouth as soon as he heard me approaching. If I didn't pour the milk down his throat immediately, he would stand there patiently with his mouth wide open, waiting. I could put the bucket on the ground and walk around him, petting him, and Beppo wouldn't close his mouth. One day I put my hand inside his mouth and patted his pink chops. The mouth remained open, those great teeth on display.

Two African giraffes were wild when they came to us. They went directly into seclusion in a high, stockade-like pen, padded on the inside so they wouldn't injure themselves. After a few days I began visiting them every morning, and they gradually lost their fear of me. Next I put granulated sugar on the top railing of their pen, then lump sugar. They loved it, and finally they were taking it from my hand. There was a ramp outside their enclosure, and as I walked by on a level with their heads, they became so bold as to bar my way with their long necks. Then they would search through my pockets for sugar. Only when the sugar was produced would they raise their necks and permit me to pass.

And there was a raven that served as the watchdog of my trailer. If any man came into the trailer except me, the raven flew into the air and attacked at eye level. This bird was also keenly aware of sex, and if it was a woman who entered, he would drop to the floor and go for her ankles. Gladys never came into the trailer unless I was there. I would call, "Raven!" and the bird would fly over and land on my arm. We used this in the Ark sequence, along with the trick of reaching into Beppo's mouth and the giraffe's game of barring Noah's way.

A bird with an ax-shaped beak that could splinter a two-by-four did a ritual dance every morning as I approached. Ever so gently he would take my hand into his beak, then climb onto my wrist and go on dancing. A blessed bird in contrast with our friend the parrot.

I proposed to Charlie Chaplin that he play Noah. He was tempted and toyed with the idea for some weeks. I thought we had him, but finally he said no; he couldn't conceive of being in someone else's picture. I then turned to Alec Guinness. There was a conflict in dates and we lost him. As actors, those two men were ideal for Noah: either of them would have given a superb performance.

But as the weeks passed, I began to realize how important it was that Noah should be on familiar terms with the animals—knowing them was as important as an actor's ability to play the role. So I decided to do the part myself.

We had two principal sets for Noah's Ark, one on the back lot and one on a sound stage: the "inside" and the "outside." The "inside" Ark, in the stage, was three stories high. A ramp led from bottom to top, past the giraffes' pen as one started to climb and on up through tiered galleries and sectioned stalls of various sizes. The heavier animals were on the bottom floor; medium-sized animals on the second floor, where Noah and his family lived, too; and smaller animals and birds on the top floor. The Ark was large enough for the birds to fly around in, so they were always airborne above us. The pens for the larger animals were constructed with a gap of a couple of feet at the bottom so they could be cleaned with rakes from the outside, and food and water could be put in for them at night without opening gates or doors. The carnivorous animals—leopards, lions and tigers—were separated from the others by heavy plate glass.

The interior of the Ark was kept scrupulously clean: there never was a sweeter-smelling barn. We had a large staff of keepers, and the animals had the best of food and bedding. All of them that could be groomed were, including two Russian bears, and they were all exercised daily. We shot inside the Ark over a period of weeks, and not a single animal ever got sick. More than once visitors came in, looked around and exclaimed, "I've never been in an Ark before!" It tells something about the utterly natural atmosphere of the place, with all those animals living together in complete harmony.

The exterior of Noah's Ark on the back lot was a beautiful structure, 300 cubits long by 30 cubits high, as specified by the Lord and executed by *The Bible*'s art director, Mario Chiari: 500 feet by 50 feet, that is. It was, of course, finished on only one side, the side to be photographed.

The road along which the animals were to parade ran through the Ark. This approach with the animals walking two by two seemed to me a prerequisite of the sequence. But how to do it? Various ideas were advanced: matte shots, glass shots, stop-camera shots, process shots . . . All the tricks that cinematography is heir to were duly considered and found wanting. At last it seemed to me the only way to get the shot would be to train the animals so that they'd actually do it—walk into the Ark two by two. No one, including the Italian animal-trainer, believed it possible. But my idea of how to go about it got the support of the German circus-owner who supplied our big cats. His opinion tipped the scale, and Dino agreed to let me try it.

First, ditches were dug on either side of the road leading into the Ark so it became a kind of causeway. While not deep enough to injure animals falling into them, the ditches served as invisible fences. The handlers started by leading individual animals along the road—through the open door of the Ark and out the other side. This road described a big circle: starting point, up the road, into the Ark, through the Ark, out and around and back to the starting place. Up, in, through, out, around, back; up, in, through, out, around, back. When one of a pair became used to this, then the other was added and the two were led side by side. The order of their appearance never varied. Behind the elephants came the ostriches, behind the ostriches, the zebras, and so forth. When the animals were well accustomed to this, the next step was to have the handlers walk in the ditches, leading their charges on longer nylon lines. Now and again men would be yanked out of the ditches by animals bolting, but it was pretty good. We could make it, as planned, with the men out of sight of the cameras, which would be shooting at ground level.

However, the animals got so used to their daily around-and-around that it suddenly struck me one morning that we might get the shot *without* the lines. Our two cameras were set up; I got into my Noah costume and took my place; the lines came off; and the animals marched right up the road, to Noah's piping, and into the Ark two by two—a parade of animals well over a hundred yards long. We knew we had it, but we did it again, and again they marched through two by two without a misstep. When we saw it on the screen in the projection room, a cheer went up. I never heard a regular theater audience applaud this scene. They seem to take it for granted, accepting it the same way that visitors to the set accepted the Ark. After all, everybody knows that animals always walk into an Ark two by two.

For me, the animals and the Ark sequences were a most satisfying and engrossing part of making *The Bible*. Yet always while shooting them we were constantly preparing for other sequences, especially the Creation. I had a stock answer in those days for anyone who asked me how things were going: "I don't know how God managed. I'm having a terrible time."

30

We tried a number of things for the very beginning of the picture, the Creation proper: dividing the waters, the firmament, light. I thought to show it not as a single event at the beginning of time but as a continuing, eternal process. Each morning is a new creation—something now and forever.

I enlisted the talents of Ernst Haas, whose work I'd known and admired ever since the Bob Capa days. His most striking photographs were of natural phenomena: ocean waves, thunderheads, rock formations—studies of the primordial.

Haas had never operated a motion-picture camera, so he underwent a crash course to learn how. Then, with a crew of four, he went to remote regions in North and South America, to the Galápagos Islands and Iceland and elsewhere. Haas' peregrinations must have cost a quarter of a million— a very expensive proposition when you consider that only three or four minutes of the material he shot was used in the picture. But there was never a complaint out of Dino. Haas brought back scenes of waters leaving the dry land; volcanos rearing up from the sea; lava building itself into smoking mountains; flowers, plants and trees groping up through mists towards the sun. And finally, animals emerging.

Our first problem with the Garden of Eden was to decide whose version of Paradise to use, and what Adam and Eve should look like. To the African nomad, for example, Paradise is an oasis with apricots and cool water. Some thought that Adam and Eve should be dark, primitive creatures not yet quite human. Eventually, however, I decided to go along with the Renaissance masters.

Michael Parks, an American actor, played Adam. He was fair-haired and had a sensitive yet somehow primitive face. A Swedish girl, Ulla Bergryd, played Eve. She was lovely looking, with long, glowing tresses and an appealing simplicity. I stayed with the fifteenth-century painters in rendering Adam and Eve as fair.

We searched for some time for the Garden of Eden before finally settling on a place about an hour and a half outside Rome: the 110-acre gardens surrounding the summer palace of Count Odescalchi. This place had beautiful, unpruned trees, gentle, rolling glades and—when I first saw it—wildflowers. It was delightful, and I gave instructions that the wild beauty of the gardens not be disturbed. The wild flowers then blooming would be gone by the time we were ready to shoot, but I instructed the greensmen to find seeds of the proper seasonal flowers and scatter them at random. On no account were the natural grasses to be touched; they were perfect for the effect I wanted. Overshadowing all were magnificent trees, ancient, yet powerful and vibrant.

At this point I left on a six-week trip to scout other locations so that there would be no delay between sequences once we started filming. Shooting *The Bible* was like doing four separate and distinct pictures, each with its own set of requirements. It would have been easier to make each of them a production on its own, but it would have cost half as much again to do so—thus every effort was made to continue uninterruptedly.

I know of no people with innovative powers to compare with the Italians. As movie-makers they are capable of miracles of creativity. By the same token, they can go wrong faster and further than any other people I know. When I returned two weeks before shooting was to commence, I was confronted with a scene of indescribable havoc in the gardens of Odescalchi.

They had put in an artificial lake. To do this, earth-movers and bull-dozers had been brought in, flattening everything for a hundred yards around. We were up to our hips in mud. Where the ground was firm, the wild grasses had been replaced by carefully cut squares of green sod for lawns, the lines around the cuts still visible; young trees had been carted in and planted because they thought the garden should look like eternal spring. They had hung paper flowers on other trees and had built a metal fence around the whole place "so that the wild animals wouldn't escape." Worst of all, they had actually stripped all the bark from the lovely old trees to make them more "dramatic." Now the trees would surely die. When Count Odescalchi saw this, he went into a rage, for which I don't blame him. It's a wonder he didn't shoot everyone concerned. I wasn't in any great humor myself. Here we were, ready to begin the Garden of Eden, and the Garden had been demolished. We could make only two or three shots there. We had little choice on such short notice but to go to a small zoological garden in Rome instead of that other beautiful place of trees, glades and wildflowers which was now but a memory.

A number of artists were used in this picture, among them Mirko, Fontana, the Russian-born American Eugene Berman and Corrado Cagli.

Our Tree of the Knowledge of Good and Evil was covered with blossoms not of this world but of a design that might have been found in the Garden before the Fall: Cagli's inspiration.

We made a number of experiments before deciding how to present the Serpent. We tried a real python; a grotesquely painted serpentine figure; a serpent with a human head, as in certain Quattrocento Italian paintings; and then discarded all these in favor of an uncomplicated, simple solution. We used a dancer who moved in a reptilian fashion through the branches of the Tree. All you saw clearly were his eyes. His body and face were covered with a skin-tight costume. When God cursed the Serpent by declaring that he should thenceforth crawl on his belly, the dancer dropped to the ground, and a real serpent—a python—slithered into view.

Mirko produced the sets for Sodom, a dark, labyrinthine place where unspeakable things took place. There were niches, alleyways and dark courtyards. The figures in the niches were either bas-reliefs or human. If human, you couldn't quite see what they were doing to one another, but you sensed it was decadent, erotic and sinful.

Besides his work on the Tree and other scenes in the Garden, Corrado Cagli designed the Tower of Babel. Actually, there were two parts to our Tower: its base and its top. The massive base, constructed on the back lot, was 100 feet high and perhaps 200 feet square. It went up toward the sky in tier after tier, like a Babylonian ziggurat. To shoot this truncated base as though it were complete, we made a "glass shot." The top of the tower was painted in perfect perspective on flawlessly clear glass. The glass was then placed in front of the camera and the scene was shot—so there were people laboring by the hundreds on the base of the Tower with the pinnacle far above them. Everything matched—even the shadows. Such glass shots are *trompe l'oeil* at its best.

The top of the Tower of Babel was built outside Cairo on the summit of an escarpment that rose straight up some 2,000 feet from the desert floor. The top itself was only a few stories high, but it was designed in such a way as to make the escarpment seem to be part of it when shooting downward. When shooting upward from the desert, only the pinnacle was shown.

The Creation of Adam was, of course, an enormously important part of the film. We discussed and rejected a variety of approaches, and I finally decided to do it in stages. The idea was to use three sculptures—progressively taking the form of a man and, finally, the living Adam. The next question was: who would do the sculptures? I thought at once of Giacomo Manzu.

I had met Manzu two years earlier. I was passing through Bergamo on my way to Venice when it came to me that this was where Manzu lived in a villa on a hilltop. I knew he was a recluse, but I wrote a note saying that if by any chance he had a few minutes to spare, I would like to meet him, and sent it to him with a driver. Back came the answer: "Please come up immediately!" I found Manzu to be a delightful man and marvelously hospitable. He showed me his sculptures in the garden and broke out the good wine. It was forenoon when I arrived and dark before I left. It was one of those instant friendships.

Dino agreed instantly to my suggestion of Manzu, and was prepared to pay handsomely for his services. But he doubted that Manzu would agree to do it. I did, too. Manzu had been working for some time on his bronze doors for St. Peter's, the first addition to the basilica's structure in over two hundred years. This task completely absorbed him. He'd had no exhibitions for two years, and none of his works were on the market. So it was with small hope that I approached him. I was quite unprepared when he replied, "Of course, John."

But Manzu had two conditions. The sculptures were in honor of our friendship; he would accept no pay. And they were to be used only for the few Creation scenes and then destroyed. No casts would be made of them.

I was overcome by his generosity and remonstrated, but he was adamant. Later on, Dino urged Manzu to let him pay for the work. "Very well, Dino. Give me a hundred lire." Manzu guessed that Dino never carried any change in his pockets, was pulling a joke on his rich friend. Sure enough, Dino searched his pockets, pulled out nothing but bills of large denomination and then, turning his pockets inside out, he grimaced and shrugged. Manzu matched the shrug. Manzu chose to do the sculptures where we intended to shoot. We went out together to inspect the place and have tents put up. The ground was bare. Manzu stooped down and dug into the ground with his hands. He examined the sample with an almost childish delight and remarked that the earth was a fine clay. He would make his sculptures out of this very earth.

Manzu mixed the clay himself and started on the sculptures. He completed them in three days. The first was little more than a mound of earth, an abstract shape; the second was of man's proportions and suggestions of man's shape; and the third an almost finished man. He started each day early in the morning and worked until late at night. It was an act of inspiration, marvelous to witness. As he completed each figure, he placed it under wet sheets to keep it moist. His reason for working at such a white heat was to finish the final piece before the first would start drying out and cracking.

We would start shooting from a height and dolly down to the first figure. Then the wind machines would start slowly; a little whorl of dust would play around the figure, and as the wind machines reached their maximum, the curtain of dust thus produced would be photographed at very high speed so that the dust would appear to be hanging in mid-air, almost standing still. Then the figures would be switched. When ready, the dust would be reduced and the camera would photograph the second figure, then the wind would blow again and the screen again would fill with dust. During each change, the golden dust filled the screen like the breath of God. The last shot in the Creation of the first man was to be when he slowly raised up and reached out his hand toward the camera— as towards the Deity.

We got it all set up and began shooting—and I'll be damned if the camera didn't break down within sixty seconds. The part that broke wasn't replaceable locally, and we had to send to London for it. A couple of days were lost tracking the part down, and even as we heard it was on its way to Rome, the figures began to crack ever so slightly. Panic reigned. The very moment the part arrived we began to shoot again. I was watching the sun drop and praying. By the time we got the last shot the figures were cracked but still retained their form. The next morning they had collapsed entirely. But we'd got it! The sequence turned out every bit as well as I had hoped it would.

I brought Manzu to see the Creation of Adam, and he was delighted. The dissolve from one figure to another was very good. When I told him how close we had come to disaster, he simply asked, "Why were you worried, John? I would have come out and done it again. You only had to ask me!"

Egypt was an experience I'd like to forget. We had assurances from the government that we would receive every assistance and cooperation. Nothing could have been further from the fact. For example, we were furnished with Army troops under the command of an Army colonel to depict the workers who built the Tower in Biblical times. We were shooting from the Tower down to the valley floor, where they were supposed to be transporting stones and other building materials on great sleds. It was a hot day. Just as we were ready for our first take, the troops got tired of what they were doing and decided to go back to their barracks. The colonel was helpless to stop them. I looked around for him, and found him on his hands and knees facing Mecca.

I trust the face of bureaucracy has changed in Cairo since we were there, but at that time it had its own peculiar physiognomy. For the most part, Egyptian higher-ups were built along the lines of Farouk—fat-assed, meaty, sallow, with pencil mustaches and great, beautiful eyes set too close together.

In Cairo an awareness of repression grew on you daily. The better suites in the hotels were bugged; agents were planted in the lobbies of all major hotels to see who among the Egyptians came to meet foreign guests; taxi-drivers reported conversations of their fares to the police. The upper classes had been pretty well "nationalized" or "sequestered," which meant they had been stripped of most of their assets, works of art and bank accounts: their businesses and in many instances their homes had been taken from them and converted into government offices. Only a few were allowed to leave the country. Corruption ran rampant, and control by the government bureaucrats was complete.

The bureaucrats who ran the Egyptian Film Board under government control did extremely well for themselves out of our pocket. For instance we were promised 6,000 extras for the "Battle of Sheva." I went to the location before dawn and saw these extras arriving by bus and truck, crammed together like cattle. Fortunately, as it turned out, there were somewhat fewer than the 6,000 promised, but it was still a goodly crowd. I asked how they had managed to get so many people together—what was their source—and was told they had been picked up at random from the streets and alleys of Cairo. Pressed labor, as it were. As the sun rose, the skies turned brassy with heat, and the people began to call out for water. The water truck finally arrived: one single truck—with one water tap—for thousands. I went to the Egyptians in charge and said, "For God's sake, what kind of an operation is this? Get more water out here at once!" Then the "food truck" arrived, and I discovered that there was one small portion of bread for each extra. When I questioned this, I was told that "these people" wouldn't expect anything more. "These people," however, had other ideas.

We were preparing to shoot a scene from a hilltop of thousands of the temporarily impressed extras—armed with rubber-tipped spears—charging "Abraham's soldiers" on the heights. The soldiers on the heights were a cadre of seventy men. They were the regulars supplied by the Egyptian Film Board—hand-picked "company" favorites from the pool of professional extras. Their spears weren't rubber-tipped; theirs had heads of sharpened steel because they would be running past the camera. A number of the "company men" on horseback had the job of keeping the rabble below in line.

The first sign of trouble was when I saw, in the distance, one of the men on horseback lashing at people with his whip. He was pulled from his horse, beaten and left unconscious on the ground. Similar set-to's began to occur. The remaining horsemen got together. The crowd went for them with a roar, and they hightailed it out of there. Then the mob turned toward us and started up the hill. The ground was covered with stones, which they picked up and began to throw. I walked forward. Stones were flying in all directions. Glancing to my left, I saw "Abraham's soldiers" come charging down the hill to do battle. I couldn't believe it! They might have killed a few of the crowd with their metal-tipped spears, but they, in turn, would have been torn to pieces. I raised my arms and shouted for them to stop. Because I was the director and they took orders from the director—and for no other reason—they came to a halt, and I sent them back uphill. At this, the crowd lost its momentum and, though a few more stones were thrown, some barely missing the camera, things calmed down. The riot was over. As we were packing up, someone who'd been down among them and spoke Arabic said the extras weren't angry with us. It wasn't the foreigners who'd caused this trouble but the Egyptian bosses. The crowd wanted them.

We got our crew into cars and began to move out, but the mob stopped each car, looking for the Egyptians responsible for this debacle. They never found them. Those sons-of-bitches had long since smuggled themselves to safety. We were paying them almost two Egyptian pounds ($5.60) per extra per day and discovered that, besides being deprived of food and water, the extras were getting about twenty cents a day!

While we were in Cairo, Gladys made friends with a family of the Farouk Era aristocracy whose wealth had been sequestered, and her experience with them deserves mention. They still had a large, well-furnished apartment, and I went there one day with Gladys. Of their few remaining art treasures, the most prominent was a standing carved wooden scribe of the eighteenth dynasty. They lived in constant fear that this piece and a few other fine objects would be seized by the government.

Gladys was going back to Rome before me, and I was aghast when she told me that she was going to take the wooden sculpture out of the country. It was estimated to be worth around $75,000. Her mission was to send it on to someone in Switzerland, where it would be sold to pay for the education of a grandson. Even though I had enormous respect for Gladys' abilities as a smuggler, I came out strongly against this caper. The penalties were just too great in case she was caught. But she assured me that the way had been paved. A member of the Italian embassy would accompany her to the airport and see her through customs. Her bags wouldn't even be opened. It would be like having diplomatic immunity.

Unfortunately, the night before she was to leave Cairo, there occurred an incident at the Rome airport which cooled relations between Italy and Egypt. A trunk being shipped under diplomatic immunity by the Egyptian legation gave forth queer sounds. On closer inspection, it began to moan and cry out, whereupon the Egyptians accompanying it fled. The trunk was opened, and a man was discovered inside, bound to a chair. Investigation revealed that he was a double agent being returned to Egypt for "questioning." This had so sobering an effect upon Italian-Egyptian relations that the man from the Italian embassy appointed to escort Gladys through customs could be of no help at all. He was virtually *persona non grata* himself.

Gladys had a number of pieces of luggage, but the customs inspector, as though by instinct, pointed to the bag containing the figure and said, "Open it." The man from the Italian embassy turned green. Gladys opened the bag, and the inspector picked up the figure and started to unwrap it, exposing an ancient wooden leg. The Italian disappeared into thin air.

"What's this?" asked the inspector.

"I brought it from Rome and I'm taking it back to Rome," said Gladys.

By all odds, Miss Hill should at that moment have been put in chains and led away. But for some inexplicable reason the inspector snapped her bag shut and passed her through.

The figure, as it turned out, was not authentic. But this, as it also turned out, was a matter of little consequence. What I did not know until I later arrived in Rome was that, in addition to the figure, Gladys had also smuggled out the family jewels—in her purse! These were the real

McCoy, worth perhaps $500,000! She delivered them to a bank in Switzerland for her friends. Had she been asked to open her purse for inspection, she would undoubtedly have spent the rest of her life in an Egyptian dungeon. I still get goosebumps thinking about it. Of course, Gladys did this with no thought of reimbursement: nor was any offered. The family knew that Gladys would have been insulted.

One of the best scenes in *The Bible*, to my mind, was never really remarked on by the critics. This was where the three angels appeared to Abraham and revealed that Sarah—in her old age—was going to have a child. Sarah's laugh when she overheard this prediction was beautifully done by Ava Gardner. I had Peter O'Toole play all three angels, because what do angels look like if not alike? To have had three different individuals would have been disturbing to me—anthropomorphizing the angelic species, so to speak. And, finally, George C. Scott was magnificent as Abraham bargaining with God in an effort to save the city of Sodom and its people. I have little use for Scott as a private person, but my admiration for him as an actor is unbounded. Christopher Fry had given Ava, Peter and Scott very fine dialogue, and all the performances were outstanding. This scene was filmed in the Abruzzi Mountains of Italy, following our return from Egypt.

Scott fell in love with Ava. He was insanely jealous, extremely demanding of Ava's time and attention, and he became violent when they were not forthcoming. This very intensity turned her off, and pretty soon she started avoiding him. Scott is an on-and-off drinker, and he was on at the time. Although it didn't actively interfere with the shooting, it did make life rather difficult on occasion.

While we were filming in the Abruzzi, the whole company stayed in a small hotel in Avezzano. One night Scott got very drunk in the bar and threatened Ava physically when she entered. In the process of trying to slow him down before he hurt someone, I climbed on his back. He's very strong, and he carried me around the room, bumping into things. He couldn't see where he was going because I had my arms wrapped around his head. Ava was persuaded to leave, and we finally got Scott calmed down.

Later, when I was editing the picture in Rome, I heard that Scott broke into Ava's suite at the Savoy, which caused a scandal. When she came back to the United States, I think Frankie Sinatra commissioned a couple of his lads to go around with her. Ava and Frank bear a great affection for each other, and when in trouble, she always turns to him. I don't know Frank well, but I admire him. He sticks by his guns and stands by his friends, ex-wives included. I respect his kind of loyalty very much.

The Bible was the most extensive thing I have ever undertaken. *The Bible* is, of course, a misnomer. We actually filmed only half the book of Genesis, the picture ending with the story of Abraham. And even though *In the Beginning* was added to the title in smaller print, the picture was popularly called *The Bible*. This was fine with Dino. He had it in mind to do the entire Bible from Genesis through Revelation. If he'd had his way, we might be up to about Ruth and Boaz by now.

Every interviewer during the filming—almost without exception—asked me if I believed in the Bible literally. I usually answered that Genesis represented a transition from Myth, when man, faced with creation and other deep mysteries, invented explanations for the inexplicable; to Legend, when he attributed to his forebears heroic qualities of leadership, valor and wisdom; to History, when, having emerged from Myth and Legend, accounts of real exploits and events of the past were handed down from father to son before the written word.

The next question would invariably be: did I believe in God? My reply was along these lines: in the beginning, the Lord God was in love with mankind and accordingly jealous. He was forever asking mankind to prove our affection for Him: for example, seeing if Abraham would cut his son's throat. But then, as eons passed, His ardor cooled and He assumed a new role—that of a beneficent deity. All a sinner had to do was confess and say he was sorry and God forgave him. The fact of the matter was that He had lost interest. That was the second step. Now it would appear that He'd forgotten about us entirely. He's taken up, maybe, with life elsewhere in the universe on another planet. It's as though we ceased to exist as far as He's concerned. Maybe we have.

The truth is I don't profess any beliefs in an orthodox sense. It seems to me that the mystery of life is too great, too wide, too deep, to do more than wonder at. Anything further would be, as far as I'm concerned, an impertinence.

I first met Carson McCullers during the war when I was visiting Paulette Goddard and Burgess Meredith in upstate New York. Carson lived nearby, and one day when Buzz and I were out for a walk she hailed us from her doorway. She was then in her early twenties, and had already suffered the first of a series of strokes that made her an invalid before she was thirty. I remember her as a fragile thing with great shining eyes, and a tremor in her hand as she placed it in mine. It wasn't palsy, rather a quiver of animal timidity. But there was nothing timid or frail about the manner in which Carson McCullers faced life. And as her afflictions multiplied, she only grew stronger.

31

More than twenty years later Ray Stark and I decided to make McCullers' *Reflections in a Golden Eye* as our second picture together. I proposed Chapman Mortimer as the man to write the screenplay, and Ray agreed.

Mortimer is a fine Scottish novelist, not well known, who has something of a cult following. I'm a member of that cult. His novels are shadowy, hypnotic, surrealistic. They move without apparent direction. The air is still in them, and surcharged with suspense. You don't know what's going to happen, but you fear it will be something dreadful; it's worse than you ever imagined.

I located Mortimer in Gisebo, a small town in Sweden. He was astonished to receive my call, and wondered how I'd found him. He was even more astonished when I told him how much I admired his work and that I'd read every book he'd written. I got the impression that he believed only a small circle of his friends—each known personally to him—read his work. I explained what I wanted, and Mortimer came to London to discuss the project.

He didn't seem to mind that he was not internationally famous, and I found him genuinely modest and content. He said he didn't know if he could write a screenplay, but I persuaded him to try, and when I received his script, I was delighted with what he had written.

We sent the screenplay to Carson, and after she'd read it, she asked me to come to see her at her home in Nyack, a little way north of New York

City. When I arrived, she was in bed, propped up on pillows, waiting for me. She ordered drinks, and they were brought by her black friend and companion, Ida Reeder, who had been with her for many years.

There was something infinitely touching about that reclining figure—so intelligent, so alert, so terribly stricken. By this time the paralysis had progressed to the point where she was left only with the partial use of her arms. She could not move her legs at all.

Carson sipped bourbon from a little silver cup with her name on it and talked, first, about the screenplay. The strokes had slowed her speech, and some words were slurred, but her observations were acute and pointed. She approved of the script. Then she wanted to hear about Ireland. I told her about the country and the people, and described St. Clerans. As I talked, an expression came into her eyes which prompted me to say, "Carson, you must come and visit me in Ireland." This wasn't something I meant seriously. It was inconceivable to me that she could make such a trip in her condition. But, to my surprise, Carson seized on the suggestion.

"When would you like me to come?"

I saw then that she was completely serious, and it was up to me to match her seriousness, so I said, "Just as soon as I've finished making *Reflections* and am back home again."

"All right, I'll come. I must get ready for it. I must prepare for it."

"Do that. I'm looking forward to it. We'll stay in touch."

That was in September of 1966. Gladys and I then went to work on *Reflections*, incorporating ideas Carson had and sharpening the dialogue. Marlon Brando came to see me in Ireland. He wasn't sure about the part. He had read the book, but doubted his suitability. As we were talking about it, the final screenplay was being typed, so I suggested that he wait and read it. Marlon did so, then took a long walk in a thunderstorm. When he came back, he said simply, "I want to do it."

During our conversation I asked Brando if he could ride a horse, and by way of an answer he assured me that he had been raised on a horse ranch. Later, during the filming of the movie, I noticed that he exhibited such a fear of horses that presently Elizabeth Taylor, who is a good horsewoman, began to be afraid also. I wondered then, as now, if Marlon got this fear because he had so immersed himself in his role. The character he played had a fear of horses. It could well be. I remember he once said of acting, "If you care about it, it's no good." Meaning you've got to get into a role to the point that you're no longer acting. You shouldn't give a damn about giving a "performance" or winning an audience's approval; you simply have to *be* the character you're supposed to be.

I can say only good things about Elizabeth Taylor. I discovered that, more than a great beauty and a personality, she was a supremely fine actress. The only sour note in my relationship with Liz came about through the machinations of Ray Stark. Elizabeth took a long time over her makeup. I understood this. It was part of her professionalism. She would not appear in front of a camera other than at her best. Ray didn't understand it. If we were ready to shoot and Elizabeth was still in her dressing room, Ray—when my back was turned—would send somebody else, some poor wretch—a second or third assistant—to tell Liz that we were ready—and waiting. It was all too obvious who was behind this, and presently Liz got her back up. I had a row with Ray about it, but Ray shrugged it off; he likes dissension.

In the film (in spite of a bad back) Liz rode a white stallion. Later, at a jeweler's in Rome, Ray saw an ivory horse set in gold and studded with diamonds. He sent it to Elizabeth with a card inscribed: "From Ray and John." But Elizabeth had been convinced since she was a child actress that all producers wanted something . . . and she was prepared to give them only what was in the contract. Ray's sending her a piece of jewelry after needling her during *Reflections* only confirmed her suspicions about him. That Ray had sent it on impulse and in good faith (which was true) never occurred to Elizabeth. And because my name, too, was on the gift, she began to distrust me also.

Some of this film was shot in New York City and out on Long Island, where we were permitted to use an abandoned Army installation, but many of the interiors and some of the exteriors were done in Italy. *Reflections* is a psychological story. Vivid Technicolor would, I felt, get between the audience and the story—a story of minds, thoughts, emotions. So I was looking for a particular kind of color. The Italian Technicolor lab exerted every effort to come up with what I wanted, I fear at the expense of other pictures they were working on. Weeks and months of experimentation were involved, starting well before the commencement of the picture and continuing after the final shots. What we achieved was a golden effect—a diffuse amber color—that was quite beautiful and matched the mood of the picture.

When I sent the final print to the United States, I thought it was something of a triumph. Warner Brothers thought differently; they didn't like the color. They ordered prints to be made in straight Technicolor. I fought this, and finally, using every threat, contact and influence I could muster, I got the studio to agree to make fifty prints in the amber color and to release these first to theaters in major American cities. The remainder would be made in standard Technicolor.

Every now and then someone comes up to me and says, "I've seen *Reflections* in the original color, and it is magnificent! Why did they ever release it in straight Technicolor?" So far as I'm concerned, the reason is that the sales department of Warners was headed by a man whose taste in color had been shaped by early "B" pirate films: "The more color per square foot of screen the better the picture."

I like *Reflections in a Golden Eye*. I think it is one of my best pictures. The entire cast—Marlon Brando, Elizabeth Taylor, Brian Keith, Julie Harris, Robert Forster and Zorro David—turned in beautiful performances, even better than I had hoped for. And *Reflections* is a well-constructed picture. Scene by scene—in my humble estimation—it is pretty hard to fault.

I returned to Ireland in February 1967 and about two weeks later was surprised to receive a letter from Carson McCullers saying that she was getting ready for her visit to St. Clerans. She had been out of bed and had sat up in a chair. Now she was making plans to take a weekend trip to the Hotel Plaza in New York City as a trial excursion. Sure enough, about a month later she did that. It was the first time she had been away from her home in more than two years. The sortie was quite successful, and she felt that she was ready for Ireland.

Carson couldn't sit up for the entire trip, of course, so I made arrangements with Aer Lingus to install a special reclining seat for her. Her visit was heralded in the Irish press. A helicopter service volunteered to transport her from Shannon Airport to St. Clerans. But there was the problem of her inability to sit upright, and though the service suggested a sling, I thought better not. (A few days before her scheduled arrival this same helicopter service managed to drop—twice—the body of a dead woman they were carrying in a sling to the island of Aran for burial. The second time, the coffin fell into the sea and was lost forever.) In the end, we settled on an ambulance as a safer, if less exciting, mode of transportation.

The great day came, and Carson arrived at Shannon Airport with Ida Reeder. I met them, and we went to St. Clerans in our ambulance. Carson was extremely tired from the trip, but she wanted to see the countryside, so I supported her, and from time to time she looked out the window at the passing fields.

When we arrived at St. Clerans, she asked for a tour, and we carried her stretcher through the downstairs part of the house, with Carson exclaiming over each room as we entered it. We lowered her stretcher

and canted it so that she could see and discuss the articles in each room.
This exhausted her utterly, and we carried her up to her bedroom. She
slept for some hours, with Ida Reeder watching over her, and I saw her
the next morning.

Carson thought that her room was the most beautiful room she had
ever been in. She exclaimed about things like the molding around the
ceiling and the curtains at the window. There was a little Epstein bronze
of a child's head, shoulders and arms called "Peggy Jean Asleep," and she
thought that was the most beautiful piece of sculpture she had ever seen.
She was delighted by a Japanese screen. She enlarged everything in importance and significance. After about an hour of talking with her I saw
fatigue set in again, and left her to go back to sleep.

Carson was adorable, and brave as only a great lady can be brave. She
was full of excitement—innocent child's excitement which touched
everything at hand. She was happy to be there, although she never left
her room the whole time. She ate hardly anything, but when she did, she
declared every mouthful to be delicious. She took bourbon in her little
silver cup, sipping from it and then putting it down beside her. After
no more than a sip or two she'd think she had finished the cup and she
would ask for another. It was as if a butterfly had touched it. Sometimes
she'd have what she thought were two or three drinks, but she never
finished more than a quarter of the small cup.

A fine Irish critic and writer from the Dublin *Irish Times*, Terence De
Vere White, called and asked if he might see Carson, and when I asked
her, she agreed eagerly. She knew his name and said, "Oh, yes! I'd like
very much to talk to an Irish man of letters." They talked about writing,
and White asked her what she conceived to be her duty as a writer. Above
Carson's bed hung a fourteenth-century Sicilian crucifix, a very heavy
wooden sculpture some two and a half feet high. It was balanced on a nail
and hung flat against the wall. In answer to White's question Carson said,
"Writing, for me, is a search for God." At this very moment the crucifix
slipped on the wall and hung sideways some ninety degrees off true.
Carson caught the motion out of the corner of her eye and began to
laugh. All three of us cracked up.

A few days after this interview Carson became quite ill. First her face
turned chalk white, then almost green. Before she came to Ireland our
local doctor, Martyn Dyar, had been in communication with Carson's
physician in New York and had been well prepared for what he might
expect. He knew what to do, but her condition didn't improve, and at
times she was only semi-conscious. Dr. Dyar was alarmed, and so was Ida
Reeder.

Finally Ida approached me and said, "I think we should go home." I was of two minds about this. It seemed to me that the trip back in her condition might very well kill her. On the other hand, there was no reason to think she would improve if she stayed where she was. The decision was made by Carson herself: she wanted to go back. I made arrangements for the same transportation in reverse, she returned to the United States, and a few months after that, Carson McCullers died.

I know the trip was hard on Carson. If she had not come, she might have lived months or even a year or two longer, but I do not regret arranging it. It was a fulfillment for her. She saw it as a liberation.

Before she left St. Clerans, she gave me the little silver cup.

I'm often asked what lies behind my choice of material, with the implication that I have a special message to convey. I don't. When I make a picture, it's simply because I believe the story is worth telling.

32 It has been said that I have a tendency to choose stories whose point is the irony of man's pursuit of an impossibly elusive goal. If this has in fact been a consistent motif of my pictures, I must confess to being unaware of it. Admittedly, certain themes trigger a deeper personal response than others, and success stories, per se, are not really of much interest to me. I'm convinced that there are more failures than men of achievement among us. Moreover, the best men tend to think of themselves as failures. Looking back on his life's work, Michelangelo expressed the desire to destroy it. Manzu told me recently that he considers himself a total failure when he compares his work to that of Phidias, Pisano and Bernini.

I made a series of films between 1968 and 1973 that were either outright failures or, at best, only moderately successful. There is no doubt about the meaning of the word "failure" in the motion-picture industry. The industry operates for profit, and a failure is a film that doesn't make money. The failures I made were *Sinful Davey*, *A Walk with Love and Death*, *The Kremlin Letter*, *Fat City*, *The Life and Times of Judge Roy Bean* and *The Mackintosh Man*.

Sinful Davey is the story, set in the mid-nineteenth century, of a young Scot who deserts from the British Army and follows in the footsteps of his father, who was a thief and an outlaw. Davey expects to end up on the gallows as his father did, but not before rivaling his father's record for sinfulness. An amusing notion. The picture was a light-hearted romp with John Hurt as Davey and, I thought, an altogether delightful affair.

Like *The Barbarian and the Geisha*, it was ruined after I delivered my final cut. I turned it in and that was that until I next saw it upon release. I was aghast! Walter Mirisch, the producer, had given full sway to his creative impulses. He had taken a scene from the end and put it at the beginning, so that the whole story became a flashback. And he had added a dreadful narration! Under the circumstances, Otto Preminger would have brought suit. I sometimes wish I were Otto Preminger!

My next two pictures, *A Walk with Love and Death* and *The Kremlin Letter*, were made for 20th Century-Fox, and both were produced by a young man named Carter De Haven. De Haven brought the first to my attention when he was visiting at St. Clerans, and I immediately saw it as a good possibility for my daughter Anjelica. Hans Koningsberger had written the novel. It was set during the Hundred Years' War and was a tale of two young people—children almost—who were in love and trying to escape from a world that was all violence and desolation. The girl Claudia, a young noblewoman, was a perfect part for Anjele; Moshe Dayan's son Assaf played opposite her in the role of the poet Heron. When Fox announced the picture and its cast at a press gathering in Hollywood, I was of course challenged. Didn't the casting of Anjelica amount to nepotism? I replied that it did indeed—that's why I was making the picture! The whole point was to launch my sixteen-year-old as an actress!

I only wish *A Walk with Love and Death* had been received everywhere as it was in Paris, where it played in three houses simultaneously and was praised to the skies. There was a certain purity about it—beautiful filming in castles, fields and forests near Vienna by Ted Scaife, magnificent costumes by Leonor Fini and authentic music by Georges Delerue.

I thought *The Kremlin Letter* had all the makings of a success. The book by Noel Behn had been a best-seller. It had, moreover, all those qualities that were just coming into fashion in 1970—violence, lurid sex, drugs. The cast was exceptionally strong—Max von Sydow, Bibi Andersson, Patrick O'Neal, Orson Welles, Nigel Green, Dean Jagger, George Sanders—and the performances couldn't have been bettered. It was extremely well photographed—there was a virtuosity, a shine to it. Gladys Hill and I wrote the script, which I considered quite good, though in retrospect it was perhaps overcomplicated. In any event, audiences rejected the picture. This surprised and disappointed me, especially as it had been aimed so directly at the box office. I felt even worse because Dick Zanuck, Darryl's son, and David Brown, as executive co-producers with 20th Century-Fox, had backed me with such good faith on both *A Walk with Love and Death* and *The Kremlin Letter*. I wished I could have given my friends, if not blockbusters, at least successful films. I still feel bad about it.

As a postscript to *The Kremlin Letter*, I should note that the picture did get good reviews in one place—Paris!

I had done bits of films in the United States, but it was a long time since I'd made an entire picture there. Ray Stark was responsible for my re-appearance on the American scene with *Fat City*, a novel by Leonard Gardner. "Fat City" is a term jazz musicians used to designate success with a capital "S." It's about people who are beaten before they start but who never stop dreaming. Its main characters are two fighters: one aging, slightly paunchy, who's had his moment of glory in the ring but whose next stop is Skid Row, and his younger counterpart who's headed in the same direction despite the living lesson before his eyes.

We had hoped to have Marlon Brando play the part of the older fighter. Ray and I met him in London. He had read the script and liked it, but refused to be pinned down, saying that he would call us by the end of the week. The time passed, we heard nothing. I despair at chasing actors, so we started looking elsewhere. (Some time later I heard Marlon had injured feelings at having been "passed over.") The man we found was another actor whose star was rising—Stacy Keach. I had never met him, but when I found that he was making a picture in Spain, I went over and paid him a visit. There was quality there. I also saw him in a beautiful, sadly neglected little film called *The Traveling Executioner*. His performance was exceptional, and I knew I was lucky to have him in *Fat City*.

Most of the other actors—apart from Jeff Bridges, who had a few pictures to his credit, and Susan Tyrell, who'd done some theater—were non-professional. Some of the cast came right out of my own past—fighters I'd known in my youth. Others turned up in Stockton itself. I remember particularly one black man we pulled out of the onion fields to try for a part. In the film he was to walk side by side with Stacy, hoeing weeds in a tomato field and telling a long story about the break-up of his marriage. This old fellow came to my apartment and read for me, his eyes glued to the pages of the script. He read as though the words were his very own. I asked him whether he thought he could learn the part.

"I already have," he said.

"What do you mean?"

"I can't read. I was just pretending." Someone had read the part to him a few times, and he had memorized it.

Then there was an arrogant sixteen-year-old black kid from the local high school. When Muhammad Ali saw him on the screen during a spe-cial showing I had for him, he stood up and shouted, "Stop the picture! That's me up there! Listen to that . . . that's me! You hear?" The kid was that good.

We shot most of the picture on Stockton's Skid Row. It's now a thing of the past; they've wiped it out. I wonder where all the poor devils who inhabited it have gone. They have to be somewhere. There were crummy little hotels; gaps between buildings like missing teeth; people—blacks and whites—standing around or sitting on orange crates; little gambling halls where they played for nickels and dimes. Many of the signs were in Chinese because the area had a large Chinese population. The police were very gentle with the derelicts. As long as they stayed within the sharply defined boundaries of the neighborhood, they could sleep in doorways, wine bottle in hand; if they wandered out, the police simply shooed them back. They were completely harmless, defeated men.

Fat City had a great reception when it was first shown, at Cannes in 1972. After the screening I walked into an adjoining hall to meet the press, and they gave me a standing ovation. When that happened, I was sure it was going to be a success. But no. Wherever it was shown, it was beautifully reviewed, but audiences didn't care for it. It's a fine picture, no question—well conceived, well acted, made with deep love and considerable understanding on the part of everyone involved. I suppose the public simply found it too sad. It has at least one devoted fan: Ray Stark considers it the best picture he has ever produced.

My next film, *The Life and Times of Judge Roy Bean*, was not exactly a failure, but you could hardly call it a roaring success. It didn't take off, as they say. Still, there were some very good things in it.

I was intrigued in the first place by the spirit of John Milius' script, which showed a splendid feeling for the old West. *Roy Bean* was in the fine old American tradition of the Tall Tale, the Whopper, the yarn peopled with outrageous characters capable of prodigious and highly improbable deeds. At the same time, it said something important about frontier life and the loss of America's innocence. "Judge" Bean insisted on hanging malefactors on the corner of First and Main, in spite of protests from townspeople who thought that that procedure ought to be conducted privately in a barn outside town. If they were ashamed of hanging people in public, the Judge maintained, they shouldn't hang people at all. (I'm sorry to say that one famous film critic took all this to be an argument in favor of capital punishment.)

I was pleased by a lot of things about *Roy Bean*. The humor had a weird and wonderful extravagance. How Grizzly Adams hibernated with the bears, for example, and lost his bear wife when she ran off with a grizzly from Montana, leaving him with a 450-pound "son" that he finds it necessary to give over into the Judge's care. The scene at the bar when the Judge and the bear get drunk and the scene where "Bad Bob" comes to town and the Judge "lets daylight through him"—literally, so that you can actually see landscape on his far side. The picture had plenty of this sort of thing. To heighten the effect, I made deliberate use of a technique that has since become much more popular, letting all sorts of events occur without logical justification. Things appear, things happen, funny, sad, comic, dramatic. Ludicrous one minute and sober the next.

Paul Newman helped all this work, of course. He is one of the most gifted actors I've ever known, and he considers his performance as the Judge one of his best. Newman will always be the Golden Lad. His political and artistic opinions are invariably correct (they coincide with my own), and his insights are rare indeed. Acting on intuition, he'll come to instant decisions that stand all the tests of logic afterward. As a performer, he's capable of those quick transformations of personality that amount to the change of a mask. Among the gods he would surely find a place as Hermes of the Winged Heels, forever in motion—graceful, stylish, with an inborn rhythm. He could have been a champion boxer or skater or gymnast. During the making of *Roy Bean* he confessed to me that he would much rather be a race-car driver than an actor, which I put down at the time as one of those idle dreams we all have. But since then he's twice become amateur racing champion of America, and not long ago he came in second at Le Mans.

John Foreman produced *The Life and Times of Judge Roy Bean*, and we became close friends. In time, we would make *The Man Who Would Be King* together, but first—to our mutual misfortune—we got involved in a picture called *The Mackintosh Man*. Somebody at Warners had come with the property to Paul Newman, who had a commitment to the studio. He brought it to the attention of John Foreman and me. We were each offered good round sums to participate. Foreman, I gathered, needed the money, and I certainly did. Besides that, the three of us had had a fine time on *Roy Bean* and were reluctant to go our separate ways. So we accepted and did the best we could with it.

From the beginning we were plagued by the screenplay's weaknesses. The worst part was that the story lacked an ending. All the time we were filming we were casting about frantically for an effective way to bring the picture to a close. Finally, during the very last week of shooting, an idea for an ending came to us. It was far and away the best thing in the movie, and I suspect that if we had been able to start shooting with it in mind, *The Mackintosh Man* would have been a really good film. But we weren't. As it is, I know of hardly anyone who has even heard of it. Like the Irish pubkeeper in Youghal, I guess I "had it coming."

I think it was in 1969, during the filming of *The Kremlin Letter*, that Orson Welles asked me to play the lead in a picture he was going to direct. He'd had the idea for some time—now he was going to write the script. "I think I'm going to call it *The Other Side of the Wind*. How do you like that for a title?"

33

"Very good."

"Will it be possible for you to start in about six months?"

I told him that we could certainly work something out, but six months went by and I heard nothing more. It must have been at least a year later that I learned that Orson was filming a picture called *The Other Side of the Wind*. I shrugged it off, thinking the picture had taken a different turn, and Orson had had second thoughts about me. He was reportedly in Switzerland shooting scenes with Lilli Palmer. But a short time later he phoned me.

"John, will it be possible for you to start in about six weeks?"

"Sure."

"Good. I'll send you the script right away."

"But, Orson, I understand you've been shooting already."

"Yes . . . yes . . . I've been shooting the scenes you aren't in, and the other half of the scenes you *are* in."

"How's that?"

"Well . . . for instance, with Lilli Palmer . . . I'm shooting her half of scenes in which she has conversations with you. I'll do your half later."

"Jesus, Orson, I've never heard of anything like that!"

"Oh, yes, it will work perfectly. I'll get the script to you right away."

That's the last I heard of the project for another year or two.

I was out in California when the director Peter Bogdanovich, a great champion of Orson's, called me. He said that Orson was going to shoot my scenes in Arizona and, if I could make it, Orson would lay plans accordingly. I said, "Well, I still haven't seen the script."

"As a matter of fact, there isn't any script. There's a kind of outline. Does it make all that much difference to you whether you see a script or not?"

"Not really."

"John, a lot of it is done right on the spot. You know how Orson is."

I'm of the school that believes you should proceed regardless of the script if you have faith in a director. I confess to being a little sensitive when I ask an actor to do something and he says, "Show me the script." He has every right, of course, but still I like the idea of an actor putting himself entirely in the director's hands.

I proceeded to do so, reporting in accordance with this latest schedule, and found an entire company living in a motel outside of Scottsdale. Orson received me with open arms and a great show of affection. I'm very fond of Orson. I have enormous admiration for him as an actor and a director, and the figure he cuts delights me. Here he was in a full-length purple bathrobe, and I don't think I ever saw him outside that bathrobe the whole time we were filming. It was a regal color, befitting Orson, and, *sans* crown, he was indeed majestic.

Orson was smoking the big cigars, and the wine was flowing. I don't mean there was any dissipation; quite the contrary. But it was a convivial affair. There were two handmaidens with Orson. One was acting in the film, and the other was a Jill-of-all-trades. These two put the lunches together, as well as the midnight suppers when we went on shooting into the night at a big house Orson had rented in the nearby town of Carefree. There were a number of cameras in evidence. Orson had a first camera-man and a second and a third, but I very quickly discovered that Orson was really the first cameraman himself. By the same token, he was his own gaffer. There were electricians around, but Orson placed the lights. There was a sound man whom Orson showed how he wanted the mixing done.

Orson had come up with an ingenious idea. It was to tell the story through cameras being held in the hands of persons being filmed by the major cameras. The plot concerns a director (my role in the film) who comes to the end of his rope. Orson denied that it was autobiographical in any way, nor was it biographical as far as I was concerned. There was indeed no script. Orson gave me a few pages containing several long speeches, but he said not to be concerned about learning them. When the time came, he would just write them on a blackboard behind the camera and I could read them. But while I'm not all that good at memorizing, I still believe that actors should know their lines. Orson saw me later study-ing these speeches on the set. "John, you're just causing yourself unneces-sary agony. Just read the lines or forget them and say what you please. The idea is all that matters." Things were somewhat complicated by the fact that during the filming I'd be saying them to a stand-in Orson instead of to Lilli Palmer, who was far away in Switzerland.

Most of the action took place during a big party to celebrate the director's birthday. It was attended by news cameramen, reporters, and people with whom he had long been associated. The whole purpose of the occasion was to pin down the financing for a three-quarters-finished picture, a situation that did put me in mind of Orson himself. There was always a camera on the director during the course of the festivities. They follow him everywhere, even into the toilet. It's through these various cameras—what they see—that the story is told. The changes from one to another—color, black and white, still, and moving—make for a dazzling variety of effects.

Orson's next-door neighbor turned out to be a drunk who didn't quite know what was going on but suspected some kind of orgy. He appeared periodically and threatened everyone, and even once brought the police in. They recognized Orson and me and were duly respectful, leading the gentleman from next door back to his own premises. After that he stood in his own driveway, shaking his fist and swearing at us. It added an appropriately bizarre note.

Orson ran out of cigars. I was a cigar-smoker, too, and though mine were not quite as big, full-bodied and rich as Orson's Havanas, he was reduced to smoking them. It crossed my mind that maybe Orson was also running out of money. This fleeting thought later proved to have substance. The inflow of funds for the picture was from Spain and Iran, and the Spanish leg man absconded with a vast sum. Undoubtedly shaken, but undaunted, Orson plowed on.

It was a delight working with him. Sometimes the scene being shot would be too hilariously funny for Orson to contain himself, and he'd break it up with his laughter. This might well have been by design: he simply wanted to cut. I wouldn't put it past him.

There was an exterior to be shot in which the director was driving a car. I haven't driven in many years. I know how to drive, but I don't like driving, particularly in cities. I like my drink and I don't think driving and drinking mix, so I've made it a rule never to touch the wheel. However, since it was required, I obliged. The director was supposed to be driving rather recklessly. I gave them all they wanted in that respect. Inadvertently I got onto a freeway going in the wrong direction, against traffic. The car was full—Orson, technicians, cameramen and myself—and the cameras were going all the while. I saw there was no fence between the freeways, so I swerved up over the curbing, crossed the dividing area and joined the flow of traffic on the other side. There was dead silence in the car for a while, and then a concerted sigh. "Thanks, John, that'll do," Orson said.

We finished shooting in Carefree except for a few effect shots that Orson planned to take elsewhere, shots that didn't require actors. I left, having had a wonderful time, and admiring Orson and his whole *modus operandi*. Some months later the incomplete picture was shown to a selected audience. Orson still didn't have the funds to finish it. I didn't get to see it, but those who did tell me it is a knockout. Unfortunately, there are problems. The picture is owned by a half-dozen different investors, some of whom, God help us, are Iranians. About two weeks more shooting is needed to finish. It's about as complicated a situation as a picture can get into. Bogdanovich at first assured me that everything would be cleared up. Now I'm beginning to wonder, and I think Peter is, too.

Orson has a wholly undeserved reputation for extravagance and unreliability. I think much of this dates from the time he went down to Rio de Janeiro some thirty years ago to get some second-unit material for a projected picture, got caught up in the drama and spectacle of the Mardi Gras and brought back a couple of hundred thousand feet or more that nobody knew what to do with. This single incident was absurdly over-publicized. I have seen the way he works. He is a most economical film-maker. Hollywood could well afford to imitate some of his methods.

Since Orson was absent at the time, I stood up and accepted an Academy Award for him not long ago. It was for his contributions to films over the years. It struck me that although he was being paid this tribute, none of the studios was offering him a picture to direct. Perhaps it can just be put down to fear. People are afraid of Orson. People who haven't his stamina, his force or his talent. Standing close to him, their own inadequacies show up all too clearly. They're afraid of being overwhelmed by him.

I've read Kipling since I was a kid. I know miles of his doggerel. You can start a line of Kipling verse, and it's an even bet that I can supply the rest of the stanza. I studied a Kipling glossary instead of algebra, and learned terms used by Kipling which were peculiar to the India or the England of his day. I knew that when a ship was "hogging," it was riding the crest of a wave, and when it was "sagging," it was in the trough between two waves; I knew that a *rissaldar* was a native leader of a troupe of Indian cavalry; that a *bhisti* was an Indian water-carrier; that *juldee* meant speed.

34

Kipling has been denounced as an unmitigated imperialist for his nationalistic views during the Boer War. Yet it has always seemed to me that Kipling's version of imperialism was by no means without redeeming value, especially in a country such as India, where, before the advent of the English, most of the population were slaves to a handful of warring rulers. India is today a democracy—shaky perhaps, but a democracy nonetheless—with an increasingly vocal and literate middle class. It is interesting to speculate whether and when this development might have occurred in the absence of imperialism's ugly head. The theme song of reproach by those who denounce Kipling is his line:

> Oh, East is East, and West is West, and never the twain shall meet.

But the point of the ballad from which these lines are extracted is that, although East and West may have basic differences in philosophy, they can and do learn from each other, and should hold each other in mutual respect:

> When two strong men stand face to face
> Though they come from the ends of the earth

I had been toying with the idea of making Kipling's *The Man Who Would Be King* into a picture since 1952, when Peter Viertel and I

discussed it briefly. In 1955, with other obligations out of the way and
Moby Dick finished, I decided to make the film. The backers of *Moby
Dick* said they would put up the money. Thus assured, I jumped at a
chance to go to India on a tiger shoot with my friend Felix Fenston, who
wangled an invitation for me from the Maharaja of Cooch Behar.

The *shikar* (hunt) in 1955 took place out of Camp Parbati in Assam,
from which one can see the foothills of the Himalayas. There were seven
in our party, but only three of us, including Felix and myself, were
shooting. Camp Parbati had four big luxury tents around a quadrangle, an
open-air bar and a wooden dining room on stilts. The service was better
than that in most first-rate hotels. At cocktails before dinner the first day
a tiny bearded man appeared and salaamed to each of us in turn. His
hands were the size of a young boy's. He wore a pale-violet turban, white
tunic, fawn-colored riding breeches and white cloth puttees that wrapped
around his naked insteps. This was Raj Kumar, and he was the Master of
the Hunt.

The elephant camp was about 200 yards from the main camp, and here
the atmosphere was completely different. There was a big fire in the
middle of the compound, and, to the sound of drums, chanting and singing, the tethered elephants were swaying as they were decked out in their
warpaint: blue, red and white designs, no two alike, painted on their
foreheads and on the meaty bases of their trunks. There were thirty in all,
and all would be used in the hunt.

Five young domestic buffaloes had been tethered out over a twelve-
square-mile area that we were to cover. In the mornings, scouts would go
out to see if any had been killed by a tiger. If so, they would come back
ringing a bell, and we would go after the tiger. No bells rang the first
morning, so a general hunt was organized. This consisted of lining up the
thirty elephants abreast—with the howdahs spaced among the beaters—
and moving forward over a broad area, shooting at whatever game was
flushed. About midday there was a scampering around my elephant's feet,
and a little hog deer darted out. I killed it. It was the only blood drawn
that day.

After that first day I began to look at elephants with different eyes.
There is a grace in them; despite their size, they can move through the
jungle more silently than a man. And, like horses, they are of many different types and breedings. Raj Kumar was his own *mahout*, sitting astride
his animal's neck. It had incredible sleekness, poise and presence. Sometimes Raj Kumar joined one of us in our howdah and his daughter rode
his elephant. She was a child of eleven or twelve, beautiful, bare-legged,

with hair down to her waist. She handled the animal with as much authority as her father.

There were no kills the second or third day, although two additional bullocks were staked out. Finally on the fourth day a little man ran into camp and reported that a tiger had killed one of his own bullocks. By ten o'clock that morning we were standing in our howdahs facing a strip of jungle where the buffalo man thought the tiger was lying up. The beaters began the drive in the distance, shouting and beating on tin pans. For sheer suspense and spectacle, I've never seen or heard anything like it. First came the clear trumpet of an elephant who scented the tiger. This was picked up by the other beater elephants, and as they approached, the trumpeting, banging and shouting rose to a cacaphonic climax.

On came the beat, out of the trees and into the grass, where we could see the elephants in line. Then the tiger: only glimpses at first—yellow-and-black flashes against the green backdrop of the jungle. When it came into full view, its movements were so graceful and effortless they seemed slow, but I knew better when I tried to lay my sights on it. It came from the right. Felix fired twice. The tiger swerved my way. As I pulled the trigger, my elephant swung around wildly, throwing me heavily against the side of the howdah. I faced about, just in time to see the tiger disappearing into the bush, and fired again, knowing I would miss. The tiger's course described a sweeping S and covered, I reckoned afterward, some 200 yards. And I am certain its time, from appearance to disappearance, was under ten seconds!

There were no kills among our bullock bait for the next four days, and another general hunt was laid on. It looked as though we had missed our one and only chance. As the elephants were getting into line, someone remarked that the scrubby terrain didn't look promising. Five minutes later I saw a tiger. It came into partial view from behind a thicket some sixty yards ahead, then disappeared behind some scrub. After a few moments it came into full view, bearing leftward and away through the grass—now about 125 yards off. I fired, and the animal disappeared. We shouted, "Tiger!" and the hunt re-formed, with the howdah elephants moving out to the right and the beaters far to the left in an encircling movement, closing on us. In about five minutes we heard a shout in the distance, and my *mahout* turned to me smiling and offered his hand. I had killed my tiger. The others called congratulations, then the beat resumed. "There may be another one," someone shouted, "better get set!"

Instantly there was the rattling, hollow, belching, infinitely fearful sound that is the growl of a tiger, and the beater elephants answered with a fanfare. I saw the tiger break cover, circling toward Felix. Felix fired both barrels, and the tiger swung toward me. I fired. The tiger reversed direction in mid-air and disappeared in an island of very high grass. Our three howdah elephants were moved up so that each faced a different side of the cover, and the beater elephants were put shoulder to shoulder and pressed forward from the fourth side. The squeals of the elephants, the yells of the *mahouts* and the growls of the tiger made a hellish din.

Then the tiger came into sight again, belly to the ground, head up. Felix fired. The tiger made a short charge on the nearest beater elephant, then slowly circled upon itself, lay down and died. It was an enormous animal, measuring over ten feet from its nose to the tip of its tail.

We then went to where my tiger had fallen. She was a young female, eight feet four inches—considered small. But it turned out that my shot was the best I ever made. The bullet had entered behind her left foreleg and had come out her right ear. It was at once a heart and a brain shot.

After the *shikari* I accepted an invitation to visit the Maharaja of Jaipur. The lives of those maharajas were of a magnificence that seemed almost to have been conjured up by a magician. I remember the approach to the palace of Jaipur at night, with torches on the ramparts, flags and banners flying and trumpets sounding. The next day it was polo, and there must have been seventy-five guests. One had the impression that there were at least six bearers for each guest.

Yet the poverty you saw in India at that time, especially in Calcutta, was shocking and depressing in the extreme. Beggars were everywhere. Many of them were professionals who deliberately crippled their own children. They attached themselves to you and smothered you with their presence. If you went to see a monument, a temple, a carving in a cave, they got between you and whatever the attraction was, staring at you with haunting, sorrowful eyes. You couldn't help feeling great sympathy, but you also could not help feeling an aversion—a combination of guilt, pity, anger and fear. There was a fear of being crushed, a fear of being drowned in their tears, and you only wanted to escape from them. Emotion poured over you. Tradesmen in shops, bearers in hotels and waiters in restaurants wept bitter tears over the country, the gods, their families, themselves, anything. People were everywhere. There was no place to be alone. Calcutta struck me as a well of sorrow and deprivation. The dead were collected off the streets in the mornings just the way garbage is collected in New York.

I went touring in the south. From a doctor in Madras, I acquired three excellent bronzes: a Vishnu, a Shiva and a Parvati. The entrance hall to

the doctor's home bears mention. Its centerpiece was a large electric re-
frigerator, on one side of which stood a life-size wax image of his father
in silk hat and tails and, on the other side, a wax image of his mother in a
sari, also life-size.

I took a hired car to Bangalore, then a boat up the Malabar Coast
through the waterways to Cochin, arriving by night. When I went into
my hotel room in Cochin, I saw mosquito netting over the bed, and I
asked the bearer if the mosquitoes were bad. He said there weren't any
mosquitoes this time of year, so I didn't let the netting down when I went
to bed. I woke up in the middle of the night consumed by mosquitoes. I
turned on the fan and drew the netting, but by then I was bitten all over.

I went out the next morning to inspect Cochin, and almost at once I
saw a man with the most hideous of all diseases: elephantiasis. One of his
legs was swollen to the size of a keg. Looking at him, I remembered that
mosquitoes were carriers of the disease. I also remembered seeing a picture of a man with elephantiasis carrying his scrotum in a wheelbarrow.
As I was ruminating on this, I looked around and it seemed to me that
every other person I saw had elephantiasis. I suppose it was only one out
of ten, or maybe one out of a hundred, but to me they were countless. I
thought, "Oh, Christ!" The more I thought about it, the more panicked
I became. I hurried back to the hotel. By the time I got there, I already
felt my scrotum swelling. I packed and left precipitately for Calcutta,
where I went directly to a hospital for treatment. The doctor there
laughed at me and explained that you have to live some time in a place
where carrier mosquitoes are located before there is any danger, and there
must be a mating in the bloodstream of the male and female filaria before
you can contract the disease. Besides, even if that were to occur, the disease
could be arrested by moving to a colder climate. My "recovery" was
miraculous.

As I traveled the backroads and byways of India, I was amazed at the
processions of people on the roads—moving, moving. Some were pil-
grims, others just going somewhere, anywhere. I was told that Calcutta
changes by as much as a million souls daily. I was fascinated by the
country, but depressed at the same time, and the day came when I could
stand the tearful gaze of India no longer. I ran away, first to Nepal, then
to Afghanistan.

I remember how in Katmandu, Nepal, the streets were teeming with
people . . . how one's senses were constantly jolted by strange sights,
sounds and smells . . . streets and alleyways that twisted away in every
direction, overshadowed by temples, shrines and stupas . . . temple friezes

embellished with animal gods and devils, everything thrown together with no sense of order, like knucklebones . . . shrines you dared not enter where women anoint Shiva's lingam with butter . . . drums, gongs, chants, songs in falsetto pitch, rattles, tinkling cymbals, chimes, bells . . . A marriage procession passes by, adding its din and color. The bridegroom is four years old. You press forward to observe some kind of ritual going on in a small square, and the surrounding crowd turns on you: a foreign dog. What's happening is not for your eyes. They motion you away. Black eyes flash angrily, and you know by the short, sharp jerks of heads and hands that they aren't fooling in the least. You don't question; you go. Perhaps it is the concatenation of religions—unorthodox Buddhism mixed with Hinduism, mixed with darkest superstition—but in Nepal there are demons and other strange gods. The place is literally jumping with devils; you can feel it.

Afghanistan is a violent country. In those days it had the highest homicide rate in the world. You never passed a cemetery without seeing the fluttering paper flags that indicated someone had recently died by violence. In the case of murder—and murder was anything that took a life, accidental or otherwise—the accused was taken before the local ruler and the evidence laid out in what is called a *durbar*, or court session. He weighed the evidence and made his decision, which was final. If a man was adjudged guilty at the *durbar*, he was turned over to the family of the murdered man, who then held—usually at night—what amounted to an auction or sale of the murderer. The man's family or friends bid for his life with camels, goats, sheep, jewelry or whatever they had of value. If the bid was acceptable, the murderer was turned over to them and the entire affair was forgotten. If he wasn't a decent fellow and had no friends or family who cared about him, the auctioneers would simply put him to death. If the crime was sufficiently heinous, no offer would be entertained, no matter how great. I once witnessed one of these "auctions." The murderer was spread-eagled on the ground, and his family had gathered to bid for his life. But the grandmother of the murdered man either didn't want the auction to be consummated or perhaps was insulted by the amount of the bid, for she grabbed a knife and cut the man's throat on the spot.

The one crime for which there was no leniency was adultery, a much more serious offense than murder because a great shame attached to it. Good men might kill each other, but it was a mortal sin to take a man's wife. If a man and a woman were discovered *in flagrante delicto*, they could be killed then and there. Both had to be killed, not just one of them.

If they weren't killed on the spot, they were usually buried up to their necks in sand and stoned to death. Sometimes they were hoisted together naked in a cage to a great height and kept there some days and nights before being dropped to their deaths.

Throughout the years and subsequent travels to India, Afghanistan and Pakistan, I continued to entertain the idea of filming *The Man Who Would Be King*. At one point I got Aeneas MacKenzie—the same Mac-Kenzie who had worked with me on *Juarez* back in 1939—to write a screenplay, and both Steve Grimes and Tony Veiller later took a hand in it. I had thought of having Bogart and Gable play the leads, and they agreed. But just when we were about to put the thing together, Bogie got sick and died. I shelved it. In 1960 Gable brought it up once more, hoping to move on to the project after finishing *The Misfits*; I was trying to cast the other part when Gable died. I put it away again.

In 1973, after we had completed *The Mackintosh Man*, John Foreman came to visit me in St. Clerans. He was browsing through the library one day when he came across the scripts (there were now three—one each by MacKenzie, Grimes and Tony Veiller) and Steve's sketches. John hadn't known about the property before, and after going over all the material and discussing it with me, he said he thought it would be great for Paul Newman. At John's urging, I sent Paul the scripts and outlined what changes I saw. Paul's immediate response was enthusiastic.

In our mutual guilt following *The Mackintosh Man*, John, Paul and I were all eager to do something we could hold our heads up about afterward.

So Gladys Hill and I went down to Cuernavaca and, incorporating a number of good things out of the other scripts, wrote yet another screenplay, sticking this time a little closer to the story by Kipling. The original story was too short to be adapted in itself, but it struck themes that lent themselves to expansion—for instance, the Masonic motif, reflected through the emblems on Kipling's watch fob, the altar stone and the treasure. Using such material as springboards, we did a lot of invention, and it turned out to be good invention, supportive of the tone, feeling and spirit underlying the original short story. Kipling's glossary served me well. I like this script as well as any I ever wrote.

I sent the new screenplay to Paul, who called me immediately and said it was one of the best things he'd read, but he'd had second thoughts about the casting of the leads, which at that point were to have been himself and Robert Redford. He said they should be played by two Englishmen. Paul, speaking not as an actor but as someone interested in the improvement of the breed, cast it right there: "For Christ's sake, John, get Connery and Caine!"

I have a great affection for Paul, and my admiration for him as an actor is unlimited, but I confess I was relieved when he said it should be two Englishmen. It was obvious on the face of things. And Paul, with his usual perspicacity, named the two ideal men. John Foreman sent Sean Connery and Michael Caine cables saying scripts would follow immediately. Within a week we received word from both men that they wanted to do the film.

The package was complete; now it was up to Foreman to get studio backing and capitalize it. Therein lies a saga. John got an estimate on the budget: it ran to over $5,000,000, a lot of money in those days. Studios were economizing, and no one of them wanted to take that big a gamble, so the backing would have to come from various sources. One source was Columbia Pictures, which agreed to go into it for the European distribution rights. Another was Allied Artists, which participated in exchange for the North and South American rights. Allied Artists also brought Canadian tax-shelter money into the deal.

In the old days, under the studio system, financing a $5,000,000 picture would have been simple. The studio would simply have put up the money. And this was not the only difference from the old days. In fact, the difficulties we encountered in making *The Man Who Would Be King* are perfect illustrations of changes in movie-making procedure. In order to understand why, it is necessary to review some history.

Many things contributed to the fall of the studio system. The studios were accused of being monopolistic and, under the anti-trust laws, were forced to sell off their own theaters. There were new tax structures; the advent of television kept many people away from theaters; the growing power of agents to demand more in salaries and benefits for their actor clients escalated production costs alarmingly. Eventually actors—having been liberated from long-term contracts and the weekly salary—were asking astronomical sums for individual pictures, and were freelancing. Some formed companies and started exercising their own creative ideas. They began to select their own material, and often shared in the ownership of the films with the studios, which would provide their facilities and the larger part of the financing. In the case of *The Man Who Would Be King*, Connery and Caine worked for a flat fee plus a percentage of the gross. I was, unfortunately, on the net.

Most pictures today are put together in much the same way we handled *The Man Who Would Be King*, although the variations can be infinite. After accepting your "package," the studio—in this case, Columbia—puts up money for specified distribution rights. Money can also be had from non-studio sources, such as Allied Artists, which function principally as a distributing organization, representing a number of theater-owners or exhibitors. The distributor is in a very privileged position, and his fee is quite high—usually starting at thirty percent of gross and graduating downward over a period of time.

The person or persons putting the package together are normally required to pay studio overhead, which is usually around twenty-five percent. This serves to support the transportation department, art and other creative departments, running salaries and even the cops at the gates, not to mention property taxes. Columbia required this of us before Columbia itself would come up with any money, even though we never shot a foot of film in its studio, everything being done on location.

And then there's "finishing" money. That is a sum that guarantees the investors completion of a film in case it runs into trouble. There are agencies that furnish these funds—for a fee. On top of everything else you also have to pay for insurance on performers. So by the time everything is paid for, the overhead has increased to a formidable figure—often to as much as fifty percent of the budget.

Studio heads now are accountants, tax experts, a sprinkling of financial wizards and ex-agents. They are hardly a creative breed. For the most part, they are illiterate when it comes to making pictures. The whole hierarchy—with a few exceptions—is made up of dismal people who imagine that because they can wheel and deal and shuffle investment money (seldom if ever their own) they have presumptive rights to opinions and dictums. Most of them assume prerogatives that would have made L. B. Mayer or even Harry Cohn blush.

So today it's something of an agony to put a picture together. I've chosen the coward's way and never have anything to do with that end of it. I'll come in and speak my piece on occasion—as I did for this picture—but no more than that. For the most part, the people who make pictures today aren't people you'd care to spend long weekends with.

As soon as we received assurances that Allied Artists and Columbia would back the project, we started scouting in earnest for location sites. It was impossible to shoot the picture on the actual ground where Kipling's story is set. Kafiristan (now usually called Nuristan) was still completely closed to foreigners, and most places along the Northwest Frontier were impractical because of their remoteness and inaccessibility. One alternative offered to us was Turkey.

It almost worked out. The Turkish government appeared interested
and cooperative, the people were amiable and the country was more
beautiful than I had ever imagined. The Greek ruins in Ephesus would
have made an ideal setting for Kipling's Sikandergul. My plans then were
to make the body of the picture in Turkey, market and street scenes in
India and some background material in Afghanistan. But the United States
and Turkey slipped into one of their recurrent disputes over that year's
poppy crop, and we were once again forced to continue scouting.

After leaving Turkey, John Foreman returned to the United States and
I went to London, where an instructive episode took place. It serves to
illustrate one aspect of the difficulties encountered in film-making today.
A Mr. Wolf, one of the owners of Allied Artists, had mentioned several
times that he would like to discuss the script with me. He was in London,
so I invited him and his lawyer (whose name, Peter, gave the duo an
obvious sobriquet) to have dinner with me in my suite at Claridge's.
When dinner was over, Wolf pulled out a few manuscript sheets and
began reading me a list of things he found wrong with the script. I
listened in amazement—he was attacking the very concept of the film.

I was shocked but not outraged. Anyone may approach me and get
a hearing. So I waited until Wolf was finished and then replied—point by
point, soberly and logically, never derisive. When I finished, Peter and
the Wolf seemed satisfied. We went on to discuss casting.

On the evening of the following day I got a call from John Foreman.
He was upset. Peter and the Wolf had gone directly to Columbia and
announced that, because of my "unapproachability," they were washing
their hands of the whole deal. They'd come to me with ideas for changes,
and I'd scoffed at them. I had in fact treated their suggestions with much
greater respect than they deserved. They had been guests in my rooms.
For that reason alone, it would have been unthinkable that I would be
anything other than polite. I'm afraid I hadn't much use for the pair of
them from that moment on.

This was the first of many "withdrawals" by Peter and the Wolf.
Finally it was agreed that they would employ as their spokesman a disin-
terested party from Columbia to arbitrate the differences of opinion. This
was done, and John Foreman and Gladys Hill took up the cudgels for our
side, taking them on point by point. The fifty or more requirements were
eventually reduced to two or three insignificant changes.

The entire operation was unfortunately typical of the kind of thing
constantly happening in picture-making today. There are ways, as I've
said, that a person or group can have a very sizable investment in a
picture and put up practically none of their own money. And not only

was this the case with Allied Artists but, as of this writing, it is in the position of having lost a lawsuit brought by attorneys for Sean Connery and Michael Caine as a result of a $4,000,000 deficit on the company books. I considered David Begelman, then president of Columbia Pictures, far and away the most intelligent and trustworthy person among the principals involved. In spite of his subsequent troubles, I'm sure I was not mistaken in this.

Not long after our trip together to Afghanistan, Steve Grimes scouted the Atlas Mountains in Morocco for possible locations. When the Turkish venture folded, John Foreman and I went in with a small group to retrace Steve's steps. There was no question but that the picture could be filmed there in its entirety. Even the market and street scenes could be shot in Marrakesh and made to look sufficiently Indian. So we settled on Morocco, and made Marrakesh our headquarters.

Marrakesh itself was an experience. The hotel was fine, the food was excellent, but the overall atmosphere was unsettling. It has since become the capital of the *haute couture*, I suppose partly because little boys are available in abundance. Depravity is looked on with an understanding eye. It is not officially condoned, but neither is it discouraged. In fact, there is an understanding between boy prostitutes and the police that, following an encounter with a foreigner, the boy is to report it to the police along with whatever else he may have been able to learn about his consort. Dossiers are kept by the police on all guests of that country who stay longer than a few days, and on all who return periodically.

From the start John Foreman and North Africa were incompatible. When we went to leave following that first scouting trip, a customs officer whom I marked as a sadistic fiend ordered the girl immediately preceding John to place all her belongings on the counter. In a search for God knows what, he even went so far as to take her phonograph records out of their slipcovers. When John's turn came, the customs man snarled disagreeably, but waved him on, picking up a piece of chalk to mark John's new Gucci bag . . . and John slapped his hand! Of course all hell broke loose. Detectives took John to an inner office and turned him inside out. From that moment John and North Africa were in disharmony.

How much baksheesh was given to corrupt officials by our company, God only knows. There was no avoiding it, for nothing could be done unless sums were forthcoming. Bribery was rampant. We soon learned that it was cheaper to pay the bribe than try to arbitrate, since our arbitrators also had their hands out and you simply wound up paying double. This kind of corruption existed on every level.

All in all, the film was a very expensive proposition. One set of the temple of Sikandergul cost around $500,000 to build. But it was a magnificent set and we were able to shoot something like half the picture in it. Other scenes were actual villages in the Atlas Mountains. The Khyber Pass scenes were shot in a very dramatic pass in Morocco with high, sheer walls that at places were no more than fifty feet apart. (The real Khyber is now an automobile road festooned with power lines.)

After we had set up camp near the Atlas Mountains, the Berbers came down from the hills. They are a bizarre, wonderful, wild people, and we employed large numbers of them, using their actual tents and other paraphernalia in many scenes. We had French-, Arabic-, Berber- and English-speaking interpreters, and I sometimes had to go through all four languages to give an order.

Alex Trauner took Steve Grimes' place as art director because Steve was otherwise engaged. Alex is as broad as he is high, and one of the toughest little men I've ever known. He had three bad auto accidents on location—all with the same Moroccan driver—and he and the driver walked away from each of them. The driver drove like a bat out of hell, but Alex was always urging him to go faster, even on mountain roads. When we tried to have the driver fired, for manifest incompetence, he put up a terrific fuss. Nothing fazed Alex, absolutely nothing—except John Wilson Apperson.

John was the head of the wardrobe department, and he had a running feud with practically everyone in the company. John bought the materials for the costumes, hand-dyed every single yard himself and had the costumes cut and sewn under his close supervision. Additionally, he dressed 2,000 extras daily and had the clothes washed and ready the next day. He was hard-working and responsible, and everyone respected his professionalism. His bearing and demeanor were those of a prim, purse-lipped maiden aunt. John had a proprietary feeling about the costumes. They were his possessions, and whoever came into the costume department was, in John's opinion, at worst an interloper and at best a guest, present only on his sufferance.

After a number of preliminary skirmishes, one day John and Alex got into a serious row. John laid one on Alex that gave him a knot over his eye. After the altercation I asked John what he had done. "I hit him with my left. I had my purse in my right hand." Alex steered clear of John after that.

Edith Head was the costume designer. They say about Edith that getting the Oscar is written into her contract; I think she's had more of them than anyone else in Hollywood. The inspiration for the designs in this instance—the manner of draping the materials, the hair styles, diadems, armlets, pins—were Greek Tanagra figurines.

Gladys went to Rome and brought back reproductions of Greek jewelry, weapons, armor, even coins. Alex designed a number of pieces, including Dravot's crown, from archaic motifs, giving to each item the same attention that he would to a work of sculpture.

I've had two great assistant directors in my life: Tommy Shaw is one, and the other is Bert Batt. The rest range from good to fair to very bad indeed. Whatever is good about *The Man Who Would Be King*, Bert Batt had something to do with it. Bert's ideas were always well thought out, and usually they were good ideas. If you didn't go for what he proposed, he didn't turn petulant, but addressed himself to the next problem. He would sometimes be up two days and three nights running, arranging something complicated like a whole troop movement; not only was he a powerhouse of energy, but he was resourceful to an amazing degree. When it came time to shoot the Khyber Pass scenes, we learned that the tribes in our area would not allow their women to be photographed. Undaunted, Bert went to the nearest cities and recruited women from the brothels. We had been warned not to touch any woman in public—even a whore was someone to be protected from foreign infidels, and the tribesmen in this place carried knives or weapons of some sort. This sequence involved a large number of people and camels moving through the "Khyber Pass," and we had already experienced great difficulties with the camels, which were agricultural camels broken to the plow but not accustomed to being loaded or ridden. Then, at a turnstile which was supposed to mark the border between Afghanistan and India, one of the women froze and refused to move. The camels were piling up behind her. All entreaties were to no avail. She simply froze and refused to budge. Bert Batt walked up behind her and kicked her right in the ass. He kicked her so hard that even I—standing next to her—felt it. The woman only had to make an outcry and Bert would have been cut to ribbons. Instead she hung her head as if to say, "Yes, Master," and moved on to join the others.

The great first assistants are all well known. They are like great top sergeants, often valued more highly than the director. When I find such an assistant, I put all my trust in him. First assistants are basically "company men," and one of their primary responsibilities is to protect the interests of the studio. Some of them carry this to extremes, basing every decision on immediate monetary savings, regardless of quality. Then there are those, like Tommy Shaw and Bert Batt, who understand that cutting corners doesn't necessarily save money. They have the ability to perceive what a director is after, and the judgment to decide whether it's good enough to warrant added expense. If it is, they are the director's champions.

A first assistant worth his salt takes over the details, leaving the director free to make creative decisions. The first assistant decides when the company moves; whether or not there should be a second unit working on the preparation of the so-called action shots; whether the action scenes should be shot together or broken up. He is a specialist in such back-up people as stunt men; he knows them by name, and knows who is best for what: falls, horses, rope-climbing, driving, piloting or motorcycling. When it comes to explosives, he picks the powder man. A good first assistant is a first-rate diplomat as well as a disciplinarian. He has the ability to command without offending people. Along with his authority he has a sense of fitness and good taste. He is able to go to the stars' dressing rooms and persuade them to his course of action without toadying to them or seeming too authoritarian. There aren't many like this.

We had contracted for Sean Connery and Michael Caine in early 1973, and the picture was delayed until the beginning of 1975, but these two gentlemen held themselves available according to their word. Their salaries had also gone up considerably during this waiting period, but they held to the originally contracted terms with no complaint. And they couldn't have been better to work with. Many of the scenes were between just the two of them, and they rehearsed together at night. Together they worked up each scene so well beforehand that all I had to decide was how best to shoot it. It was like watching a polished vaudeville act—everything on cue, and perfect timing.

Originally I'd intended to have Roxanne a fair girl, blonde and blue-eyed. You see them occasionally in Kafiristan—the setting of Kipling's story—and they are reputed to be descendants of Alexander's soldiers. But there are no fair-skinned people among the Moroccans, and I soon realized that I had to change my concept and go with a dark-skinned beauty. Michael Caine's wife was Indian and fitted the bill perfectly. I asked Mike if she could do the role, and he agreed with some reluctance. She couldn't act. In fact, they both assured me, she had no acting ability whatsoever. But then none was required, except perhaps in the final scene, where in terror she bites Dravot. When we got to that scene, I discovered that Mike and Shakira had only spoken the truth: she couldn't pretend being afraid—her brand of honesty forbade such dissembling. I solved the problem by getting her to roll her eyes back so that only the whites showed. She looked drugged, swooning, out of control. It served marvelously.

John Foreman's tribulations in Morocco continued throughout our stay. He was hounded and harassed to the bitter end. In trying to protect me so I'd only have to worry about making the picture, he took on all the small, dirty jobs as well as the major production problems. The payroll never got to the bank on time. It was Allied Artists' money, and I suspect it was held up until the last moment in order to squeeze out the last cent of interest before sending it on. This was a source of constant embarrassment to us. Once, to cover the payroll, John was forced to write a personal check for an amount which he didn't have in his account. The problems with customs and other petty Moroccan officials multiplied, and John was in the middle of every controversy. Baksheesh was only a part of it. Each time raw film stock arrived, John had to negotiate its clearance, even to keeping the customs officials from opening the tins. But throughout he managed to control himself admirably. He was the perfect diplomat—right up until the gold-medallion incident. That capped it for John Foreman.

Sean Connery's wife, Micheline, had been born in Morocco, and through her efforts obtained an audience for John with the King. It was hoped that, hearing about our problems, he'd intercede with customs. Micheline also arranged for the King's jeweler—a favorite at court—to accompany John to Rabat, to show him the ropes. It was a long drive, four hundred miles, and in the way of polite talk John inquired about the possibility of making a gold medallion—three medallions, actually—that would be keepsakes for Sean, Michael and me. The jeweler nodded.

Upon arrival in Rabat they proceeded to the palace, were admitted and passed from official to official. Eventually they were ushered into the presence of the King. He looked up from what he was reading, shook hands with John and said, "Welcome to Morocco." That was it. They were dismissed. John was a bit put out, to say the least, having spent two days and traveled 400 miles for this exciting moment. And of course we got no help at all from the King. Quite the contrary.

Two days after their return to Marrakesh the jeweler brought John the three gold medallions. He also presented him with the bill: $15,000!

John was stunned. "I'll have to think this over."

"There's nothing to think over. The gold in these medallions is a gift from the King. You have to take them, otherwise it would be an insult to the King."

"Well, if it's a gift, what's the fifteen thousand for?"

"For my work."

John exploded and said he wouldn't pay. Someone then pointed out to him that Micheline was caught in the middle of this. She had recommended the jeweler and she had paved the way for John's "audience" with the King. John paid. Morocco is not a recommended topic of conversation with John Foreman these days.

I could have spent three times as long on *The Man Who Would Be King*, but I'm not sure it would have been a better picture for it. It doesn't strive for perfection. But then Dravot and Carnehan aren't themselves perfectionists in any sense. "We are not little men," they say. Flawed they may be, but they're the stuff of heroes. The picture has its faults, I suppose—but who gives a damn? It plunges recklessly ahead. It swims toward the cataract.

One day I saw an old man. He was standing on one leg, leaning on a staff. I thought he was one-legged until I approached him and he put his other foot down. He was bearded. I was the only other person there with a beard. He came forward and pulled it, then muttered some words of approval. He didn't look it or act it, but it turned out he was over a hundred. It struck me that he might be right for Kafu Selim, the High Priest in the picture, so I got him to stand in front of a camera and put questions to him through an interpreter. He thought it was all hilariously funny. Laughing, he did a little impromptu dance.

So we got him two assistant "priests," one a partriarch in the local mosque and the other an ancient Berber from the high mountains. They were all very good indeed. You couldn't tell them what to do, you could only try to make them understand what the scene was about and then let them do it. Once they got the drift of it, they acted it out naturally.

Toward the end of the picture I had these three old men come in and see themselves on film. They had never seen a motion picture, although they had heard of them. After the lights came up, they talked rapidly and excitedly among themselves. Finally they appeared to come to some kind of agreement.

I turned to the translator. "Ask them what they think of what they saw."

Kafu Selim answered for them: "We will never die."

I read without discipline, averaging three to four books a week, and have since I was a kid. Gram used to read aloud to me books by her favorite authors: Dickens, Tolstoy, Marie Corelli. She also read speeches from Shakespeare to me, and had me repeat them to her. When I was in my early teens, we'd talk about the "style" of an author. I puzzled over the meaning of the word. Was an author's style his way of arranging words to set himself apart from other writers? An invention, so to speak? Surely there was more to style than that! One day it came to me like a revelation: people write differently because they *think* differently. An original idea demands a unique approach. So that style isn't simply a concoction of the writer, but simply the expression of a central idea.

I'm not aware of myself as a director having a style. I'm told that I do, but I don't recognize it. I see no remote similarity, for example, between *The Red Badge of Courage* and *Moulin Rouge*. However observant the critic, I don't think he'd be able to tell that the same director made them both. Bergman has a style that's unmistakably his. He is a prime example of the *auteur* approach to making pictures. I suppose it is the best approach: the director conceives the idea, writes it, puts it on film. Because he is creating out of himself, controlling all aspects of the work, his films assume a unity and a direction. I admire directors like Bergman, Fellini, Buñuel, whose every picture is in some way connected with their private lives, but that's never been my approach. I'm eclectic. I like to drawn on sources other than myself; further, I don't think of myself as simply, uniquely and forever a director of motion pictures. It is something for which I have a certain talent, and a profession the disciplines of which I have mastered over the years, but I also have a certain talent for other things, and I have worked at those disciplines as well. The idea of devoting myself to a single pursuit in life is unthinkable to me. My interests in boxing, writing, painting, horses have at certain periods in my life been every bit as important as that in directing films.

I have been speaking of style, but before there can be style, there must

be grammar. There is, in fact, a grammar to picture-making. The laws are
as inexorable as they are in language, and are to be found in the shots
themselves. When do we fade-in or fade-out with a camera? When do we
dissolve, pan, dolly, cut? The rules governing these techniques are well
grounded. They must, of course, be disavowed and disobeyed from time
to time, but one must be aware of their existence, for motion pictures
have a great deal in common with our own physiological and psychological processes—more so than any other medium. It is almost as if there
were a reel of film behind our eyes . . . as though our very thoughts were
projected onto the screen.

Motion pictures, however, are governed by a time sense different from
that of real life; different from the theater, too. That rectangle of light up
there with the shadows on it *demands* one's whole attention. And what it
furnishes must satisfy that demand. When we are sitting in a room in a
house, there is no single claim on our awareness. Our attention jumps
from object to object, drifts in and out of the room. We listen to sounds
coming from various points; we may even smell something cooking. In a
motion-picture theater, where our undivided attention is given to the
screen, time actually moves more slowly, and action has to be speeded up.
Furthermore, whatever action takes place on that screen must not violate
our sense of the appropriate. We accomplish this by adhering to the
proper grammar of film-making.

For example, a fade-in or a fade-out is akin to waking up or going to
sleep. The dissolve indicates either a lapse of time or a change of place.
Or it can, in certain instances, indicate that things in different places are
happening at the same time. In any case, the images impinge . . . the way
dreams proceed, or like the faces you can see when you close your eyes.
When we pan, the camera turns from right to left, or vice versa, and
serves one of two purposes: it follows an individual, or it informs the
viewer of the geography of the scene. You pan from one object to another in order to establish their spatial relationship; thereafter you cut.
We are forever cutting in real life. Look from one object to another across
the room. Notice how you involuntarily blink. *That's a cut.* You know
what the spatial relationship is, there's nothing to discover about the
geography, so you cut with your eyelids. The dolly is when the camera
doesn't simply turn on its axis but moves horizontally or backward and
forward. It may move closer to intensify interest and pull away to come
to a tableau, thereby putting a finish—or a period—to a scene. A more
common purpose is simply to include another figure in the frame.

The camera usually identifies itself with one of the actors in a scene, and it sees the others through his eyes. The nature of the scene deter-mines how close the actors are to each other. If it's an intimate scene, obviously you don't show the other individual as a full-length figure. The image on the screen should correspond to what we experience in real life. Seated a few feet apart, the upper body of one or the other would fill the screen. Inches apart would be a big-head close-up. The size of their images must be in accordance with the proper spatial relationship. Unless there's a reason: when actors are some distance apart and the effect of what one is saying has a significant impact upon the person he's talking to, you might go into a close-up of the listener. But still his distance, as he views the person who is speaking, must remain the same. Going into a big-head close-up with dialogue that is neither intimate nor significant serves only to over-emphasize the physiognomy of the actor.

Usually the camera is in one of two positions: "standing up" or "sitting down." When we vary this, it should be to serve a purpose. Shooting up at an individual ennobles him. As children we looked up to our parents, or we look up at a monumental sculpture. On the other hand, when we look down, it's at someone weaker than we are, someone to laugh at, pity or feel superior to. As the camera goes higher and higher looking down-ward, it becomes God-like.

The conventional film-maker usually shoots a scene in full shot—a master scene—followed by medium shots, close shots and close-ups . . . at various angles . . . then decides in the cutting room what to use. The opposite way is to find the one shot that serves as an introduction to a scene; the rest will follow naturally. Again there's a grammar to it. Once you write your first declarative sentence, the narration flows. Un-derstanding the syntax of a scene implies that you already know the way the scene will be cut together, so you shoot only what's required. That's called "cutting with the camera."

I work closely with the cameraman and with the operator, the man who actually manipulates the camera. He looks through the lens, execut-ing what you've specified. At the end of a shot you look to him to see if he's brought it off. The camera is sometimes required to take part in a sort of a dance with the artists, and its movements timed as if they were to music, and I've noticed that most good operators have a natural sense of rhythm. They usually dance well, play drums, juggle or do something that requires good timing and balance.

Cameramen—most of them ex-operators—are really lighting experts. They like to be known not as cameramen but as directors of lighting. Young directors are, as a rule, somewhat frightened of their cameramen.

This is understandable, for cameramen often proceed in an independent fashion to light each scene precisely as they please. Lighting is their first interest, since other cameramen will judge them by it.

As an actor, it's been my opportunity to observe the working methods of other directors. For the most part, they go by the book. Inexperienced directors put great stock in the master scene—which is shot as though all the actors were on a stage; you see everybody at once, and all the action. Their idea is that if they've missed something in the closer work with the camera that they should see, they can always fall back to the master shot. They think of it as a way of protecting themselves. I've often heard cameramen advise such a procedure, but a cameraman is not a cutter. The fact that falling back to the master scene interrupts the flow of the whole scene and breaks whatever spell has been evoked through good close-up work is of no concern to him. Obviously I am not speaking about all cameramen. There are any number of outstanding professionals who are just as concerned with getting that ideal sequence of shots—whatever the cost— as any director.

So many things can go wrong while filming a scene. If only everything bad that's going to happen would happen at once and be over with! You're seldom that fortunate. Instead, it's the camera, or an actor forgetting his lines, or the sound of an airplane, or a car backfiring, or an arc light that flickers. When things of this kind occur, you simply have to start again. It can drive a director up the wall. I recall an incident involving one especially volatile director who was making a film in Africa. During one take a native baby began crying, and that stopped the scene. He started over, and a lion began roaring when it wasn't supposed to. The director shouted: "Cut! I can see that there's only one way to get this God-damned scene! Throw the fucking baby to the fucking lion!"

Now, if you can make use of two or even three set-ups—going from one balanced, framed picture to another without cutting—a sense of richness, grace and fluency is evoked. For example, one set-up might be a long shot of a wagon train moving slowly across the screen. The camera moves with it and comes to two men standing together, talking. Then one of the men walks toward the camera, and the camera pulls back to the point where he encounters a third individual, who stands back to the camera until the other man has passed on out of the scene. Then he turns and looks after him, in close-up. Three complete set-ups—without cutting. Of course, the set-ups must be carefully laid out and perfectly framed, and this multiplies the chances of something going wrong. But I've discovered that, even with the increased possibility of error, the time spent is not much more than would be spent on three separate set-ups.

Such linked shots are the mark of a good director. The scenes I have put together in this fashion have scarcely—if ever—been remarked on by an audience or a critic. But the fact that they have gone unnoticed is, in a sense, the best praise they could receive. They are so natural that the audience is caught up in the flow. This is the exact opposite of the kind of thing people tend to think of as clever—somebody's distorted reflection in a doorknob, for instance, a stunt that distracts one's attention from the scene. It is important to say things on the screen with ingenuity, but never to belabor the audience with images that say, "Look at this!" The work of the camera with the actors, as I mentioned before, often amounts to a dance—panning, dollying, following the movement of the actors with grace, not cutting. There's a choreography to it. Not many picture-makers are up to this. I'd say a dozen or so.

It is best to shoot chronologically. In this way you can benefit by accidents, and you don't paint yourself into corners. However, if the picture begins in India and ends in India, with other countries in between, it is economically impractical not to shoot all the Indian material at one time. When you are on a distant location, you do everything that calls for that location. That is a compromise, but making a picture is a series of compromises. It is when you feel that the compromise will affect—or risks affecting—the overall quality of the picture that you must decide whether or not to go along with it.

Plain, ordinary judgment plays a big part. For instance, you may well get what seems to be the ideal scene on your first take. Then you must question whether you have been sufficiently critical. Is the scene truly as good as you first thought? Inexperienced directors are inclined to shoot almost every scene at least twice, in the fear that something may have escaped them. They may be blessed and not realize it—and, in trying to improve upon something that doesn't need improving, may run into these technical problems that I mentioned earlier. If the action is right and the artists have been everything you desire, then a second take will do you no good. If something is wrong with the film or the lighting, it will be wrong on the second or third take, too, so that's no kind of insurance. A director has to learn to trust his judgment.

Each time you get a good scene is a kind of miracle. Usually there is something wrong, however slight, and you must consider the importance of the error. As you repeat a scene, your demands in terms of quality tend to increase proportionately. You've got to watch this, and not become a fanatic.

I've come onto sets where a director has prepared all the lighting and designated all the action before bringing in any of the performers. In some cases it was an inexperienced director following the advice of his cameraman—in others, a matter of such a tight schedule that every second counted. But simply to light a set and say, "Now you sit here. You stand there," without any preliminaries, is only to embalm the scene: The actors are put into strait-jackets. The best way, the only way, is to search out that first shot—that first declarative sentence which I mentioned earlier—and the rest will follow naturally. It's not easy to come by, especially when there are a number of people in the scene. But until you get that shot you're at sea. The answer is not simply to pull back for a full shot. Instead, look for something that has style and visual energy, something in keeping with your ideas for the picture as a whole. You have the actors go through their paces and you still don't see it. Now, don't panic. Don't worry about what the actors and the crew may think (that the director doesn't know what the hell he's doing!). This anxiety may force you into something false. And if you get off to a false start, there's no correcting it. Given time and freedom, the actors will fall naturally into their places, discover when and where to move, and you will have your shot. And given all those shots, cut together, you will have your microcosm: the past on the winding reel; the present on the screen; the future on the unwinding reel . . . inevitable . . . unless the power goes off.

These observations are seldom remarked upon by picture-makers. They are so true, I suppose, that they are simply accepted without question as conventions. But they are conventions that have meaning—even for mavericks.

In 1962, Otto Preminger phoned me in Ireland and asked me to be in a picture he was about to make, *The Cardinal*. The last time I'd acted in a film was when I played the man in the white suit in *The Treasure of the Sierra Madre*, fifteen years before.

36

Telling someone what to do and doing it yourself are two entirely different propositions. Actors, save for a notable few, have not made good directors—the exceptions being Charlie Chaplin, Orson Welles and, more recently, Paul Newman. By the same token, the directors who've acted in pictures have not fared all that well either—the exceptions being Paul Newman, Orson Welles, and Charlie Chaplin.

Despite all that, I put up very little resistance to Otto's proposal. He would send me the script, he said, and if I would agree to playing the part, I would be paid the sum allocated to it in the budget. In other words, I was not to look on it as a favor to a friend. When the deal was presently made, I took two Jack Yeats paintings instead of money.

Otto is the kindest and most considerate of men in everyday life, but he is notorious for his behavior on the set. His tirades are legendary. It usually turns out that a reputation like Otto's has little basis in fact, but as I came onto the set the very first day I was to work, Otto was already roaring like a lion, and his roars never ceased. He didn't roar at me, or if he did, it was a muted roar. Most of his roaring was at Tom Tryon. They were a couple of weeks into the picture, and I was told he'd been roaring at Tom since the opening shot. Poor Tom was a wreck!

We had a scene where we entered a room together. Standing outside the door, waiting for the cue light to flash, I could actually feel Tom quaking beside me, and I put my arm around him to steady him. He said in an undertone, "I'm going to quit acting." After we played the scene, I drew Otto aside and told him that I thought, as things were going, Tom was heading for a nervous breakdown. "He's a bundle of nerves. If you don't get him to relax, he might not finish the picture." Otto was astounded. He hadn't even realized that he was raising his voice at Tom.

Tryon's next scene was practically a monologue, and he wasn't doing all that well with it. He was tense. His eyes were desperate, and in a final rehearsal I heard him groan once between lines. He got through the scene somehow. Otto said, "Cut!" Then he rose, walked up behind Tom, who stood isolated and miserable, and screamed into his ear, "*Relax!*"

True to his word, Tom Tryon left acting and became a writer of best-sellers.

Otto's eccentric behavior is confined to the set. Time and time again he has demonstrated his courage, his morality and his fearlessness. He was, for example, the first to hire one of the Hollywood Ten when they emerged from prison. He did not penalize the man financially or keep his name off the credits, as was often done. Otto fought—and lost—a lawsuit against a great network for cutting his films for television. I could go on —but this will give you an idea of the kind of adversaries he takes on.

Since *The Cardinal* I've acted in a number of films indiscriminately. Whether the pictures were good or bad or indifferent was of no conse-quence, as I don't take that part of my life seriously. Each episode has been a lark—and they actually pay me to do it. In recent years I have found myself doing a good bit of acting. I have no intention of acting at the expense of directing. Always and forever, I'm a director.

Early in 1978, when I was in Las Caletas, I received a copy of Flannery O'Connor's novel *Wise Blood* from a man I did not know named Michael Fitzgerald. The book was followed by a telephone call from Fitzgerald, who said he was hoping to make a movie of it and wondered if I would be interested in directing it. I replied that I would, and a few days later he put in an appearance.

Michael Fitzgerald turned out to be a young man with shoulder-length hair, a golden beard and delicate features. His manner was a combination of reticence and formality. I found that he spoke four languages fluently, including Chinese, and came from a family of scholars. His father, Robert Fitzgerald, Boylston Professor of Rhetoric and Oratory at Harvard, was well known for his definitive translations of Homer's *Iliad* and *Odyssey*, as well as other works. The Fitzgerald family was, moreover, closely involved with Flannery O'Connor; Michael's father was her literary executor, and his mother had recently edited a collection of O'Connor letters.

Flannery O'Connor died some fifteen years ago. During her lifetime she had a devout but small audience; now she is coming into her own as an important American literary figure. *Wise Blood*, the novel Michael Fitzgerald had sent me, is set in Georgia and is the story of a young religious fanatic's brief rebellion against Christ. It is both funny and dire. From page to page you don't know whether to laugh or to be appalled. In any case, it was hardly the sort of thing to attract investors. It didn't take Michael long to learn this.

From time to time during the next year I'd get calls from him—New York, Los Angeles, Germany, Italy—telling me how things were going. A time or two it looked as though he had the money, but then he'd be disappointed. I began to feel guilty about having encouraged him. I said perhaps he was mistaken in pursuing it any further, that he might better put his time and effort into something else. I then discovered there was steel beneath Mike's silky exterior. He said he had no intention of giving up. He made me feel ashamed of having lost faith. And, sure enough, not long after that, Mike called to say he'd got the money—some $2,000,000. Not much, as today's budgets go, but enough if managed well.

I advised Mike to try to get Tommy Shaw—the best American first assistant I'd ever worked with (now a production manager)—and let him run the show. It all worked out to something close to perfection. Tommy put together the production unit *par excellence*. The entire crew consisted of only twenty-five persons—the lowest number I'd ever had before was, I believe, fifty. Everyone worked for a minimum wage.

We undertook to make the picture in forty-eight days, and Tommy cut more corners than Andretti in the Monte Carlo. He had three of his children working on the picture—one in the office and two on the set. My son, Tony, was second assistant. Michael's mother and his wife, Kathy, did the clothes and the interiors. Nepotism was the order of the day. The screenplay, by the way, was written by Mike and his older brother, Benedict.

Tommy made friends with the mayor and others of the city fathers of Macon, Georgia, where the major portion of the film was shot. Everybody, including the firemen and policemen of Macon, proceeded to break their necks to help us in every conceivable way. Even the weather conspired. We had sunshine when we needed it, and rain when we needed it. No one got sick. There were no casualties. The picture went off without a hitch.

We brought the picture in for almost one third less than the budget. Tommy Shaw was primarily responsible for this. When all was finished, I said to Mike, "Wouldn't it be a good thing to cut Tommy in on the profits . . . if any?"

"I already have, John."

I must take my hat off to young Michael.

To my knowledge, this is the first time that Tommy Shaw, or any other production manager or assistant, has ever been given a percentage of a picture.

There were seven outstanding performances in *Wise Blood*. Only three of those seven actors have any reputation to speak of: Brad Dourif, Ned Beatty and Harry Dean Stanton. The other four are unknowns. They are all great stars, as far as I'm concerned. Nothing would make me happier than to see this picture gain popular acceptance and turn a profit. It would prove something. I'm not sure what . . . but something.

Walking along the beach I see a man hitting something with a stick while a little boy looks on. I come up to them. The man's killing a snake—a sea-snake. Most Mexicans believe all snakes are poisonous. There's no such thing as a harmless reptile. They kill every snake they can find. The only poisonous snake in this latitude is the coral snake—and who's ever heard of anybody being bitten by one?

37

I tell the man the snake is harmless—was—it's now a dead snake about a foot and a half long, reddish brown with a flat tail like the blade of an oar. I hold forth on the harmlessness of most reptiles, how they really do good, keeping down all the rodents. It's the little boy I hope to enlighten and, through him, the next generation.

They hear me through and then turn away and start off down the beach. Out of earshot the father will of course tell his son that all gringos being crazy, it was best not to argue with me, and that he should kill all snakes whenever and wherever he finds them.

I go on a few steps and see a second snake coiled up in a coconut husk. I have an inspiration. Here's my chance to prove the snake's harmlessness. I call to the man and the boy. I will put my finger in the snake's mouth. I shout after them, but they don't hear me above the sound of the surf. Then they are too far off to bring back. I pick the snake up and throw it back into the sea where it belongs, wondering what makes some sea creatures cast themselves up onto dry land as though seeking immolation.

A few days later I am with an amateur herpetologist. The talk comes round to sea-snakes, and he informs me that they are one and all deadly. The snake I picked up is related to the cobra, only more venomous. The species is not aggressive, however. You'd practically have to put your finger into the snake's mouth to get it to bite you, the herpetologist says.

Although I'm well pleased it didn't happen, I cannot conceive of a more appropriate end for yours truly—sufficiently absurd in both the existential and purely comic senses.

During the making of *The Misfits* I was, like Calvin Coolidge and other clowns before me, adorned with a feather headdress and adopted into an

Indian tribe. I was given the name "Long Shadow." Since then, whenever I'm at a self-imposed disadvantage—making a fool of myself, that is— Pearson called to express his delight at Long Shadow's appearance in a friends of mine, old knowing friends, so address me. For instance, Billy television commercial in which he abjured the ways of the gambler and counseled the audience to put its money in the bank.

I'm under no illusions regarding my management of money. Three times I tried using money to make money: a gold mine, a hotel and a silver mine, all in Mexico. Needless to say, I'd have done better to take my money to the nearest race track. I've made several millions but I've never had a million dollars at one time. But none of this should be construed as a complaint. I've never lived any way but the best. Except for that one bad time in England, I've always managed to give dinner parties at The Colony, Maxim's and the Grand Vefour, have suites in the finest hotels and smoke Havana cigars.

With a few exceptions the making of my films since the war has been described in considerable detail. Not so my personal life; over the last twenty years things have happened that were more important to me than any film.

In January 1969, I received word that Ricki had been killed in an automobile accident in France. We had been legally separated for ten years, but her death was a tragic blow. We had lived in different worlds but had remained friends. During our separation I had a second son—my beloved Danny. His mother, Zoë Sallis, lives in Rome; Danny was born there in 1962. They have spent almost all of their summers and Christmases with me in Ireland and Mexico. Also during our separation, Ricki had a daughter, Allegra, born in London in 1964. She bears my name and is as dear to me as Tony, Anjelica and Danny. I brought her and her nurse to live with me in Ireland after her mother died. Allegra graduates this year from high school. She was with me in Las Caletas most of last summer and again at Christmastime, helping to edit this manuscript.

I named some names in the beginning pages of this book—surviving friends, wives and lovers. Some of them have gone unmentioned thereafter because their roles in the events of my life are not as important as their places in my heart. Uppermost among them is Suzanne Flon. Her affection over the years has been my blessing on earth, and I would not trade it for any other.

In 1972, three years after Ricki's death, I married for the fifth time. This was tantamount to putting my finger in the sea-snake's mouth. I survived—but barely. Enough said about that.

In addition to Gladys Hill and Maricela, Hank Hankins, the pilot I originally met in Africa, has come to live with me in Las Caletas. After *The African Queen* he went to Mexico and was for some years President Miguel Aleman's personal pilot. When illness forced him to give up commercial flying, he went prospecting in the hills of Guerrero. I go with him sometimes on his forays into remote places. His eyes still glitter like a squirrel's but he claims his vision is failing. The other day, however, he identified a gray whale half a mile away by its flukes.

The animals in my Las Caletas family are a Rotweiler, Don Diego; two pet deer, Nadia and Nijinsky; a squirrel, Panchito Sunshine (so named by Maricela); a macaw who's called simply Bird; a boa, Lechuga; a coatimundi; an ocelot; two cats and a pet pig. I hope to add to this collection— perhaps some otters from the Quimixto River, a puma, a jaguar. . . .

So there you are, for what it's worth. The whole story has not been told, of course. I've refrained from making any dark disclosures regarding my secret life. My misdeeds are not sufficiently evil to justify their being put on display. They are insignificant. Damningly so. On the other hand, I haven't recounted some of the more decent things I've done. They, too, lack sweep and magnitude. They are about on a level of insignificance with my wrong-doings. There have been times when I confused the two lists: found myself cringing at the memory of a good deed and glowing at the memory of a bad one.

My elder son, Tony, not long ago married Lady Margot, one of the daughters of Marquis and Marchioness of Cholmondeley of Cheshire in England, and I've recently become a grandfather. As a grandfather I'm entitled to a few words of advice to the young, based upon my long and unvarying experience as a transgressor. I can sum them up with these answers to the oft-repeated question, "What would you do or not do if you had it all to do over again?"

> I would spend more time with my children.
> I would make my money before spending it.
> I would learn the joys of wine instead of hard liquor.
> I would not smoke cigarettes when I had pneumonia.
> I would not marry the fifth time.

INDEX

A NOTE ON THE TYPE

The text of this book was set on the Linotype in Janson, a recutting made directly
from type cast from matrices long thought to have been made by the Dutchman
Anton Janson, who was a practicing type founder in Leipzig during the years 1668–87.
However, it has been conclusively demonstrated that these types are actually the work
of Nicholas Kis (1650–1702), a Hungarian, who most probably learned his trade
from the Dutch type founder Dirk Voskens. The type is an excellent example of the
influential and sturdy Dutch types that prevailed in England up to the time William
Caslon developed his own incomparable designs from them.

Composed by Maryland Linotype Composition Company, Inc., Baltimore, Maryland
Printed and bound by the Haddon Craftsmen, Inc., Scranton, Pennsylvania
Inserts printed by The Murray Printing Company, Forge Village, Massachusetts

Designed by Margaret M. Wagner